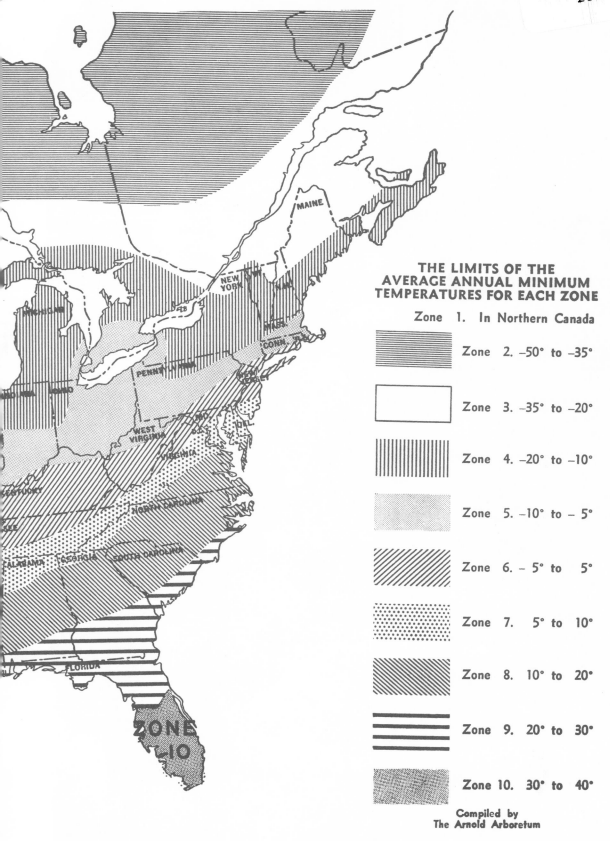

THE LIMITS OF THE AVERAGE ANNUAL MINIMUM TEMPERATURES FOR EACH ZONE

Zone 1. In Northern Canada

Zone 2. −50° to −35°

Zone 3. −35° to −20°

Zone 4. −20° to −10°

Zone 5. −10° to − 5°

Zone 6. − 5° to   5°

Zone 7.   5° to 10°

Zone 8. 10° to 20°

Zone 9. 20° to 30°

Zone 10. 30° to 40°

Compiled by
The Arnold Arboretum

KNOWING YOUR TREES

By

G. H. COLLINGWOOD
and
WARREN D. BRUSH

Revised and Edited

by DEVEREUX BUTCHER

With more than 900 illustrations showing typical
trees and their leaves, bark, flowers, and fruits

1978

THE AMERICAN FORESTRY ASSOCIATION
Washington, D. C.

First printing, 1937
Twentieth printing, edited and revised, 1965
Twenty-eighth printing, revised, 1974
Twenty-ninth printing, 1975
Thirtieth printing, revised, 1978

© 1978, by The American Forestry Association
1319 Eighteenth Street, N.W.
Washington, D. C. 20036
Library of Congress Catalog Card Number 78-52994 ✓

PRINTED IN THE UNITED STATES OF AMERICA

FOREWORD

We Americans are an outdoor-loving people. At every opportunity we turn to natural beauty for relaxation and enjoyment. Some find it in their own gardens, in the surrounding countryside; others follow highways and byways to distant forests and parks. But whether at our own doorstep or at timberline on some mountain peak, the greatest single factor in this quest is trees.

As individuals, trees shelter and beautify our homes, shade our streets and highways, give charm and dignity to our parks, life and character to our landscapes; in tree communities, they form our hillside woodlands, our forests that sweep to the horizon. Just as products of the forest contribute in a thousand and one ways to our day-by-day life, so do living trees contribute at all seasons of the year to our relaxation and enjoyment.

Thus to know more about trees is to enhance the pleasure we derive from them. And to this purpose KNOWING YOUR TREES is dedicated—to bring to the American people, in picture and in story, the characteristics and important contributions trees make to society. Identification is made easy by actual photographs of the tree, both winter and summer, its leaves, fruit, bark and, when significant, its flower. To obtain such a comprehensive assembly of photographs, The American Forestry Association for years has been searching collections and working directly with photographers in every corner of the nation.

Initial work on KNOWING YOUR TREES was begun in 1932 by G. H. Collingwood, then forester for the Association, and in 1937 the first edition was issued. This was revised in 1941. At this juncture Dr. Warren D. Brush, nationally recognized authority on woods, took up the work and contributed material for additional trees.

By 1963, texts were out of date and the original page forms had become so worn from repeated printing, that it was necessary to edit the texts and reassemble hundreds of photographs or take dozens of new ones for future printings. That work, which required a year, was done by Devereux Butcher who, back in 1941, had served on the editorial staff of *American Forests* and, in 1942, became executive secretary of the National Parks Association as well as editor of *National Parks Magazine*. In 1957, he resigned from the National Parks Association and, in 1959 through 1962, with his wife, edited and published a monthly newspaper, *National Wildlands News*. Between 1947 and 1965, he authored three books—two on national parks and one on national wildlife refuges. It was immediately following cessation of the newspaper that Butcher became the third author-editor of KNOWING YOUR TREES. To this and the preceding edition, he has added eighteen new tree species, bringing the book's total to 188 species.

Nearly fifty maps in these latest editions have been redrawn to make the ranges conform more closely to the latest knowledge about tree ranges as shown in the *Atlas of United States Trees, Vol. 1, Conifers and Important Hardwoods*, by Elbert L. Little, Jr. (U. S. Dept. Agr. Misc. Pub. 1146, 1971). The author-editor wishes also to express his appreciation to Dr. Charles T. Mason, curator, University of Arizona Herbarium, for his kind help with regard to certain southwestern trees that have been added to these editions.

Common and scientific names used in the text conform generally to those accepted and published in *Standardized Plant Names* as prepared for the American Joint Committee on Horticultural Nomenclature, although in several cases common names in widespread usage have been retained.

Sources of photographs have been acknowledged throughout.

EASTERN WHITE PINE
Soft pine, Weymouth pine
Pinus strobus Linnaeus

WHITE PINE, monarch of eastern forests, flourishes from Newfoundland to Lake-of-the-Woods, Manitoba, southward through eastern Minnesota and eastern Iowa east to New England and south along the Appalachian Mountains to eastern Georgia.

The sturdy, gradually tapering trunk and horizontal limbs of blue-green foliage of white pine are characteristic of our northern forests, where trees with trunks six feet in diameter and heights of 250 feet were reported by the early lumbermen. Next to the sugar pine of California, eastern white pine is the largest United States pine.

The needles, three to five inches long, are in bunches of five, and remain on the tree from one to three years. A papery sheath surrounds their base during spring and early summer.

In May and June, yellow staminate, pollen-producing blossoms appear on the new shoots of the lower branches. At the same time, small bright pink, cone-bearing ovulate flowers with purple scale margins occur on the ends of the young upper shoots. The staminate blossoms wither and fall soon after they lose their pollen, but by the end of the first season's growth the tiny upright, green cones are about an inch long. Early in the second season, these turn down with the increasing weight and become brown, maturing in August. In September they open to release winged seeds which are carried as far as a quarter mile by the wind. The scientific name *strobus*, derived from the Greek and Latin words for pine cone, probably refers to the conspicuous cones.

Bark on branches and young trunks is thin, smooth and greenish brown, becoming fissured, ridged, darker and heavier, varying from less than an inch to four inches thick.

During its first few years, white pine develops a moderately long taproot, with spreading lateral roots. With maturity, these develop and form a shallow root system similar to that of spruce.

White pine lumber ranks among the principal economic woods of North America. Creamy white to red brown, it is soft, straight-grained, may be cut with ease, polishes well and, when seasoned, warps but little. Almost everything from ships' masts to matches, including doors, flooring, framing, trim, crating and novelties have been made of this wood. A cubic

Devereux Butcher

Eastern White Pine is typified by a straight trunk and a narrow, irregular crown supported by whorls of horizontal branches

4

foot when air dry weighs twenty-four to twenty-seven pounds. It is probably the least resinous of all the pine woods, but has a mildly resinous odor. Although not noted for its strength, it compares favorably with ponderosa pine, cottonwood and basswood. The original stand of white pine in the United States and Canada was approximately 750,000,000,000 board feet, of which 600,000,000,000 was in the United States. King of American commercial woods before the present century, it is now exceeded in quantity of lumber produced by the southern pines as a group, Douglasfir, the oaks and ponderosa pine and hemlock.

White pine thrives on deep sandy loams, but will grow under a variety of soil conditions where adequate moisture is available. It grows in nearly pure stands and in mixture with hardwoods, as well as with hemlock and red pine. White pine of the original forests grew to be two hundred to two hundred and fifty years old, with occasional trees of three hundred to three hundred and fifty years. Under modern economic conditions, however, trees are usually cut at sixty to eighty years when they measure from twelve to seventeen inches in diameter and are from eighty to one hundred feet tall. In the original forests, trees from thirty to forty inches in diameter required at least two hundred and forty years to grow. White pine reproduces readily from seed, and with fair soil, sunlight and moisture, will reach heights of ten feet in ten years, twenty-five feet in twenty years, sixty feet in forty years, thus averaging fifteen to eighteen inches each year. Similar trees forty years old may measure from seven to nine inches in diameter and yield fifty to eighty board feet of merchantable material. It is the most rapid growing northern forest tree, occasionally averaging a yearly growth of one thousand board feet an acre over periods of forty to eighty years. It responds to silvicultural treatment and has been more widely planted than any other American tree.

Fire, white pine blister rust and white pine weevil are the white pine's principal enemies, although other pests, such as white pine scale, the pine sawyer and several root fungi and rots, cause heavy damage. Forest fires are particularly damaging to the young growth. Fire is an enemy common to all trees, but white pine blister rust, which entered this country from Europe about the year 1907, is peculiar to the five-needled pines and takes a heavy toll. This can be controlled by destroying all gooseberry and currant bushes, which are intermediate hosts of the disease, that are found growing within the forest in the vicinity of the trees to be protected. Without the leaves of these plants the disease can neither complete its life cycle nor infect other white pines.

Throughout parts of its range the leader shoots of white pine are killed by the white pine weevil. The tree is not killed, but frequently is so deformed as to make it valueless for lumber. No satisfactory control of the weevil has been developed.

White pine is seldom used for street or roadside purposes, but its vigorous growth and attractive color cause it to be favored as an ornamental tree for lawn and park purposes, as well as for a background for other plantings. It is successfully grown considerably beyond its natural range, and has long been planted in northern Europe.

J. Horace McFarland

Long tapering cones, slender bluish green needles bunches of five, and clusters of yellow pollen-bearing blossoms

U. S. Forest Service

Broad, flat-topped, dark gray longitudinal ridges characterize Eastern White Pine bark

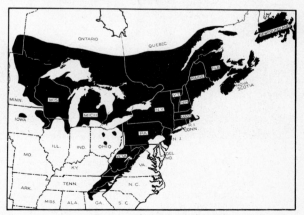

Natural range of Eastern White Pine

WESTERN WHITE PINE
Finger-cone pine, Idaho white pine
Pinus monticola Douglas

Weldon F. Heald

The tall shaft of Western White Pine reaches heights of one hundred feet or more and supports a narrow, symmetrical, pyramidal crown of short drooping branches. This open-grown tree has an unusually long crown. Frequently, more than half of the trunk is clear of branches

WESTERN WHITE PINE, the silver pine of the Northwest, is native to the region from southern British Columbia across northern Idaho, Montana and Washington, southward through Oregon into California. True to its name, *monticola*, it is confined to the mountains, where in Idaho and Montana it is found at elevations of 2,000 to 5,000 feet above sea level, somewhat higher in Washington and Oregon and up to 10,000 feet in California.

Ranking among the important timber trees of America, western white pine frequently grows in dense stands and develops a tall, slender shaft with a peculiarly short-branched, narrow, symmetrical crown. The trunk is usually clear for a half to two-thirds of its length, has little taper and the slender drooping branches seldom extend more than twelve to fifteen feet. These trees may reach heights of 175 feet and be eight feet in diameter at breast height, but they are more often ninety to 110 feet high and two to three feet in diameter. Rapid growth is combined with long life, for trees of 200 to 500 years are not uncommon.

The silvery gray bark sometimes takes on a tone of purple and is broken into small oblong or rectangular blocks. Trees exposed to the wind become distinctly cinnamon in color. Even on mature trees the bark is seldom more than one and a quarter inches thick, while that on young trees and branches is thin, smooth and bright gray. Very young twigs and shoots are covered with a fine reddish down, which helps distinguish this tree from other white pines.

The pale bluish green leaves or needles are two to four inches long, commonly with a white, frosty appearance and are borne in bundles of five. They differ from the needles of eastern white pine in being thicker and more rigid. They remain three or four years or longer.

The yellow pollen-bearing, staminate flowers or catkins are borne during early spring in clusters of six or seven on the lower branches, while the pale purple ovulate flowers occur on long stalks near the ends of the high branches. From these higher blossoms develop green or dark purple cones, which first stand erect, then become pendulous by the close of the first season. By the end of the second summer they turn yellow-brown and mature to a length of six to ten inches, or occasionally fifteen inches. The slightly curved cones are longer than those of eastern white pine and are so slender as to give rise to the name "finger-cone pine." Trees seldom bear fertile cones before forty to sixty years of age, and then infrequently at intervals of two or more years. Under each cone scale may be found two pale red-brown seeds about a third of an inch long attached to a narrow wing from three-quarters of an inch to an inch long. The seeds are shed in September and October after the cones ripen and may be carried by the wind several hundred feet from the parent tree. Buried in duff and well shaded, seeds retain their vitality several years. Over most of its range the tree reproduces sparingly and the seeds germinate best on exposed moist min-

6

eral soil, or on humus which keeps moist through the growing season. Many stands of white pine came into being as even-aged forests following the forest fires of 1889 and 1910, from seeds stored in the duff or released from cones that escaped destruction. Seedlings and young trees will endure shade, but, as the tree becomes older, more and more sunlight is demanded.

The pale brown to nearly white wood weighs only twenty-four to thirty pounds to the cubic foot, is straight-grained and easily worked. Although not strong, it is harder and stronger than eastern white pine and for many purposes compares favorably with cypress, any of the spruces and Douglasfir. Its high commercial value is attested by the fact that, among the species with which it is associated, few command a higher price. It is used widely for structural purposes, window and door frames, moldings, matches, and pattern stock.

Western white pine develops greatest size and highest economic importance in deep porous soils, on gentle north slopes and flats in northern Idaho and Montana. It seldom grows in pure stands and is most frequently associated with western hemlock, Douglasfir, the several western firs and lodgepole pine. Deep snowfall, a mean annual precipitation of fifteen inches in California to sixty inches near Puget Sound, and a comparatively short growing season characterize the regions where this pine thrives.

While subject to disastrous losses from fire, protection against which is essential, its most dangerous enemy is the white pine blister rust. This fungus disease, first reported on the west coast in 1910, has made serious inroads upon scattered stands of young growth as far south as California. The fungus must find opportunity to live for a period upon the leaves of currant and gooseberry bushes before going over to the white pines, and cannot live where either the white pine or currant-gooseberry hosts are absent. Accordingly vigorous efforts are being made by the federal government, supported by the states and private landowners, to control the disease by destroying all the bushes in localities where the white pine is of commercial value.

The mountain pine bark beetle, *Dendroctonus monticolae*, is the principal insect enemy and causes losses amounting to thousands of dollars each year. Control can be secured by felling the infected trees, peeling the bark and burning it. It is subject also to pests common to eastern white pine, but no others are of special significance in its natural range.

David Douglas, the Scottish explorer and botanist, first reported western white pine on the slopes of Mount St. Helens in Washington in 1825. Soon after, seeds were sent to England, where the tree grows successfully. Because of its extreme hardiness, attractive color, compact pyramidal form and rapid growth during the first years, it is highly desirable for ornamental purposes on home grounds in the Northwest, and as far north as Ottawa, Ontario.

Western white pine is characterized by blue-green needles in bunches of five, cones six to ten inches long, and blocky bark that is gray, grayish purple, or cinnamon in color

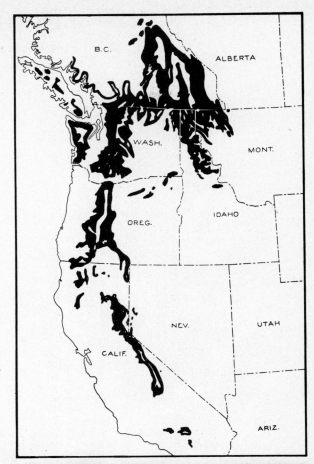

Bu. Entomology and Plant Quarantine

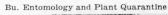
Bu. Entomology and Plant Quarantine

7

SUGAR PINE
Purple-coned sugar pine
Pinus lambertiana Douglas

SUGAR PINE is the tallest and most magnificent of all the pines. It is one of the *Quinae*— or five-leaves-in-a-bundle pines—and is confined to a narrow strip about 1,000 miles long extending from southwestern Oregon, along the western slopes of the Sierra Nevada and coast ranges of California at elevations of 1,000 to 9,000 feet above sea level, to lower California. Heights of 245 feet, and diameters, breast high, of twelve to eighteen feet have been recorded, but trees 160 to 180 feet high and four to seven feet in diameter are more common. The straight cylindrical trunk of mature trees frequently rises fifty to eighty feet to the first few long horizontal limbs which form the base of a wide crown. These great branches sweep outward and downward in graceful curves. With maturity, the spire-like outline of sugar pine assumes a flattened top similar to that of old eastern white pines. Trees attain ages of 300 to 500 years, and occasionally nearly 600 years, and stand on a broad, shallow root system.

First recorded in 1825, on the Multnomah River in southern Oregon, by David Douglas, it was named *Pinus lambertiana* in honor of his friend, Dr. Aylmer Bourke Lambert, a distinguished British botanist of that time, and author of a book on pines. The name sugar pine refers to the white, crisp globules of resin which exude from the bark after injury. These are sweet, with a pleasant suggestion of pitch flavor, and possess certain cathartic qualities.

As with all true white pines, the deep blue-green needles, which have a whitish tinge, are borne in groups of five. They are two and a half to four inches long stout, stiff, twisted, and remain on the twig through the third year. In early spring light yellow, pollen-bearing flowers, half an inch to an inch long, are borne in clusters on young twigs, simultaneously with light green or pale purple ovulate cones. Before maturing, the cones become dark purple-brown, and stand erect, giving rise to the name "purple-coned sugar pine." By August of the second year, the cones, which are the largest of all pine cones, become pendulous. They attain lengths of eleven to eighteen inches, or occasionally twenty-one inches, and two and a half to three and a half inches in diameter. In October the scales expand to release hundreds of dark, chestnut-brown, winged seeds. Each has a wing one and a half to five inches long, and an edible kernel

U. S. Forest Service

Largest of all pines, the Sugar Pine, magnificent Pacific Coast tree, attains mature heights of 200 to 245 feet

about the size of a grain of corn, which is relished by many birds and mammals. The cones remain on the tree for two or three years. Heavy seed crops occur only at intervals of four to six years and trees under twenty inches in diameter seldom bear. The seeds are carried by the wind about the same distance as the height of the tree. They germinate best on loose, moist soil with a little litter of decayed leaves.

The bark of mature trees is deeply and irregularly grooved into long plate-like ridges, covered with loose purple-brown to cinnamon-red scales, and is two to three inches thick. On young trees the bark is thin, smooth and dull dark gray in color.

The light colored, soft, straight-grained wood is fragrant, and satiny when planed. It is similar to that of eastern white pine, except that it is whiter, changes color less on exposure, has more conspicuous resin ducts, and has a slightly coarser texture. The wood weighs twenty-two to twenty-five pounds to the cubic foot when air dry. Although not as strong or stiff, it enters into all the uses of eastern white pine. Its remarkable freedom from any tendency to warp and twist with changing moisture, its durability in contact with the soil, and the large boards which are possible, cause it to be used for general construction, interior trim, patterns, and model making. Sugar pine is produced only in Oregon and California where it ranks in volume and value with redwood.

It grows at elevations of 1,000 to 2,000 feet in the coast range, and from 6,500 to 9,000 feet in the Sierra Nevada, in loose, deep, moist but well-drained sandy loams where air humidity, as well as soil moisture, are favorable. Best growth is found in the mountains where the annual precipitation is forty inches or more. Western yellow pine, white fir, Douglasfir, incensecedar, Jeffrey pine and giant sequoia are its principal associates.

Seedlings and trees up to twelve inches in diameter are easily damaged by fire. Thereafter the thick bark and high crown protect the trees against ordinary fires. Lightning is a frequent source of damage because the larger trees stand out above their fellows. Young trees are occasionally attacked by mistletoe, which kills or stunts them. Snow frequently accumulates to a depth of ten or fifteen feet, causing severe breakage to small trees, followed by insect damage, but until white pine blister rust entered the western forests, sugar pine was remarkably free from serious enemies. Because of its great value, the federal government is cooperating with California and Oregon and with private owners to control the disease by destroying all currant and gooseberry bushes within its commercial range. The fungus must spend part of its life on these bushes before it goes on to the pine.

Sugar pine sustains a rapid rate of growth to a remarkably advanced age. During its first century of life, favorably located sugar pine will average one foot in height-growth each year. Many acres with 192,000 board feet of merchantable timber have been recorded, while 75,000 to 150,000 board feet to the acre are not uncommon. The ability of young sugar pine to endure shade enables it to start among other species, but as it grows older it demands more and more sunlight. It meets severe competition, however, from ponderosa pine.

Although not widely planted for reforestation or ornamental purposes in the West, individual specimens for sugar pine have been established in a number of eastern states. It has proved hardy in sheltered locations, as far north as Massachusetts, but under these conditions grows more slowly than the native eastern white pine, *Pinus strobus*. David Douglas introduced sugar pine in England in 1827, and occasionally specimens are now found among collections of trees on estates and in parks there.

George E. Stone

Sugar pine has the largest cones of all—ten to twenty inches. The bark is three inches thick, gray-brown, broken into ridges

U. S. Forest Service

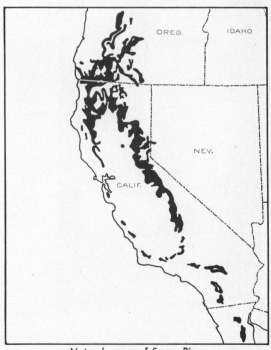

Natural range of Sugar Pine

LIMBER PINE
Rocky Mountain white pine
Pinus flexilis James

LIMBER PINE is one of the smaller white pines. It is usually bushy, with branching trunks, and when growing near timberline may be only a dwarf ground cover. It grows singly or in small groups throughout the higher eastern slopes of the Rocky Mountain region from Alberta and Montana to western Texas and northern Mexico, and westward into Nevada and southern California. It is fairly common at elevations between 4,000 and 12,000 feet on exposed, rocky slopes, the tops of ridges and foothills, and sometimes in moist canyons or along the banks of mountain streams.

Usually a low, many-branched tree, limber pine occasionally develops an undivided trunk thirty, fifty, or even eighty feet tall, whose diameter is two to five feet. Ordinarily, however, the trunk tapers rapidly, and is seldom clear of branches for more than ten to twenty feet. Distinctly regular whorls of slender, tough branches stand out at right angles to the main trunk of smaller trees, and may extend to the ground. Larger trees have extremely long branches which bend gracefully toward the ground. The outer ends of the branches of the upper crown tend to assume a vertical position, giving a peculior up-reaching effect. The twigs and branches are capable of being bent to such an amazing extent that it is called limber pine, and scientists named it *flexilis*.

Growth is slow, but its life is fairly long. Individual trees may take 200 years to attain diameters of nine or ten inches, while others may reach eighteen to twenty-two inches in 200 to 300 years. Some trees are believed to live 1050 years or more. Trees of greatest size are found in the high mountains of Arizona and New Mexico.

Each stout, stiff, dark green needle is one and a half to three inches long in closely pressed clusters of five. The needles remain on the twig for five or six years. They are forward pointing, densely crowded and compressed rather than flaring, and appear as short tufts on the ends of the branches. Under a magnifying glass the margins are smooth with only an occasional semblance of teeth.

Limber Pine is a white pine of the high mountains. It has a relatively short trunk and long slender branches

Reddish, pollen-bearing, staminate flowers are borne on spikes throughout the crown, while the bright red-purple ovulate cone-bearing ones are generally in clusters near the top. The relatively thick, oval cones mature in late summer or early autumn of the second year, and shed their seed in September or early October. The cones are three to ten inches long, peculiar in that their broadly oval, light yellowish brown scales are greatly thickened, but without prickles, and are green or rarely purple at maturity. Instead of hanging down from the branch they remain erect, and at maturity stand out horizontally or decline only slightly. By early winter they fall from the trees without breaking up. The hard shelled, deep reddish brown seeds are mottled with black and are from a third to a half inch long. Each narrow, rudimentary wing generally remains on the inner cone scale so as to leave a clean seed. Large seed crops occur at irregular intervals, but small quantities are released locally nearly every season. They are sought out by birds and rodents, which play an important part in disseminating them.

The cone, seed and needle characteristics of both limber pine and whitebark pine (*Pinus albicaulis*) help to distinguish these two species from the other American pines. With certain mountain pines of the old world, they are classed as *cembrae* or stone pines, in distinction to the more common and usually larger white pines of the *strobi* group.

The bark on old limber pine trunks is dark brown or almost black, one and a half to two inches thick, with deep furrows between wide rectangular blocks. On trees eight to twelve inches in diameter the bark is broken into small, thin, gray-brown plates, while on younger trees it is a bright gray, often silvery, thin and smooth.

The tree's exceedingly slow growth and limby structure cause the light, soft wood to be dense and usually full of knots. The heartwood is pale lemon yellow, while the thin layer of sapwood is nearly white. The wood is very heavy when green, but a cubic foot when air dry weighs only about twenty-eight pounds, and is seldom found in commercial sizes. It is occasionally used for rough construction lumber, as well as for log cabins, fuel and mine props.

Pure stands of limber pine are sometimes found, but this species is more common as an individual, or in small groves in mixture with mountain hemlock, Lyall larch, whitebark, lodgepole and bristlecone pines at high elevations, and with Douglasfir, white fir, Engelmann spruce, and ponderosa pine at lower elevations. It is less abundant in the Pacific Coast states than in the Rocky Mountains region.

Young trees, especially, suffer heavily from surface fires, but the long taproot and the flexible limbs make limber pines resistant to wind damage. As with other five-needled pines, it is subject to white pine blister rust, but the generally scattered distribution seldom calls for special protective measures.

While not suited for forest planting, the slow growth and unusual outline of limber pine, resulting from the horizontal and pendulous branches, indicate possibilities for landscape use. It prospers under most western conditions, and thrives in the Northeast when planted in well drained soil at the base of a moist slope.

U. S. Forest Service

One- and two-year-old cones grow among the forward-curved needles which are in bundles of five

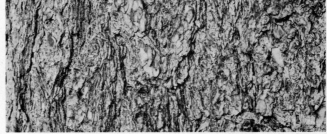

U. S. Forest Service

The gray bark of youth turns brown and rough with maturity

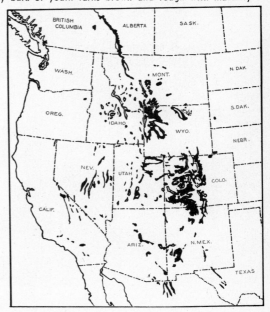

Natural range of Limber Pine

11

WHITEBARK PINE

Pinus albicaulis Engelmann

THE wind-distorted crown of whitebark pine is a feature of high mountain areas from north central British Columbia, southward irregularly along the Rocky Mountain summits of Alberta, Montana, Idaho, northwestern Wyoming, and northern Utah, and again along the summits of the Cascade Mountains and Sierra Nevada into southern California. In its northern range this pine grows at elevations of 6,000 to 7,000 feet. Southward it thrives at increasing elevations up to 12,000 feet in the Sierra Nevada. On high summits temperatures of sixty degrees below zero are relieved by a scant three months of frosty summer, and prevailing winds often blow with such unabating force that most of the stout, flexible limbs develop on the leeward side of the thick, squatty trunk. At lower elevations and in protected coves, better soil and more encouraging surroundings combine to produce rela-

tively tall and symmetrical trees. Even here, however, heights of more than sixty feet or diameters exceeding two feet at breast height are rare. Where undisturbed by wind, the side branches, and especially those of the upper crown, stand almost erect.

Whitebark pine has five stout, stiff, slightly incurved needles in a bundle, therefore belonging to the white pine group. The needles are one and a half to two and a half inches long, marked on the back with one to three rows of light colored pores or stomata. The needles are usually clustered toward the end of the stout, orange branchlets, and remain from four to eight years before they are shed.

Scarlet male and female catkins appear during early July on the growth of the preceding year. In late summer of the second year, the ovulate ones develop into small round, almost stemless cones which are one and a half to three inches long. They ripen in August and are ordinarily a dark purplish brown. Inside and at the base of each cone scale are two sweet-kerneled, winged seeds, plump on one side and flattened on the other. They are nearly half an inch long and about one-third of an inch in diameter. The narrow translucent wings stick to the sides of the cone scale so that the seeds must break loose. They are shed slowly through the late autumn and early winter. Squirrels, chipmunks, and other small animals and birds seek them greedily and are largely responsible for their distribution. The busy rodents often store the seeds in narrow rock crevices on high, exposed elevations where germination may take place. Too often the tender young seedlings are whipped and worn in two against the sharp granite rocks by constant winds. At high elevations the surviving trees may sprawl over the rocks to form low springy mats of tough limbs, which provide shelter for mountain goats, bears, deer, and other animals, and not infrequently for an occasional traveler or sheep herder. Heavy snows keep the trees flattened during most of the year, leaving little time for the limbs to lift themselves. The bark of the larger trunks sometimes carries a whitish cast, while young trunks and twigs

Devereux Butcher

A dweller of high places, subject to unabating winds, Whitebark Pine develops a thick, squatty form which with age and depending on exposure may become distorted in shape

12

are clothed with fine, white pubescence. This is responsible for the common name "whitebark," as well as for the scientific name *Pinus albicaulis*, which may be translated as "the pine with the white stem."

The bark is scarcely more than half an inch thick and comparatively tender. For many years it remains characteristically smooth, but with maturity develops narrow vertical and horizontal cracks with the outer surface covered by thin light gray to brown scales. Beneath the scales, the inner bark is reddish brown. The winter buds are more or less egg-shaped, and about one-third to one-half inch long.

Whitebark pines are seldom large enough or in sufficiently heavy stands to be of commercial importance. Occasionally, however, individual trees at lower elevations may be cut for fence posts or lumber. The wood is light in weight, nearly white, brittle, and marked by many close annual rings. Superficially, it resembles the wood of western white pine and, no doubt, small quantities are sawn and marketed with this more important relative. No figures are available for the stand estimate.

During its early development, whitebark pine is fairly tolerant to shade, but with maturity it demands full sunlight. Its growth is so slow that timberline trees scarcely five feet high have been found to be fully 500 years old. Other trees only three and a half inches in diameter have revealed as many as 225 annual rings. John Muir, with the aid of a magnifying glass, is reported to have counted seventy-five annual rings in a twig only one-eighth of an inch in diameter. A veteran tree with a trunk seventeen inches in diameter is recorded as being 800 years old.

Ordinarily whitebark pine associates with other hardy mountain trees such as alpine fir, limber pine, Engelmann spruce, foxtail pine, Lyall larch, western juniper, Rocky Mountain juniper, and knobcone pine. Of all these trees, whitebark pine is most frequently confused with limber pine, *Pinus flexilis*. In general the range of whitebark pine is more northerly, but the two trees may occupy the same area in several regions. Both are five-needled pines with many common characteristics. They are best distinguished by their cones. Limber pine cones are three to ten inches long, with slightly reflexed scales, while those of whitebark pine are only one and a half to three inches long and more nearly cylindrical, with thickened scales armed with sharp points. The rows of light colored pores or stomata are on all sides of the limber pine needles instead of being limited to the back side, as with whitebark pine.

Like all five-needled pines, whitebark pine is susceptible to the white pine blister rust. Because of its scattered growth and relatively low commercial value, however, no special protective efforts are being made. Bark beetles also take a fairly heavy toll, but the greatest enemy is fire. Its natural habitat makes it particularly susceptible to lightning.

Whitebark pine is suitable for ornamental purposes and is so used to a limited extent. Trees selected from high elevations may maintain an inherited tendency to develop low spreading forms suitable for many landscape purposes.

Asahel Curtis

Whitebark pine has stout, stiff, in-curved needles, one to two and a half inches long, in bundles of five. The cones are small, almost stemless and dark, purplish brown

Devereux Butcher

The pale gray cast of the bark and stems gives Whitebark Pine its name

The natural range of Whitebark Pine

PINYON
Colorado pinyon, Nut pine
Pinus edulis Engelmann

Low, round-headed Pinyon trees, with far-reaching horizontal branches, grow in open stands over the lower slopes of the southern Rocky Mountains

U. S. Forest Service

PINYON, the two-leaved nut pine of the Southwest, grows in scattered groves and open stands on the dry foothills, mountain slopes, and canyon sides of the southern Rocky Mountains, at elevations between 5,000 and 8,000 feet above sea level. Small isolated specimens are found up to elevations of 9,000 feet.

A stand of pinyon scattered over the arid slopes reminds one of an old apple orchard. It is one of the first trees to gain a foothold on the lava overflows so common throughout the Southwest, and often forms the advance growth as the forest encroaches upon more arid lands. Less resistant to frost and drought than the neighboring junipers, pinyon will succeed on exposed slopes where the average annual precipitation is less than thirteen inches, and the annual range of temperature extends from 110° F. to 25° below zero.

This is one of four nut pines of the Southwest. Chief among the numerous details by which they may be distinguished is the manner in which the leaves or needles are borne. The Parry pinyon, *Pinus parryana*, has the needles in clusters of four; the Mexican pinyon, *Pinus cembroides*, usually in clusters of three; the singleleaf pinyon, *Pinus monophylla*, usually has single leaves; and the stout, dark, yellowish green needles of *Pinus edulis* are borne in pairs or occasionally in clusters of three. The ranges of these pines overlap, but all are confined to the Southwest. The needles of *Pinus edulis* are sharp-pointed, often curved, with smooth margins, and seven-eighths of an inch to one and three-fourths inches long. Those of seedlings and of new growth are a bright bluish green. They remain on the branches as long as nine years but begin to fall with the fourth season.

This small, scraggy nut pine grows in association with the western junipers, ponderosa pine, Gambel oak, the

14

mountain mahoganies, and in pure stands over small areas. As the range of this species extends principally throughout southeastern Utah, southwestern Colorado, northern Arizona and almost all of New Mexico, it forms a woodland type of considerable local importance. Best growth is attained on mesas and slopes where the sandy or gravelly soil is moderately deep and rich, but the tree is more frequently found on poor rocky soils.

In the early spring elongated clusters of dark red, pollen-bearing, staminate flowers cover the tree, while on the ends of the twigs are short-stalked, purplish, ovulate blossoms. The staminate flowers soon drop, but the ovulate ones develop in August and September of the second year into egg-shaped, shiny, yellowish brown cones about an inch to two inches long. The cone scales are relatively few in number and without prickles. In pairs, on the scales near the middle of each cone, are two to thirty red-brown, mottled, nut-like seeds.

Piñon (pin-yone) is the name given by the early Spanish explorers. The tree was described by Cabeza de Vaca in 1536. Although several other pines produce edible seeds, the scientific name *Pinus edulis* refers specifically to the large seeds of this tree.

Although pinyon bears abundant crops of seeds at intervals of two to five years, only a small percentage is fertile, and the power to germinate is soon lost. So large a part of the crop is eaten by birds, small animals, and gathered by Indians or local settlers that natural reproduction is poor. Weevils may also enter the seed before the cones open. For these reasons, the maintenance and reproduction of natural stands is difficult.

Pinyon nuts were formerly a staple item in the fall and winter diet of southwestern Indians and Mexicans, but they are now sold largely for use as a delicacy. To prevent the seeds from spoiling and to retain their flavor, they are usually baked immediately after being gathered.

The reddish brown bark is irregularly furrowed with shallow diagonal ridges and varies from half an inch to an inch thick.

The pinyon tree is usually only fifteen to twenty feet high, but reaches heights of thirty-five to fifty feet. The trunk is rarely free from branches for more than six or eight feet. Trees may attain breast high diameters of twelve to thirty inches in 150 to 375 years, but the growth is always slow. The root system is shallow.

The wood is soft, without special strength, and weighs about thirty-seven pounds to the cubic foot when air dry. Considerable quantities are used locally for fuel, fence posts, corral posts, telephone poles, mine logging, charcoal, and general construction. It is not durable in contact with the soil.

Pinyon is seldom injured by fire, but excessive grazing may destroy the seedlings. The worst enemy is probably a two-host fungus disease similar to white pine blister rust. As in the case of the white pine pest, the alternate host of the "pinyon blister rust" is a wild currant. Damage is chiefly sustained by seedlings and younger trees.

Although peculiar to the Southwest, this tree has been successfully planted in the eastern states where it has proved a hardy, slow growing, compact, bushy evergreen as far north as Massachusetts.

Dark, yellowish green needles are borne in pairs, and the large edible nuts grow in egg-shaped cones, at the ends of the branches

Mature trunks are clothed with reddish brown bark whose shallow irregular ridges may be broken into small detachable scales

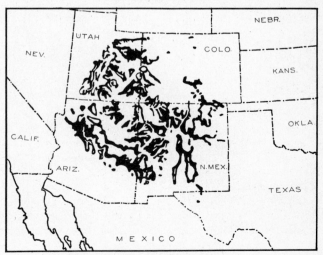

Natural range of Pinyon

15

SINGLELEAF PINYON

One-leaf pine

Pinus monophylla Torrey and Fremont

SINGLELEAF PINYON is unique among all American species of pine in that its needles occur singly (or occasionally in twos), from which it derives the name *monophylla*, meaning one leaf. Its range is principally in Nevada, except for the northwestern part of the state, and it extends westward to the eastern slopes of California's Sierra Nevada and southward to the eastern slopes of the San Bernardino Mountains. Stands occur also in extreme southwestern Utah, with scattered sites in northern Utah and western Arizona. It is found mostly on dry, low mountain slopes, canyon sides and foothills, where it frequently forms pure open stands over large areas between 2,000 and 7,000 feet above sea level. The largest trees and heaviest stands occur at the lower elevations.

Singleleaf pinyon is characteristically a low, spreading tree. In protected and otherwise favorable situations it may reach a height of from thirty-five to fifty feet but, as a rule, it does not exceed twenty-five feet in height and from twelve to fifteen inches in diameter. The short trunk, which is rarely straight, is often divided near the

Devereux Butcher

Characteristically a low spreading tree, Singleleaf Pinyon may reach a height of from 35 to 50 feet

low them, from the underside of the lower branches, hang the elongated, scaly, pollen-bearing, staminate flowers, which drop soon after releasing their pollen. The cones, like those of other true firs, maintain an erect position and in early September mature as close-packed cylinders of cone scales, three to five inches long, ranging in color from ashen-tinged olive-green to purple.

The seeds, which develop at the base of the scales, are a dingy yellow-brown with shiny, clear, rose-tinged wings. They are released to be carried fifty to one hundred feet by the wind as the thin, close-packed, overlapping cone scales gradually fall away from the central spike-like axis. Good seed crops occur at irregular intervals of two or three years, and, while most abundant during the years of the tree's rapid growth, continue to maturity. The erect, woody spikes of the cone cores remain attached to the branches for several years. In no cone-bearing trees except the eastern baldcypress do the cones break up as do those of the firs.

White fir wood is white, straight-grained, and fine-textured. It has no resin ducts and only a slight distinction between sapwood and heartwood. Unseasoned lumber has a disagreeable odor, which is so entirely lost with seasoning that it has been successfully used for butter tubs. Its slight resistance to decay makes treatment necessary wherever the wood is to be used in contact with the soil or where termites are prevalent. The wood weighs about twenty-six pounds to the cubic foot when air dry, or 1,550 to 1,600 pounds for every thousand board feet of sawed lumber. It compares favorably with eastern hemlock, spruce and ponderosa pine in strength and is used largely for the construction of small houses and for boxes and crates. It holds paint well, and is successfully used for cupboards and interior trim. Pulp material suitable for newspaper and wrapping paper can be produced from white fir, but there is a small prospect of any immediate market developing within the tree's range.

The stand of all the western true firs is estimated at about 100,000,000,000 board feet, more than one-third of which is white fir, about seventy percent of it in California.

While the seeds have a relatively low percentage of germination, they grow readily on almost any seed bed. The tree reproduces naturally on exposed denuded lands, as well as under its own shade. The seeds will grow under cultivation and small trees are readily transplanted.

White fir is widely used as an ornamental tree, and is growing successfully in many eastern states from Virginia north into New England. Its dense symmetrical crown and ability to survive under heavy shade render it especially suitable for landscape planting.

The mature cones are three to five inches long and they stand erect on the topmost branches

With age the resin pockets, or "balsam blisters," disappear and the ashy gray bark becomes deeply furrowed, hard, horny, and fire-resistant

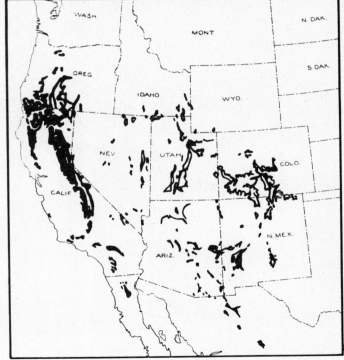

Natural range of White Fir

MEXICAN PINYON
Three-leaved pine, Mexican nut pine, Stoneseed pine
Pinus cembroides Zucce.

IN the United States, Mexican pinyon, handsomest of the pinyons, is distributed in the mountains of the border country, including the Chisos in Big Bend National Park, Brewster County, the Davis Mountains, Jeff Davis County and the Guadalupe Mountains in Guadalupe Mountains National Park, Culberson County, Texas, west to the Mogollon and Big Burro Mountains, Grant County, and the Hatchet Mountains, Hidalgo County, in southwestern New Mexico. In southeastern Arizona, the tree thrives in the Chiricahua and Huachuca mountains, Cochise County, the Santa Rita Mountains, Santa Cruz County, the Santa Catalina and Baboquiviri mountains in Pima County and as far north as the San Francisco Mountains, Greenlee County, the latter just west of the Mogollons of New Mexico.

It inhabits the oak-juniper belt on slopes from 4500 to 7500 feet, sometimes going as high as 8000 feet elevation.

Younger trees are symetrical and broadly conical with a short trunk clothed almost to the ground with many slender, spreading branches. Older trees, with trunks of a foot to one and a half feet in diameter and heights up to thirty-five feet and occasionally higher, develop stout branches to form a broad, rounded crown.

The bark on young stems and branches is rough and red-brown to gray; while that on older trunks is dark gray, deeply grooved, with thick ridges of thin scales.

The stout, slender twigs are dark gray-brown or yellow-brown, coated with pale, matted hair. Long and sharply pointed, the buds are protected by glossy brown scales.

The dark, slender, blue-green, curved needles are one and a half to two and a half inches long. They grow more densely toward the ends of the twigs, are triangular in cross-section, with rows of white stomata along the inner side and are three, rarely two, to a bundle.

Male or pollen-bearing flowers are erect, brown to yellow and catkin-like, and a half to three quarters of an inch long, borne in a cluster at the base of the new growth in spring. The small, dark red female or cone-producing flowers along the twig of the previous year, are globular, stalkless or on a short, stout stalk and, when developed, the cones are light brown, one to two and a half inches long, almost spherical or egg-shaped. When the thick, blunt, upper scales open, the cones are one and a half to two and a half inches broad at the base. The lower scales, flat and sterile, remain closed.

The dark choco-

Devereux Butcher

Conical in youth, Mexican Pinyon develops a well rounded head of dense, dark foliage with age

18

late-brown, hard shelled seeds or nuts are smooth, a half to three quarters of an inch in length, flattened on one side, oily, sweet, edible and are referred to as pinyon or pine nuts. A narrow, light brown, rudimentary seed-wing remains within the cone scale when the nut falls.

Because of the tree's small, broken range in our country, the nuts are not plentiful enough to be used widely here as food. They are sold in markets throughout Mexico, however, because the tree is much more widely distributed there. They are important also to small mammals.

Wood of Mexican pinyon is rather hard, coarse-grained, brittle, light yellow with thin, nearly white sapwood. It contains considerable amounts of pitch and has little value except for fuel.

An abundant tree within its scattered range, this pinyon associates with alligator, one-seed and drooping junipers, Arizona cypress, Chihuahua pine and a number of deciduous oaks, as well as evergreen ones, such as Emory, Grey and silverleaf.

One of the finest, as well as most easily accessible, stands of Mexican pinyon is to be seen in Green Gulch, Big Bend National Park, Texas, where a road ascends the gulch to The Basin in the heart of the Chisos Mountains. It is the only pinyon in the park and the largest, most numerous species of pine, and it cannot be mistaken there. Another stand can be seen along the Mount Lemmon road, toward the upper limits of the oak and juniper belt on the southern slope of the Santa Catalina Mountains, near Tucson, Arizona.

Devereux Butcher

The slender, blue-green, curved needles are triangular in cross-section, a half to two inches long, growing more densely toward the ends of the twigs

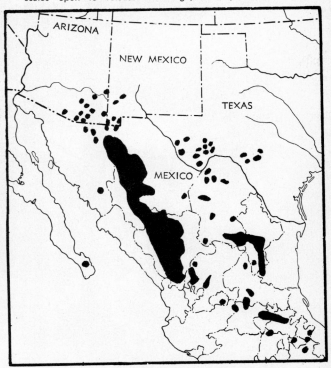

Devereux Butcher

Before opening, the light brown cones are nearly globular, becoming flat and about two inches broad when the upper scales open to release the large, brown, edible nuts

Devereux Butcher

Bark on young trunks and branches is rough and red-brown or gray, but on older trunks it is dark gray and deeply fissued into thick ridges of many thin scales

Natural range of Mexican Pinyon

CHIHUAHUA PINE

Yellow pine, Pino real
Pinus leiophylla var. *chihuahua* (Engelm.) Shaw

THE COMMON NAME, Chihuahua, pronounced *cheewawa*, derives from the Mexican state of Chihuahua, where the variety was discovered. From as far south as northern Durango, Mexico, the range of this pine extends northward through the mountains of Chihuahua and eastern Sonora, reaching its northern limits on Animas Peak and San Luis Pass in extreme southwestern New Mexico and in the Pinal, Chiricahua, Santa Catalina and Santa Rita mountains in southeastern Arizona, at altitudes generally between 5500 and 8200 feet above sea level.

This pine, inhabiting a scattered range in the Transition Zone north of the border, thrives best on coarse, gravelly soils on warm slopes and flats. Although occasionally developing pure stands, it associates with Apache and ponderosa pines, as well as with several species of live oak that inhabit the same elevations in the mountains of southern Arizona and New Mexico. A medium size tree, Chihuahua pine seldom attains heights above forty to fifty feet, with trunk diameters up to two feet. In Mexico, it reaches larger proportions. The straight, slightly tapering trunks of mature trees may be clear of branches for two thirds of their height. Lower branches tend to droop, but those above are horizontal, becoming increasingly ascending toward the top to form a rather narrow, open, irregular, pyramidal or rounded crown of comparatively sparse foliage. Growth is slow, maturity being reached in 250 to 300 years. Young trees are not tolerant of much shade.

The slender, blue-green nee-

A tree of sparse foliage and straight, slowly tapering trunk, Chihuahua Pine seldom is taller than forty or fifty feet, except in Mexico

20

dles, two to four inches long, are arranged in fascicles or bundles of three. Triangular in cross section, each one of the three sides is marked by conspicuous rows of pale or white stomata, and the needle margins are minutely toothed. At the base of each fascicle is a papery, light brown sheath, which, unlike those of other pines, drops off when the needles are fully grown. After remaining on the tree through their first year, each needle falls singly.

The slender twigs are bright orange during their first season, turning dull red with age. Bark on the lower trunk of mature trees is three quarters to one and a half inches thick, deeply broken by orange-red fissures into dark gray or black flat topped ridges of tightly appressed scales.

Flowers appear in July, the male or pollen-producing ones occurring in a cluster around the base of the new growth. Soon after the pollen has been dispersed by wind, they fall away. The female or seed-producing flowers are yellow-green, later developing into an ovoid or egg-shaped cone one and a half to two inches long, borne on a half inch stalk. Cone scales are light brown and lustrous, turning gray with weathering. Paler in color at their slightly thickened tips or umbos, which are armed with a small deciduous prickle, the scales may remain closed for several years before opening to release the seeds, which mature in September of their third year. The oval seeds, about a quarter inch long, are covered by a thin, dark brown husk attached to a thin membranous wing about five eighths of an inch in length. The abundance of cones that remain on the tree for many years is a distinguishing characteristic of Chihuahua pine.

Essentially, the wood of this pine is comparable to ponderosa pine. It is pale orange, with thick, paler sapwood; is light in weight, soft, lacks strength, but is durable under normal weathering. In the United States it has little commercial value because of a scattered, limited range, being used locally for lumber and fire wood.

A characteristic that is rare among pines is this tree's ability to sprout from the stump after logging. Although seed production in this species is abundant, reproduction from that source is sparse, but the deficiency is at least partly compensated by sprouting, which sometimes results in thickets of trees.

Chihuahua Pine cones, ovoid and one and a half to two and a half inches long, are borne on a short stalk. Their lustrous, light brown scales are paler at their thickened tips, which bear a deciduous prickle

The slender, blue-green needles, two to four inches in length and arranged in bundles of three, held at their base by a deciduous sheath, are triangular in cross section, with margins minutely toothed. Each of the three sides is marked by pale stomata

The gray or black bark of Chihuahua Pine usually is about one and a half inches thick, broken by orange-red fissures into scaly ridges

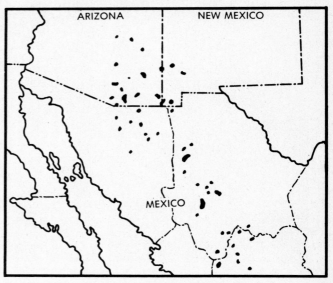

Natural range of Chihuahua Pine

BRISTLECONE PINE

Hickory pine, Foxtail pine

Pinus aristata Engelmann

BRISTLECONE PINE gets its name from the long, slender, bristle-like prickle which is borne at the end of each cone scale. The name foxtail refers to the brush-like needle tufts at the twig ends, and is perhaps best applied to the related species *P. balfouriana* Grev. and Balf.

This is a tree of the high mountain regions, from 8,000 to 11,000 feet elevation. It maintains its existence under adverse circumstances where it is cold and stormy in winter and where the brief growing season is subject to excessive drought. At the upper limit of its growth, it clings to stony ledges and wind-swept ridges, where the ungainly trunks are welcome to the traveler, miner, or sheepherder who is in need of shelter or of firewood for his camp.

Bristlecone grows from the Rocky Mountains of Colorado and northern New Mexico to Utah, eastern Nevada, the Inyo and White mountains of eastern California and the San Francisco Mountains of Arizona. Rarely forming pure stands, it is usually scattered on thin rocky soil, mainly on south slopes, with little or no underbrush. It is most abundant at higher levels where its only associate is limber pine, which it somewhat resembles in manner of growth. The two can be readily distinguished, however, by the shorter needles of the bristlecone pine.

The tree varies in height and form from a half-prostrate, twisted shrub at very high elevations, to a bushy-crowned tree from thirty-five to forty feet in locations more favorable for its growth. Ordinarily, bristlecone pine grows from fifteen to thirty or, at the most, forty feet high, and it has a short stocky trunk twelve to eighteen, or sometimes thirty, inches in diameter, which is commonly clothed for the greater part of its length in a dense, wide, irregular crown. In older trees, the upper branches are erect and much longer than the usually pendulous lower branches. The rather wide bushy crown of long, drooping lower branches and of irregularly long, upright top limbs is characteristic of single trees or those in open stands on wind-swept slopes. In denser stands, in less exposed situations, the crown may be narrower. Young trees have a distinctly pyramidal crown with short, rather thick branches which stand out from the stem at right angles.

The stout, light orange - colored

Arnold Arboretum

In favorable locations at high elevations, Bristlecone Pine is a bushy-crowned tree from thirty-five to forty feet tall. Elsewhere it is a twisted shrub

twigs turn to dark gray-brown, or nearly black, with age, and are clothed at the ends with long, compact, brush-like tufts of foliage.

Because of the small size, poor form and inaccessibility of trees, bristlecone pine contributes little or nothing to the nation's timber supply. This species provides, nevertheless, valuable cover on many of our high western watersheds. The tree is recognized as the oldest living tree in the world, with specimens in California's White Mountains estimated to be 4,000 years old. Part of the Inyo National Forest has been set aside to protect these trees.

The stout, curved, deep green needles, five to a bundle, are densely clustered at the ends of the twigs. Each mature needle is one and a quarter to one and a third inches long, lustrous on the back, and often showing minute but conspicuous whitish resin flecks on the surface. The leaves of each season's growth persist for fourteen to seventeen years.

Dark orange-red pollen-bearing flowers are borne on spikes throughout the crown; while the dark purple female ones are borne at the ends of the twigs. The cylindrical, nearly stemless cones mature at the end of the second season and are then two and a half to three and a half inches long, deep chocolate-brown, tinged with purple. They hang at the very tips of the branchlets, opening and scattering their seeds about the first of October. Each cone scale is armed with a sharp, slender, and very fragile incurved prickle nearly one-fourth inch long, often covered with brown, shiny droplets of resin.

The seeds are nearly oval, light brown, often mottled with black, with long, thin terminal wings. The trees begin to bear cones when they are about twenty years old and seeds are produced every season, with especially heavy crops at intervals of several years. The large winged seeds are carried a considerable distance by the wind, often as far as 600 feet from the parent tree. Nevertheless, reproduction is usually sparse and scattered because many of the seeds are eaten by rodents, and others never find conditions suitable for germination.

Bristlecone pine bark is thin, smooth and grayish white on the stems and branches of young trees. On the trunks of old trees, it is a dull reddish brown, one-half to three-quarters of an inch thick, and is rather shallowly furrowed. The main flat ridges, irregularly connected by narrower slanting divisions, are covered with small scales.

The narrow-ringed wood is light, soft, weak, pale brownish red with a thin layer of whitish sapwood, and weighs thirty-five pounds to the cubic foot in an air-dry condition. Because of the small size of the tree and its poor timber form, the wood is of little value, except in localities where better timber is scarce. There it is in demand for mine props, railway ties, fence posts and fuel. Although it is low in resistance to decay, fence posts and ties made of this wood may have a fairly long life when used in dry regions.

Bristlecone pine can be grown on the plains as an ornamental evergreen. In cultivation, it is usually a handsome low shrub, with ascending branches densely clothed with appressed leaves sprinkled with white grains of resin, a characteristic by which the species is easily distinguished from other shrubby pines.

Stout, curved, deep green needles are densely clustered at the ends of the twigs. Each cone scale bears a sharp, curved point

Young bark is thin, smooth and light gray. On old trunks it is dull reddish brown, thick, scaly and shallowly furrowed

Base map © J. L. Smith, Phila. Pa.

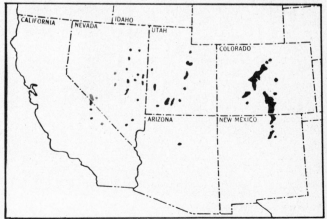

The natural range of Bristlecone Pine

23

BALFOUR PINE
Foxtail pine
Pinus balfouriana Grev. and Balf.

A CLOSE RELATIVE of bristlecone pine, *P. aristata*, Balfour pine is a tree of far more limited range. It occurs in but one area of the southern Sierra Nevada of California and, 375 miles distant, in three, small, separate areas in the northwestern corner of California. The Sierra Nevada location, the largest, is high on the eastern slope of the mountains, above Owens Lake, extending to the western slope on the Kern River watershed, lying across the southeastern boundary of Sequoia National Park southward into the Inyo National Forest.

The largest of the three northerly areas is approximately eight miles northwest of Clair Engle Lake, in the Shasta National Forest, Trinity County. Another, twenty miles to the northeast, is in the Scott Mountains, principally in Siskiyou County, also within the Shasta National Forest, about eight miles southwest of Weed; while the third, a little farther north and west, is in the Marble Mountains of the Klamath National Forest, Siskiyou County, twenty-five miles south of the Oregon state line.

The ranges of *P. balfouriana* and *P. aristata* do not overlap, the closest point between them being the twenty miles or so across the Owens Valley separating the Sierra Nevada from the Inyo Mountains to the east. Although both, at their highest elevations, are tree-line species, with *P. balfouriana* going from 5000 to 6000 feet above sea level in the northern part of its range, to 11,500 feet in the Sierra Nevada and, although both trees take on a weather-beaten, shrubby or sprawling form at the highest altitudes, they are readily distinguished by their ranges and by the longer cones of *P. balfouriana*.

The lustrous, dark green needles of Balfour pine are stout and stiff, measuring from three quarters of an inch to an inch and a half long and are marked on their under sides by several rows of pale stomata. Borne in bundles of five, which places this species in the white pine group, the needles are thickly clustered toward the twig ends to form long, thick masses of foliage that suggests the common names foxtail and bottle-brush. The needles remain on the tree for as long as a dozen years.

Male or pollen-producing flow-

Short branches, a narrow crown and heights of forty to sixty feet typify Balfour Pine in its windy, snowy mountain top habitats

ers, in the form of small, dark orange-red aments, appear in spring at the base of the new growth; while the female or seed-producing flowers are dark purple, developing into oblong ovate cones measuring three to five inches in length and turning dark red-brown when mature, but weathering gray with age. The cone scales are protected at their thick tips by a small, incurved prickle.

Mottled with dark purple, the pale seeds are one third inch in length, rounded at the apex, tapering toward the base and are attached to a wing about an inch long by a quarter inch wide.

This species attains heights of from forty to sixty feet and, in optimum sites, occasionally as much as ninety feet, with trunk diameters ranging from one to three and sometimes five feet.

Because of winter snow and ice and severe winds at the high altitudes, branches tend to be comparatively short, forming an irregular, narrow crown of minutely hairy or downy branchlets, which become smooth, turning gray or almost black, bearing the brush-like foliage only at their outer ends. With age, trees in exposed locations often die back until sometimes no more than a branch or two remain alive—a characteristic also of the related *P. aristata*.

Bark on the trunks and branches of young trees is smooth and thin and light gray; while that on mature trunks becomes red-brown, three-quarters of an inch thick and deeply furrowed into broad, flat, rectangular plates of closely appressed scales.

The pale brown, rather heavy wood is soft and brittle and of little commercial value because of its rarity as a timber-producing tree. Balfour pine grows in association with limber pine in the Sierra Nevada and with whitebark pine, mountain hemlock, red fir, *A. magnifica*, and California incensecedar in the northern localities of its range.

U. S. Forest Service

Three- to five-inch cones are dark red at maturity, each scale tipped by a small, incurved prickle. Stiff, dense and lustrous, the needles are three-quarters to one and a half inches long

G. B. Sudworth, U. S. Forest Service

Bark on young trunks is thin, smooth and nearly white, while on mature trunks it is red-brown, three-quarters of an inch thick and deeply furrowed into broad, flat, rectangular plates

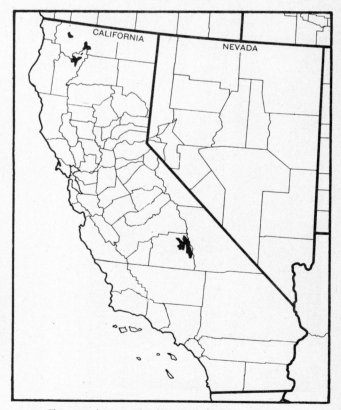

The natural range of Balfour Pine does not overlap that of the closely related Bristlecone Pine

25

PONDEROSA PINE
Western yellow pine, Blackjack pine
Pinus ponderosa Douglas

KNOWN until recently as western yellow pine, and by a variety of other names, this tree of the western mountains is now recognized as ponderosa pine. It grows in fairly open stands from British Columbia and the Black Hills of the Dakotas southward in the Pacific and Rocky Mountain regions to western Texas, New Mexico, Arizona and on into northern Mexico and Lower California. Northern and Pacific coast forms have been differentiated from the southwestern ones, but this description includes all forms under the single heading. In different parts of its range there is noticeable variation in length and thickness of the needles, size of the cones, color of the bark and texture of the wood.

It grows on well-drained uplands and mountain slopes up to elevations of 12,000 feet in the southern part of its range and in dry valleys at lower elevations in the north. In the Colorado plateau of northern Arizona and New Mexico, ponderosa pine constitutes over four-fifths of the stand in vast valuable forests at elevations of 6,500 feet to 10,500 feet above sea level.

Members of the Lewis and Clark expedition first reported this tree in 1804, while going up the Missouri River. Twenty-two years later, David Douglas found it growing near the Spokane River in eastern Washington. He suggested the name *ponderosa,* because of the tree's ponderous bulk, and he sent seeds to European gardeners.

Ponderosa pine trees attain heights of 150 to 230 feet and five to eight feet in diameter at breast height. They may be 350 to 500 years old and the regular spire-like head surmounts a massive trunk, the irregularly divided scaly bark of which is cinnamon-brown to orange-yellow. Until the trees are eighty to one hundred years old, the bark is less broken and is dark brown to nearly black. This accounts for the name blackjack pine and the occasional idea that the dark barked trees are unrelated to the older trees with the brighter colored bark.

Grouped botanically among the pitch pines, ponderosa pine has needles five to ten inches long which are borne in clusters of two and three. Normally these remain on the twigs from three to seven years.

Asahel Curtis

Forest-grown trees may reach heights up to 200 feet and live for 500 years. The map shows the natural range of Ponderosa Pine

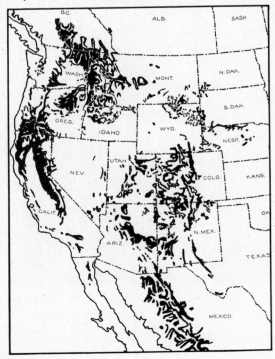

The brown cones are three to six inches long and are frequently in a cluster. Before the seeds ripen the cones are bright green or purple and stand erect on their short stalks. As they ripen they become a reddish brown, turn down, and the scales spread open for the winged seeds to escape. Ordinarily there are two triangular seeds under each scale.

The hard, strong, comparatively fine-grained wood is light red with a narrow band of nearly white sapwood and weighs twenty-five to twenty-eight pounds to the cubic foot when air dry. The light weight has led to its confusion with white pine. A fungus known as "blue stain" frequently disfigures the sapwood of trees cut in warm, damp weather, but does not materially reduce its strength. The wood is widely used for general construction, interior finish, boxing and crating. It is not strong enough for heavy construction and is too easily attacked by fungi to be used in contact with the soil.

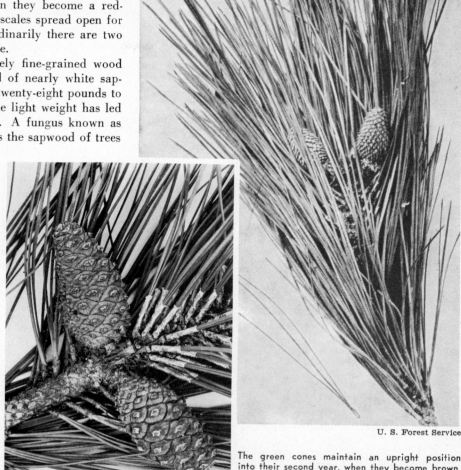

Ponderosa pine grows vigorously from seed and adapts itself to forest plantings. It has been successfully planted over its natural range, and to a considerable extent in the eastern states, but is not generally a rapid grower. There are so many other trees better adapted to eastern conditions that it is not recommended for planting outside of the area where it is native.

The green cones maintain an upright position into their second year, when they become brown, turn down and release the seeds from between the back-spread scales. Usually three, but occasionally two needles are held in a cluster

Although subject to a number of insect and fungus enemies, the trees' resistance to them is evidenced by its wide distribution, the large areas of forest in which ponderosa pine predominates, and the great age and size that it frequently attains. Next to fire, the two most serious enemies of ponderosa pine are the *dendroctonus* bark beetle and mistletoe. Attacks by bark beetles may follow fire damage and these attacks frequently accompany mistletoe.

Two common forms of needle disease either distort the needles or cause them to die. Neither disease kills the tree, but materially reduces the rate of growth.

In Oregon and other parts of the West, caterpillars of the pandora moth have eaten the needles from large areas of merchantable pine. Infestations reach epidemic proportions at fairly regular intervals of twenty or thirty years, and continue for six to eight years.

The size of the trees, the great area over which they grow and the relative inaccessibility of many of the timber stands make absolute control of this pest impracticable. Although mature trees are fire-resistant, foresters in charge of forests of ponderosa pine face a problem in keeping its enemies within bounds.

Close pressed papery layers or scales make up the bark which is cinnamon-brown to orange-yellow in the older trees, but nearly black in trees younger than eighty or 100 years

27

JEFFREY PINE
Bull pine
Pinus jeffreyi Greville and Balfour

JEFFREY PINE, known also as bull and black pine, is scarcely less magnificent in size than its associate ponderosa pine, which it so closely resembles that some botanists consider it a variety of the latter. From the forester's point of view, there appears to be no practical reason for distinguishing them, as they occur in practically the same region, are nearly of the same form and have similar wood.

Jeffrey Pine is found from southern Oregon down along the Sierra Nevada slopes to Lower California. Beautiful and symmetrical in form, mature trees are often 180 feet high

Woodbridge Metcalf

Botanically, however. Jeffrey pine, discovered in northern California in 1850 by John Jeffreys, differs in many respects from ponderosa. The needles are bluish green, compared to the yellow-green foliage of ponderosa; moreover, the huge, thick cone of Jeffrey pine, five to fifteen inches long, contrasts conspicuously with the smaller cone of ponderosa, which measures from three to six inches. The prickles on the Jeffrey pine cone scales are longer than those on ponderosa pine, but they turn inward and hence the cone can be handled without the prickly feel typical of ponderosa cones.

The tree grows from southern Oregon southward along both slopes of the Sierra Nevada to Lower California. It mingles with ponderosa pine but can endure greater extremes of climate, and east of the Sierra, where conditions are much more rigorous, it is the more important species. Mature trees attain heights of 100 to 180 feet, with short, spreading, or often pendulous, branches, the uppermost ascending, forming an open pyramidal and sometimes narrow spire-like head. Trees from 200 to 400 years old have trunk diameters of from three to six feet.

The bluish green needles are from five to ten inches long. They remain on the twigs longer than those of ponderosa pine, thus giving the foliage a heavier and denser appearance. The twigs of a year's growth are considerably thicker than those of ponderosa and distinctly purple when young, compared to brownish green in ponderosa pine. When cut or bruised, they exhale a fragrant, violet-like or pineapple-like aroma, whereas twigs of ponderosa give off a turpentine or orange peel odor.

The male pollen-bearing flowers are yellow-green; the female, or ovulate flowers, which occur in clusters or pairs at the ends of the upper branches are purplish. The drooping, short-stalked cones are shaped something like an old-fashioned beehive, thick in proportion to their length, and purple in color when mature at the end of the second season. The cone scales terminate in a long, slender, incurved prickle, which is occasionally deciduous. After shedding their seeds, the cones turn a light russet-brown. They fall in September.

The seeds are yellowish brown mottled with purple, similar to those of ponderosa pine, but are larger—often nearly one-half inch long. The wings are also larger—from one to one and three-quarter inches long. It takes about 3,100 seeds to weigh a pound.

The oblong winter buds are only slightly resinous on the surface; in ponderosa pine, they are profusely dotted with resin droplets. Although the bark is similar in appearance to that of ponderosa, it is a darker cinnamon-red and is usually tinged with lavender or purple, particularly on old trunks.

While Jeffrey pine is a prolific seeder, it produces seed only at a rather advanced age. Large numbers of the seeds are eaten by birds and rodents. Their weight prevents them from being blown far from the parent tree. Jeffrey pine reproduces more vigorously at higher altitudes than does ponderosa pine.

Jeffrey pine is an ornamental tree, mainly because of its symmetrical habit when young and its long, pale bluish leaves, which are longer than in most other hardy species. It is occasionally planted as an ornamental in eastern Europe and has been cultivated with some success in eastern United States. It is hardy in sheltered positions as far north as Massachusetts.

The species is subject to the same insect and fungus enemies as ponderosa pine, the two most serious being the *dendroctonus* bark beetle and mistletoe. Attacks by bark beetles may follow fire damage and they frequently accompany mistletoe. They channel beneath the bark of the trunk and kill the tree more quickly than does mistletoe, the latter a parasite, which centers its attack principally upon the limbs and branches. Two forms of needle disease are also common. These either distort the needles or cause them to die, though in neither case do they kill the trees. They materially reduce the rate of growth, however.

In Oregon and other regions of the West, caterpillars of the pandora moth have eaten the needles from large areas of pine. They reach epidemic proportions at fairly regular intervals of twenty or thirty years, and continue abundant for six to eight years.

Jeffrey pine is found in the same regions where ponderosa pine grows, and the two species are not kept separate in the lumber trade.

The wood of Jeffrey pine is similar to that of ponderosa in appearance, properties and uses. That from the outer portion of large trees is comparatively soft and light in weight, often bearing a close resemblance to white pine. In young trees and in the heartwood of older trees it is generally heavier, harder and stronger. In general, the wood of Jeffrey pine, because it occurs largely in regions of low rainfall, where the growth is somewhat slower, is lighter and softer than that of pon-

George B. Sudworth

Five to fifteen inches long, the cones resemble an old-fashioned beehive. They are thick and purple in color when mature. The characteristic bark of Jeffrey Pine (left) is dark cinnamon-red, tinged with lavender or purple. The map shows the natural range of Jeffrey Pine

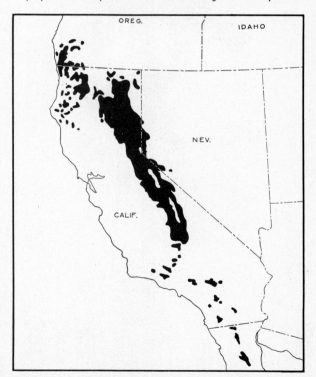

George B. Sudworth

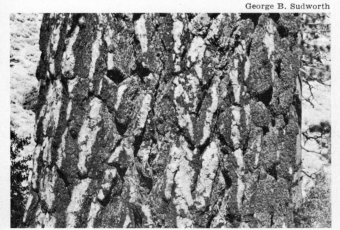

derosa pine. This lighter, softer wood, as well as that of ponderosa, is especially suitable for window sash, doors and inside finish of houses. Lumber that contains defects, such as knots, is used in making boxes, for which it is well adapted because of its moderate weight, light color and the ease with which it can be worked and nailed. Much of the heavier, denser wood is cut into sheathing, joists, and rafters for house construction.

LODGEPOLE PINE

Bird's eye pine, Screw pine, Tamarack pine

Pinus contorta Loudon

LODGEPOLE PINE has been referred to as the most common conifer of the northern Rockies. It grows from sea level to elevations of 11,500 feet, extending from the Yukon River down the coast of Alaska and British Columbia, through Washington, Oregon and California, and most of the Rocky Mountain region. Along the seacoast and in the bogs of the far North, the tree is frequently gnarled and stunted so as to deserve the name "scrub pine." Doubtless, the technical name, *Pinus contorta*, refers to the twisted branches of the botanical type characteristic of the coast, which is also reflected in the local name, "screw pine." In parts of the Rocky Mountains, where it grows with Douglasfir, Engelmann spruce, alpine fir, and other trees, lodgepole pine is of commercial importance.

While commonly sixty to eighty feet high, it occasionally reaches 150 feet, and thirty to forty inches in diameter. Trees mature in about 140 years and may live to be 300 years old. It develops stands of more than 10,000 board feet to the acre. By far the greater part of the lodgepole pine stands in the United States are in the Rocky Mountains, with the remainder in the Pacific Northwest.

Some botanists recognize the more upstanding tree of the high mountains as a distinct species, while others call it a variety of lodgepole pine. Accordingly, it may be referred to as *Pinus murrayana*, or *Pinus contorta* variety *latifolia*.

The needles or leaves are bright yellow-green, occur in pairs, range from one inch to three inches, but average about two inches in length, and remain on the trees six to eight years.

Fertile cones are borne nearly every year after the trees are fifteen years old. Heavy seed crops occur at intervals of three or four years. The cones are glossy, light yellow-brown, three quarters of an inch to two inches long, and often occur in clusters of a half dozen or more. Each thin scale is armed with a slender more or less recurved prickle. The cones ripen in August or September of the second season, but may hang on the branches for years before opening and liberating their seeds. Lodgepole pine seeds have been known to show life after forty years.

In dense stands, tall, clean, gradually tapering shafts with short, round, small-branched crowns are developed. Such shafts, five or six inches in diameter, and flexible, were used by Indians to make their lodges or tepees, whence the name "lodgepole pine." Open stands result in dense rounded or pyramidal

U. S. Forest Service

Lodgepole Pine of the Rocky Mountains frequently grows in dense, even-aged stands, attaining a height of one hundred and fifty feet, with diameters of three feet or more

crowns of large, much-forked branches which may extend down to the ground.

The wood is hard, stiff, somewhat brittle and straight-grained. The heartwood is usually light brown, tinged with red, while the thick sapwood is nearly white. A pebbled appearance on some boards has led to the name "bird's eye pine." The wood from coast trees is heavier, stronger and more dense than that from trees grown in the mountains, a cubic foot weighing about thirty-six pounds as compared with about twenty-five pounds for the mountain form. Lodgepole pine is used for railroad ties, construction lumber, fence and corral poles, house logs and fuel.

Although native only to the West, lodgepole pine has been successfully planted in various parts of the East. Specimens growing in the Arnold Arboretum, in Massachusetts, were planted about 1877, and others have been grown successfully at Letchworth Park in western New York since 1912 and 1914. Under natural conditions it avoids limestone soils and demands full sunlight for best growth.

The thin scaly bark of the trunk is pale brown with a grayish tinge, from half an inch to an inch thick, and irregularly divided by vertical and cross fissures into small oblong plates. The inner bark is prepared as food by the Indians of the Northwest and of Alaska. The Indians also work it into baskets.

Fire destroys large areas of valuable lodgepole timber, but at the same time it prepares ideal conditions for the seedlings by exposing the mineral soil, removing competing vegetation and killing or driving away the birds and rodents that would otherwise feed on the seed. In dense lodgepole stands, fires quickly develop into disastrous crown blazes, which destroy everything in their path. Even surface fires quickly burn through the thin bark and severely damage the stands. The cone scales, however, insulate many of the seeds against damage, yet they open most readily in the presence of heat, so that a heavy distribution of seeds frequently follows a fire. The resulting lodgepole seedlings grow quickly in the fire-cleaned area, producing a dense stand without competition from other kinds of trees.

Mistletoe distorts many lodgepole trees, causing them to have thin crowns, sickly, pale, short needles and slow growth. Trees badly covered with mistletoe should be cut and removed when practicable. Heart rot in lodgepole pine is caused by canker infections from several kinds of wood-destroying fungi.

Serious damage is done great areas of lodgepole pine by western pine bark beetles, which bore under the bark and eventually girdle and kill the trees. Bark beetles can be controlled by peeling the bark from the trunk and stump of the tree and then burning it. Porcupines prove a lesser menace by gnawing off the bark from many trees, killing branches and sometimes whole trees.

U. S. Forest Service

The bright yellow-green needles are about two inches long and borne in pairs. The cones range up to two inches long. Natural range of Lodgepole Pine is shown in the map

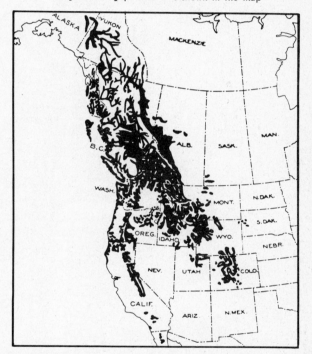

U. S. Forest Service

The pale brown bark of the main trunk is made up of many thin, irregular scales and is seldom more than an inch thick

31

COULTER PINE
Big-cone pine
Pinus coulteri **D. Don**

ALTHOUGH smaller than ponderosa pine, Coulter pine, in general appearance, resembles the young or middle-age trees of that species, with which it is sometimes associated. However, Coulter pine is easily distinguished by its stiff, much heavier foliage, stouter twigs and huge cones. It is sometimes called big-cone pine. Other common names applied locally to the Coulter pine are pitch pine and nut pine.

Ordinarily it is from forty to sixty feet high, with an irregularly open, heavy-branched crown. The clear trunk is short—from ten to fifteen feet—and from eighteen to thirty inches in diameter. Occasionally, trees reach a height of nearly seventy-five feet and a diameter of three and a half feet. The big lower branches are long, bending downward often to the ground, with an upward curve at their ends, and the upper branches are short and ascending, forming a loose, unsymmetrical, often picturesque head.

The stout twigs are dark orange-brown at first, becoming nearly black at the end of three or four years, and roughened by the persistent bases of the bud scales. The winter buds are oblong egg-shaped and resinous, sharp and often abruptly pointed. Bud scales are fringed.

On dry warm slopes and ridges, as well as sometimes on more moist sheltered north slopes, Coulter pine occurs on the coast ranges of southern California, generally at elevations of from 3,000 to 6,000 feet. At lower altitudes, it occurs singly or in groups on summits and in sheltered ravines and hill coves. Coulter pine never forms pure forests but is commonly associated with incense-cedar, ponderosa pine, big-cone-spruce, su-

Coulter Pine is distinguished by a heavy-branched crown, short trunk, stiff, heavy foliage and huge cones

gar pine and live oak. The stout, dark, bluish green leaves, three to a bundle, are from six and a half to twelve inches long. They occur in immense bunches at the ends of the branchlets and are deciduous during their third and fourth seasons.

The staminate, or male, flowers are in crowded, cylindrical and somewhat curved clusters; their anthers are yellow. The pistillate flowers are oblong-oval, their scales ovate and dark reddish brown covered with a whitish bloom and contracted into long incurved tips.

The huge, armed, extremely heavy cones distinguish this pine from all its relatives and associates. Coulter pine produces the heaviest cones of any American pine. The largest, when green, have weighed from four to five pounds. Measuring from ten to fourteen inches in length, they are egg-shaped, short-stalked and pendant. The thick, broad, light yellow-brown cone scales terminate in flattened elongated knobs armed with more or less incurved flat claws, one-half to one and a half inches long. Those near the base of the cone are the longest and exhibit the greatest curvature. The scales are dull dark purple on the exposed surfaces.

The cones mature by August of the second summer and, during October, open partly and continue to shed a few of their seeds for several months. Some of the cones remain attached to the branches for six years or more. The oval, compressed, dark chestnut-brown seeds, about one-half inch long, are thick-shelled and encircled by a thin wing with a thickened inner margin, broadest near the oblique apex. The wing is nearly twice as long as the seed and is shiny brown, striped with darker lines. The seeds were formerly gathered in large quantities and eaten by the Indians of southern California.

The bark is roughly broken, even on young trees. That of old trunks is from one and a half to two inches thick, dark brown to nearly black, and deeply furrowed, with broad, rounded ridges which are roughly scaly and irregularly connected with one another.

The wood is coarse-grained, light and soft, with light red or reddish brown heartwood and thick, nearly white sapwood. It is suitable for low-grade lumber, but is rarely cut except for fuel. It formerly was used in large quantities for the production of charcoal for blacksmith shops.

Although some seed is produced every year and large crops are released about every third year, reproduction is never dense. The heavy seeds usually fall close to the parent tree and many do not encounter conditions suitable for germination. Too, the seed retains its vitality for a comparatively short time. However, seed is produced at an early age and cones are often borne on trees only ten to fifteen feet high.

Coulter pine is a slow growing species. Trees from twenty to twenty-six inches in diameter are 110 to 125 years old. It probably does not reach a greater age than 200 years. The tree cannot endure shade except when very young, when it competes successfully with chaparral.

In European countries this is a popular ornamental pine and is planted chiefly for its great golden-brown cones. It is also planted somewhat as an ornamental tree in the United States.

Dr. A. E. Hubbard

The egg-shaped cones, the heaviest of any American pine, weigh four to five pounds when green

L. C. Miller

Even on young trees the bark is roughly broken. On old trunks it is dark brown and deeply furrowed

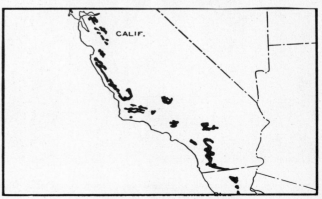

The natural range of Coulter Pine

DIGGER PINE

Gray pine, Grayleaf pine

Pinus sabiniana Douglas

THE DIGGER, or gray pine, is one of the small group of distinctively California pines. The tree was discovered in 1831 near Monterey by the young Scottish botanist and explorer, David Douglas, and named by him for his friend Joseph Sabin, then secretary of the Horticultural Society in London. The common name of Digger pine derives from the fact that the first Europeans to reach California called the native Indians "Diggers," and found them subsisting during a part of the year on the large rich seeds, or nuts, of this pine.

This pale, dusty, gray-green, gaunt tree is characteristic of California's dry interior. Its distribution is limited largely to the foothills, lower mountain slopes and high valleys, and although it is found as low as 500 feet elevation and as high as 4,000 feet above sea level, in general it likes altitudes of 1,000 to 2,500 feet. Growing well in dry, shallow, coarse gravelly soils, where no other pine can survive, Digger pine adapts itself to sites with rainfall as low as five inches and temperatures from ten to 110 degrees Fahrenheit. It is found mainly on the south slopes of the Klamath Mountains, eastward to Owens Valley, in the Sierra Nevada, and southward to the San Bernardino Mountains.

Digger pine, which belongs to the pitch pine group, does not form pure forests, but grows mostly in open groups or singly. At the lower elevations it mingles with ponderosa, Coulter and knobcone pines. Best growth is attained at elevations ranging between 2,000 and 3,000 feet, where it competes only with chaparral. In early life it endures shade very well, but later on demands the fullest sunlight.

Its mature form is very irregular, with one or more large limbs curving upward from a usually crooked trunk, or separating into several forks similar to a hardwood. Its odd form, with its rapidly tapering trunk, gray-green, sparse-foliaged crown and lower drooping branches, make the tree readily recognizable at a considerable distance.

Old trees vary in height from fifty to eighty feet, with trunk diameters of from two to four feet. Little is known definitely of its longevity, but it appears to reach its average size in sixty to eighty

Devereux Butcher

A crooked trunk and open crown characterize Digger Pine—gaunt, hardy tree of California's dry interior foothills

34

Sparse gray-green needles, up to twelve inches long, are borne in clusters of three

Scales of the large, heavy cones are reddish brown, sharp-pointed and incurved

Dark brown, irregularly ridged bark on mature trees is two inches thick

Natural range of Digger Pine.

years. Recurrent fires may prevent a possible survival up to a hundred and fifty years. Young trees have a rounded or pyramidal crown branching from a short, thick stem, with dull gray bark. The bark in mature trees is about two inches thick, roughly furrowed, with wide, irregular scaly ridges. It is dark gray-brown, tinged with purple-red when unweathered.

The needles of Digger pine are light blue or gray-green, from eight and a half to twelve inches long, and grow three to a bundle in thin, drooping clusters. They remain on the tree for three or four years.

Cones are six and a half to ten and a half inches long. Among American pines, only those of Coulter pine are larger and heavier. Those of the Digger pine occur annually in varying quantities, mature by September of the second year following the blossom, but remain firmly attached to the branches for years. The scales are sharp-pointed and incurved toward the stem, making them difficult to handle. Opening slowly, the cones shed seed during several months. The Indians used to gather the cones, hasten their opening by fire, and eat the rich, meaty nut-like seeds.

The short-winged seeds of Digger pine are dark chocolate or blackish brown. The heavy nuts are seldom scattered by the wind, falling near the seed trees where natural reproduction is usually found. Seeds germinate during the winter rainy season, producing seedlings with fifteen or sixteen seed leaves, usually under shade and on rough, bare mineral soil.

The dark yellowish brown wood, often tinged with red, is soft and light. Because the tree grows in the open or in scattered stands, the wood is very coarse-grained. It is weak and brittle, a cubic foot of dry wood weighing slightly over thirty pounds. Distillation of the wood produces a nearly colorless aromatic liquid, abietene, used to some extent in making stains. The small commercial value is largely confined to local use for fuel. The tree's greatest value is as a soil-holder in watershed protection. When planted for ornamental purposes, in fertile, irrigated soil, the needles are stouter, the appearance is more thrifty, and the cones are usually smaller.

TORREY PINE

Soledad pine, Del Mar pine, Lone pine

Pinus torreyana Parry

TORREY PINE has the smallest range of any pine of the United States. It is confined to a narrow strip of coast, a few miles long, in southern California just north of San Diego, and the neighboring Santa Rosa Island. It is found only in open, scattered stands with little or no other growth, except the thin chaparral, on the highlands adjacent to the sea and on the sides of deep ravines and washes leading to the coast.

Along the coast, where it is exposed to high winds, Torrey pine is a low, crooked, bent or sprawling tree from twenty-five to thirty-five feet in height and eight to fourteen inches in diameter. Away from the sea winds, it grows to a height of fifty to sixty feet, with a straight trunk, as much as two and a half feet in diameter. The largest trees are found on sheltered sides of hills and spurs of canyons. The crown is small, rounded and often composed of only a few large, greatly developed branches.

The stout twigs are bright green in their first season, becoming light purple and ultimately nearly black.

Torrey pine is readily distinguished from other pines of the Pacific coast by its long, heavy needles which vary from seven and a half to thirteen inches in length and occur five to a bundle. The foliage is dark gray-green and clustered in large tufts at the ends of the stout branches.

The blossoms appear from January to March. The yellow staminate flowers occur in short, dense heads while the purplish pistillate flowers are borne on long stout stems. The deep russet or chocolate-brown cones are broadly ovate, from four to five inches long and about as broad as long. Strongly attached to the branches by thick stems, they ripen early in August of the third season, and by the middle of September some of the seeds are shed. The cones usually remain on the tree for

Ralph D. Cornell

Along the coast where exposed to winds, Torrey Pine is a low, crooked, sprawling tree twenty-five to thirty feet tall. Away from the sea winds it attains greater height and has a straight trunk

Dark gray-green needles occur five to a bundle.
The russet cones are four or five inches long

Yellow staminate flowers occur in short dense
heads. The pistillate are borne on long stems

On old trees bark is dull gray and spongy,
irregularly divided into broad, flat ridges

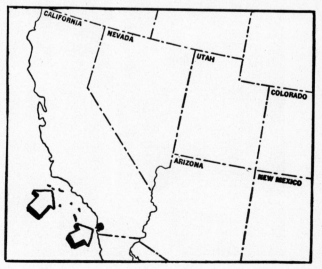

Found only in southern California, Torrey Pine has
the smallest range of any pine in the United States

four or five years.

When the cones fall, a few cone scales remain attached to the branch of the tree. These thick scales are armed with minute spines, and the large edible seeds, from three-fourths of an inch to an inch long, are dark brown, with areas of yellow-brown. They are nearly surrounded by thin dark brown wings, often nearly one-half inch long. They are edible, and may be eaten raw or roasted.

Seeds are produced in large quantities every year, trees bearing well when from twelve to eighteen years old. Most of the seeds are discharged from the cones during their third year. Germination usually takes place in crevices and washed mineral soil. Reproduction is good and seedlings are quite numerous in the vicinity of parent trees.

The bark on young trees, as well as that on the branches of old ones is spongy and dull gray. On the trunks of old trees it is about an inch thick, irregularly and deeply divided into broad, flat ridges covered by wide, thin, light reddish brown scales.

The light, soft, wide-grained wood is low in strength properties. The heartwood is pale reddish brown and the sapwood nearly white. Because of the small size of the tree and its limited occurrence, the wood is of no commercial importance. It is occasionally used for fuel.

Torrey pine is a slow growing species. Trees ten to twelve inches in diameter are from seventy-five to eighty years old. It is also short-lived by comparison with other pines, usually reaching an age of 100 to 150 years, with a maximum of 200 years.

Several names have been applied to this tree, including Soledad pine, Del Mar pine and lone pine—but Torrey pine or Torrey's pine is the one by which it is most commonly known.

RED PINE
Norway pine
Pinus resinosa Aiton

THE straight clean trunk and reddish brown bark of the red pine is a familiar feature of the forest stands of the Northeast from southern Canada throughout the northern states from Maine to Min-

Devereux Butcher

Red Pine attains heights of eighty feet or more

nesota, and south as far as Pennsylvania. Scattered specimens are found in West Virginia. This species reaches its optimum development on sandy plains in the Great Lakes region, as well as on dry, gravelly ridges of the northeastern states.

Known widely as Norway pine, this tree is usually from sixty to eighty feet high with trunk diameters of two to three feet at breast height. Occasional trees attain a height of 140 feet with a diameter of four and a half feet. It seldom reaches an age of more than 300 years and declines in vigor after 200 to 230 years. During the first sixty or seventy years, the red pine is capable of an average height growth of one foot a year. Thereafter, the rate of growth gradually declines until it practically ceases at around one hundred years. The crown is symmetrically conical, and the whorled branches extend at right angles from the main trunk. Under forest conditions the trunk may be free of branches for one-half to two-thirds of the total height.

Stands in Massachusetts have attained an average height of ninety-one feet with breast high diameters of sixteen inches in eighty-eight years, while average trees in a Minnesota stand were over 200 years old and measured nearly nineteen inches in diameter.

The dark green, glossy leaves are borne in pairs held together by long, persistent, membranous sheaths. Each leaf is four to six inches long, flexible, and sharply pointed. Leaves occur in tufts near the ends of the branches and remain on the tree four or five seasons.

In May or June dense clusters of dark purple staminate blossoms about half an inch long occur at the base of the current season's growth, while near the ends of the upper branches on the same tree are the less evident pairs of short-stalked, broadly egg-shaped, scarlet, ovulate flowers. The short, compact character of the ovulate flower is retained as the cone develops to maturity through the succeeding two seasons.

The light, chestnut-brown, broadly conical cone is about two inches long, and grows without a stalk, at right angles to the parent stem. Each cone scale is slightly thickened at the end, and unarmed. No other pine, native to the northeast except white, has cone scales without a spine or bristle. Although the cone may remain on the tree through the winter, most of the winged seeds are shed early in the autumn. Ordinarily, a bushel of cones will yield a half to three-quarters of a pound of mottled brown, oval seeds approximately an eighth of an inch long. About 50,000 are required to make a pound. Never a prolific seed bearer, red pine produces its cones high in the crown, at intervals of two to four years. Except during logging operations, seeds are difficult to gather, but they bring relatively high prices.

An outstanding feature of the tree is the reddish brown bark, divided by shallow fissures into broad, flat ridges, with thin, irregular, flaky scales. The bark is three-fourths to one and a half inches thick, and rich in tannin. The color is partly responsible for the common name.

The species name *resinosa* is not particularly appropriate in that it indicates a pine "full of resin." Living red pines have never been a source of turpentine, but gum spirits are sometimes produced in small quantities by burning the stumps in especially constructed stills. An accepted name—Norway pine—is credited to an early explorer who confused the tree with Scotch pine, *Pinus sylvestris,* which grows in Norway.

The pale red, close-grained heartwood, surrounded by a moderately thick layer of light yellow sapwood, weighs thirty to thirty-four pounds to the cubic foot when air dry. It is used for general construction, piles, door and window frames, sash, flooring, boxes, crates, ship masts, and ship flooring. It is not durable when used without treatment in contact with the soil.

While pure stands occur in the lake states, red pine more frequently grows with white and jack pines and hardwoods.

The thick bark of red pine is fairly resistant to fire. The species has the ability to reproduce heavily after fire, and to grow rapidly during the seedling and sapling stages. It is more resistant to insects and diseases than white pine.

Red pine is frequently used for forest planting in the northeastern states. Its rich color, attractive form, vigorous growth, and the ease with which it may be transplanted make it popular for ornamental purposes, while the quality of the lumber gives it a place of increasing importance in forest management.

William M. Harlow

Each pair of needles is four to six inches long, and the cone has no spines or prickles

U. S. Forest Service

The reddish brown bark flakes off in irregular scales

Devereux Butcher

In May or June, dark purple, crowded clusters of staminate or pollen-producing flowers in half-inch catkins appear at the base of the current season's growth

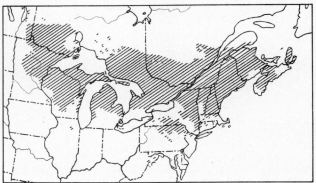

Natural range of Red Pine

39

PITCH PINE

Southern Pine
Pinus rigida Miller

PITCH PINE belongs to the group of hard pines, and is the only three-needled pine of the northeastern states. Its wide, scraggy top is common to the rougher, sterile slopes, but it is found occasionally in swamps from southern Maine to northern Georgia, west along the slopes of the Appalachians in eastern Tennessee and Kentucky.

Trees from forty to fifty feet high with trunks one to two feet in diameter are common; while broad-crowned individuals of about 200 years may attain heights of eighty to 100 feet, with a trunk up to thirty inches in diameter. In youth pitch pine is fairly symmetrical, but with age the wide crown may become irregular or even scraggy and grotesque. It is generally considered a slow-growing tree, for where other pines mark each season's growth with a single whorl of branches and one growth ring, pitch pine may put on two or sometimes three whorls of branches, and as many growth rings in a single year. Reports indicate that trees will attain a height of fifty feet in as many years. With increasing age, the growth slows down, so that at one hundred years the tree may be seventy-five feet high and about eighteen inches in diameter.

The Latin name *rigida* refers to the stiffness of the wide-spreading, sharply pointed, yellowish green needles, which are often twisted and two and a half to five inches long. They are usually in clusters of three, bound at the base by a fibrous sheath. Each leaf stands out almost at right angles to the twig where it remains for two years.

In April or May clusters of yellow, cylindrical, staminate flowers are produced at the base of the new season's g r o w t h, and they send forth clouds of yellow pollen. More or less simultaneously with these, o v u l a t e flowers appear as individuals or in clusters along the sides of the new twigs. Two years after fertilization, these mature as two to three inch, dark green, pointed cones closely attached to the parent stem. They may remain on the tree for years. Each cone scale

Devereux Butcher

The hardy Pitch Pine assumes an unconventional form with age, and ordinarily attains heights of fifty to eighty feet with trunk diameters at breast height of about two feet

is broadly thickened at the end and armed with a stout recurved prickle. In the fall or winter, the cones may open to release many brown, winged seeds, so small that 65,000 to 75,000 are required to make a pound. Because the cones frequently hang on several years before opening, the crown may be filled with cones of varying ages. Pitch pine seeds that are shed in midwinter are sometimes an important source of food for squirrels, quail, and small birds. While the species depends primarily upon seeds for reproduction, vigorous stump sprouts will grow to merchantable size. This ability to sprout has been observed in trees up to four to eight inches in diameter.

On young trees and branches, the rough bark is broken into reddish brown scales, while on mature trees it is deeply furrowed and broken into large irregular plates. It is very resistant to fire. Clusters of leaves and short branches known as "water sprouts," may be produced along the trunk and main branches, which, like the ability to reproduce from stump sprouts, it is a unique characteristic among northern pines. Such considerable quantities of pitch flow when the bark is broken, that at one time logs and branches were destructively distilled for naval stores as far north as Pennsylvania. This is no longer done to any extent, but the name "pitch pine" persists.

The soft, coarse-grained, yellowish wood is only moderately strong and is full of resin. It weighs about thirty-two pounds to the cubic foot, and is used for rough construction, mine props, fencing, fuel, pulp, crating, and railroad ties. When grown under favorable conditions, the wood is of good quality and is as valuable as that of the other eastern hard pines.

Pitch pine has few enemies, and no pine east of the Mississippi River maintains itself under such unfavorable conditions. It is not demanding as to soil or moisture, and will grow under a variety of soil and climate conditions. Accordingly, it is frequently found on dry, burned-over, gravelly slopes, on rocky cliffs at high elevations and also in swamps. Best growth is frequently found when the tree is in association with hardwoods. It can be established either directly from seed or by means of nursery-grown seedlings and transplants.

The stiff, yellow-green needles are usually in clusters of three, while the scales of the broad-based cones have thick ends, each armed with a short recurved prickle

Deeply furrowed reddish brown bark, sometimes an inch and a half thick and highly fire resistant, is found on mature Pitch Pine trees

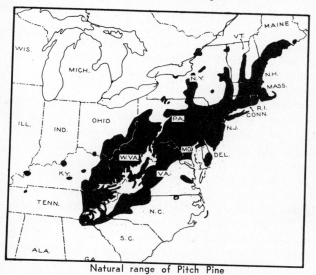

Natural range of Pitch Pine

41

JACK PINE

Banksian pine
Pinus banksiana Lambert

Devereux Butcher

Jack Pine frequently attains heights of sixty feet or more, and young trees usually carry branches well down to the ground

TYPICAL of light sandy soils and the heavy snow country of the North, jack pine grows in much of northern New England, northeastern New York, the greater part of the lake states, and south as far as the Illinois shore of Lake Michigan. In British Columbia the range lacks scarcely 300 miles of being transcontinental, extending from the southern shores of Hudson Bay to the upper waters of the Mackenzie River. Approaching to within one and a half degrees of the arctic circle, it is the most northern of all American pines. The range reaches some 1,600 miles to the south, and the spread from east to west is 2,500 miles.

Generally considered an inferior tree, as implied by the name "jack," it is scrubby and dwarfed on its outer limits of distribution, but under favorable conditions of soil and climate attains heights of twenty-five to sixty feet and breast-high diameters of eight to twenty inches. Occasional trees attain heights of seventy-five to ninety feet, with diameters up to two feet. It reaches its largest size on the sandy barrens northwest of Lake Winnipeg in the provinces of Manitoba and Saskatchewan.

Barren, sandy or rocky land at elevations from 100 feet to 1,200 feet above sea level are its usual habitat, but the largest trees develop on moist soils of good quality. Jack pine is given little consideration in New England, but it is assuming increasing importance in the lake states.

Jack pine is essentially a pioneering tree in that it takes over the land after lumbering operations and fires to provide shelter for more desirable species that may follow. During the first twenty to twenty-five years jack pine grows faster than either red pine or white pine, but eventually these species will overtake it and dominate the stand. Open-grown trees six to fifteen inches in diameter may be twenty-five to eighty-five years old, while trees growing in dense stands may take seventy-five years to attain a diameter of six inches. Naturally short-lived, the oldest jack pine trees do not exceed 125 to 150 years.

Botanists classify jack pine with the twenty-four hard, pitch or "yellow" pines, which grow throughout the country, and until 1905 was known as *Pinus divaricata*. The stubby, flat, grayish green needles, two in a cluster, are among the shortest of the entire pine group. They vary from less than an inch to an inch and a half in length, are scanty and somewhat clustered at the ends of the twigs and remain two or three seasons before dropping.

After the trees are four to eight years old, crowded clusters of yellow, pollen-bearing, cone-like blossoms appear in the early spring on the ends of the past season's growth, while the upper branches of the same tree carry clusters of dark, purple ovulate flowers. After fertilization, the ovulate ones grow to about one or two inches in length, by a half inch to an inch in diameter, and become lopsided. These ripen during September of the second season. Pressed closely against the stem or sometimes growing more or less at right angles to it, these light, clay-brown cones may remain attached and closed for twenty-five years or longer. They open irregularly to release some of the small, brown-winged, blackish seeds, which drift before the wind for long distances. The unusual capacity of this tree to retain its seeds and liberate them during warm weather or after a fire, and the fact that many of the seeds, which land on open soil, grow to seedling or sapling stage, frequently causes jack pine to be the first to reclothe burned land. In fact, jack pine's greatest usefulness is to clothe poor, sandy, or gravelly land with tree growth and hold the ground for other species to follow.

The relatively thin, dull red-brown bark of mature trees is narrowly ridged and furrowed. The irregular, main, vertical ridges are connected by smaller lateral ones.

Taken as a whole, the tree is easily identified by its short leaves, which are always in pairs, its persistent curved cones, and by its many crooked branches.

The brownish yellow heartwood, surrounded by a layer of creamy sapwood, varies in texture and weighs twenty-nine to thirty pounds to the cubic foot when air dry. It lacks strength, is brittle, and decays rapidly when left in contact with the soil. Clear lumber resembles that of red pine, and is so marketed, but it is usually low grade and knotty.

Used locally for fuel and rough lumber, there are increasing demands for it as pulpwood, crates, slack cooperage, mine timbers and ties.

Jack pine has few enemies other than fire and from this it reseeds itself with remarkable ability. While not satisfactory as a street or shade tree, the peculiar green of its foliage makes it desirable for some ornamental purposes.

First reported by French explorers and early settlers in eastern Canada, it was planted in England as early as 1735. It has, however, proved better adapted to the soil and climate conditions of Germany and Russia than of England.

Devereux Butcher

Short, flat needles borne in pairs cluster toward the end of tough branches, and the lopsided cones may retain their seed for years

U. S. Forest Service

The dull red-brown bark consists of narrow, intermeshed ridges of closely pressed scales

Devereux Butcher

When trees are four to eight years old, crowded clusters of yellow, pollen-producing blossoms appear in early spring at the base of the current year's growth

The range of Jack Pine extends into west central Mackenzie, which gives this tree the distinction of being the most northerly pine on the continent

LONGLEAF PINE

Longstraw pine, Georgia pine, Southern yellow pine

Pinus palustris Miller

IN THE ORIGINAL southern pine forest, longleaf pine outranked shortleaf, loblolly and slash pines, and was comparable to the present rank of Douglasfir in national importance. The temperate almost sub-tropical climate, combined with ample rainfall of the coastal plain, from southeastern Virginia through North and South Carolinas, Georgia, Florida, Alabama, Mississippi, Louisiana and eastern Texas, furnishes desirable growing conditions. Trees of best development are found on moist but well-drained, deep, sandy loam, but they grow well on all sandy and gravelly soils within this range.

Literally translated, its botanical name *Pinus palustris* means the pine that lives in marshy places, but it grows on many different kinds of soil. Frequently growing with shortleaf, loblolly, and slash pines, it shares with them the common name of southern yellow pine. In certain respects, commercially, it is the most desirable of them all.

The leaves, or needles, are eight to eighteen inches long, held three in a bundle, and drop off before the end of the second season. Like all other pines, separate male and female flowers are borne on the same tree during early spring. The male flowers appear as dark rose-purple catkins around the base of young shoots and bear yellow pollen. These shrivel and fall shortly after the wind has carried the pollen to fertilize the ovulate or female blossoms, which appear in pairs or small clusters at the ends of the upper branches. During the second season after fertilization these grow into cones five to ten inches long, and having matured, release the winged seeds which develop in pairs under each of the cone scales.

Longleaf pine frequently grows to heights of 100 to 120 feet, with a tall slightly tapering trunk from two to three feet in diameter. The orange-brown bark of mature trees is made up of many closely pressed papery scales and may be a half-inch thick.

The light red to orange-yellow heartwood is exceedingly hard, strong and durable, and within the tree is surrounded by a thin nearly white layer of sapwood. A cubic foot of the wood weighs forty to forty-three pounds when air dry. Its great strength and the large sizes in which it is available cause it to be favored above most others for construction. It is used for heavy girders in buildings and bridges, masts and spars, railway ties, flooring, interior finish and general construction, as well as for fuel and charcoal.

The southern pine stand ranks second in our national storehouse of forest wealth, being exceeded only by Douglasfir.

U. S. Forest Service

Longleaf Pine, aristocrat of the southern pines, frequently attains heights of 100 to 120 feet in the light sandy soils of the coastal plain from southeastern Virginia to western Texas

The pollen-bearing male catkins (top) are dark rose purple. The female flowers develop into cones five to ten inches long

Warren D. Brush

No description of longleaf pine is complete without reference to the naval stores industry. This general term applies chiefly to turpentine and resin, the principal products derived from the distillation of the pitch or crude gum which exudes from pine trees when "chipped" or wounded. It also is applied to similar products obtained by distilling the pine wood. Longleaf and slash pines are the chief gum-running trees from which naval stores are secured. Most of this is produced in the region from South Carolina to Mississippi. Paint and varnish, soap, shoe polish, paper, and printing ink use up most of the naval stores. Chipping of the trees and distilling of the gum employs several thousand people and is one of the major forest industries in some parts of the Southeast.

Longleaf pine produces vigorous seedlings which grow slowly above ground during the first few years because of the energy spent developing a long taproot and large root system. After four or five years the longleaf saplings begin to grow rapidly and continue for thirty-five to fifty years, producing in that period trees fifty-five to eighty feet tall and seven to eleven inches in diameter. Timber growth of 300 to 500 board feet an acre a year in full stands is not uncommon throughout the longleaf area.

Fire and hogs are the worst enemies of longleaf pine. During the early seedling stage, light grass fires do comparatively little harm, but this apparent immunity becomes less effective as the trees get taller. While the small trees have what is sometimes called an "asbestos bud," their sweet succulent roots appeal to hogs that range much of the southern pine country. A single "razorback" hog with a taste for pine roots may destroy hundreds of little trees in a day.

Again, after the trees have attained a fair size and have been wounded or "faced" for gum, they are easily damaged by fire. These faces start a few inches from the ground, and being covered with dry gum or pitch, burn easily. In spite of constant preventive efforts, fires continue to rob the South of millions of dollars in present and future timber values.

Various insects and fungus diseases attack longleaf pine, but the one most generally recognized is the southern pine beetle. Attacks by these tiny insects upon the living trees may be partially prevented by not cutting timber in the hot season, or if it must be cut, by piling and burning the brush as quickly as possible. Infested trees should be used at once, and all brush and bark should be burned.

Longleaf pine bears large crops of seeds at intervals of three to five years, with a few seeds from open stands nearly every year. Where seed trees are left, and fire and hogs are kept out, it re-establishes itself after a lumbering operation. Where seed trees are not available seedlings may be grown in a nursery and transplanted after the first year.

Tenn. Coal, Iron and R. R. Co.

The orange-brown bark of Longleaf Pine is furrowed and broken into closely pressed, papery scales and may be a half inch thick

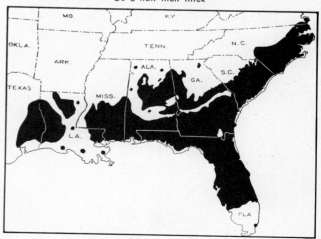

Natural range of Longleaf Pine

Apache Pine

Arizona longleaf pine
Pinus engelmannii Carr.

APACHE PINE in some respects resembles the longleaf pine, *P. palustris*, of the southeastern states. This is especially so when the tree is in its earliest stages of growth, because of the exceptionally long needles of both trees at that time. In other respects Apache suggests the ponderosa pine of the West, to which it is closely related and with which it associates in some localities of the Apache's range.

Apache occurs principally in the Transition Zone at altitudes of from 5500 to 8200 feet above sea level, ranging northward from the Mexican states of Zacatecas, Durango, Sinaloa, Chihuahua and Sonora, to the mountains of extreme southwestern New Mexico—Gillespie Mountain, Animas Peak, Black Point and San Luis Pass—and in extreme southeastern Arizona—the Chiricahua, Huachuca, Dragoon and Santa Rita mountains. Attaining heights of from fifty to sixty feet and rarely seventy-five feet, it has trunk diameters of one to two feet and rarely larger.

The needles borne in fascicles or bundles of two to five, but usually three, remain on the tree for two years. They are noticeably longer than those of other western pines, especially as seedlings, when the needles, during a grasslike stage, reach fifteen inches in length. In older trees they are eight to twelve inches. A bright, clear green, they are slightly coated with a pale bloom and are rectangular or triangular in cross section, with edges minutely toothed. The pale brown, papery basal sheaths, exceptionally long, are from one to two inches.

Male or pollen-producing flowers, appearing in spring, grow in clusters at the base of the new growth and, before the pollen has been dispersed by wind, are pale yellow. The purple female or seed-cone-producing flowers, borne on short stalks, occur mostly on the higher branches in pairs or in whorls of as many as five. The cones, when fully developed, are broadly egg-shaped or conical, oblique, five to seven inches in length and are pale brown and lustrous. At maturity their prickle-tipped scales open to release the dark brown, winged seeds.

Devereux Butcher

Apache Pine, native to our Southwest and Mexico, is closely related to Ponderosa Pine. It attains heights of fifty to sixty feet and rarely taller

Twigs, comparatively sparse on this pine, are stiff and gray-brown. The bark on mature trunks is broken by furrows into flat ridges, dark at first, but turning lighter and slightly yellow-tinged with age.

The wood, similar to that of ponderosa pine, is light yellow or white, smooth and fine-grained. It may be harvested with ponderosa in some localities, although because of its limited supply and scattered range, it has little commercial value in the United States except locally.

Seedling Apache pines develop tap roots to depths as much as six feet; until the tree reaches the age of six and perhaps more, however, it grows slowly. In appearance the sapling stage is striking. The slender, branchless stem, two to three feet tall, is crowned by a magnificent head of needles twelve inches and longer, the lower ones slightly dropping, the upper ascending.

The scientific name honors George Engelmann (1809-84), a German-born physician and botanist of Saint Louis, Missouri, who had originally given the tree another name.

Devereux Butcher

The bright green needles of Apache Pine are rectangular or triangular in cross section, with edges minutely toothed. In the seedling stage, they are about fifteen inches long and up to twelve inches on the mature tree

Devereux Butcher

The bark on mature trunks of Apache Pine is broken by furrows into flat-topped ridges of appressed scales, dark at first, but turning lighter and slightly yellow-tinged with age

Devereux Butcher

Apache Pine cones, borne on short stalks, are broadly egg-shaped or conical, oblique when the scales open, and are five to seven inches long, pale brown and lustrous

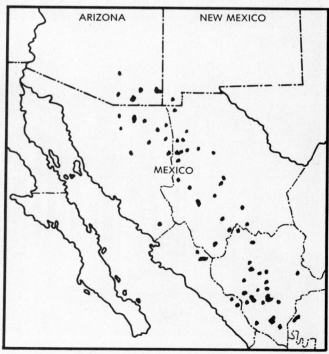

Natural range of Apache Pine

SLASH PINE

Pinus elliottii Engelm. var. *elliottii*

SLASH PINE ranks high among the rapid growing, early maturing pines of the southern coastal plain. Because of its ability to produce heavy stands of timber and its yield of high quality resin, it is probably the most profitable of all southern timber trees.

It grows on low ground and on hummocks in swamps or moist "slashes" from southern South Carolina to central Florida and westward across Georgia, Alabama, and Mississippi to eastern Louisiana. It occurs in pure stands or in association with other native pines. Another variety, *Pinus elliottii*, Engelm. var. *densa*, grows from the Florida keys to north of Lake Okeechobee and sixty miles farther north along both coasts. The species *Pinus caribaea*, Morelet, inhabits Central America, Cuba, the Isle of Pines and the Bahama Islands.

Best growth and purest stands are attained in Florida and southern Georgia, where trees rise to heights of eighty to 150 feet and attain trunk diameters of two to three feet. The average hight is about 100 feet, with clear lengths of sixty or seventy feet surmounted by a dense, rounded crown of heavy horizontal limbs. During its first twenty to fifty years, slash pine exceeds all of the southern pines in growth, reaching heights of forty-five feet and diameters of six inches in twenty years, and attains over eighty feet in height and fifteen inches in diameter by fifty years. Trees mature at about one hundred years, but may reach 150 to 200 years.

The dark lustrous green needles grow in bundles of two, three, or more—but are most frequently in pairs. They are eight to twelve inches long, forming dense clusters near the ends of the branches, and drop off in their second season.

In spring the reddish brown terminal bud elongates into a light gray "candle" about the thickness of a large pencil, in contrast to similar "candles" from the larger terminal buds of longleaf pine, which are an inch or more in diameter.

During January and February, before leaf growth starts, dark purple staminate flowers appear in crowded clusters at the base of twigs of the previous year's growth, while at the ends of the same or similar twigs are pink ovulate flowers on long stems which develop into small erect cones. These hang down during the second season, and by October have matured into glossy, leathery brown, egg-shaped cones three to six inches long. The thin, flexible cone scales are each armed with a slender, slightly recurved prickle. These prickles, borne on the varnished end of each cone scale, are peculiar to slash pine.

Under each cone scale is a pair of mottled dark gray winged seeds. Large crops of seeds

U. S. Forest Service

The rapid growing, early-maturing Slash Pine is one of the profitable timber trees of the south Atlantic and Gulf states

are borne every two or three years, which are carried by the wind to assist in this tree's aggressive reclamation of old fields and cutover areas. There are 16,000 to 18,000 seeds to the pound, with sixty to ninety out of every one hundred seeds fertile.

The bark is clear orange to red-brown, one-half to three-quarters of an inch thick, consisting of many overlapping, irregular plates or scales which form broad flat ridges on the trunk. Turpentine workers invariably associate the orange bark with free-flowing resin qualities, for slash pine excels all other southern pines in production of rosin or gum containing a large content of spirits of turpentine.

The light brown to rich orange wood is coarse-grained, resinous, brittle, without durability in contact with the soil, and a cubic foot weighs — when air dry — about forty-eight pounds. Accordingly, it is the heaviest of all pines and comparable to the hickories and white oaks. The wide sapwood is nearly white. It so closely resembles the wood of longleaf pine that a distinction is seldom made when the lumber is marketed. Large quantities of second growth timber are cut for railroad ties, increasing amounts for wood pulp, and mature trees are used for general construction and interior trim.

The moist location of most slash pine stands provides natural protection against fire, but trees are often subject to red heart rot.

Slash pine is one of the most rapid growing and early maturing of all eastern forest trees. Because of its capacity to produce wood pulp, fuel, lumber, and naval stores, as well as its adaptability to moist, sandy soils within its range, it has been extensively planted in several of the southern coastal states. Moreover, it is recognized for its beauty as an ornamental.

William M. Harlow

The short-stalked, three- to six-inch cones are armed with distinct prickles on each cone scale

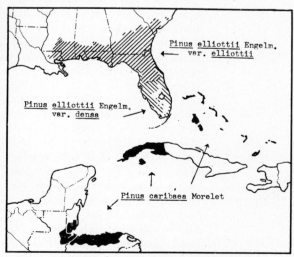

The natural range of Slash Pine. Var. *densa* grows in the Florida keys north to central Florida; while *P. caribaea*, in the Bahamas, occurs on Abaco, Grand Bahama, Andras and New Providence—the islands nearest to Florida

Daniel Todd

Irregular orange-colored plates lie one over the other to make a half-inch layer of bark

SHORTLEAF PINE

Shortstraw pine, Arkansas pine, North Carolina pine
Pinus echinata Miller

SHORTLEAF PINE—one of four important southern yellow pines—attains commerical importance in Arkansas, Virginia, Missouri, Louisiana, Mississippi, Texas, South Carolina and North Carolina, but is found in varying abundance from Long Island and south central Pennsylvania south and westerly to eastern Texas and Oklahoma. It prefers well-drained light sandy or gravelly clay soil. On moist soils along the coastal plain it is crowded out by loblolly pine and longleaf pine with which it is often sold as lumber. A very hardy tree, shortleaf pine can withstand lower winter temperatures than any of the other important native southern pines.

The long clean trunk has little taper and is surmounted by a relatively short, pyramidal or rounded crown. Trees from eighty to one hundred feet high and two to three feet in diameter are not uncommon.

Shortleaf pine reaches maturity at about 120 years and occasionally lives more than three hundred years. The bark of old trees is yellow, tinged with cinnamon-red, broken into irregular plates which peel off into thin scales. Bark on young trees and branches is smooth and green, becoming brown and scaly with age.

The slender dark bluish green leaves are three to five inches long, occur in clusters of two or three, and remain on the tree for from two to five years.

In April or May the pale purple pollen-bearing staminate blossoms cluster at the base of the new leaf growth, while the cone-bearing ovulate flowers are borne two or four in a whorl on stout erect stems below the new growth. The short-stalked, dull brown, egg-shaped cones reach a length of one and a half to two and a half inches and mature in two seasons. They are the smallest cones of the four important southern pines. Each cone scale is terminated with a temporary prickle or broad-based spine. This characteristic is responsible for the scientific name *echinata* derived from the Latin word *echinus*, meaning hedgehog. Under each central cone scale are two pale brown triangular seeds about three-sixteenths of an inch long, each provided with a wing about a half inch long and one-eighth of an inch wide. When the cone opens the seeds drop out and may be carried several hundred feet by the wind. They germinate evenly and quickly, and frequently find places for growth in abandoned open fields, which gives rise to the common name "old field pine."

Maryland State Department of Forestry

Shortleaf Pine frequently grows in open fields and is commonly called "old field pine." Its broad, rounded, dark bluish green crown, with long somewhat drooping branches, surmounts a straight cinnamon-red trunk

It is unusual among the pines because of its ability to sprout from the stump, or when injured by fire. This ability is characteristic of young trees and is lost after they are six or eight inches in diameter.

The yellowish wood is noticeably grained, moderately hard, strong and stiff. It resembles that of longleaf pine, with which it is frequently sold, but is lighter and less strong. A cubic foot of air-dry shortleaf wood weighs thirty-six to thirty-nine pounds, as compared with forty to forty-four pounds for longleaf pine. It is used extensively in house-building, including framing, ceiling, weatherboarding, panels, window and door frames, casing and carved work. The grain shows well in natural finish or when stained. Frames of overstuffed furniture, chairs, desks, agricultural machinery, excelsior, wood pulp, mine props, barrels and crates are also made of this pine.

Shortleaf pine grows in association with lobolly pine, oaks, hickories and sweetgum, but extensively in stands comprised only of shortleaf pine. Whole stands frequently attain an average height of fifty or sixty feet and nearly nine inches in diameter in thirty years. Such a stand may contain nearly fifty cords of wood capable of being cut into about 6,000 board feet of lumber.

Shortleaf pine, along with all other southern forest trees, suffers from the yearly burning of the woods. Not only are the immature trees killed, but the mature ones are seared and weakened, leaving them prey to injurious insects and fungi. The ability to sprout only partially offsets the damage and in no case makes up for the removal of the natural mulch of leaf litter from the soil. Next to the loss from fire is that from attacks of the southern pine beetle. This insect attacks the living trees and is particularly active after long dry periods, but will not live through winter temperatures of zero or colder. Other enemies include such insects as the pine sawyer, the Nantucket tip moth, and fungus diseases, such as "red heart," whose spores frequently enter the tree through wounds caused by fire. "Littleleaf" disease has been a problem on poor sites.

Aside from its value for timber, the broad pyramidal head, straight symmetrical trunk, and vigor result in shortleaf pine being recognized as a handsome park or lawn tree.

Both the short leaves and short cones help to distinguish shortleaf pine from the three other important southern pine species

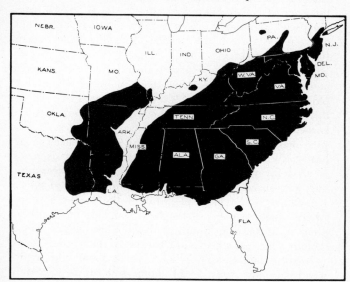

Natural range of Shortleaf Pine

The scaly bark of mature trees is almost cinnamon-red and broken into more or less rectangular plates

LOBLOLLY PINE
Old field pine
Pinus taeda Linnaeus

LOBLOLLY PINE is one of the four important southern yellow pines. Its range extends over the coastal plain and lower Piedmont sections from southern Delaware, south and west into the river valleys of eastern Texas and southern Arkansas. It often grows in moist de-

pressions locally called "loblollies"—hence the name. loblolly pine. The tall, straight, cinnamon-colored trunk supports a relatively short, open, spreading crown. Trees have attained a height of 170 feet with a breast-high diameter of six feet, while trees ninety to 120 feet high and three to four feet in diameter are not uncommon. The trunk may be sixty to eighty feet to the first limb. Trees occasionally reach an age of 200 years, and sometimes even more.

The red-brown to cinnamon-colored bark is deeply furrowed into broad, flat oblong plates made up of many thin, closely pressed scales, and is usually from three-quarters of an inch to one and one-half inches thick. The slender brown twigs have a tinge of yellow and may be distinguished from other three-needled pines by a fine bloom or fuzz during their first season. The pale green needles are five to nine inches long, are borne in threes, held together at the base by a fibrous sheath, and stay on the twig for three or four years. They are slender, stiff, slightly twisted and tipped with a rigid sharp point. The buds are without resin.

From the middle of March to the first of April yellow pollen-bearing staminate flowers appear crowded at the base of the lower twigs, while higher up in the trees are single or occasionally clustered yellow ovulate flowers. At the end of the second season these mature into light reddish brown, broad, more or less egg-shaped cones three to six inches long. Each woody cone scale is tipped with a stout triangular spine.

Blackish, winged seeds are discharged from October to late November of the second season, but the cones remain on the trees for months before they break off, leaving a short stock. The seeds are carried considerable distances by the wind and usually germinate the following spring. They grow best on exposed mineral soil, such as abandoned agricultural land. Accordingly, the tree is called "old field pine." Open grown trees may seed abundantly when twenty to thirty years old, and the seeds are highly fertile. Loblolly pine is essentially moisture-loving.

The light brown, coarse-grained wood is resinous and, while lighter and softer than the wood of longleaf pine, is nearly as strong. It weighs about thirty-four to thirty-eight pounds to the cubic foot when air dry and is used for construction, interior finish, bridges, freight cars, barrel shooks, boxes, crating and tobacco hogsheads. When treated with creosote to prevent decay, it is used for railroad ties and piling. More recently it has been successfully used in the manufacture of paper.

Loblolly is the most plentiful of the southern pines. About ninety percent of the total stand of the southern pines is in the deep South, and probably half of this is loblolly pine, principally in Georgia, Alabama and Texas.

Because loblolly pine has a thick bark and grows mostly on low sites or in damp soils it is relatively resistant to fire. Heavy losses occur on higher land. Fire

U. S. Forest Service

Loblolly Pine usually grows on flat moist land and develops a clean, straight trunk and broad open crown

is used to control brush to allow seedlings to grow. This species also is subject to attacks from the pine sawyer, the southern pine bark beetle, and a bud moth which destroys the terminal shoots of young pines. The first two insects are small beetles which bore into the bark and cambium. Insect attacks may be controlled by cutting all infested trees as soon as the foliage begins to brown. While the logs may be used, the bark and branches should be burned as quickly as possible. Similarly, when trees are cut from May to October, the logs should be peeled and the bark burned, together with any limbs or fresh woody trash.

Loblolly pine grows faster over long periods than any other southern pine. In fairly open stands, with ample space for the branches and roots of each tree to spread, it may attain diameters of nine to fourteen inches and heights of forty-seven to seventy-five feet in thirty years, depending upon the character of the soil. Where natural seeding fails, loblolly pine seedlings may be planted.

A well-stocked acre may produce from 300 to more than 1,000 board feet of saw timber yearly. The production depends, as with other crops, upon the character of the soil, and the protection from fire and pests. Individual stands have been measured that had averaged 1,800 board feet a year on each acre for thirty-two years. After seventy years on fair to good growing sites 30,-000 to 40,000 board feet of timber is a reasonable yield, and stands may produce an income from thinning for pulpwood within twenty years.

Each scale of the three to six-inch reddish brown cones is armed with a sharp, triangular spine

Deep furrows break the cinnamon-red bark into flat, oblong, scaly plates

This shows a crowded cluster of yellow pollen-bearing blossoms and the early spring growth of a young Loblolly Pine

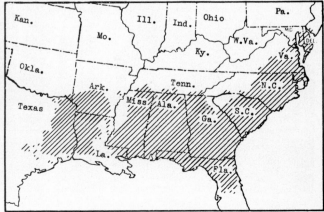

Natural range of Loblolly Pine

53

POND PINE

Marsh pine, Bay pine, Pocosin pine
Pinus serotina Michaux

W. R. Mattoon

Pond Pine is a relatively small, usually shaggy looking southern hard pine

ONE OF THE least important of some twenty-two so-called hard pines, pond pine prefers to have its roots in moist, sandy soil. This usually shaggy looking, comparatively short trunked tree inhabits stream banks, the border of ponds, or small swampy areas, as well as undrained peaty soils, and low, wet, sandy flats and islands. Full details of its range are not reported, but it grows from southern New Jersey southward along the coastal plain nearly to Lake Okeechobee in Florida and west into southeastern Alabama. Occasionally it occurs as far inland as the eastern edge of the Piedmont Plateau in North Carolina.

Pond pine bears such local names as marsh pine, bay pine, and pocosin pine. The latter is a local name for a dry swamp. It is closely related to pitch pine, *Pinus rigida*. The name *serotina* means "late." This probably refers to the habit of retaining the cones for several years and the somewhat delayed dispersal of seeds. As a result, the first impression made by pond pine on most people is of an irregular crown, overloaded with cones. Many of these, however, are old and empty, so that the tree is not as prolific a seeder as might be supposed.

With trunk diameters of one to three feet, it ranges from forty to eighty feet high. Only under most favorable locations does it approach a hundred feet in height. When grown in crowded stands, the trunk is clean and fairly straight. The stout, sometimes contorted, branches tend to be pendulous at the ends, forming an irregular and open crown or top. The numerous slender twigs are dark green, turning orange in their first winter and brown to almost black by the fourth or fifth year.

The dark, reddish brown bark is irregularly broken by narrow grooves into broad, squarish flat plates of thin closely pressed scales. It is a half to three quarters of an inch thick and resembles that of loblolly pine.

The slender, dull yellow-green needles are in clusters of three, or occasionally in fours. They resemble those of pitch pine but are longer, measuring six to eight inches or occasionally ten inches. Moreover, they are slightly twisted, marked with several rows of stomata or tiny breathing pores on the three faces, and hang on until the third or fourth year. The tendency for the trunk and limbs to sprout bunches of leaves and short twigs is noticeable in pond pine.

Spring finds the trees adorned with crowded spikes of dark orange staminate catkins, while the greenish pistillate ones are borne in pairs or clusters on stout stems near the ends of the twigs. Like pitch pine, many mature cones remain closed for several years, while others open during the first fall or early spring. They are reddish brown, turning gray when weathered, two to two and a half inches long, and like those of pitch pine are short and broadly pyramidal, or like a long pointed egg. The thin, almost flat scales of the newly mature cones are tipped with a slender prickle which soon drops off.

The seeds are about an eighth of an inch long, nearly

The broadly egg-shaped, red-brown cones are about two inches
long, while the long slender needles are usually in clusters of three

triangular, sometimes ridged beneath, and fully rounded at the side. The thin, dark, rough shell forms a wide
border, and the wings, narrowed toward the ends, are
broadest in the middle. They measure a scant quarter
inch in width and three quarters inch in length.

Trees growing in close stands seldom bear seed before
thirty or thirty-five years of age, but thereafter with fair
abundance. The cones often hang on the trees for six
or more years, but usually they are empty and seedless.
The seeds, however, are credited with retaining their
vitality for several years. They germinate readily when
they fall on ground which has sufficient moisture. There
the young trees quickly take possession of poorly drained
and otherwise valueless land, or of open and abandoned
pastures and fields. In common with pitch pine and a
few others, young pond pine reproduces from stump
shoots, which appear after the tree is cut or killed by fire.

Although pond pine trees do not grow rapidly, they
develop into merchantable timber of fair quality. The
wood ranks as medium heavy for pine, weighing thirty-
eight pounds to the cubic foot when dry. It is soft,
coarse-grained, resinous and brittle, without any qualities of special importance. The dark orange heartwood
is surrounded by a wide area of pale sapwood. Its qualities of strength and flexibility are comparable to those of
slash pine, pitch pine, and longleaf pine, with which the
lumber is frequently marketed. Pond pine wood is sparingly used for construction, small masts for local demands,
and for other general uses. When pond pines occur with
slash or longleaf pines, they are occasionally tapped for
turpentine, often by mistake of the operator.

Like other pines, pond pine is not very satisfactory as
a shade tree, but its pleasing foliage and form encourage
its use as an ornamental in southern parks, where the
soil is wet and sandy. Because of its natural moist habit,
it seldom develops a taproot. The wet sites, however,
usually offer partial protection from fire. Moreover, the
tree has no severe insect or fungus enemies.

Many thin, angular plates serve
to build up the thin brown bark

Natural range of Pond Pine

MONTEREY PINE
Insignis pine
Pinus radiata   D. Don

MONTEREY PINE is one of those Pacific coast species having a limited natural range. A handsome tree of wide-spreading branches and broad rounded crown, especially when open-grown, it has rich, dark green, dense, luxuriant foliage and reaches heights of seventy feet on the coast, to a hundred feet inland, with a trunk of two to three feet in diameter and sometimes larger. Growing at elevations from sea level to nearly 1000 feet, it ranges as far as six miles inland on northerly slopes. It thrives on a variety of soils and sites, preferring well drained, moderately deep acid, sandy loams.

The species formerly had a much wider distribution, as shown by fossil records, but an increasingly dry climate forced it to retreat to a few localities along the humid coastal belt of central California, principally on and near the Monterey Peninsula, hence the name Monterey pine. The tree occurs also in a small area at Swanton, a few miles up the coast. Another concentration lies about eighty-five miles to the south in the vicinity of Cambria, with a small stand six miles north of there. A related form of the Monterey pine, *P. radiata* var. *binata* (Englm. Lemmon), thrives nearly 500 miles away, at elevations of 1300 to 4000 feet above sea level on the northern tip of Mexico's Guadalupe Island, 150 miles off the coast of Lower California.

Monterey pine grows in association with California live oak and, locally on and near the peninsula, with Gowen and Monterey cypresses and bishop pine, as well as with such shrubs as manzanita, ceanothus, California huckleberry and coyote brush. In the Swanton area, it associates

Devereux Butcher

With dark, dense foliage, an open-grown Monterey Pine develops a head of wide-spreading branches and rounded crown

56

with California-laurel, redwood, Douglasfir and knobcone pine, hybridizing naturally with the latter.

Bark on mature trunks, one and a half to two inches thick, is dark brown to black, deeply furrowed into broad plates. Young trees are easily fire-killed, while older trunks may be scorched if not killed.

The root system of Monterey pine is shallow, seldom going deeper than a foot; but it is wide-spreading on older trees, reaching forty feet from the trunk and giving anchorage against wind-throw. Where trees are close, roots intertwine and frequently graft. Selected cuttings from trees two to seven years old root successfully, but stumps are not known to sprout.

The slender, flexible, dark green needles are four to six inches long, borne in bundles or fascicles of two or three. The slender yellow twigs, which later turn red-brown, are roughened by the persistent bases of the bud scales. Needles of the Guadalupe Island variety occur in bundles of two.

In late winter or early spring, the flowers appear, the light brown to yellow, catkin-like, pollen-bearing ones forming dense clusters at the base of the new growth; while the dark purple female ones develop into curved, oval, pointed cones three to seven inches long, in groups of three to seven on trunks or branches. These cones mature in the late summer or fall of the second year, and are chestnut-brown and lustrous, their scales thickened toward the outer side of the cone's base and thinner on the inner side and at the apex, with purple on the inside surface of the scales. Each scale is tipped with a small, straight or incurved prickle. The cones are persistent, some remaining closed for several years unless subjected to the heat of fire, but normally, new cones exposed to the spring sunshine will open during the first warm days of spring. Others open in summer when easterly winds bring hot, dry air from the valleys. Every year, abundant crops of the oval, compressed, roughened, black-shelled seeds, with a laterally-striped wing, are dropped, and trees begin to bear cones at four years. Trees raised from cuttings bear at three. A large mature tree may contain several thousand cones, each cone producing 125 to 200 seeds. Young trees bear the largest cones, which produce the greatest number of seeds, and the wind may carry the winged seeds as far as 200 feet from the parent tree. Viability of the seeds is high and persistent.

Monterey pine wood is soft, brittle, light, pale yellow-brown and coarse-grained. Because of its scarcity it finds little use in this country, except locally for rough lumber and fuel. The tree has been planted within and beyond its natural range as an ornamental and as a windbreak; while commercial forest plantings have been established in New Zealand, Australia and South Africa.

The species has a number of virus diseases in addition to insect pests, such as red turpentine beetle, Monterey pine ipse and weevil, and the California four- and five-spined ipse. Two kinds of rot attack the roots, and the trunks and branches are subject to attack by dwarf mistletoe and coastal and western gall rusts.

The scientific name, *radiata*, probably refers to either or both the wide-spreading branches and roots.

The persistent, curved, pointed cones of Monterey Pine are three to seven inches long, lustrous chestnut-brown, often remaining on the tree unopened for many years. The dark green, slender, flexible needles, four to six inches long, occur in bundles or fascicles of two or three

Bark on mature trunks, dark brown or black and deeply furrowed in broad plates, is about two inches thick, but offers the tree little protection from fire

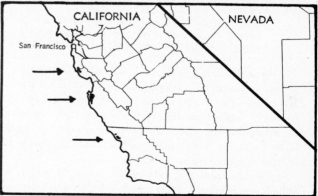

Natural range of Monterey Pine

57

VIRGINIA PINE

Jersey pine, Scrub pine
Pinus virginiana Miller

G. H. Collingwood

Virginia Pine is seldom over fifty feet high. It usually has a short trunk and an open scraggly crown. (Right) Natural range of Virginia Pine

Young trees are roughly pyramidal in form and grow frequently in dense stands. With maturity the crown becomes flat topped, open and scraggly—supported on a relatively short trunk, with long horizontal or tortuously pendulous branches in remote whorls. Over most of its range the usual heights are thirty or forty feet with breast high diameters up to eighteen inches, but occasional heights of 110 feet with diameters of three feet are attained. It matures in fifty to 100 years and seldom lives longer than 150 years. Ordinarily Virginia pine grows on poor, light sandy soils, and always demands full sunlight. While it prospers on moist, fertile soils it usually suffers from competition with other species and is crowded out.

The stiff, divergently twisted, sharp pointed, grayish green leaves are one and a half to three inches long, and usually in pairs. They are closely distributed along the smooth, tough branchlets and are shed irregularly during the third and fourth years. The purplish, waxy bloom on the slender young shoots distinguishes *Pinus virginiana* from other two-needled pines.

With early spring, clusters of yellowish brown staminate flowers appear at the base of the new growth, and they scatter clouds of fine yellow pollen. The purplish, long-stalked ovulate blooms appear like small prickly cones on the same branches. They may be single, in pairs, or in whorls, and unlike most pines are produced in all parts of the crown.

After two growing seasons they mature in the autumn as dark reddish

FROM LONG ISLAND and the sand barrens of New Jersey to northern Alabama, and westward on shale hills and mountain bases across the Alleghenies to eastern Kentucky and Ohio, the Virginia pine is a common and occasionally important forest tree. It grows from sea level to about 3,000 feet, and is rare on the southern coastal Atlantic plain.

Appearing under a variety of names, it is frequently called scrub pine. Over much of the northern coastal area it is Jersey pine, and throughout a considerable portion of the south it is spruce pine—or simply spruce.

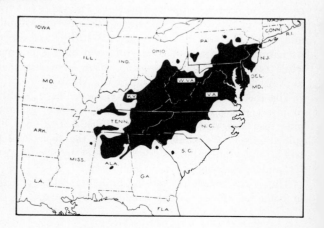

brown cones one and a half to two and a half inches long, growing tight to the parent stem. Each thin cone scale is armed with a slender, persistent spine or prickle. The cones may open any time during the next three or four years to shed the small, pale brown, winged seeds.

The dark brown bark is broken by shallow fissures with flat scaly ridges. It is smoother than the bark of any of its associated pines, and seldom is more than a quarter to a half inch thick.

Until recently the light orange to yellow wood, which is soft, coarse-grained, brittle, and knotty, had little value. Because of its small size its use was largely limited to mine props, railroad ties, rough lumber, and fuel. Early settlers burned the wood in kilns for tar and charcoal. More recently, however, the pulp-wood market has opened up a steady demand, and from Pennsylvania southward it is recognized as an important feature of the forest. A cubic foot when air dry weighs about thirty-three pounds.

Trees bear seed by their twentieth year and produce heavy crops every two or three years thereafter. While the wings are too small to carry the seed far, seedlings usually appear in all surrounding places where the soil is exposed. This means that, with the aid of a comparatively few seed trees, direct planting is unnecessary to secure satisfactory restocking of the land.

Pure stands of young Virginia pine frequently follow on old fields when agriculture is abandoned, but they persist only in the more sterile sand and clay areas of its range. Elsewhere pure stands of this tree are temporary in character and eventually give way to other competing conifers and hardwoods, leaving only individual Virginia pines or small groups of them. Because of its extensive range, this pine grows in combination with a variety of hardwoods and conifers, such as red maple, black cherry, dogwood, white oak, together with pitch, loblolly, and shortleaf pines, depending upon the locality. Seeds are produced early and in abundance, and they germinate readily on open land. For this reason its greatest value is probably to reclothe worn out or neglected lands, and as a nurse crop for more useful trees.

Over much of its range Virginia pine shows a growth rate sufficiently rapid to warrant its encouragement. This can be accomplished by selective cutting or by cutting to a diameter limit. By combining this with a reasonable amount of weeding, the encroaching hardwood trees can be kept under control.

Virginia pine has few enemies, other than fire, to which it quickly succumbs, because of its thin bark and relatively shallow root system. Although not considered a vigorous species, its habit of retreating to poor soils, where there is little competition, gives assurance that its ranks may never be seriously reduced.

L. W. Brownell

Yellowish brown staminate and purplish cone-like ovulate flowers develop during early spring at the base of the new growth

Warren D. Brush

The thin, shallowly furrowed, rather scaly bark becomes dark brown with maturity

U. S. Forest Service

Each scale of the narrowly conical red-brown cone bears a persistent prickle or spine

SAND PINE
Ocala sand pine, Choctawhatchee sand pine, Scrub pine
Pinus clausa (Chapm.) Vasey

SAND PINE is confined to Florida, except for a small area at the southern tip of Baldwin County, Alabama. The tree's original range has been reduced by fire, real estate development and other causes. The largest remaining tract is within the Ocala National Forest, the eastern half of Marion County, in the north central part of the peninsula. Other tracts are in eastern Seminole County, southern Osceola County, central Highlands County and central Volusa County, with a narrow, broken belt along the east coast from southern St. Johns County to northeastern Broward County. A few isolated stands remain on the gulf coast from northern Pasco County southward to Collier County. A third coastal belt lies along the shore of the Florida panhandle from the vicinity of Port St. Joe west to the eastern shore of Mobile Bay, Alabama. A number of coastal islands also support stands of sand pine.

Elevations within the range of this tree vary from sea level along the coastal sand dunes to 200 feet inland.

Usually somewhat curving, the slender trunks attain breast-high diameters of about a foot to sixteen inches and heights of from fifty to sixty feet. On preferred sites, diameters of two feet and more and heights up to seventy feet and higher have been recorded. The numerous branches and smooth, stiff, red or pale gray twigs produce a conical or cylindrical crown of dark green to gray-green, slender, flexible needles from two to three and a half inches in length, marked by rows of white stomata. They are borne in bundles or fascicles of two. During March and April, the needles acquire a coating of resin which increases flamability.

The bark on the lower trunk of old trees is deeply fissured into irregular oblong plates broken on the surface into thin, closely appressed gray-brown scales; while on young stems and limbs it is thin, smooth and pale gray. It offers meager protection against fire, and once the crowns of a dense stand are reached, the flames spread rapidly from crown to crown, consuming acres of forest in a short time.

Botanists recognize two strains or races of the species—the Choctawhatchee of the panhandle coast and the Ocala on the peninsula. The variations between the strains are not based on any morphological differences, but on the fact that the cones of the western strain open when the seeds have matured; whereas the peninsula cones persist and may remain tightly closed for years, opening only when subjected to heat from forest fire or, following harvest, when slash has been trimmed and dropped, subjecting the cones to direct sunlight and increased warmth close to the ground. Dispersal of seed at that time is important to regeneration.

The one-inch-long male or pollen-bearing cones appear in spring, developing in clusters of erect, dark orange spikes at the base of the new growth. The two- to three-and-a-half-inch, seed-bearing cones, borne on short, stout stems are conical at first, becoming ovoid when open, and stalkless or nearly so. They develop at the ends of the previous year's growth, usually in groups of four or five, often tipped toward the trunk. Each cone scale

Devereux Butcher

Confined almost entirely to Florida, east coast Sand Pines develop a westward lean is armed with a short, deciduous prickle. One cone produces up to seventy-five black seeds less than a quarter inch long attached to a half inch, glossy, dark brown wing. Seed viability declines with age in the Ocala strain. Trees of this strain accumulate large quantities of cones through many seasons, the older ones turning ash gray and sometimes gradually becoming imbedded in the expanding growth of the branches.

Seedlings put on most of their first year growth twice— through March and April and again usually in early September. Under normal conditions, the trees average three feet in height by their third year, and in fifty or sixty years they reach commercial maturity.

The soft, strong but brittle, light orange or yellow wood with thick, pale sapwood formerly was considered valueless, but now is harvested on the Ocala National Forest as pulpwood for the manufacture of paper.

Well established trees usually are able to resist the effects of drought and extreme temperatures and, unless weakened by fire, there is little chance of fatal attacks by such pests as the black turpentine beetle, southern pine beetle, ipse engraver beetle, red-headed pine sawfly, the pitch moth larvae, certain borers and a rot known as red-heart.

The common name, sand pine, has been suggested by the sandy soil in which the tree grows; while the scientific name, *clausa*, means "closed" and refers to the closed cones of the Ocala strain.

Because of a wide-spreading root system, sand pine seldom blows down, but where strong prevailing winds occur, such as the easterlies along the Atlantic coastal belt, all the trees in a stand tilt characteristically westward at the same angle.

Soils are light, sandy, comparatively infertile and acid, with only slight variations in composition.

Sand pine is the tallest tree among its associates, which include Chapman, scrub, turkey, live and sand live oaks.

Devereux Butcher

Bark on the lower trunks of old trees is broken into irregular, oblong, gray-brown scaly plates, while that on young trees and limbs is thin, pale gray and smooth

Devereux Butcher

Young cones at the base of the previous year's growth are inconspicuous among the needles, which occur in bundles of two and are two to three and a half inches long

Devereux Butcher

Two to three and a half inches long and pale gray, the cones on peninsula trees remain closed for years, while those on panhandle trees open when seeds are ripe

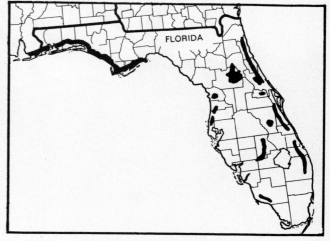

Natural range of Sand Pine

BISHOP PINE
Swamp pine, Dwarf marine pine, Obispo pine, Bull pine
Pinus muricata   D. Don

CONSIDERED a variable species, bishop pine is a rare and comparatively small tree, as pines go, seldom eighty feet tall and usually no more than thirty to sixty feet, with diameters up to two and rarely three feet. The trunk, often leaning, sends out numerous stout branches at varying angles, which develop a spreading, rounded or slightly conical crown of rich foliage. Younger trees have dense, pyramidal crowns.

The natural range of bishop pine extends intermittently along the California coast from Mendocino County to San Luis Obispo County and from sea level to 1000 feet, and a mile or two inland, including a stand on the southwestern shore of Tomales Bay on the Point Reyes Peninsula in Marin County, with isolated occurrences on the Monterey Peninsula in northern Monterey County, where this species hybridizes with *P. radiata*. Santa Rosa and Santa Cruz islands, twenty-five miles off the coast, south of Santa Barbara, support a half dozen small stands. A closely related species, *P. remorata*, (Mason), differing from bishop pine in that it has symmetrical instead of lopsided cones, also has been identified on these islands. One small stand of bishop pine has been found on the west coast of Lower California, about eight miles west of Valle San Vicente, just south of Ensenada, and two small areas discovered on Cedros Island, off Lower California's coast, a dozen miles northwest of Point Eugenia, may be *P. muricata* var. *cedrosensis*, (Howell).

The bark of bishop pine, four to six inches thick, is light gray and deeply furrowed into long, sinuous ridges, which sometimes lack horizontal furrowing.

Young twigs are stout, dark yellow-green and smooth, becoming yellow-brown and later turning purple-brown, roughened by the persistent bases of bud scales. The sharply pointed buds of the following year's growth are ovoid and covered by red-brown protective scales having hairy margins.

The dark orange catkin-like male or pollen-producing flowers are in clusters at the base of the new growth, and the female or cone-producing ones occur in whorls of three to seven on the twigs of the preceding year, and sometimes on the twigs of the year. They are attached by stout stems, their ovate scales narrowed into points and the large bracts nearly round. The cones, erect when young, mature by the second fall and lean toward the trunk, which gives them a lopsided form. They are two to four inches long, chestnut-brown and lustrous, their scales armed with a flattened spine, incurved above the middle of the cone and recurved toward its base. Some cones remain on the tree for years, but unlike those of other pines whose cones persist, such as those of

Devereux Butcher

Often with leaning trunk and stout branches at varying angles, Bishop Pine seldom attains eighty feet

62

P. clausa, these are not enveloped later by the increasing diameter growth of the branch. Instead, the expanding branch breaks the cone's stem, and the cone is pushed away by the diameter growth, the stem held only by the bark.

The dark brown, roughened, winged seeds, shed in September or October, are somewhat triangular. Large seed crops are produced almost every year; germination is good and seeds keep their vitality for several years when retained within the closed cone.

The dark green, stiff, sharply thick-tipped, coarse needles persist for two years or longer and are marked with rows of pale colored stomata. Three and a half to five and a half inches in length, they are borne in bundles of two, and are noticeably dense, particularly at the ends of the branches.

The light brown, hard, strong wood is coarse-grained, has thick sapwood, is nearly free of resin and finds little use in the market, except locally for fuel or rough lumber.

Bishop pine thrives in a variety of soils, including dry, gravelly, sandy soil, peat bogs and cold clay soils.

Among the associates of bishop pine are California live oak, Monterey pine, Gowen cypress, Douglasfir, madrone, tanoak, bigleaf maple, California laurel, and various shrubs, such as ceanothus and rhododendron.

Devereux Butcher

Persisting for two years, the dark, coarse needles are three and a half to five and a half inches long, borne in bundles of two, and are dense at the branch ends

Devereux Butcher

Lustrous chestnut-brown, two to four inches long and with each scale armed with a stout prickle, the cones are lopsided from leaning back toward the trunk

Devereux Butcher

The deeply fissured, pale gray bark is four to six inches thick and sometimes contains long ridges lacking horizontal breaks

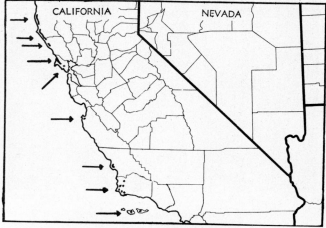

Natural range of Bishop Pine

SPRUCE PINE

Cedar pine, Poor pine, Walter pine, Bottom white pine
Pinus glabra Walter

Warren D. Brush

Spruce Pine is a medium-sized tree, eighty to ninety feet high, with spreading branches and narrow crown, which sometimes grows to a height of 120 feet

SPRUCE PINE is one of the less important yellow, or hard, pines of the Southeast. It usually occurs singly or in small groups, never forming pure stands over any large area. Chiefly confined to the coast region, it grows in southeastern South Carolina, southern Georgia, Alabama and Mississippi, northern Florida and extreme eastern Louisiana.

Requiring a moist soil, spruce pine commonly occurs along rivers, especially on low terraces subject to overflow. It seems to require a warm, humid climate for its best development. Sometimes it is found mixed with shortleaf and loblolly pines. Nowhere abundant, it is of greatest economic importance in western Florida where it is common over areas of considerable extent and attains its largest size.

While usually a medium-sized tree eighty to ninety feet high and two to two and a half feet in diameter, it has been known to attain a height of 120 feet and a diameter of three and a half feet. The bole is commonly unsymmetrical with much taper, and the limbs formed along the trunk persist until the tree is nearly mature. The limbs are horizontal, dividing into spreading branches, and the crown is comparatively long and narrow. The slender, flexible branchlets, light red and tinged with purple at first, ultimately become dark reddish brown. The sharp-pointed buds have brown scales with whitish matted hairs on their margins.

On young trees and on the limbs and upper trunk of older trees, the bark is smooth and light gray in color. On old trees, it is from one-half to three-fourths of an inch thick, and irregularly divided by shallow fissures into flat, connected ridges broken into small, thin, closely appressed, light reddish brown scales. The specific name, *glabra*, meaning smooth, is well-used in describing the spruce pine, since its smooth bark readily distinguishes it from other pines within its range.

The soft, slender, dark green needles, from one and a half to three inches long, occur two to a bundle. They are sharp-pointed. At the end of their second and in the spring of their third year they fall from the tree. The male or staminate flowers are yellow and grow in short, crowded clusters at the base of the twig, while the pistillate are purplish and are borne on slender, slightly ascending stems at or near the ends of the twigs.

Spruce pine has the smallest cones of any of the eastern pines. They measure from one half to two inches long, are nearly spherical or somewhat egg-shaped, and are on short, stout, bent stalks. They are reddish brown and they open and shed their seed soon after ripening. Each thin, slightly concave cone scale is armed with a minute, weak, erect prickle, which is usually deciduous. The seeds are nearly triangular, about one-eighth of an inch long, with a thin, dark gray shell mottled with black, and thin, delicate wings five-eighths of an inch long and one-fourth of an inch wide.

L. W. Brownell

The egg-shaped cones, smallest of any of the eastern pines, are from one-half to two inches long and are attached by short, bent stalks

On old trees the bark is divided into flat ridges, broken into small, thin, light reddish brown scales and is a half to three quarters of an inch thick

Warren D. Brush

L. W. Brownell

Dark green needles are slender and sharp-pointed. They occur two to a bundle and fall in three years. Male flowers are yellow, the pistillate purplish

Although classified botanically as a hard pine, the wood is light in weight, and is moderately soft and weak. The heartwood is light brown and the thick sapwood nearly white. Although the tree is not well adapted for conversion into lumber, because of its poor form and rather small size, sawmills sometimes segregate the lumber and sell it to manufacturers of sash, doors and interior finish, for which it is very suitable. Also it is being used increasingly for pulpwood together with other southern pines. However, its principal use is for fuel. Other names applied to it are cedar pine, poor pine, Walter pine and bottom white pine.

Spruce pine is a tree of very rapid growth, attaining an average diameter of from four to four and a half inches, and a height of thirty-five feet, in twenty years. Although fully grown at about seventy-five years, it may live to an age of 150 years or more. It thrives and propagates in the shade and will even crowd out other trees by the rapidity of its growth. Seed, which germinates best in half shade, is produced abundantly at an early age, often at ten years. Under favorable conditions, this species will reproduce and take possession of cleared land and abandoned fields.

Spruce pine's natural habitat, on low, moist land, helps to protect the tree from fire. The wood is not highly resistant to decay, however, and overmature trees often have heart rot from butt to top.

Occasionally planted as an ornamental tree because of its attractive form when young and open grown, it is not hardy in cultivation except in the South.

Base map © J. L. Smith, Phila. Pa.

Natural range of Spruce Pine

TABLE-MOUNTAIN PINE

Mountain pine, Prickly pine

Pinus pungens Lambert

TABLE-MOUNTAIN PINE obtains its name from being confined in its natural distribution mainly to the dry, gravelly tablelands, ridges and slopes of the Appalachian Mountains, from southern Pennsylvania to North Carolina and to eastern Tennessee and northern Georgia. In the northern part of its range it is generally scattered among other trees such as pitch and Virginia pines, oaks and hickories, but in the southern Alleghenies it often forms pure forests of considerable extent.

Generally a small tree, in some localities it reaches a sufficient size to be of commercial importance. When crowded in the forest, a height of sixty to seventy feet and a trunk diameter of two and a half to three feet is not uncommon. The fairly long, clear trunk is crowned near the summit by a few short branches forming a shallow, narrow, round-topped head. In the open it is usually only twenty to thirty feet high with a short thick trunk frequently clothed to the ground with long horizontal branches. The lower ones are pendulous toward the extremities, sometimes touching the ground, and the upper ones sweep in graceful upward curves, forming a flat-topped, often irregular head. The stout branchlets are light orange and smooth when they first appear, later becoming rather rough and dark brown.

In crowded clusters of two, or occasionally three, the stout, stiff and often twisted, dark green needles are about two and a half inches long. They fall from the tree during their second or third year.

Blossoms appear in April or May. The yellow, staminate flowers are borne in long, loose clusters at the base of the current season's growth, while the short-stalked purplish ones, which develop into cones, grow laterally along the new growth in whorls of two to seven.

Table-mountain pine has a characteristic, heavy, egg-shaped cone, the scales of which are much thickened at the ends and are armed with conspicuous, stout, hooked spines. These light brown cones measure from two to three and a half inches in length. They are stemless and usually grow in clusters of three or four or occasionally seven or eight. The thin, tough cone-scales are much thickened at the ends, and have a prominent transverse ridge. The strong, curved prickles are incurved above the middle of the cones and recurved below it. The scales near the base are often much-thickened knobs. The cones ripen in autumn of the second season, opening as soon as ripe and gradually shedding their seeds.

George Washington National Forest

Generally a small tree, Table-Mountain Pine often reaches sufficient size to be of commercial importance, with a height of 60 to 70 feet and a diameter of two feet

However, they sometimes remain closed for two or three years, frequently remaining on the branches for eighteen or twenty years. The rounded triangular seeds are nearly a fourth of an inch long, with thin wings one inch long and a fourth of an inch wide, broadest near the middle and gradually narrowed toward the ends.

The oblong, obtuse, winter buds are dark chestnut-brown. On old trunks the dark reddish brown bark is from three-fourths to one inch thick and is broken by shallow fissures into irregularly shaped plates, separating on the surface into thin, loose, brown scales tinged with red. On young stems and old branches the bark is not so thick and rough, but is broken into thin dark brown scales.

The wood of table-mountain pine is moderately heavy, hard, stiff and strong, a cubic foot of the air-dry wood weighing about thirty-six pounds. The heartwood is pale reddish brown with thick, nearly white, sapwood. It is little used except for fuel.

The tree grows rather slowly and probably does not live to be more than 250 years old.

Seeds are produced at an early age. Trees only five years old and two to three feet tall can often be found bearing cones and large numbers are borne on mature trees. Although the cones shed their seeds very irregularly, large numbers fall to the ground every year and considerable reproduction takes place. It is a very aggressive tree and often takes possession of old abandoned fields and rough land unsuited for agriculture, where it serves as a protection against erosion.

Table-mountain pine does not make a suitable shade or street tree. As a single specimen, however, it may serve as an ornamental. It is attractive when young, especially when planted in the open.

J. Horace McFarland Co.

Cone-producing flowers are short-stalked and purplish. The yellow staminate flowers are borne in long loose clusters

A. Varela

The heavy egg-shaped cone bears conspicuous stout spines. Stiff and often twisted needles occur in clusters of two or three

George Washington National Forest

On old trunks, the dark reddish brown bark is broken by shallow fissures into irregularly shaped, scaly plates

Base map © J. L. Smith, Phila. Pa.

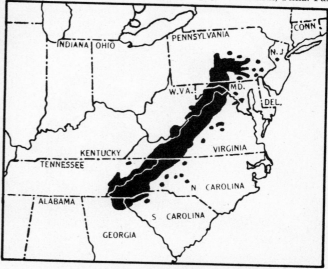

Natural range of Table-Mountain Pine

SCOTCH PINE

Scots pine

Pinus sylvestris Linnaeus

SCOTCH PINE has been more extensively planted for forestry purposes in eastern North America than any other European tree. Its irregular crown, and the orange-red bark of the upper trunk and limbs are seen in many parks and cemeteries. Plantations, windbreaks, and ornamental plantings from western North Carolina to Quebec, and across the lake states to Saskatchewan and northwestern Nebraska testify to this tree's indifference to soil and climate conditions. In its native Europe it is found over most of the continent and much of north-ern Asia, comprising the bulk of the forested area of northern Germany and enormous forests in Russia. It thrives on well drained sites where the soil is deep and moist, as well as on dry, sterile sands and thin soils of rocky outcrops to elevations of 8,000 feet in the Caucasus Mountains.

Although commercially important in Europe, Scotch pine has an unhappy record as a timber producer in this country. Early plantings were largely from seed of low, stunted, high mountain trees, producing crooked trunks and poor quality wood. Since 1920, increasing numbers of trees from seed of selected origin have been planted, including a variety from the vicinity of Riga, in northeastern Europe. The American grown trees of this variety are expected to inherit their parents' tall, straight form.

Scotch pine attains heights of sixty to ninety feet in America, with diameters of one to three feet, but under favorable western European conditions it reaches 150 feet and diameters of five feet. When young, it has an irregularly pyramidal crown, but with age a broad, irregularly round-topped head, often described as picturesque, develops. Forest-grown trees are tall and have a straight, un-branched trunk of relatively little taper and a short crown. Trees grown in the open retain their branches well down toward the ground, several of which may become long, and horizontal in form. At a distance this tree resembles pitch pine.

The needles are one and a half to three and a half inches long, borne in sheathed clusters of two or rarely three. They are dull blue-green, appreciably flattened, rigid sharp-

Devereux Butcher

Field grown Scotch Pine has a short trunk, an open, irregular crown, and heights of sixty feet or more

pointed and usually twisted. The needles are shorter than those of red pine, stouter than shortleaf pine, and more blunt pointed than table-mountain pine. They extend along the length of medium thick, grayish yellow twigs, which are rougher than those of Virginia pine. Each twig is terminated by blunt orange-red buds whose small scales turn backward.

Dense clusters of egg-shaped, yellow, pollen-bearing, cone-like staminate blossoms about two-fifths of an inch long are borne near the base of the new growth in May or June. The seed-producing ovulate blooms appear simultaneously, singly or in pairs near the ends of the new growth in the upper crown. These mature in the second season as backward pointing, somewhat curved, dull, tawny yellow, short-stalked cones, one to two and a half inches long. The cone scales are swollen at the base and are usually armed with a tiny prickle. The small, dark gray, winged seeds may be carried several hundred feet on the wind.

The bark of the upper trunk and larger limbs is orange-red, thin, and peels off in papery flakes. That of the older trunks is grayish brown, about a half inch thick near the base, with longitudinal scaly plates and irregular furrows, which reveal streaks of orange-red inner bark.

The pale reddish brown resinous heartwood is hard, tough, and moderately light—a cubic foot weighing thirty-three to thirty-four pounds when air seasoned. The heartwood becomes increasingly distinguishable from the lighter colored sapwood on prolonged exposure to the air. The annual rings are clearly apparent. It is moderately durable in contact with the ground, drys well in the air, but is susceptible to blue stain, and is suitable for outside work. Throughout Europe, Scotch pine is widely used for general construction. Its many uses include buildings, bridges, scaffolding, ships' masts, mine props, fencing, paving, and the better grades are selected for joinery. The wood gives good results with paint or varnish, can be effectively stained, and is easily glued.

Within its European range, and especially on poor soils, Scotch pine forms pure stands of considerable extent. On better sites, it associates with Norway spruce, silver fir and European larch. In the Scottish highlands it is found with European white birch, and on the peat moors with aspen and alder.

In America, Scotch pine is reasonably free of fungus diseases and insect pests, but in Europe no other tree is more susceptible to injurious insects. Bark beetles, weevils, wood borers and various needle feeding insects are especially active where trees grow on poor soil. Fungus diseases also do considerable damage. The thin bark makes young trees susceptible to ground fire damage, but the thicker bark on older trees resists fire to a considerable extent.

Scotch pine has proved a hardy pioneer, especially when planted on long-abandoned, trampled pastures, and on blow sand. Even on such sites, however, native species will grow with equal or greater vigor, and the resulting forest products are usually superior. Like other trees from Europe and Asia it shows strong tendencies to establish itself by natural seeding. Extensive stands of volunteer second generation Scotch pine may be expected over the northern and eastern states, and the better strains may provide this country with sources of good timber.

Devereux Butcher

Clusters of yellow pollen-bearing blossoms appear at the base of the new spring growth

Devereux Butcher

The gray-brown bark near the base of old trees is broken by shallow, longitudinal fissures

Devereux Butcher

Two flat, twisted, blue-green needles are in each sheath. The cones may be two inches long

AUSTRIAN PINE

Black pine

Pinus nigra Arnold

A NATIVE of Europe and western Asia, Austrian pine has been cultivated for many years in the United States as an ornamental, having been introduced here as early as 1759. The symmetrical, stout, spreading branches and thickly set, dark green needles of a well-developed tree make a handsome appearance. In its native habitat, Austrian pine attains a height of 100 and occasionally 150 feet with a trunk diameter up to six feet. In the United States, however, trees more than fifty feet high are exceptional. In youth its form is pyramidal, with the slightly ascending branches arranged in regular whorls, but with age it develops a broad, round or often flat-topped head.

The stout branchlets are usually yellowish or light brown and the ovoid or oblong-ovoid winter buds are light brown tinged with white, the lowermost scales loose and the uppermost bound together by white resin.

The dark green needles occur two in a sheath and measure from three to six and a half inches long. They resemble in appearance those of red or Norway pine (*Pinus resinosa*), but are stout and stiff, while those of the latter are slender and flexible.

The male or pollen-bearing flowers, in clusters of three to ten or sometimes more, are borne on the lower half of the branchlets of the current year's growth. The female flowers, bright red in color, occur singly or in twos or threes at the top of the young branchlets. They develop into small, globular cones, which ripen at the end of the second year. Austrian pine cones resemble those of red pine, but are somewhat larger and usually have prickles, which are absent in the latter. The mature cone is egg-shaped, stemless, yellowish brown, glossy, and measures from two to four inches in length. The end of each cone scale is depressed, conspicuously ridged, and usually provided with a very short prickle at the tip. The gray, winged seed contained under each scale is about one forth of an inch in diameter. The cones are deciduous at maturity.

The dark gray bark is deeply fissured on old trees and divided into irregular, longitudinal scaly plates.

The wood is hard and strong, the heartwood reddish brown and the sapwood pale yellow. In lower Austria, where this species occurs abundantly, timber of good quality is obtained from trees frequently more than a hundred feet tall, with stems clear of branches for as much as two-thirds of their height. In the other countries where it grows naturally it is a valuable timber tree. The wood is used for general construction purposes and for most of the products for which pine timber is suitable. Austrian pine is not important as a source of commercial timber in the United States, but is commonly grown here for ornamental purposes instead.

Arnold Arboretum

As a young tree, the Austrian Pine has a pyramidal form and in maturity develops a round, flat-topped head. The tree attains a height of 50 feet

The male flowers occur in clusters of three to ten. The female flowers are bright red and occur singly or in twos or threes

The dark green needles occur two in a sheath. The mature cone is egg-shaped, yellowish brown, and from two to four inches long

Austrian pine is, in fact, one of the most common exotics used in ornamental planting in the United States because of the symmetrical form of the tree and its dense, dark green foliage. Of pyramidal form in youth, it will maintain its lower branches for thirty to forty years, if given ample space, usually showing vigorous growth for at least sixty or seventy years. The broad, flat top of older trees also gives a striking appearance. Although more severe and not so graceful as other trees, such as the white pine and hemlock, it is well liked as a single or lawn specimen. When planted in mass for landscapes, the dense, dark green foliage is considered by some to give a somber and depressing effect. This may be relieved, however, by interplanting groups of trees with brighter foliage.

The tree is hardy in eastern United States as far north as New England and southern Ontario. It is not very particular as to soil, growing well in sandy soil, as well as in heavy loam and clay. It often serves ideally as a windbreak for gardens and orchards because the dense foliage and stiff branches will withstand strong wind and heavy snow.

Because of its extraordinary hardiness and rapid growth, Austrian pine is a suitable tree for field planting and for covering rocky land. It is also used for the improvement of land by fixing sand dunes. During the first sixty or seventy years, Austrian pine may average a foot of height growth a year. Thereafter it gradually slows down until it almost ceases at about a hundred years.

The dark gray bark is deeply fissured on old trees and divided into irregular, longitudinal scaly plates. The wood is very hard

TAMARACK

American larch, Eastern larch, Black larch, Hackmatack, Alaska larch
Larix laricina (DuRoi) Koch

FROM the Atlantic to the valley of the Yukon, north to the limit of tree growth near the arctic circle and along the shores of Hudson Bay, tamarack, or eastern larch extends south throughout much of Canada, New England and New York, into Michigan, Wisconsin and Minnesota.

stands are crowded. One by one, its tree companions drop out, from south to north, until the last to remain are black spruce, red spruce, aspen, paper birch and, finally, the willows. Toward the arctic circle, growth is scattered and dwarfed. This tree sustains itself from sea level to elevations of 4,000 feet; from the relatively mild climate and humidity of the Atlantic coast to the interior of Alaska.

The broad, shallow root system is adapted to swampy ground, but best growth is made in fresh, well-drained soils.

The straight, slender tamarack is seldom more than fifty to sixty feet tall, with a trunk eighteen to twenty inches in diameter, but on the low benches north of Lake Winnipeg, trees reach one hundred feet or more

Devereux Butcher

Slender and sparsely foliaged, Tamarack is often fifty or sixty feet tall

Its slender, sparse and feathery, clear green summer crown contrasts with the dark green heavier foliage of other conifers. In winter its bare orange-brown branches form a delicate tracery.

On the well-drained uplands and occasional cool sphagnum bogs of its southern range, tamarack grows in mixture with black, red, and white spruces, hemlock, balsam fir, aspen, paper birch, alder, northern white cedar, willow and red maple. The occasional even-aged, pure

U. S. Forest Service

From late September until April the crown and horizontal branches are bare of foliage with diameters of two feet.

In youth the crown is narrowly pyramidal, with a flexible terminal shoot. With age trees become irregular, and those grown in the open maintain a low broad head. The slender upper branches are horizontal or slightly ascending, the lower ones drooping in long sweeps. The straight trunk tapers rapidly. Trees grown within the forest may be clear of branches for half or more of their length.

Clusters of twelve to twenty bright green, soft leaves grow on wood of the previous year, or singly on the new shoots. They are three-quarters of an inch to an inch and a quarter long and triangular in cross section. The upper side is rounded, and the lower sharply keeled. In early spring the new leaves are marked with breathing pores or stomata. By September or October the leaves turn yellow and fall.

The delicate green tracery of the spring foliage is punctuated with clusters of inconspicuous, stemless, yellow staminate or pollen-bearing blooms on the one- or two-year-old orange-brown branchlets. The more showy ovulate cones grow on short lateral stalks of one- to three-year-old twigs. They are like small flattened spheres, with green-tipped, rose-colored bracts growing out between the red scales. At first they stand erect, with scales spread ready for pollination. Later they droop and close their scales when the seeds develop. By autumn they stand erect again, are chestnut-brown and one-half to three-quarters of an inch long. During the fall and winter the scales spread to liberate the chestnut-brown winged seeds.

The reddish brown bark of mature trunks is a half to three quarters of an inch thick. Its surface is broken into thin, brown, closely pressed, nearly round scales. Young bark is smooth and light orange.

A cubic foot of the tough, resinous, coarse-grained wood when dry weighs about thirty-nine pounds. It is light brown, with thin, nearly white sapwood. Because it is durable in contact with the soil it is used for railroad ties, posts, sills and for boats. Its other uses include excelsior, cabinet work, interior finish and telephone poles.

Next to fire, the worst enemy of this tree is the larch sawfly, which often kills large areas of tamarack forest.

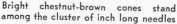
Devereux Butcher

Bright chestnut-brown cones stand among the cluster of inch long needles

Natural range of Tamarack

The reddish brown bark has shallow furrows and is about half an inch thick

WESTERN LARCH
Montana larch, Mountain larch, Western tamarack
Larix occidentalis Nuttall

THE most important, as well as the largest and most massive of all the larches or tamaracks, is western larch, whose natural range is restricted to the high mountain valleys and slopes of southeastern British Columbia and the upper Columbia River basin bounded by the Rocky Mountains on the east and the Cascade Mountains on the west. This tree is seldom found below 2,000 feet or higher than 7,000 feet above sea level, and attains its greatest size and abundance in Montana.

Short, horizontal branches on a tall straight trunk form a crown whose narrow, pyramidal form runs to a slender point. The crown usually occupies from one-half to one-third of the total height, so that trees 160 to 200 feet tall may have sixty to over one hundred feet of clear trunk. Such individuals, which occasionally attain diameters of six or seven feet, may be 600 or 700 years old, while trees sixteen to twenty inches in diameter may be 250 to 400 years old.

The larches and the southern cypress are unique among coniferous trees in that they shed their leaves in the autumn. The light green, flatly triangular, pointed needles are one to one and five-eighths inches long. First appearing singly in spirals on the twig, they later develop on a scaly spur in bundles of thirty to forty. They turn yellow in the fall and drop off.

Separate male and female flowers are borne close together on the same tree during the early spring, on growth of the previous year. The yellow-green, pollen-bearing male flowers are about the size of a pea, while developing on the same twigs are small scaly, bright purple or red ovulate flowers, each of which is surrounded by a bundle of leaves. These ovulate flowers, when fertilized, develop into broadly egg-shaped cones, one to one and a half inches long, with a characteristic slender bract extending beyond the tip of each cone scale. In the early fall the small, chestnut-brown, winged seeds are shed, and by the end of October or November the cones have dropped from the trees.

The conspicuous bract extending beyond the cone scale, as in the case of Douglasfir cones, the white woolly coating of hairs near the base of the cone, the larger cones and needles, and the fine hairy growth on the young twigs help distinguish western larch from the other larches. The leaves or needles are triangular in cross-section, and are longer than those of the other larches.

Mature trees have deeply furrowed, dull, reddish cinnamon-brown bark composed of innumerable overlapping rounded plates broken to form a zig-

Western Larch attains heights of over two hundred feet and develops a slender symmetrical crown covered with satiny, pale green foliage

74

zag pattern of many imperfect diamonds. It is three to six inches thick near the base. Higher up on the trunk and on the branches, the bark is relatively thin, scaly and more brown than red. The thick bark on the lower trunk often proves an effective protection against fire. This, together with the natural tolerance of the tree, helps explain the pure stands of western larch which frequently follow the destruction of lodgepole pine and other associates by fire.

The hard, fine-grained, reddish brown wood is not only the heaviest of the larches, but one of the heaviest of all the conifers. It weighs thirty-six to thirty-nine pounds to the cubic foot when air dry, and is remarkably durable in contact with the soil. It works well with tools and is used to an increasing extent for interior finish, boxes, boats, and furniture, as well as for telephone poles, railroad ties, mine timbers, and posts. Its largest use is probably as rough lumber in local construction. The butt logs, however, are so heavy, and frequently so full of defects that they are often left in the woods.

Western larch sometimes occurs in pure open forests, but is usually associated with other species. In mixture with ponderosa pine in eastern Oregon, stands of about 2,000 board feet an acre are common, while in western Montana in mixture with western white pine, Douglasfir, lodgepole pine, lowland white fir, alpine fir, and Engelmann spruce the stand may reach 10,000 to 12,000 board feet to the acre.

Throughout its range, the natural reproduction is increased by fires, because the seedlings require a large amount of light, and because of the relative resistance which large trees have to fire. In this respect, western larch finds lodgepole pine its chief competitor.

The precipitation through much of the range of western larch is from twenty to thirty inches, with long seasons of moderately heavy snowfall, frequent rains in the spring and fall, but hot dry summers.

Western larch is subject to the attack of a number of wood-destroying fungi, the most common of which is a chalky, quinine fungus that causes a brown heart rot. The tree also is subject to what the lumbermen call "shake"—a breaking or disintegration along the growth rings of the lower trunk.

Of the nine species inhabiting the world, four are native to North America. In addition to western larch, there is the eastern tamarack common to the northeastern states with its range extending westward to southern Alaska, alpine larch found in the high mountains of the Northwest, and Alaska larch limited to a part of that state.

Larix occidentalis may be translated directly to mean the larch of the western world. David Douglas first observed and described the species in April, 1826, in northeastern Washington.

Elongated cones one to one and five-eighths inches long grow on the twigs among the fine, flexible needles, which occur in clusters of thirty to forty

U. S. Forest Service

The dull cinnamon-brown bark, composed of many small irregularly rounded plates, may be three to six inches thick near the base of the trunk

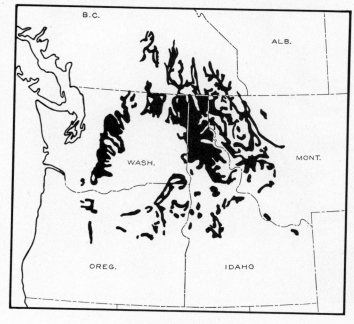

Natural range of Western Larch

RED SPRUCE

Eastern spruce, He-balsam

Picea rubens Sargent

THE NARROW, dark yellow-green crowns of red spruce pierce the forest skyline from southeastern Canada through New England, eastern New York and along the Appalachian Mountains to North Carolina. On swampy sites and on mountain tops, the species sometimes occurs in pure stands, but in the northern part of its range, on well-drained soils near sea level, it occurs in association with white pine, eastern hemlock, balsam fir, sugar maple, yellow birch and beech. In the Adirondack Mountains of northern New York, it grows at altitudes up to 4,500 feet, while in the southern Appalachian Mountains, particularly on the high ridges and peaks of western North Carolina and southwestward along the summits of the Great Smoky Mountains of western North Carolina and eastern Tennessee, it ranges between 5,000 and 6,000 feet and higher.

Red spruce of the North reaches heights of sixty to eighty feet, with trunk diameters of nearly two feet. Larger sizes are attained in the southern Appalachians, with occasional trees over one hundred feet high and up to four feet in diameter. (Some botanists classify the southern mountain spruce as *Picea australis*.) The crown of red spruce is less regularly symmetrical than that of most other spruces, and with maturity becomes open and wide-spreading. Numerous large, irregular branches droop as they extend outward and turn up at the tips.

The plump, four-sided, dark, shiny, yellow-green needles are about half an inch long and grow singly from all sides of the twigs and branches. They are slightly incurved, usually blunt-pointed, and have a prominent midrib on the lower surface. They remain on the twigs about six years. A reddish coat of down persists on the slender new twigs through the first year. This, together with the shortness and the incurving of the needles helps to distinguish red spruce from all but black spruce, the

Devereux Butcher

The open, wide-spreading crown of Red Spruce
reaches heights of sixty to one hundred feet

needles of which are more nearly blue-green, and do not have the midrib on the lower surface. Red spruce's warm green is distinguished from white spruce's blue-green needles.

Bright red, oval, pollen-bearing staminate flowers, about half an inch long, grow close to the twig near the ends of the previous year's growth in April and May. The ovulate flowers appear simultaneously, but on the ends of different branches of the same tree. They are reddish green, oblong, cylindrical cones about three quarters of an inch long. Standing erect at first, they hang down after being fertilized, and in the autumn of the same year mature as elongated egg-shaped cones one and a half to two inches long. Purplish or light green during the spring and early summer, they become a light, glossy, reddish brown when ripe. The rounded, entire margins of the scales help distinguish these cones from those of black spruce. Also, the cone scales are thicker and less flexible than those of white spruce. The dark mottled brown seeds are shed through fall and early winter, and the cones drop by the end of the following year. The seeds are about an eighth of an inch long, and, with the full rounded wing, are nearly half an inch long.

The scientific name *rubens* was suggested by the red coloring of the young cones. The name originally was applied by Sargent.

Old trunks have dark, reddish brown bark often appearing as if washed with gray. It is hard, firm, and about half an inch thick.

The light, soft, narrow-ringed wood is faintly tinged with red, but a layer of sapwood often two inches thick is almost white. Averaging about twenty-eight pounds to the cubic foot when air dry, the wood is easy to work, free from pitch or distinctive flavor, and holds paint fairly well. The combination of strength and stiffness in relation to weight gives spruce a special place in the construction of ladder rails, canoe paddles, and light oars, while the long straight fibers and light color make it suitable for the manufacture of paper. Spruce furnishes a large part of the pulpwood for American paper manufacture.

Fire is the worst enemy of spruce. Fortunately, however, its preference for damp situations usually retards a serious conflagration. Occasionally, heavy accumulation of debris under the trees becomes dry. At such times, if fire gets in, it may sweep into the crowns with disastrous results. The less spectacular ground fires are especially damaging to the young growth.

Of the many insects which prey upon the foliage, bark, wood, and twigs of spruce, the European spruce sawfly is the worst.

Devereux Butcher

Glossy red-brown cones emerge from last year's dark yellow-green needles

The dark reddish brown bark of mature trunks is hard and firm, often appearing as if washed with gray

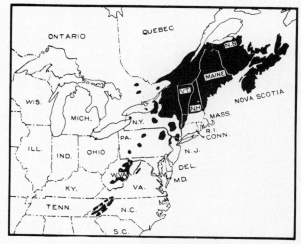

Natural range of Red Spruce

BLACK SPRUCE

Bog spruce, Swamp spruce, Shortleaf black spruce
Picea mariana (Miller) Britton, Sterns and Poggenberg

WHILE the form of black spruce varies according to site, its most noticeable characteristics are its slender, straight trunk, irregular open conical crown, comparatively short branches, and small cones. In favored situations at the southern extremity of the range, it sometimes attains a height of one hundred feet with a trunk diameter of two or three feet, and on good sites in the North it occasionally grows to seventy feet or more with a trunk that measures ten or twelve inches in diameter. As a rule, however, it is only thirty to fifty feet tall. Toward the northern limits of its range, the tree is reduced to a shrub with heights up to twelve feet. A moisture-loving species, it inhabits cold sphagnum bogs, springy swamps and lake shores. It also occurs on sandy or rocky hillsides and uplands.

Black spruce is a slow growing tree, especially when in swampy locations. Trees in these sites will add only an inch or two to their trunk diameters in seventy-five or a hundred years. In such areas there is little competition so that it is most abundant and develops thick pure stands. It grows also on glacial drift and clay soils, but best growth occurs in well-drained alluvial soils that are constantly moist. On upland sites in the North it occasionally grows to seventy feet or more. Black spruce does not demand deep soils because the root system is shallow. It is a fairly long-lived tree, and specimens of average size are from one hundred and twenty-five to two hundred years old.

The range of black spruce is transcontinental, extending from Labrador, Newfoundland and Nova Scotia southward through New England, New York and northern New Jersey and Pennsylvania. In the lake states it occurs in northern Michigan and Wisconsin and northeastern Minnesota, and thence from Hudson Bay and southern Manitoba northwestward in a broad belt to the west coast of Alaska.

Bark on the mature trunk is a quarter to a half inch thick, dark reddish brown turning gray with age, and is broken on the surface into flaky, thin, rather closely pressed scales. Trunks of trees growing in the open are clothed to the ground with branches, the upper ones being horizontal, while the lower ones droop and turn upward at the tips. Occasionally the basal branches of isolated trees sweep the ground taking root and sending up shoots. Middle-aged trees in dense stands have their trunks clear of branches for half their height, and trees forming thick, pure stands in bogs often have only a few short branches clustered at the top of the tree.

The sharp-pointed buds of black spruce are covered with light reddish brown overlapping scales and measure an eighth to a third of an inch long. Twigs of the year are yellowish brown, covered with short reddish brown hairs, later turning dark brown and becoming scaly. The four-angled, blunt-tipped needles measure a quarter to three-quarters of an inch in length and are slightly incurved above the middle. They are dark bluish green with a whitish bloom, and have rows of tiny white stomata on each of the four sides. They grow in spirals along the twig, standing out on all sides from it, and remain on the tree for from seven to ten years.

Flowers of the black spruce appear in May or June, and are situated near or at the tips of the branches and measure about one-eighth of an inch in length. The staminate or pollen-bearing ones are dark red and nearly stemless, while the ovulate or seed-producing flowers are purple and are composed of rounded scales.

The clustered, drooping, grayish brown cones, measuring one-half to one and

The most noticeable features of Black Spruce are its slender straight form, comparatively short branches and small size

a half inches in length, mature in August. When the scales open the cones are nearly round. They fall entire, but remain on the trees for twenty or thirty years, the oldest being at the base of branches nearest the trunk. Scales are brittle, rounded, slightly hairy, and have notched, uneven edges. The dark brown, winged, oblong, pointed seeds measure a half-inch in length and an eighth inch in width. Black spruce bears large seed crops only at infrequent intervals. Seeds retain their vitality for a long time. Their rate of germination is fairly high, and is best on constantly moist mineral soil or humus, or on wet decayed wood, needle litter, or moss. During their first year or two, seedlings require little or no direct sunlight. Older trees also are very tolerant of shade, especially on wet sites, and up to an advanced age are able to recover from suppression. Though often forming pure forests, this tree is found in mixture with larch, aspen, willow, alder, cottonwood, balsam fir, northern whitecedar, and black ash. Black spruce, eastern larch and willow, all three of dwarf size, make the most northerly outpost of trees, where their ranges draw close to the edge of the Beaufort Sea in the Mackenzie Bay region.

Heavier than the wood of any other North American spruce, that of black spruce weighs about thirty-three pounds to the cubic foot when dry. It is pale buff yellow or with a reddish tinge, and has a few inconspicuous resin ducts. Because of slow growth, the annual rings are narrow and the sapwood thin. It is soft, straight-grained, not strong, and is commercially less important than the other two eastern spruces—red spruce and white spruce—because the tree is small and slow growing. The wood, however, has much the same properties as the others. The chief use to which black spruce is put is in the manufacture of paper pulp, for which it is ideally suited owing to the long white fibers that make up the wood and that need little or no bleaching. It is used also for canoe paddles, oars, ladder rails, construction, ship building, and for many other purposes requiring a light, stiff wood. Chewing gum is made from the resin, and formerly spruce beer was made by boiling the branch tips. Today young trees are increasingly in demand for the Christmas tree market.

Other common names for black spruce are blue spruce, spruce pine, eastern spruce, bog spruce, and swamp spruce. The scientific name *Picea mariana* means Maryland spruce.

Its thin bark and resinous exudations on the trunk make black spruce susceptible to injury by fire, but this is lessened by the wet locations in which it grows. The tree is attacked by several kinds of fungi and by insects, especially the spruce budworm.

Black spruce is rarely planted as an ornamental tree because it is short-lived in cultivation. Moreover, it has an uneven, unkempt appearance owing to an accumulation of dead branches.

G. B. Sudworth

The grayish brown cones are clustered and drooping, and the bluish green, four-angled needles grow in spirals along the twigs

R. K. LeBarron

At first reddish brown, the bark turns gray with age, and is broken into thin, closely pressed scales

Natural range of Black Spruce

WHITE SPRUCE

Cat spruce, Canadian spruce, Skunk spruce
Picea glauca (Moench) Voss

THE RANGE of white spruce stretches from Labrador to Alaska, southward to Montana, the lake states, northern New York and northern New England. Its most westerly, and perhaps most northerly stand is near the Arctic Ocean, in Alaska, at latitude 68°. One of the two most widely distributed of the seven American spruces, it is of less commercial importance than red spruce, but of greater importance than black spruce, which accompanies it across the continent. It grows best on moist, well drained, porous soils, from sea level to elevations of 5,000 feet.

Ordinarily a tree forty to seventy feet tall, with trunk diameters of one to two feet, it sometimes reaches heights of eighty to 140 feet, with diameters up to four feet. Such trees may be 250 to 350 years old. In British Columbia and Alberta, white spruce attains large dimensions and constitutes the bulk of the forest. Toward the northern extremity of its range in Alaska, it is dwarf, but it attains fair size on higher ground along streams. This species almost invariably has a straight central trunk. When grown in the open it forms a narrow, regular spire clothed nearly to the ground with whorls of long, thick branches, which bend toward the ground, then turn up. As the tree matures, numerous small side branchlets droop down from the main branches, and the crown becomes wider and less pointed. In dense forest conditions, the straight, smooth trunk may be clear of branches for a third to two-thirds of its height. It often grows in dense pure forests, or in mixture with black spruce, Engelmann spruce, larch, birch, and aspen.

There is some confusion regarding its scientific name. *Picea glauca*, as adopted in this description, has been approved by three leading American dendrologists—Sargent, Sudworth, and Rehder. Some botanists use *canadensis*, published in 1768 by Philip Miller, the English botanist and contemporary of Linnaeus, but Miller seems to have described white and black spruces and hemlock under this name. The word *glauca* applies to the pale blue, hoary, or even whitish tinge of the new needles, and provides one reason for the common name, white spruce.

The four-angled, pointed needles are one-third to two-thirds of an inch long and grow singly from all sides of the twig. When crushed or bruised they give off a polecat odor, which explains the local names of cat or skunk spruce. They remain on the stout twigs seven to ten years before beginning to fall off. The young shoots are slender and without the fine hairs characteristic of other associated spruces.

In May or early June, conspicuous pale red catkins half an inch or more in length, with stalks of nearly equal length appear near the twig ends throughout the crown. These are the staminate flowers whose wealth

Devereux Butcher

Open-grown White Spruce develops a pyramidal "crown," and under forest conditions it rises to heights of from forty feet to more than a hundred and forty feet

of pollen soon makes the catkins more yellow than pink. On the ends of neighboring branches in the upper part of the same tree are also reddish or yellowish green, cone-like ovulate flowers of about the same size.

With fertilization, the fruit blossoms bend down and mature by the end of summer as pendulous, oblong-cylindrical, slender cones, about two inches in length. The thin, flexible, rounded cone scales are at first a light grass-green tinged with rose-red later becoming pale brown and lustrous. One of the means of distinguishing white spruce from black and red spruce is by the shape and length of the cones. Also the cone scales of white spruce appear as if abruptly cut off at the ends, whereas in red and black spruce they are rounded. Most of the cones begin dropping from the trees immediately after the seeds are released, but some hang on until the following spring. In New England, heavy seed crops are borne at intervals of about eight years. The seeds are only moderately fertile and germinate best on moist moss over organic soil. The seedlings thrive under heavy shade for many years.

New twigs are orange-brown. On young trunks and branches the bark is ashen gray, smooth or slightly roughened, while on older trunks it is about a half inch thick, broken into pale gray scales.

The pale yellow-white wood is soft, straight grained, and has narrow growth rings. A cubic foot weighs about twenty-eight pounds when air dry. In this respect it ranks midway among the seven native spruces. It is an important source of paper pulp, general construction lumber and interior finish. As is the wood of other spruces, that of white is prized for sounding boards of musical instruments.

White spruce is an easy victim of fire, because of its thin bark, resinous exudations, and extremely inflammable foliage. It is also subject to attack by trunk and root fungi and by various insects.

White spruce was introduced into England about 1700. Its ability to endure extremes of temperature, as well as drought, and its attractive light bluish green foliage have caused it to be widely used for ornamental purposes. Fully a dozen subspecies distinguished by the color of the foliage, size of tree, and other features, are known to the nursery trade.

The shiny brown cones, which are about two inches long, grow at the ends of twigs clothed with blue-green, sharp-pointed needles

The gray bark is scaly and is about half an inch thick

In early May or June, pale red, erect male catkins a half inch or longer, borne on short stems, appear near the ends of the twigs throughout the tree's crown

Natural range of White Spruce

SITKA SPRUCE

Coast spruce, Tideland spruce, Yellow spruce
Picea sitchensis (Bongard) Carrière

LARGEST of the eighteen species of spruce inhabiting the northern hemisphere and towering over the six other spruces occurring in North America is the Sitka spruce of the north Pacific region. From sea level to elevations of 3,000 feet, it occupies a narrow coastal ribbon forty to fifty miles wide and some 2,000 miles long from Mendocino County in northern California to the eastern end of Kodiak Island, Alaska.

Ranking with redwood and Douglasfir, Sitka spruce is one of America's fastest growing conifers. Heights of over 200 feet have been attained in 100 years, yet it may live 800 to 850 years. Trees are ordinarily eighty to 125 feet high and three and a half to six feet in diameter, but heights over 280 feet have been recorded. In low, wet valleys and flatlands, they reach 160 to 200 feet with diameters of eight to ten feet above the buttressed base. The swollen buttresses of the long clean trunks and the protruding roots help distinguish Sitka spruce from associated redwoods, western redcedars, lowland firs, and yellow cedars, as well as the smaller Pacific yew and black hemlock, with which it is frequently associated. It also grows in company with Douglasfir, broadleaf maple, vine maple, alder, black cottonwood, and willows. Northward into Alaska it forms pure stands or associates with western hemlock. In the extreme Northwest, where it extends beyond all other conifers, it is reduced to a low shrub.

In dense stands it is clear of branches for forty to eighty feet and has a thin, open conical crown of small branches. Open - grown individuals seldom attain the height of those in the forest, and the rapidly tapering trunk is clothed to the ground with huge sweeping branches.

Sitka spruce is unique among American spruces in having thick, flattened leaves, the four angles of which are indistinct. The needles grow on smooth stems, are bright bluish green, half an inch to a little over an inch long, keenly pointed and have broad silvery bands of stomata usually confined to the lower surface. In the tops of tall trees, the leaves are thicker, more crowded, and have stomata marking the upper surface. The prickly needles stand straight out around the twig.

Dark red, pollen-bearing flowers adorn the ends of the drooping side

Devereux Butcher

Sitka spruce towers above all other spruces.
Open-grown trees reach heights up to 160 feet

branches in early spring, while high up on stiff terminal shoots are the short-stalked oval female cones. A single growing season matures these as pale yellow or reddish brown, flexible cones two to four inches long, which hang conspicuously on the pendulous branches. They ripen in the early fall, and from their thin, papery, oval scales, whose margins are unevenly toothed, are shed tiny, clay-brown winged seeds. Heavy crops of fertile seed may occur every two to three years. They will germinate on any wet or constantly moist soil.

Deep reddish brown or dark purple bark, with the surface broken into large, thin, easily detached scales, clothes old trunks to a thickness of about half an inch. On branches and trunks of young trees the bark is scaly and dark grayish brown.

Without odor or taste, the pale pinkish brown wood is soft, straight grained and light—a cubic foot weighing about twenty-five pounds when air dry. It works easily and the planed surfaces have a silky sheen. Remarkably strong for its weight, it is easily kiln dried and shrinks and swells only moderately.

Sitka spruce wood is used for boxes and crates, furniture, planing mill products, doors, blinds, sash, and general mill work. Much is cut for pulp, which indicates its excellence for the manufacture of paper. Small quantities of slowly grown, highly resonant timbers are specially selected for piano sounding boards. During both world wars Sitka spruce was used in airplane construction, but this proved hazardous to aviators because of splintering by bullets.

Nearly all of the Sitka spruce in the United States is situated in western Washington, western Oregon and Alaska. There also are large quantities in British Columbia.

While the thin bark makes individual Sitka spruce trees easy victims of fire, the humidity of its coastal range habitat helps to protect old stands from severe damage. Organized fire protection during the two or three dry summer months is, however, essential to the natural reproduction that follows logging. Sitka spruce frequently is harmed by one of the bark beetles, and is defoliated by the Douglasfir chermes. Although attacked by two rust diseases, and by several wood rotting fungi, this spruce is more free from decay than either Douglasfir or western hemlock.

Archibald Menzies, a distinguished English traveler, is credited with discovering Sitka spruce on Puget Sound, in 1792. For a time it was known as Menzies spruce, *Picea menziesii*, but botanists now accept the geographical name, *Picea sitchensis*, in which the French botanist Bongard recognized the heavy stands near Sitka, Alaska.

Sitka spruce demands a cool, humid climate and is successfully grown for forest, as well as ornamental purposes in England and western Europe.

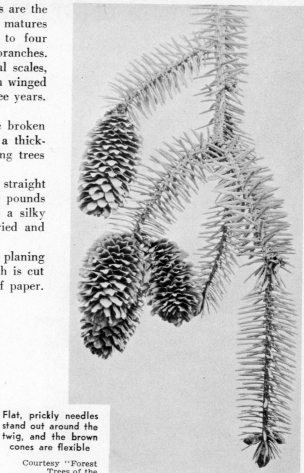

Flat, prickly needles stand out around the twig, and the brown cones are flexible

Courtesy "Forest Trees of the Pacific Slope" by W. A. Eliot

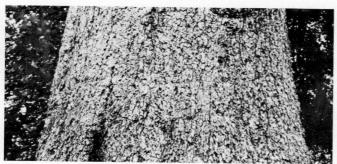

U. S. Forest Service

The reddish brown scaly bark is about half an inch thick

Natural range of Sitka Spruce

ENGELMANN SPRUCE

Columbian spruce, Mountain spruce
Picea engelmanni Parry

The deep blue-green spires of Engelmann Spruce dominate the landscape of the Rockies from British Columbia to Arizona

THE narrowly pyramidal, deep blue-green crown of Engelmann spruce is a feature of the high Rocky Mountains from British Columbia to Arizona. In the western Cascade Mountains of Oregon and Washington, it grows at elevations of around 6,000 feet, and at steadily increasing elevations as the range extends southward into Arizona and New Mexico, where it is found from 8,500 to 12,000 feet above sea level. As a rule it finds sufficient soil moisture only at higher elevations, so that its lower range is limited to moist canyons and north slopes. In dense stands, Engelmann spruce has a straight, slightly tapering trunk and a fairly short, slender, tapering crown of small branches. The lower branches droop and, when grown in the open, extend to the ground. Numerous tassel-like side branchlets hanging from the main horizontal branches give a compact appearance to the crown. Trees attain heights of eighty to 110 feet, with diameters at breast height from eighteen inches to thirty-six inches, and clear trunk lengths of twenty-five feet. Such trees may be 500 to 600 years old. At high altitudes exposed to wind and low temperatures, trees two to four feet high with slender, spike-like stems may live for 100 years or more.

The blue-green leaves or needles are an inch or more in length, four-angled, more or less directed forward, rather soft and flexible to the touch, with a relatively short, flat point. On young trees and on those that do not bear cones, the needles are spreading and evenly scattered, while on the cone-bearing twigs they are commonly crowded and usually shorter. Ordinarily deep blue-green, some trees are decidedly silvery. This is particularly true of the younger trees. The young shoots, which are covered with fine hairs for the first three years, and the leaves, give off a disagreeable odor when crushed. Engelmann spruce can be distinguished from Sitka spruce and blue spruce by the needles which, in the latter two species, extend out at right angles from the twig and are sharp-pointed; and by the longer cones of these two species. While the leaves are four-sided in blue spruce, as in Engelmann spruce, they are flattened in Sitka spruce.

The dark, purplish brown or russet-red bark is one-quarter to one-half an inch thick, and broken into thin, loosely attached, small scales.

In the spring each tree carries dark purple male flowers and bright scarlet female flowers that resemble little catkins, near the top of the tree. The latter develop by the following August into cylindrical, light brown cones, an inch to three inches long. The small, dark brown, winged seeds are soon shed and by early winter the empty cones drop from the trees. Large crops of seed are borne at intervals of three or four years from the time the tree is about twenty-five years old to an advanced age. While the seed crops are heavy and seeds that lie protected in the forest duff continue to be fertile for four or five years after being shed, natural reproduction is usually sparse.

The light yellowish or faintly reddish brown wood is fine-grained and lighter in weight than white pine. A single cubic foot when air dry weighs about twenty-three pounds. It is strong for its weight, and carefully selected spruce lumber was used in the early airplanes. It is used locally for telephone and telegraph lines, and also for doors, window sash and interior trim.

Picea is the Latin name for spruce. It is derived from *pix*, meaning pitch, while *engelmanni* refers to George Engelmann, a distinguished botanist of St. Louis, Missouri, whose identifying description of this spruce first appeared in 1863.

Commercially, this is the most important of the Rocky Mountain spruces. It is cut chiefly in Colorado, with smaller amounts in Idaho, Montana, Wyoming and Utah. While Engelmann spruce grows at the upper limits of tree growth, varying from 6,000 feet above sea level in the north to 12,000 feet in the south, with variations according to local climatic conditions, the merchantable sizes are found at the middle and lower levels. Even these are relatively high elevations, however, and the resulting inaccessibility is the chief reason for its comparatively minor commercial importance.

Within its range, Engelmann spruce is frequently the dominating species. It is commonly associated with alpine fir, white fir, lodgepole pine, limber pine and Douglasfir. In the North it also may be found with western white pine and in the South with corkbark fir. Because it surpasses most of its associates in its tolerance of shade, the forest invariably contains Engelmann spruce of all ages and sizes, varying from seedlings and saplings to trees of sawlog size. These are more tolerant in youth than in old age, but the small, suppressed growth shows remarkable ability to respond after it has been released by the removal of larger trees. Even after years of shading, trees will make good growth after the source of suppression is removed.

Fortunately the season of great fire hazard at high elevations is relatively short, but once started, fire is almost impossible to control when it gets into the heavy crowns of this spruce. Fire, as well as extensive timber cutting, may be followed by considerable windfall because of the tree's shallow root system.

Engelmann spruce has few insect or fungus enemies, but is susceptible to the spruce budworm. Control under the mountainous forest conditions would be difficult, but thus far the attacks have never been extensive.

Although native to the high western mountains, Engelmann spruce can adapt itself to eastern conditions and has been successful as an ornamental tree on northern exposures in relatively moist clay loam soils. However, it is unable to withstand the hot dry winds of the open prairies. The singular beauty of color and form makes Engelmann spruce increasingly favored for landscape purposes. Even though the tree may lose some of its symmetry with age, it retains its lower branches for forty or fifty years, and it is always beautiful.

The flexible, four-angled needles are an inch or more long and the cones one to three inches long

Many small, loosely attached scales are laid one over the other to form the thin, russet-red bark

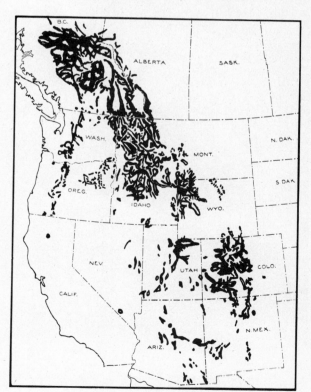

Natural range of Engelmann Spruce

BLUE SPRUCE

Colorado spruce, Colorado blue spruce
Picea pungens Engelmann

M. W. Thompson

The symmetrical, pyramidal crown of Blue Spruce with its crisp, cool, blue-green foliage is frequently seventy to ninety feet high or higher

BLUE SPRUCE is one of the most admired and widely known of all North American evergreens. It grows naturally in a relatively limited area within the central Rocky Mountain region, where the pyramidal crown and cool, crisp, silvery blue foliage of the young trees is frequently a striking feature of the landscape. After the tree is thirty-five to fifty years old, the crown becomes thin and irregular, the lower limbs disappear, revealing a clean, tapering trunk a fourth to a half the total height of the tree, and the silvery blue hue of the foliage gives way to a less distinctive green. Trees commonly attain heights of seventy to ninety feet with breast-high diameters of sixteen to twenty-four inches in 275 to 350 years. Occasional trees in favorable locations may be 110 to 130 feet high and four feet in diameter. Growth is often extremely slow, but trees may live from 400 to 600 years.

Pure forest stands of blue spruce are seldom found, but individuals or scattered groves are fairly common along stream banks. There it grows in moderately rich, dry to moist gravelly or rocky soils and is commonly associated with Douglasfir, Engelmann spruce, alpine fir, and occasionally with narrow-leaf cottonwood. Although usually found at elevations of 6,000 to 8,500 feet above sea level, trees may ascend to nearly 10,000 feet.

While blue spruce is found as far north as Fremont County in eastern Idaho, its principal distribution is in central Utah, the mountains of Colorado, northern New Mexico and sporadically southward.

The stiff, sharp-pointed, four-angled, single needles are a half inch to an inch and a quarter long. They range from dull gray-green to blue-green or silvery white depending upon the age of the tree and the location of the leaves. The frosted, silvery appearance is due to a fine powdery substance on the surface of the needles. Most of this may be removed by rubbing them between the fingers. New growth carries more of the silvery blue hue than does the old foliage. Accordingly, the trees assume their most striking appearance in mid-summer, shortly after the new foliage is fully grown. The leaves remain on the twigs eight or nine years and become darker with age. Each needle is borne on a brown, stalk-like base which remains on the twig several years after the green leaf has fallen. These leaf-bases give the branchlets, from which the needles have fallen, a rough appearance.

Blue spruce differs from Engelmann spruce in having more definitely blue, very stiff, keenly-pointed leaves. This gives rise to the local name "prickly spruce," and to the scientific name *pungens*, which comes from a Latin word meaning "to prick." The crushed leaves of blue spruce do not smell as rank as do those of Engelmann spruce, and are largely free of the "catty" odor.

The light ashy brown bark is composed of many thin scales divided into vertical ridges, while the bark of Engelmann spruce is seldom ridged or furrowed. The bark of mature blue spruce trees is a half inch to more than an inch thick. That of young trees is thinner, less broken, and often tinged with cinnamon-red. The twigs are stout and smooth, differing from those of Engelmann spruce, which are pubescent.

In the early spring each tree may bear male and female flowers near the ends of twigs of the previous year's growth. The drooping, pollen-bearing, staminate blooms are yellow, tinged with red, and may develop over much of the tree. Usually higher on the tree and on the ends of the branches are green to purple, ovulate, female cone-like flowers. While in blossom, these stand erect with broad, oblong scales expanded to catch the wind-blown pollen. Soon after being fertilized they turn down and become pendulous. By the following autumn they mature as shiny, light brown cylindrical cones two to four inches long. This is nearly twice the length of the Engelmann spruce cone. Under each of the thin cone scales may be two small chestnut-brown seeds, each fitted to a pale yellow-brown wing. The seeds are discharged in the late autumn or early winter.

The wood is light, moderately soft, nearly white in color, brittle and weak. It is frequently knotty, is one of the least commercially valuable of the American spruces, but is used locally for corral posts and poles, fuel, house logs, and occasionally for railroad ties and temporary mine props.

Blue spruce is best known as an ornamental tree, for which purpose it is widely used in northern Europe, as well as throughout the United States. Seedlings may show a wide variety in the intensity of the blue color of the foliage. The bluest specimens are selected by nurserymen for ornamental planting. Koster's blue spruce, with its brilliant silvery blue foliage, is a particularly fine form of this spruce, which is propagated by being grafted upon spruce seedlings or transplants. For economical reasons, most of the selected blue specimens are grafted on stock of Norway spruce, *Picea excelsa*, but any other spruce may be used.

Forest-grown trees are subject to fire injury and to several insect and fungous pests, many of which extend their activities to the trees planted for ornamentation. Spruce gall aphis and red spider are common enemies, and as with other spruces, blue spruce is subject to defoliation by the European spruce sawfly. While difficult to control under forest conditions, all these pests can be combated successfully when the trees are growing on lawns or in parks.

Devereux Butcher

Chestnut-brown cones about three inches long are borne at the ends of the preceding year's twigs near the top of the trees. They mature in a season

M. W. Thompson

The ash-brown bark of old tree trunks may be an inch or more thick

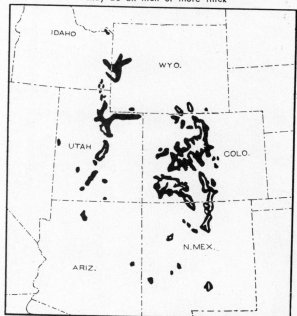

Natural range of Blue Spruce

WEEPING SPRUCE

Brewer spruce
Picea breweriana Watson

WEEPING SPRUCE is limited to the Pacific slope where it is generally restricted to the Siskiyou and Shasta mountain regions of northern California and adjacent areas in southwestern Oregon.

On steep north slopes of mountains and ridges, it may extend to timberline at elevations of 5,000 to 7,000 feet above sea level. It may also grow about protected heads of mountain streams, to form open, park-like stands or, more often, at lower elevations it may associate with mountain hemlock, Douglasfir, white fir, and sugar pine. Its long, pendulous side branches fringed with plummet-like branchlets and its slender pointed top set it apart from its neighbors.

Sterile specimens of what are thought to be weeping spruce were collected in 1863, near the base of Mount Shasta, by the California botanist, Professor William H. Brewer. Hence the fact that it is frequently known as Brewer's spruce. However, definite identification was not achieved until 1884, when Thomas J. Howell of Arthur, Oregon, found individual trees on the north side of the Siskiyou Mountains, near the headwaters of the Illinois River, in northern California. Even then, the actual naming and botanical description awaited Sereno Watson, in 1885.

Of some forty species of spruce, seven are native to the United States. All frequent the cooler regions of the northern hemisphere. They range from within the arctic circle south to Arizona and the Carolinas in North America, to the Pyrenees Mountains in Europe, to the Himalaya Mountains and central China, in Asia, and the island of Formosa.

Picea is the classical name for spruce. It derives from the Latin *pix* meaning pitch, which refers to the resinous exudation in the bark. The pitch is a source of gum and spruce beer. More significantly, it is the base from which some varnishes and medicinal compounds are derived. The name "spruce" may have derived from Prussia, where spruce is one of several native forest trees.

Weeping spruce, in company with Sitka spruce, differs from the five other American spruces in that the cross sections of the leaves are flattened or obscurely triangular rather than four-sided. Each needle is three-quarters to one and an eighth inches long, somewhat flexible, and blunt ended. The rounded under surface is slightly ridged, dark green and shiny in contrast to the flattened upper surface on which four or five rows of stomata parallel each side of the midrib. They grow from all sides of the twigs, to give a bushy or spray effect. Flat-leaved spruces are a separate group known as *Omorica*, in distinction to the four-sided *Eupiceas*.

A unique feature of weeping spruce is the multitude of fine, string-like branchlets that hang in a four- to eight-foot fringe from all but the topmost limbs.

A long, pointed crown and heavily drooping branches carrying many slender, slightly hairy, pendulous branchlets,

F. W. Cleator and Ed. Cliff

The long, pendulous branchlets and slender, pointed top are characteristic of mature Weeping Spruce

with dense foliage that is a bright but deep, yellow-green are added features of this singular tree.

Dark purplish green cones, two to four inches long, hang from the slender twigs. The cone scales are broadly rounded and have smooth edges in contrast to the thin elongated and toothed cone scales of Sitka spruce. Like other spruces, they mature in one year. After the dark chocolate-brown, winged seeds are shed late in September and October, the cones turn dull brown. The seeds are about an eighth of an inch long, with relatively short wings. Many remain in the cone until the end of the second autumn.

The trunk swells at base, tapers rapidly to the top, and the dull red-brown mature bark is about three-quarters of an inch thick. It consists of layers of long, thin, firmly pressed sheets or scales.

The wood is not only scarce, but usually inaccessible and has small commercial importance. Little is known of its qualities. It is soft, light brown or nearly white, fine-grained and rather heavy. The sapwood is indistinct. The branching habit results in many knots.

Mature trees may reach eighty to one hundred feet high, with diameters of eighteen to thirty-six inches. A tree growing near Miller Lake in southwestern Oregon has been reported with a breast-high circumference of twelve feet and two inches—comparable to forty-three inches in diameter.

J. B. Sudworth

A unique feature of Weeping Spruce is the multitude of fine, string-like branchlets which hang like fringes around the dark purple-green cones

Oliver V. Matthews

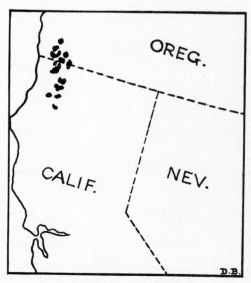

Natural range of Weeping Spruce

Bark is red-brown, with thin scales

NORWAY SPRUCE

Picea abies (Linnaeus) **Karaten**

NORWAY SPRUCE, the common spruce of Europe, is widely planted in the United States. Its native range extends beyond Norway to nearly all of middle and northern Europe. It is at home from sea level to the higher mountain slopes where moisture is abundant.

Early introduced in this country, Norway spruce is hardy in all of our northern states as far west as North Dakota, and in many other western states. Like other spruces, it grows naturally in cool humid climates, but may be planted with some success as far south as the southern highlands of Georgia, Tennessee, and Arkansas. Although preferring well drained, sandy loam, it has been successfully planted on almost all soils except those which are sour or permanently water-soaked. It has been widely planted for windbreaks and shelterbelts in the western prairies, but is happier in the more humid regions of the northern, eastern, and Pacific states.

Occasionally attaining a height of 150 feet, with diameters of three feet or more, American-grown Norway spruce usually begins to deteriorate before reaching sixty feet, and it seldom lives more than 100 years. Young open-grown trees up to a height of twenty-five or thirty feet are symmetrically cone-shaped, with a single straight tapering trunk, and branches arranged more or less in annual whorls. The branches become heavier and more spreading with age, and may be retained to the ground through the life of individual trees. With increasing age, the tree assumes a ragged, unkempt appearance, for the foliage becomes thin.

The bark is reddish brown, scaly and seldom more than half an inch thick. Reddish or light brown cone-shaped winter buds, without resin, form before late summer, and each needle or leaf is attached to the twig separately. Although the shiny dark green needles point upward and forward, their bases entirely surround the twig. They are a half to three-quarters of an inch long, have four sides, each with tiny white lines, and remain on the twig for six or seven years.

U. S. Forest Service

As Norway Spruce attains maturity the spread of the branches increases and the pendulous branchlets become more apparent

Unlike the pines, the spruce trees mature their cones and seeds in a single season. In the spring, male and female blossoms may be found on the same trees. The male or staminate flowers are like little yellow catkins on the ends of the twigs, while the ovulate ones are usually higher on the tree and range from green to purple. They stand upright on the twig until fertilized, and gradually turn down until they mature in the fall as pendulous, cylindrical cones four to seven inches long and light brown in color. During the late winter and early spring the scales spread back to release the winged seed.

The scientific name, *Picea excelsa*, was given this tree by a Swedish botanist named Link in 1841. *Picea* is an ancient Latin word for spruce, derived from *pix* meaning pitch, while *excelsa* means elevated or tall.

The wood of Norway spruce is soft, weighs about twenty-five pounds to the cubic foot, is straight-grained and easily worked. Although not durable in contact with the soil it is widely used for construction purposes. The heartwood is yellowish white, and the thin sapwood is white. It is an important source of pulp for the manufacture of paper, and has been planted in many of the northern and eastern states for that purpose.

Although extensively planted for forest purposes in many parts of the North and East, Norway spruce has proved especially successful as an ornamental tree and for farm windbreaks and shelterbelts in the middle west. It may be pruned and can be used for hedges. Christmas tree plantations have proved financially successful, but the needles soon drop off in a warm house.

Norway spruce has relatively few enemies of importance. Chief among them are the red spider and several parasitic fungi. Ornamental trees probably suffer most for lack of moisture and because the soil around the roots becomes too tightly packed. Grass fires may do severe damage, and in many localities, late frosts may destroy the leader.

The shiny, four-sided, dark green needles point outward and often forward, and grow from all sides of the twig

J. Ben Hill

Young cone, left, develops in twelve days to the size in center, and by midsummer reaches maturity, right

The circular growth in the reddish brown bark is where the stub of a former branch has been overgrown

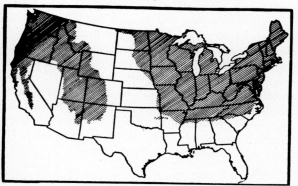

Approximate areas within the United States where Norway Spruce may be grown

EASTERN HEMLOCK
Canada hemlock, Hemlock spruce
Tsuga canadensis (Linnaeus) Carrière

EASTERN HEMLOCK, with its irregular crown of dark green foliage, its slender, gracefully drooping leader, and its massive trunk, is a feature of the forest and open country throughout the northeastern states. It inhabits cool, moist slopes and well drained, fertile valleys from eastern Canada to northeastern Minnesota, south through Wisconsin, southern Michigan and Indiana, and southward along the mountains from Pennsylvania and West Virginia into northern Alabama and Georgia.

Of relatively slow growth, eastern hemlock reaches maturity in 250 to 300 years and may live for 600 years or more. While many trees are sixty to eighty feet high and two to three feet in diameter, heights of more than 100 feet and diameters exceeding four feet are not uncommon. Occasional individuals 160 feet high and six feet in diameter have been measured.

The flat, narrow leaves are one-third to two-thirds of an inch long, rounded or minutely notched at the end, shiny dark green above, light green below, and marked with two parallel lines of white dots or stomata beneath. Each leaf or needle grows on a thread-like stem or petiole, and, while borne spirally on the branchlets, they appear to be two-ranked, like a flat spray. The early spring foliage is a delicate light yellow-green contrasting with the darker green of previous years. The needles remain on the twigs for three or more years, and upon falling, the base of the petiole remains, giving the twig a roughened appearance.

Early in May each tree bears separate male and female flowers on twigs of the previous year. The small, yellow, globular male blossoms appear singly in the axils of the previous season's leaves and occasionally near the ends of the twigs, while the small seed-bearing female flowers are erect and greenish, with circular scales, from the upper surfaces of which may appear thin bracts. Blossoms occur on all parts of a tree, from the top to the lowest branches. By October, at the end of one season, the fertilized ovulate flowers develop into broadly oval, green to purple cones, one-half to one inch long, which become reddish brown and hang down singly from short stalks as they reach maturity. These are among the smallest of all tree cones. Under each fertile scale are two light brown seeds whose transparent wings help carry them on the wind. The partially empty cones remain on the twigs through the fall and much of the winter. A single seed is about one-sixteenth of an inch long, and 400,000 weigh one pound. In spite of the many seeds produced each year, hemlock reproduces poorly. Seed-

U. S. Forest Service

Hemlock reveals its rugged beauty and massive proportions when growing in the open or near the edge of a forest. Trees may attain heights of seventy-five to 160 feet and diameters of two to four feet or more

92

The male flowers are yellow, globular, and inconspicuous

Devereux Butcher

lings cannot endure strong light and reproduction is best in moist, shady places. Later, when the roots have developed, they respond to increased light.

The tiny, reddish brown buds are alternate and the slender, yellowish brown twigs are coated with fine hairs in the first winter, but later become smooth and dark gray or purplish brown.

Deeply divided cinnamon-red to brown bark covers the rapidly tapering trunks of mature trees. It is from two to three inches thick, broadly ridged, and covered with fine scales. The tannin-bearing bark may comprise fifteen to nineteen percent of the cubic volume of a tree. For years the value of the tannin was so high by comparison with the lumber that great trees frequently were left to decay in the forest after the bark had been removed. The bark is peeled off in rectangular sheets about four feet square. It is still so much in demand by the leather industry that lumbering operations are usually confined to spring and summer when the bark "slips" easily.

With scarcity of other lumber, the light buff, soft, coarse-grained wood of hemlock has become of increasing importance. It weighs only twenty-eight pounds to the cubic foot when air dry, is practically without taste or odor, is not durable when exposed to the elements, and is frequently splintery and subject to windshake. The lumber is used for boxing, crating, general construction, and railroad ties, and recently as a source of chemical pulp for the manufacture of paper. Hemlock possesses unusual power to hold nails and spikes. It is low in fuel value.

In the North the common associates of hemlock are white pine, beech, yellow birch, and the maples, while in the southern mountains it grows with tuliptree, red maple, the hickories and oaks.

Hemlock is a member of the pine family and is of ancient origin. Remains of leaves, cones and wood have been found in geological strata of America and Asia. Of the ten known species, four are found on this continent, two being native to the eastern states and two to the Northwest. The others are in Japan, China, and the Himalaya Mountains between India and Tibet. There are no native hemlocks in Europe.

The name *Tsuga* was first applied to the genus in 1847 by the dendrologist, Stephen L. Endlicher, and is a Japanese word meaning yew-leaved, while *canadensis* means Canadian. Eastern hemlock actually is so abundant south of the international boundary that it is ranked among the important sources of timber in the United States. Since June, 1931, it has been the state tree of Pennsylvania.

Except for the flat-headed borer, eastern hemlock has few enemies of importance, and these seldom occur in epidemic proportions.

Hemlock ranks high among the coniferous evergreens for ornamental planting, and in its juvenile stages it lends itself to border and background plantings.

George J. Baetzhold

The needles, set in two-ranked sprays, are rounded or notched at the tip, and the cones are a half to one inch long

U. S. Forest Service

The cinnamon-red bark, broken into broad ridges, may be two to three inches thick

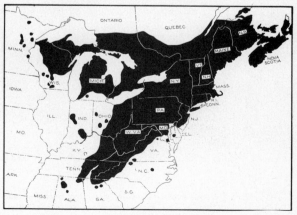

Natural range of Eastern Hemlock

93

CAROLINA HEMLOCK

Tsuga caroliniana Engelmann

THIS COMPARATIVELY rare tree is found principally along the rocky banks of streams in the Blue Ridge Mountains of the Appalachians from southwestern Virginia through western North Carolina into northern Georgia, at elevations of 2,500 to 3,000 feet. It generally grows singly, sometimes on almost inaccessible rocky ridges and cliffs, or in small scattered groves, often in company with eastern hemlock, eastern white pine, silver-bell tree, and various oaks and hickories.

The usual height of the tree is forty to fifty and occasionally seventy feet, with a trunk rarely exceeding two feet in diameter. The many short, stout, often pendulous branches form a handsome, compact, pyramidal crown which usually extends for two-thirds the height. The slender twigs are light orange-brown, covered at first with soft, fine hairs, later becoming smooth and dull brown.

The dark green leaves or needles differ from those of eastern hemlock in two respects: they are slightly longer, one-third to three-fourths of an inch, and stand out in all directions from the branchlets instead of being conspicuously two-ranked. They are frequently notched at the end, and the upper surface is lustrous with a conspicuous central groove, while the under surface shows white bands on each side of the midrib made up of seven or eight rows of stomata.

The male or staminate flowers are small, nearly spherical, yellow bodies tinged with purple. They are borne singly from buds at the bases of the leaves near the ends of the branchlets to which they are attached by thread-like stems. The purple, erect, female flowers, which produce cones and seed are smaller, and grow at the ends of the twigs; they have broadly ovate bracts that are irregularly toothed on the margins and are about as long as their scales.

The short-stalked, oblong cones are somewhat larger than those of eastern hemlock, measuring from one to one and a half inches in length. The cone scales are narrowly oval, much longer than wide, and spread nearly at right angles to the axis of the cone at maturity; in contrast, the cone scales of eastern hemlock are no longer than broad and do not spread so widely when mature. There are two seeds about one-sixth of an inch long under each fertile scale. The seeds are about one-fourth as long as the pale lustrous wings, which are broadest near the base, narrowing toward the rounded apex.

The dark chestnut-brown buds are more or less spherical in shape, nearly one-eighth of an inch long and are covered with fine soft hairs.

On the trunks of mature trees, the reddish brown bark, one to one and a half inches thick, is deeply divided

Arnold Arboretum

Attractive foliage, compact crown, drooping branches and an ability to do well in shady locations make Carolina Hemlock an increasingly popular ornamental tree

94

into broad, flat, connected ridges covered with thin, closely appressed, plate-like scales.

The wood of Carolina hemlock is similar to that of eastern hemlock. The heartwood is pale brown, tinged with red, and is not distinct from the thin sapwood, which is somewhat lighter in color. Because the supply is so small and so much of it is inaccessible, Carolina hemlock timber is of little commercial importance. Where it is cut, however, it is put to the same uses as eastern hemlock. The wood is coarse and uneven in texture, moderately light in weight, fairly hard, rather weak, and somewhat low in ability to resist shock. It lacks durability when subjected to conditions favorable to decay.

The principal uses for hemlock lumber are for building construction and for boxes and crates. The wood is also very suitable for the manufacture of paper pulp by the chemical process. Hemlock bark is an important source of tannin used for converting hides and skins into leather.

Carolina hemlock bears seed frequently, but usually not in abundance. Because of their small size and the large wings, the seeds are carried considerable distances from the parent trees by the wind. Seedlings grow best and are more abundant in moist, shady locations than on sites open to strong sunlight.

The tree is very desirable for ornamental purposes and has the advantage over many other conifers in that it does well in the shade. The attractive foliage, compact crown and drooping branches have served to make it increasingly popular for this purpose. It is often planted in the eastern United States and occasionally in Europe.

Carolina hemlock seems to have no serious fungus diseases or insect enemies. When growing on thin soil the tree is sometimes thrown by the wind because of its shallow root system, and forest-grown trees are often killed by ground fires which burn through the humus.

U. S. Forest Service

Carolina Hemlock needles are longer than those of the more abundant Eastern Hemlock, and they stand out in all directions along the twig. The drooping cones, too, are larger than those of Eastern Hemlock, measuring from an inch to an inch and a half in length

Davey Tree Expert Co.

The reddish brown bark on mature trees is divided into broad, connecting ridges, and it measures as much as an inch and a half thick. It is rich in tannic acid, which is used extensively for tanning hides and skins into leather for shoes, belts and other products

Base map © J. L. Smith, Phila. Pa.

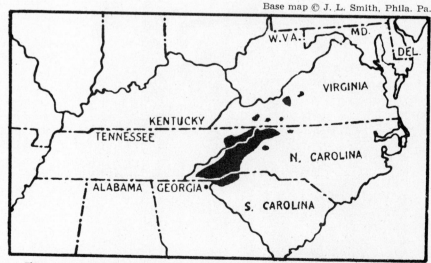

This comparatively rare tree is found along rocky banks of streams in the Blue Ridge Mountains of the Appalachians, at elevations of from 2,500 to 3,000 feet

WESTERN HEMLOCK

Pacific hemlock, West coast hemlock
Tsuga heterophylla (Rafinesque) Sargent

WESTERN HEMLOCK, a tree of increasing economic importance, is found in the deep forests of the humid coast regions from Prince William Sound in Alaska south a thousand miles to Marin County, California, just north of San Francisco, and inland as far as northern Idaho and northwestern Montana. It grows best in cool, moist locations on the seaward side of the Cascade Mountains, at elevations from 1,500 to 3,500 feet above sea level, but ascends from sea level to altitudes of 6,000 feet.

Growing to greater dimensions than its eastern relatives, this tree, under favorable conditions, may become 130 to 150 feet high and from seventeen to twenty-one inches in diameter in one hundred years. Occasionally, western hemlock reaches an age of 500 years or more, when it develops to heights of 175 to 250 feet, with diameters ranging to eight or ten feet.

Everywhere it is a dignified tree, with grave and massive outline, but in the dense forest the crown of irregular, slender, pendulous branches is narrow and pyramidal. The long, clean, cylindrical trunk has little taper, and the base is often abruptly buttressed. Open-grown trees have a broad crown which may extend to the base of the trunk. Being tolerant of shade, it clears its trunk of branches somewhat slowly.

The flat, narrow, distinctly grooved leaves are a dark, highly lustrous green from one-third to three-fourths of an inch long. They remain on the branchlets three to six years. Closely resembling the leaves of eastern hemlock, the ends are distinctly rounded, although the two bands of white stomata on the under side of each leaf are less well defined.

Tsuga is the Japanese name for hemlock, while *heterophylla* is derived from two Greek words meaning other or different leaves. Apparently it was applied by Rafinesque in an effort to indicate the slight distinguishing differences of the leaf from that of *Tsuga canadensis*, the eastern hemlock.

Male and female blossoms are borne separately on sprays of the preceding season, on different parts of the same tree. Yellow, pollen-bearing, male flowers grow singly at the base of leaves near the ends of the branchlets, while the small, purple, scaly female flowers are at the ends of the sprays.

By the middle or end of August, the reddish

K. D. Swan

Western Hemlock, largest of ten hemlock species, attains heights of 150 to 250 feet, and diameters up to eight or ten feet clay-brown cones, which develop from the pistillate blossoms, are mature and ready to discharge their winged seeds. These cones hang from the ends of the branchlets, are considerably larger than those of eastern hemlock, being three-fourths to one and a fourth inches long, and are more acutely pointed. Each cone is attached by a short thread-like stem, and drops during the succeeding winter. The thin, overlapping scales are faintly downy on the outer surface. Under each scale there may be two light brown seeds, about one-eighth of an inch long. The comparatively large wings of these seeds permit them to be carried away from the parent tree by the wind for considerable distances.

Open-grown trees begin to bear seed when twenty-five to thirty years old, but those growing in dense forests at a much older age. Some seeds are produced nearly every year, but heavy crops occur at intervals of two or three years. The seeds, which are borne in large quantities, are fairly high in germinative ability, retain their vitality for several years, and develop best on wet moss, decaying wood or moist humus. This tree reproduces freely under a variety of conditions, and the seedlings endure dense shade, but grow more rapidly in sunlight.

On old trunks the dark russet-brown, deeply furrowed bark may be one and a half inches thick. It is even richer in tannin than that of eastern hemlock, having twelve to fifteen percent, as compared with ten to thirteen percent for the eastern species.

The pale, yellowish brown heartwood contrasts with the narrow area of white sapwood, and weighs about twenty-nine pounds to the cubic foot when air dry. Western hemlock is heavier, harder, and stronger than the wood of eastern hemlock, is less splintery, and because of its soft, fine, non-resinous texture and straight grain is finding an increasing demand in commerce. The wood is relatively resistant to attacks by termites, but is not durable when used untreated under conditions that favor decay. When commercially dry it is suitable for all but the heaviest construction work, and is extensively used for framing, house sheathing, planing mill products, boxes, barrels, railroad ties, concrete forms, and is becoming one of the most important pulp woods grown on this continent.

The comparatively thin bark and shallow root system make western hemlock highly susceptible to fire injury and to windfall. While less frequently damaged by "wind shake" than the eastern hemlock, it suffers heavily from insects and fungi, against which little can be done.

Western hemlock's natural beauty and its ability to withstand shade make this tree desirable for ornamental purposes. For best results, however, such plantings should be confined fairly closely to the areas that lie within the natural range of the species.

The flat, glossy green leaves are round-tipped. The pointed, pendant cones are three-fourths of an inch to an inch and a quarter long

The deeply furrowed russet-brown bark is over an inch thick and rich in tannin

The natural range of Western Hemlock

MOUNTAIN HEMLOCK

Black hemlock

Tsuga mertensiana (Bongard) Carrière

MOUNTAIN HEMLOCK, with dense, blue-green foliage, frequently stands silhouetted against high mountain skylines, such as on the rim of Crater Lake, Oregon, where it grows luxuriantly and frames incomparably beautiful vistas.

It inhabits the mountainous country from the south fork of the Kings River Canyon in California, north through Oregon, Washington, northern Idaho, Montana, British Columbia and Alaska. In southern Alaska it grows at elevations from tidewater to 4,000 feet above sea level. On the slopes of the Cascade and Olympic mountains of Washington, it grows at elevations from 5,000 to 7,000 feet, while in California it is found at 6,000 to 11,000 feet. Northern exposures are usually preferred because of the cool, moist soil conditions. At high elevations it occurs in mixture with whitebark pine, alpine fir, alpine larch and Engelmann spruce. At lower elevations its associates are lowland white fir, lodgepole pine, and western white pine.

The sharp-pointed, narrowly pyramidal crowns bear little resemblance to the western hemlock of lower elevations, but it has the same drooping branches and deeply furrowed, dark reddish brown trunk. On steep slopes the trunk may be bent in a wide curve like a sled runner or a great saber—the result of being bent down by heavy snow when the tree was a sapling.

Like other timberline trees, mountain hemlock is usually short and distorted, reaching only twenty-five to sixty feet in height and ten to twenty inches in diameter. Trees exposed to buffeting winds may be low and sprawling and only a few feet high. On gentle slopes and at the heads of moist valleys, trees seventy-five to eighty feet high are not uncommon, with occasional heights of 100 to 150 feet and diameters of two and a half to three and a half feet. Such trees are undoubtedly of great age, for trees eighteen to twenty inches in diameter are 180 to 260 years old. In contrast to the rapid growth of low country trees, those that grow on wind-swept ridges may take sixty to eighty years to reach five to

U. S. Forest Service

Mountain Hemlock occurs in the high mountains of the Pacific Slope

seven inches in diameter.

The blue-green, bluntly pointed leaves, a twelfth of an inch to an inch in length, are plump but flat, arranged spirally, so as to stand out from all sides of the twig. Because of the needle arrangement, the tree is sometimes mistaken for a spruce. Like the leaves of all other hemlocks, each stands on a separate petiole or stem, and unlike the three other American hemlocks, both leaf surfaces are marked with parallel lines of white stomata. The leaves drop off during the third and fourth years.

Richly colored male and female flowers are borne on the same tree. Violet-purple staminate ones hang on slender, drooping, hairy stems of the previous year, while erect lustrous purple or yellow-green ovulate ones appear near the ends of the branches at about the same time. These develop into broad scaled, blunt-pointed cones three-fourths of an inch to three inches long. They stand erect until half grown and then become pendulous, ranging in color from yellowish green to a bluish purple. Under each cone scale there may be two small, light brown seeds with large wings capable of being carried considerable distances on the wind when they ripen in September or October. Large quantities of seed are produced annually, but relatively few germinate. The young trees will endure shade and suppression for years, and resume normal growth when given full light.

The dark cinnamon to lavender-brown bark is an inch or more thick, with deep, narrowly furrowed, rounded ridges.

The pale brown to red, close-grained, soft wood, while light in weight, is the heaviest of all the American hemlocks, weighing thirty-three pounds to the cubic foot when air dry. It is without special strength and is used locally only for cabins and rough log shelters.

Mountain hemlock is a tree of unusual beauty suited for ornamental planting in cool moist soils in the northern Pacific states and in the East as far north as Massachusetts. Outside its natural habitat, however, it seldom achieves the grace and vigor of the wild mountain trees.

The name *mertensiana* honors a German physician and naturalist, Karl Heinrich Mertens, who lived from 1795 to 1830. *Tsuga* (tsü-ga) is the Japanese name for the hemlock genus.

Purple cones up to three inches long are produced near the branch ends

U. S. Forest Service

The rich brown, narrowly furrowed bark is an inch or more thick

Asahel Curtis

Natural range of Mountain Hemlock

DOUGLASFIR

Douglas spruce, Douglas yew, Oregon pine

Pseudotsuga menziesii (Mirbel) Franco

Asahel Curtis

In the mountains of the Pacific Northwest, Douglas-fir attains magnificent proportions, sometimes reaching a height of over two hundred feet

DOUGLASFIR is a widely distributed western tree. It grows naturally throughout the Rocky Mountains, from their eastern base to the Pacific coast, and northern Mexico and the mountains of western Texas, southern New Mexico and Arizona to British Columbia. It attains its largest size near sea level in the coast region of southern British Columbia, Washington, Oregon and on the western foothills of the Cascade Mountains. No attempt is made in this description to distinguish between the Oregon variety and the slower growing, more hardy Douglasfir native to Colorado and the interior mountains. Although the tree has a number of common names, Douglasfir is generally accepted.

Three hundred and twenty-five-foot heights have been recorded, with trunk diameters of ten to seventeen feet, and trunks often clear of branches for a third of their height. The larger trees may be from 400 to a thousand years old. The reddish brown bark of large mature trees is broken into oblong longitudinal plates and may be ten to twelve inches thick. The smooth, thinner bark of young trees is more the color of ashes, and it has resin blisters like the true firs.

The tree is rather a botanical puzzle, for it bears strong resemblance to spruce and fir, as well as to hemlock and yew. Accordingly, the botanists went to the Greek to describe it as a "false hemlock with a yew-like leaf." It was first discovered by Dr. Archibald Menzies, in 1791, on the west coast of Vancouver Island; later it was rediscovered by the Scottish traveler David Douglas, who introduced it into England in 1827. Since then it has been widely planted in the British Isles.

The soft, flattened, slightly pointed gray-green needles are a half to one and a half inches long and grow around the twig so as to give it a full rounded appearance. They are grooved on the upper surface, and have a white band on each side of a prominent midrib beneath. When pulled off they leave an oval scar on top of a little projection. They remain on the trees five to eight years before they fall. Frequently the dark orange-red pointed terminal bud is one-fourth of an inch long, while the side buds are about half as large.

The oval cones are pendulous like those of the spruce and pine. They are an inch and a half to four and a half inches long and mature in the first autumn from reddish ovulate flowers that grow well out on the ends of the branches. The three-lobed bracts—the "Neptune's trident"—is especially noticeable in the blossom stage. On the same tree are the bright red staminate or male flowers, which appear in the early spring on the under surface of the previous year's growth. The thin, rounded scales of the cone are thrust over conspicuous three-pointed bracts, and under each scale are two seeds, each with a single wing. The parent trees scatter these seeds so effectively that they quickly take possession of burned forest areas. Trees may begin producing cones at twelve years, and continue to bear crops nearly every year.

The wood is usually yellowish to light red, with a narrow band of white sapwood. It is fairly light, strong, firm and works well. Compared with other American woods it is the strongest of all in terms of weight. The immense size of the trees permits the manufacture of timber remarkably free from knots and other defects. It is important in the lumber industry and building trade. When air dry a cubic foot weighs thirty-one pounds. It is used for many kinds of construction, as well as railway ties, and piles, is resistant to decay, and can be attractively stained for interior trim.

Douglasfir may be grown from seed under nursery conditions, and successfully transplanted to forest plantations. Under natural conditions it grows from sea level where more than 100 inches of rain falls each year, to altitudes of nearly 11,000 feet where the annual precipitation is fifteen inches. In deep loam soils, Douglasfir develops widespreading root systems. In moist, well drained soil, trees will grow to a height of thirty-five feet in twenty-five years. The trees prefer northern and western exposures, but will withstand wind fairly well and endure considerable shade. The young trees are hardy and attractive for ornamental planting. They may be planted close together and pruned for hedges. The symmetrical young trees, whose soft, rich green needles hang on long after the tree is cut down, are being used in increasing numbers for Christmas trees.

Photographs by U. S. Forest Service

The reddish brown deeply fissured bark of mature trees is sometimes a foot thick

Above: — The three-pointed bracts extending beyond the cone scales, the flexible, bluntly pointed green needles, and dark orange-red winter buds help identify Douglasfir

Below:—When young, Douglasfirs are dense-foliaged and symmetrical. They are planted over a wide area to decorate home grounds, for windbreaks and for future stands of timber

Douglasfir is particularly subject to fire damage during its early years, but as the bark grows thicker it becomes increasingly resistant. Not only does fire destroy many trees, but it also causes unfavorable soil conditions, and the fire scars furnish places where insects and fungi may enter. It may be attacked by a long list of insects, fungi and mistletoe, but is little affected by most of them. The worst insect enemy is a beetle which bores between the bark and the wood, frequently killing the tree.

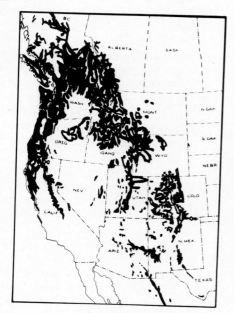

Natural range of Douglasfir

BALSAM FIR

Canada balsam, Eastern fir

Abies balsamea (Linnaeus) Miller

TYPICAL of cold climates and well drained, moist situations, the arrow-headed spires of balsam fir add a note of deep green to the northern forests. Ranging from sea level to elevations of over 5,600 feet, the species grows in New England and Labrador west and north across New York, the lake states, and Ontario to within a few degrees of the Pacific Ocean, at the headwaters of the Yukon River. Most important of the two eastern true firs, *Albies balsamea* is one of ten firs native to the United States and Canada. This large genus of evergreens is characterized by disk-like leaf scars and erect cones which, soon after the seeds ripen, drop their scales and leave a woody core standing on the branch.

Often associated with red spruce, black spruce, tamarack, and hemlock, occasional pure stands of balsam fir are formed. On drier sites it is mixed with yellow birch, beech, and maple.

Perhaps the most symmetrical of all northeastern evergreens, it averages twenty-five to sixty feet in height and occasionally reaches eighty to ninety feet. Trunk diameters range from ten inches to twenty-eight inches. With maturity, long slender branches develop in somewhat distinct whorls. At high elevations and on wind-swept mountain summits, dense mats of dwarf trees are formed. Capable of enduring deep shade in early youth, balsam fir may grow rapidly, but it shows defects within ninety years and seldom lives more than 150 years.

The deep blue-green, narrow leaves are about an inch long, and are shiny on the upper surface. The ends are blunt, frequently indented, conspicuously light colored on the under side and marked near the ends with rows of stomata. Arranged spirally on the twig, they usually part in two ranks like the teeth of a double comb to form a V-shaped depression on the upper side of the twig. The upper crown leaves are short, plump, incurved, and almost erect as compared with the longer leaves near the base. They adhere to the twigs about eight years and furnish winter food for deer and moose. The aromatic needles are widely used for stuffing balsam pillows. Oil of fir, sometimes used in pharmacy, may be distilled from either needles or bark. The young shoots are smooth, with fine, grayish hairs, and the stout, blunt winter buds are resinous.

In early spring each tree produces male and female blossoms. Yellow catkin-like staminate blooms about one-quarter inch long emerge from the under side of the leaf axils on most of the past year's growth, but the erect, purple, three-quarter-inch cones containing the ovulate blooms are confined to the upper branches. These ripen in September as dark purple, slightly tapering, cylindrical

Devereux Butcher

The deep blue-green spires of Balsam Fir reach heights of sixty feet and more cones two to four inches long and one to one and a quarter inches wide. They stand erect like tapers on a candelabrum, and lose their overlapping fan-shaped scales soon after the seeds ripen. Each light brown, resinous seed is about a quarter inch long with a shining wing of about the same length. Heavy cone crops occur at intervals of two to four years. The winged seeds drift considerable distances on the wind, to germinate in moist, exposed soil and on moss-covered stumps. Many are eaten by grouse and small animals. Some natural reproduction occurs when the lower pendent branches become covered with soil and take root.

The dark purple cones stand erect amid the plump, upturned foliage of the upper crown

The bark of mature trees is dull, red-brown with many thin scales and is about half an inch thick. That of young trees and branches is thin, smooth, ash-colored and underlain with many resin blisters. These are the source of Canada balsam—a greenish yellow, transparent, sticky fluid which dries into a transparent mass. It is used in pharmacy and as a medium in which to mount material on microscopic slides.

The wide-ringed, yellowish brown wood has a narrow band of white sapwood one to two inches thick, and weighs twenty-four to twenty-nine pounds to the cubic foot when air dry. It is soft, brittle, and quickly perishable. Its major use is for paper pulp, but considerable lumber goes into interior trim, crates, and packing boxes. It is often sold with spruce. Large numbers of small to medium sized, symmetrical Christmas trees are cut. Not only are their form and fragrance attractive, but the rich green, blunt needles remain firmly attached and retain their color long after the tree has dried out.

The ash-colored bark of young trees is underlain with many balsam blisters

In moist locations, balsam fir suffers comparatively little fire damage. However, when fire occurs on drier sites, the large number of resin blisters under the bark cause intense heat. The shallow root system makes balsam fir easily wind blown, and dangerous fire traps may result.

Balsam fir's worst enemy is the spruce budworm, whose ravages extend from the Atlantic coast to Minnesota and central Ontario. Several fungi are also damaging.

This fir seldom prospers as an ornamental tree because of its susceptibility to city smoke and gases, and because it needs constant soil moisture. It has proved satisfactory in cool, moist, sheltered locations for about fifteen years before becoming ragged and less attractive.

The natural range of the Balsam Fir

103

FRASER BALSAM FIR

Southern balsam fir

Abies fraseri (Pursh) Poiret

FRASER BALSAM FIR is found only on the highest peaks of the southern Appalachian Mountains at altitudes of from 4,000 to 6,000 feet, in southwestern Virginia, western North Carolina and eastern Tennessee. It clothes the dry summits with forests of considerable extent in pure stands or in company with red spruce, mountain-ash and yellow birch. Its occurrence in dry localities is in contrast with the more northerly balsam fir (*Abies balsamea*), which prefers moist locations. The name southern balsam fir is sometimes applied to this species, and locally it is commonly called "she balsam" by the mountaineers to distinguish it from the red spruce or "he balsam."

Growing to a usual height of thirty to forty feet, the tree sometimes attains seventy feet with a trunk diameter of from one to two and a half feet. In isolated locations the rather rigid branches form an open symmetrical pyramid. When crowded by other trees, the lower branches generally disappear at an early age. The stout branchlets are densely covered with short reddish hairs for three or four years. They are pale yellow-brown during their first season, becoming dark red-brown, often tinged with purple.

The flat, stemless leaves are one-half to nearly one inch in length. They are obtusely short-pointed or occasionally slightly emarginate at the apex and, spreading upward and forward, they are crowded on the upper side of the twig. Dark green, lustrous and centrally grooved above, they are silvery white beneath, with eight to twelve rows of stomata.

In May, male and female flowers appear separately on the same tree, the staminate very abundant on the lower side of the branches above the middle of the tree and the pistillate usually on the upper side only of the topmost branches. The staminate are yellow tinged with red and the pistillate purple with scales much broader than long and shorter than their oblong, pale yellow-green bracts which are rounded at the broad apex and terminate in a slender, elongated tip.

The oblong-ovate or nearly oval cones mature in September. They are rounded at the somewhat narrowed apex, about two and a half inches long and one and an eighth inches thick. The cones differ from those of balsam fir (*Abies balsamea*) in that the scales, which are twice as wide as long, are nearly half covered at maturity by their much longer reflexed bracts which are oblong, rounded, and short-pointed at the wide denticulate apex.

J. Horace McFarland Co.

Generally 30 to 40 feet tall, Fraser Balsam Fir grows in pure stands and also with red spruce, mountain-ash and yellow birch. It often resembles an open symmetrical pyramid

104

The bark of young trunks has numerous resin blisters. On older trunks the bark is from one-fourth to one-half inch thick and is covered with thin, closely appressed, bright cinnamon-red scales, generally becoming gray on old trees.

The light, soft wood is low in strength properties and in resistance to decay. The pale brown heartwood is surrounded by nearly white sapwood. Because of its inaccessibility, the wood is little used, although it is valuable for the same purposes as balsam fir. It has been occasionally manufactured into lumber for the construction of hotels and other buildings at high elevations on the mountains of North Carolina and Tennessee, but little of it enters commerce. Like the balsam fir, Fraser balsam fir is very desirable as a Christmas tree, not only because of its symmetrical form, but also because the needles remain on the twigs for a comparatively long time after the tree is cut. The needles are much used for making balsam pillows.

Fraser balsam fir is occasionally planted in the parks and gardens of the northeastern states and of Europe. It is hardy as far north as southern Ontario and New England, but is short-lived and not very satisfactory under cultivation.

Wooly aphids, a serious pest transported by automobiles, threatens the remaining stands. Control efforts so far have been ineffective. Lumbering and pulpwood operations in the southern Appalachians, frequently followed by fires, have greatly reduced the timber-producing areas of this species. Forest land acquired by the United States government in this region embraces large areas where the tree grows naturally and protection from destructive cutting operations may insure future stands. In its natural habitat near the summits and on elevated slopes of the southern Appalachians, conditions are not conducive to destructive forest fires. There is frequent and abundant rain there, and the forest shade usually keeps the ground too moist for fire. When severe damage is done by fire, however, a second stand of timber is unlikely because of the inability of the tree to seed itself on tracts that have been severely burned.

Fraser balsam fir grows quite rapidly in youth, but more slowly as it becomes older. When young it will grow in the shade of other trees, but later it requires full light for its best development.

The flat, stemless leaves are dark green and centrally grooved above and silvery white beneath with 8 to 12 rows of stomata

The nearly oval cones, which mature in September, are about two and a half inches long and one and one eighth inches thick

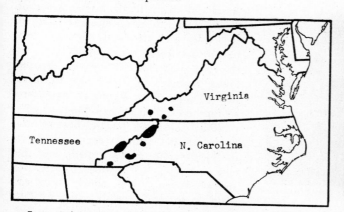

Fraser Balsam Fir is found only on the highest peaks of the southern Appalachian Mountains at 4,000 to 6,000 feet

The bark of older trees is covered with thin, closely appressed bright cinnamon-red scales, generally becoming gray in old trees

WHITE FIR

White balsam

Abies concolor (Gordon and Glendinning) Lindley

WHITE FIR is the most important of seven true firs inhabiting the forests of the Pacific slope and of the Rocky Mountains. It grows generally on north slopes at moderate altitudes from southern Oregon through California into Lower California, and from Nevada, Utah and southern Colorado, through Arizona and New Mexico.

This species reaches greatest growth in northern California on northerly and easterly slopes and at the heads of streams. While thriving best on fairly deep, rich, moist loams, white fir does well on all moderately moist soils, except heavy clays, and frequently grows on dry, coarse, disintegrated granite. It is a massive tree whose dense, heavily-foliaged crown may extend to the ground in open-grown trees or from a third to a half the way down the straight, ashy gray, gradually tapering trunk of forest-grown trees. The lower and middle crown branches droop conspicuously, while the upper branches tend upward. With great age, growth slows down and the trees develop a rounded top. Occasional trees grow to 100 feet high and six feet and more in diameter.

Daniel Gellerman

White Fir is a massive tree, is tolerant of shade and frequently retains its branches all the way to the ground

Young trees have comparatively smooth, pale gray bark with a brown tinge, whose conspicuous resin blisters, like those of the other true firs, give rise to the popular name, "balsam." This clear material has several medicinal and scientific uses. With age the bark thickens to four or six inches, takes on a distinctly ashy gray color, breaks into deep furrows, and becomes hard, horny and fire resistant.

The flat, plump, blunt-pointed leaves are yellow-green, but have a bluish cast in the first few months of growth. With maturity this becomes more pale and takes on a whitish cast, which, with the light-colored bark, gives rise to the name, white fir. The leaves are arranged spirally on the twigs and remain five to ten years before dropping. They stand out distinctly from two sides of the twig, and those on the lower part of the tree are frequently longer, less curved and more sparse than those on the upper branches. Leaves on the lower branches may be one to three inches long, while the upper leaves are seldom more than an inch long.

Both male and female flowers are borne on the same trees on branches of the previous year's growth, and the cones develop to maturity during a single season. The short, rounded, scaly cone and seed-bearing ovulate flowers stand erect and singly on the uppermost branches of the crown. Below them, from the underside of the lower branches, hang the elongated, scaly, pollen-bearing, staminate flowers, which drop soon after releasing their pollen. The cones, like those of other true firs, maintain an erect position and in early September mature as close-packed cylinders of cone scales, three to five inches long, ranging in color from ashen-tinged olive-green to purple.

The seeds, which develop at the base of the scales, are a dingy yellow-brown with shiny, clear, rose-tinged wings. They are released to be carried fifty to one hundred feet by the wind as the thin, close-packed, overlapping cone scales gradually fall away from the central spike-like axis. Good seed crops occur at irregular intervals of two or three years, and, while most abundant during the years of the tree's rapid growth, continue to maturity. The erect, woody spikes of the cone cores remain attached to the branches for several years. In no cone-bearing trees except the eastern baldcypress do the cones break up as do those of the firs.

White fir wood is white, straight-grained, and fine-textured. It has no resin ducts and only a slight distinction between sapwood and heart-wood. Unseasoned lumber has a disagreeable odor, which is so entirely lost with seasoning that it has been successfully used for butter tubs. Its slight resistance to decay makes treatment necessary wherever the wood is to be used in contact with the soil or where termites are prevalent. The wood weighs about twenty-six pounds to the cubic foot when air dry, or 1,550 to 1,600 pounds for every thousand board feet of sawed lumber. It compares favorably with eastern hemlock, spruce and ponderosa pine in strength and is used largely for the construction of small houses and for boxes and crates. It holds paint well, and is successfully used for cupboards and interior trim. Pulp material suitable for newspaper and wrapping paper can be produced from white fir, but there is a small prospect of any immediate market developing within the tree's range.

The stand of all the western true firs is estimated at about 100,000,000,000 board feet, more than one-third of which is white fir, about seventy percent of it in California.

While the seeds have a relatively low percentage of germination, they grow readily on almost any seed bed. The tree reproduces naturally on exposed denuded lands, as well as under its own shade. The seeds will grow under cultivation and small trees are readily transplanted.

White fir is widely used as an ornamental tree, and is growing successfully in many eastern states from Virginia north into New England. Its dense symmetrical crown and ability to survive under heavy shade render it especially suitable for landscape planting.

The mature cones are three to five inches long and they stand erect on the topmost branches

With age the resin pockets, or "balsam blisters," disappear and the ashy gray bark becomes deeply furrowed, hard, horny, and fire-resistant

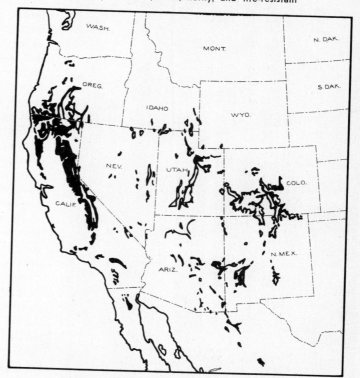

Natural range of White Fir

107

PACIFIC SILVER FIR

Cascades fir, Amabilis fir, Pacific silver fir

Abies amabilis (Douglas) Forbes

Oliver V. Matthews

Characterized by its beautiful spire-like form and lustrous foliage, the Silver Fir grows to a height of 200 feet

SILVER FIR or Pacific silver fir, as it is also called, is so named for the striking silvery white appearance of the under side of its needles. Another name applied to it is lovely fir—implied by *amabilis*—because of its beautiful pyramidal or spire-like form in comparison with the usually dome-like crown of noble fir and lowland white fir, with which it is often associated. The pleasing form of silver fir shows to best advantage in open situations where it is densely clothed to the ground with comparatively short branches. These branches sweep downward and outward in graceful curves.

The tree grows to a height of 200 feet, with a trunk diameter of three to five feet. It attains its largest size in the Olympic Mountains of Washington, where it is the most common fir. Its range extends from the southern extremity of Alaska southward along the British Columbia coast through the State of Washington to southern Oregon. It occurs near sea level in Alaska and British Columbia and at elevations of from 1,000 to 6,000 feet or more in Washington and Oregon.

Preferring deep moist soil and a southern and western exposure, silver fir is usually found on well-drained lower slopes of canyons, benches and flats. It grows in small pure stands, but more commonly in mixture, usually associated with lowland white fir, Douglasfir, Sitka spruce and western hemlock. At higher altitudes it occurs with alpine and noble fir, Engelmann spruce, Alaska cedar, western larch and western white pine.

The needles of silver fir grow in four irregular ranks along the twig, forming a spray that is flat below and rather bushy above. The upper rows point noticeably forward, toward the end of the twig. Dark green and grooved on the upper surface, the needles are three-fourths to one and one-half inches long, often broadest above the middle. Those on the underside of the twig are longer than those on the upper side. On the lower branches they may be obtuse and rounded or notched or occasionally acute at the apex; needles on the upper branches are usually pointed.

The winter buds are nearly spherical, one-eighth to one-quarter of an inch thick, very resinous, and covered with overlapping lustrous scales. The red staminate flowers hang singly from the lower side of the branches and drop soon after releasing their pollen, while the purplish ovulate ones grow erect in clusters on the topmost branches.

The mature purple cones are conspicuous objects on the tree, measuring from three and one-half to six inches long. They are oblong, slightly narrowed to the rounded and often indented tip. Cone scales are one to one and one-eighth inches wide, nearly as long as broad, and about twice as long as the reddish bracts which adhere to the backs of the cone scales, and terminate in long slender tips. The cones, which mature at the end of the first season, ripen in September and shed their seeds in October. These seeds are light yellow-brown, half an inch long, and have pale brown, lustrous wings about three-fourth of an inch in length.

On stems up to about three feet in diameter, the bark is ashy gray and smooth, with large, irregular, chalky colored blotches and numerous blisters filled with resin. On larger trunks it becomes rougher and irregularly divided into plates covered with small, closely appressed, reddish brown or reddish gray scales.

The heartwood of silver fir is pale brown, the sapwood nearly white. The wood is soft, light, and low in strength properties and in resistance to decay. It weighs about twenty-seven pounds to the cubic foot in air-dry condition, and is used in the form of lumber principally for framing and sheathing in small house construction and for boxes and crates. It is well adapted to the manufacture of paper pulp, but markets for this use are limited.

Growth is slow, and trees two feet in diameter are frequently 200 years old. A century is usually required to produce a tree of small sawlog size. Although large seed crops are produced every two or three years, the percentage of germination is low and the vitality of the seeds transient. Moreover, the seedlings cannot develop in contiuous dense shade. Like other western true firs, silver fir is free from insect pests and fungal diseases.

Because of the beautifully shaped crown and dense, lustrous foliage, silver fir is cultivated as an ornamental tree in the eastern states and in western Europe. Unfortunately, however, it often does not fully develop its beauty of form when grown away from its native forests. In the East, it is hardy in sheltered positions as far north as Massachusetts.

A. Varela

The mature cones are conspicuous. Purple, they measure from three and a half to six inches long

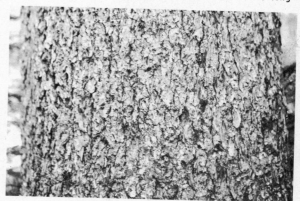

U. S. Forest Service

The bark is ashy gray, with large chalk-like blotches and many resin blisters

U. S. Forest Service

The name of Silver Fir derives from the silvery white under side of its needles

Natural range of Silver Fir

GRAND FIR

Lowland white fir, Yellow fir
Abies grandis (Douglas) Lindley

Downward-sweeping limbs with upcurved ends characterize the Grand Fir, which attains heights of 250 or more feet

GRAND FIR is found throughout the Pacific coast region from the northwestern end of Vancouver Island, British Columbia, to Sonoma County, California, and east through Washington and Oregon into northern Idaho and Montana.

It thrives from sea level to 7,000 feet, where it seeks moist situations on gentle mountain slopes, and alluvial stream bottoms. Best and most abundant growth is on stream bottoms at low levels along the coast. The deep root system favors fairly deep, porous, well-drained soils. Best known of all the western firs because it is common in the valleys, as well as on the mountains, grand fir is a stately, narrow-crowned tree rising to heights of 150 to 200 feet. Exceptional trees are 250 to 300 feet tall, with a trunk three to four and rarely six feet in diameter.

Also known as lowland white fir, it fully lives up to its name *Abies grandis*, or grand fir. This is particularly true, if the word *Abies* is derived, as some authorities have suggested, from the Latin word *abeo*, and used in an ascendant or upreaching sense. Certainly, of the ten North American firs, this is probably the tallest, but it does not attain the large dimensions of some of its western relatives. On less favorable sites the tree may be only eighty to 125 feet tall, with trunk diameters of eighteen to thirty inches. In the high mountains it tends to be small.

Standing alone or in the open forest, trees hold their long, graceful, downward-sweeping branches to within a few feet of the ground, while in close-grown stands the straight, gradually tapered trunk may be clear of branches for sixty to 100 feet or more. With advanced age, height growth becomes less rapid, and the side branches continue to extend, so that the narrow tapering point develops into a rounded top. All except the topmost branches have a distinct downward and upward swing. These branch characteristics sometimes make the rather open crown appear widest in the middle.

Ring counts on the stumps of felled trees have shown a diameter of thirty-four inches in 196 years, indicating that this fir is only moderately long-lived, but capable of attaining an age of 200 to 250 years.

The dark, yellow-green leaves are shiny on the upper surface and so silvery white below as to be partly responsible for the name of white or silver fir, which confuses it with *Abies concolor*. The leaves are one to two inches long, about one-eighth of an inch wide, thin, flexible, deeply grooved on the upper surface, and rounded and usually distinctly notched at the tip. The undersides are marked with two parallel lines of white stomata. Arranged spirally, the needles appear to be on opposite sides of the twig with alternate long and short leaves. They spread out flat like a comb on the lower branches, and are probably the most conspicuously flat and glossy of any of the native firs. Those in the upper crown, and especially on cone-bearing branches, are shorter, more densely crowded and curve upward, while the scattered leaves of the leader are distinctly pointed. They persist for five or ten years before being shed.

The round, resin-covered buds, as well as the twigs, are pale russet-brown, and the latter are covered with fine hairs through the first season. Like all true firs of the genus *Abies*, male and female flowers are borne on branches of the previous year's growth, on different parts of the same tree. The female flowers, which mature in one season into seed-bearing cones, are short, scaly, yellow-green bodies, which stand erect in the upper branches of the tree. In contrast, the pale yellow, pollen-bearing male flowers hang singly from the lower sides of branches beneath those that bear female flowers.

The mature cones are bright yellow-green, roughly cylindrical and slightly indented in the end. They stand upright in clusters on the twigs of the upper crown. Each is two and a half to four and a half inches long, and one to one and a third inches in diameter, and consists of many, closely packed scales that conceal broad, square-ended bracts. The cones break apart soon after maturity to release the pale yellow, resinous seeds, the broad wings of which may carry them on the wind 100 feet or more from the parent tree. Only the central cores remain through the winter and early spring to show where the cones had been. Trees may begin to bear cones after the twentieth year, and heavy seed crops are produced at intervals of two or three years. Under ordinary conditions the seeds do not retain their vitality longer than one year, and seldom are more than half of them capable of germinating.

Chalky areas on the smooth, ashy brown bark of young trees and branches contribute to the common name white fir, while the deeply but narrowly-ridged bark of old trees is a pale red-brown with an ashen tinge. It is hard, close, and horny, rarely more than two inches thick, but scarcely an inch thick on trees up to twenty inches in diameter. Like all true firs the young bark carries many blisters or resin pockets filled with clear aromatic resin, which with the aromatic odor of the crushed leaves, accounts in part for the earlier name *Abies aromatica* given the tree by Rafinesque in 1832.

Grand fir makes up more than ten percent of the total stand of the true firs. Lumber and pulpwood are products of the soft but firm, moderately wide-ringed and straight-grained wood, which varies in color from pale yellowish brown to very light brown. A cubic foot of dry wood weighs about twenty-eight pounds, which is heavier that that of other firs. Although easily worked, its brittleness and lack of strength and durability has limited its use principally to boxboards, packing cases, slack cooperage, interior trim, and rough construction lumber.

Grand fir occurs only rarely in pure stands, but usually in mixture with Douglasfir, western redcedar, western hemlock, Pacific yew, and vine maple. At low levels in Oregon and Washington, silver fir and noble fir, bigleaf maple, and black cottonwood are added to its associates. In the low coast region it is found with Sitka spruce.

George C. Stephenson

Green cylindrical cones stand erect on the upper branches, whose thin flexible leaves have a silvery white undersurface

U. S. Forest Service

The hard, narrowly-furrowed bark of mature trees is pale red-brown with an ashen tinge and barely two inches thick

Natural range of Grand Fir

111

NOBLE FIR

Abies procera Rehder (*A. nobilis* Lindley)

AS ITS name suggests, this tree is an aristocrat among the true firs. In its native forest environment and growing at its best, it is a magnificent specimen, lifting its crown on a clean and symmetrical trunk a hundred and fifty to two hundred feet into the sky. Rarely it attains 250 feet with a trunk girth at base exceeding twenty feet.

In its crown, too, there is character that helps to distinguish it from other firs within its range. Standing out rigidly and somewhat sparsely, its branches grow at right angles to the trunk in widely spaced whorls or groups to form a round-topped cone, which at distant view often marks its identity. In the dense, mature forest, its straight and symmetrical trunk is often clear of branches for a hundred feet. Open-grown, however, branches may clothe its stem to the ground, the lower ones tending to droop.

Locally, noble fir is also known as feather-cone red fir, bracted red fir, larch and Tuck-Tuck, the last an Indian given name. Lumbermen have given it the name "larch" for marketing reasons. Wood of noble fir is superior to that of the other true firs and to offset the market prejudice against the latter, the trade name of larch has been used. *Abies procera*, referring to height, is now applied in place of *Abies nobilis*—a name previously given a fir of Central Europe.

Noble fir grows in the Cascade Mountains southward from Snohomish and Chelan counties, Washington, to Klamath County, Oregon, and it occurs sporadically in the coast ranges from Pacific County, Washington, south to the Siskiyou Mountains in northern California. The principal commercial range is in the central part of the Cascades in southern Washington and northern Oregon.

While demanding an abundance of soil moisture, the tree grows on many kinds of soil, but reaches its best development on deep, rich soil. It occurs on gently sloping ridges, valleys, and plateaus at elevations from 1,400 to 6,000 feet above sea level, through a zone of uniformly mild, damp climate.

Growth of noble fir is fairly rapid, offering equal competition with its associates, which are usually Douglasfir, western white pine, western hemlock, and less frequently mountain hemlock, lodgepole pine, and silver and alpine firs. Pure stands of noble fir are rare and small in area. Little is known about the age of this species, but probably it is the longest lived of the firs.

Oliver V. Matthews

The trunk of Noble Fir is straight and symmetrical, while the sparse, short branches, arranged in whorls, form a round-topped conical crown

The bark of noble fir is thin, averaging one or two inches thick on older trees. Grayish brown in color, it is broken by narrow grooves into irregular, soft plates covered with closely pressed scales that flake off, revealing a ruddy-colored underbark. On young trees the bark is gray and has the resin blisters common to the bark of young trees of other firs. The rounded reddish winter buds are about an eighth of an inch long, coated with resin, and the twigs are slender, hairy and reddish brown.

The curved needles of noble fir vary in color from pale to dark blue-green and appear to grow in a crowded mass along the upper sides of the twigs. Needles of the lower branches usually are notched at the tip, and are about one or one and a half inches long, while those of the upper branches, noticeably four-angled, are about five-eighths to three-quarters of an inch long, and nearly always sharply pointed. All needles are grooved on their upper surface. In the vicinity of Davis Lake, Oregon, where the ranges of noble fir and red fir overlap, this groove characteristic offers a means of distinguishing the two species. Needles of red fir, instead of being grooved, are ridged on the top.

Flowers are borne on twigs of the previous season. The purple staminate or pollen-bearing ones hang singly from the branches of the lower crown, while the reddish or yellowish green ovulate ones, with broad rounded scales and long bracts, stand erect and scattered on the topmost branches. The erect, oblong, round-tipped cones are four or five inches long and are strikingly different from the cones of other firs, in that they have sharply pointed bracts which entirely cover the scales and give them a shingled appearance. Ripening early in September, the cones start to drop their scales and liberate the seeds in October.

Pale reddish brown, the seeds measure about a half inch in length, and are blunt and slightly rounded at the tip. The species is a fairly prolific seeder, some seed being produced every year, with abundant crops occurring at irregular intervals. Trees up to sixty years of age produce seed, but the largest crops are produced by older trees. The rate of germination is low, and seeds do not long retain their vitality. Seedlings grow best on mineral soil and humus in the open or in partial shade, but will not develop in continuous shade. Forest clearings or burned areas soon support an abundant growth of seedlings when parent trees are present.

A cubic foot of noble fir wood when dry weighs twenty-eight pounds. It is hard, strong, very close-grained, firm, and in color is light brown marked with reddish brown streaks which add to its beauty. Sapwood is darker than the heartwood. It is low in fuel value, but works easily and takes a good polish. Uses include flooring, interior finish, doors, window sash, boats, crates and boxes.

The thin bark makes the tree subject to injury by fire, but as it usually grows in moist locations, this danger is lessened. There is some loss in old trees due to fungus decay, but attack by insects is almost unknown.

In Europe noble fir has been successfully planted as an ornamental tree. In eastern United States, it will survive the winter cold as far north as central New England.

The erect, oblong cones have sharply pointed bracts covering the scales like shingles

The thin grayish brown bark is broken by narrow grooves into irregular, soft, scaly plates

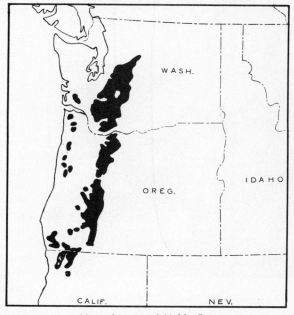

Natural range of Noble Fir

RED FIR

Red-barked fir, Shasta fir, Golden fir
Abies magnifica Murray

Weldon F. Heald

At elevations of 7,000 to 9,000 feet above sea level in Oregon and California, Red Fir develops into a tall symmetrical tree

RED FIR, also known as red-barked fir, Shasta fir and golden fir, is found on meadows and on high, western slopes of the mountains, from southern Oregon and northern California southward to the divide between the White and Kern rivers. It grows at elevations from 4,800 to 9,000 feet above sea level, and forms extensive forests in the Sierra Nevada and on Mt. Shasta, at altitudes of 7,000 to 9,000 feet, where it is associated with western white pine, Douglasfir and Jeffrey pine. Its largest size is attained on moist, sandy or gravelly loam soils, where deep snows frequently cover the ground from November to June, but where the temperature seldom falls to zero.

True to its name, *Abies magnifica* becomes a magnificent, symmetrical tree commonly sixty to 125 feet and occasionally 175 feet high, with trunk diameters from one to five feet. The narrow, cone-shaped crown is composed of numerous horizontal strata of fan-shaped sprays. Too little is known regarding the longevity of red fir, but trees are known to have lived 350 to 370 years. The scientific name is credited to the botanical studies and descriptions of Andrew Murray, who, as secretary of the Oregon Botanical Association of Edinburgh, Scotland, sponsored the botanical expedition of John Jeffrey into northern California in 1852. The specimens and field notes of this expedition are in the Herbarium of the Royal Botanical Garden at Edinburgh.

There are some twenty-five species of fir distributed over the northern hemisphere. Eleven of these are native to the United States and seven are native to the western mountains.

In close stands the trunks of red fir are clear of branches for sixty to eighty feet. The central and lower branches droop, while those near the crown have an upward trend. Only in the densest stands are medium-sized trees clear of branches for as much as half of their length.

The deep purplish brown or dark red bark of mature trees is two or three inches thick, hard, rough, with deep furrows and narrow, rounded ridges, which give a peculiar diagonal or zigzag trend. In youth the bark, like that of many larger branches, is relatively smooth and conspicuously chalky white. As with other true firs, balsam blisters are evident under the thin bark of young trees and branches.

The dark blue-green, four-angled, flat leaves have wide blunt ends, are five-eighths of an inch to a little over an inch long without a twist, and are densely incurving so as to hide the upper side of the branch. The leaves frequently have a whitish tinge and the new growth is light green. They are arranged spirally on the branches and persist for five to ten years. Branches from which the leaves have fallen are marked by conspicuous circular scars, where the leaves were once attached. The twigs divide in a horizontal plane, developing numerous fan-shaped sprays of foliage which give the tree an appearance of being stratified. The leaves on the lower branches differ slightly from those in the middle and upper parts of the tree. The leaf buds are light, chocolate-brown.

The greenish red ovulate flowers are about three inches long and stand erect and singly on branches of the uppermost part of the tree. They develop from buds formed during the previous season on twigs of that year, and grow during a single season from dull purple objects to erect deep purple or occasionally brown cones. They are broadly oval, four to eight inches long, two and one-half

114

to three and one-half inches in diameter, with broad scales whose edges are upturned, partly concealing the irregular tongue-like points of membranous bracts. The dark reddish purple, pollen-bearing flowers hang like long cylindrical cones from the under side of branches of the previous year's growth, and on the same tree with the ovulate flowers. They occur most plentifully in the upper half of the tree, but below the cone-bearing flowers. The cones mature in August of the first year and maintain their erect or nearly erect position, which is characteristic of all firs. They break up during September, liberating numerous seeds with large shiny purple or rose-colored wings. Only an erect spike, or central axis, six to nine inches long, is left through the winter. The baldcypress of the South is the only other native cone-bearer whose mature cones break up as do the firs. Good crops of seeds are produced every two or three years. Seeds may be carried by the wind two hundred feet or more from the parent tree and germinate abundantly on exposed moist mineral soils, or in light shade. Seedlings grow rapidly and frequently cover high slopes or openings cleared by fire or storm. As the tree grows older it becomes less tolerant of shade.

The wood has a reddish tinge, is soft, light, rather brittle, and has a straight, fine grain. It is more durable in contact with the soil or exposure to the weather than the wood of any of the other native firs. Weighing twenty-nine pounds to the cubic foot when air dried, it ranks as the heaviest of all the true firs. It is used largely for rough lumber, packing boxes, bridge floors and mine timbers. Red fir occurs in largest quantity in California and contributes, though to a smaller extent, with white fir (*Abies concolor*), to the lumber cut.

The blisters on the bark are the source of an oleo-resin known as Canada balsam, used for mounting microscopic specimens, for medicinal purposes and in the manufacture of some varnishes. An essential oil used in pharmacy is also obtained from the leaves, which give off a turpentine-like odor when bruised.

The dense foliage and frequent exudation of balsam on the bark make young stands of red fir susceptible to fire; but with increasing age, the thicker bark resists damage from the heat of ground fires. Dense young stands are also seriously weighed down and bent by heavy snow.

Small, woolly, sucking insects known as adelgids sometimes cause extensive injury to the leaves and buds of this and other firs. No satisfactory control measures have been developed for forest trees, but soapy solutions containing nicotine are usually effective when sprayed on infested ornamental trees during late winter or early spring.

The handsome, regular habit of red fir, together with its ability, when young, to grow in crowded, shady stands, makes it desirable as an ornamental tree. It has proved successful on cool moist sites in the eastern states and in northern Europe.

The purplish brown, six- to nine-inch cones, the longest of the native true firs, stand singly and erect on twigs of the previous year's growth.

Deep zigzag furrowings in the hard, rough, dark red bark are characteristic of Red Fir

Natural range of Red Fir

ALPINE FIR
Subalpine fir, Downy-coned fir
Abies lasiocarpa (Hooker) Nuttall

ALPINE FIR, whose slender spires are supported by dense blue-green whorls of flat foliage sprays, is a characteristic feature of large areas of high country in the western mountains. Although relatively small and unimportant, this tree is the most widely distributed fir in western North America. It grows as far south as the Pinalino Mountains of southern Arizona and the Mogollon Mountains of New Mexico. It is common in Colorado, Montana and Idaho, westward through the mountains of Oregon and Washington into the high ranges of British Columbia and northward beyond all the other western firs to sixty degrees latitude in Alaska.

True to its name, Alpine fir grows in cool, moist situations at elevations of 3,500 feet to 10,500 feet and occurs commonly at timberline, as well as in protected valleys at the heads of streams, about mountain lakes and on moist meadows. Trees of largest dimensions are found growing on fairly deep, loose, moist soil at elevations of 5,000 to 8,000 feet. It does not thrive on heavy, clay soils. Within its range it is frequently associated with Engelmann spruce, lodgepole pine, mountain hemlock, western white pine, whitebark pine and, toward the South, with aspen and corkbark fir *Abies lasiocarpa* var. *arizonica*.

The long, slender, narrowly-conical crown terminating in a conspicuous spire distinguishes alpine fir from its associates. In the open, the narrow crowns of old trees, as well as young, extend down to the ground, while in dense forest stands the trunks of old trees are occasionally free from branches for twenty to forty feet. The dense, tough branches at the base of the crown droop and are often sharply curved or bent down upon the trunk. The twigs are commonly covered with tiny rusty brown hairs for two or three years.

Ordinarily, alpine fir attains heights of sixty to ninety feet, with trunk diameters at breast height of fourteen inches to twenty-four inches. Occasionally, trees 175 feet high, with diameters of three to five feet, have been reported. Although moderately long-lived, the largest trees are probably not older than 250 years, while trees ten inches to twenty inches in diameter are often 140 to 210 years old.

Two kinds of deep blue-green leaves or needles ranging from less than an inch to one and three-quarters inches long are commonly found on each tree. The leaves occur singly and are arranged alternately on all sides of the twigs. Those of the lower branches are relatively long, flat, blunt and all are distinctly upward pointing. On the higher limbs and branches the leaves are thicker, somewhat shorter, pointed and retain the feature of being distinctly massed and upward pointing. Each new season's growth of foliage has a silvery tinge.

Flowers of both sexes are borne on twigs of the previous year, on different parts of the same tree. The solitary staminate or pollen-bearing flowers are dark blue, later turning violet, and occur abundantly on the lower branches in the axils of the leaves. The scaly ovulate flowers are

Devereux Butcher

The slender, dark blue-green spires of Alpine Fir are striking features in many areas of the western mountain region

116

fewer in number, are violet-purple and stand erect on the upper branches. The latter mature during a single season into downy, deep purple cones whose cylindrical form is contracted toward the tip. They are from two and one-quarter to four inches long, about one and one-half inches in diameter, and stand erect on the upper branches to form a purple cluster in the top of the tree.

The scientific name *Abies lasiocarpa* is derived from the Greek words *lasius*, meaning hairy or woolly, and *carpous*, meaning fruit. Literally translated, this means "the fir with a hairy fruit."

Beneath each rounded cone scale are two ivory-brown seeds about one-fourth of an inch long, with a large lustrous purplish or violet tinged wing. The cones swell when they ripen, releasing the scales, as well as the winged seeds, so that the central cores of the cones remain on the tree for one or more seasons. The seeds retain their vitality only for a short time, but during that period their capacity for germination is relatively high. Trees produce cones as early as the twentieth year and continue to bear abundant crops of seed at intervals of about three years. During some seasons, however, cones throughout large areas may fail to mature.

The rounded winter buds, consisting of light orange-brown scales, more or less covered with resin, may be a quarter of an inch thick.

The flinty bark of the trunk is usually gray, but sometimes is a chalky white. It is relatively thin, seldom more than an inch and a quarter thick and is marked by the blister-like resin pockets characteristic of all the firs or "balsams." Even on large trees the bark is little broken except for occasional narrow, shallow cracks near the base of the trunk.

Alpine fir is of little commercial importance. The pale, straw-colored wood is fine-grained, soft, and, except for frequent small knots, works easily, but is not durable in contact with the soil. Weighing only about twenty-one pounds to the cubic foot of dry wood, it is the lightest of all the firs. Dead timber is used locally for fuel, house logs and corral logs, while standing timber is occasionally cut and sawed into rough lumber for local use. Alpine fir is important primarily in preventing soil erosion on steep slopes at high elevations.

Natural reproduction is usually abundant in the open on exposed mineral soil and on moist duff under light or comparatively heavy shade. Seedlings grow thickly on the north sides of groups of trees and under parent trees.

Fire is the chief enemy of alpine fir. Insects seldom threaten the lives of these trees, but aphids or "plant lice" sometimes kill the lower branches.

Although naturally subjected to a rigorous climate, with forty degrees below zero in winter and heat of ninety degrees in summer, alpine fir has not proven hardy for planting in the northeastern states, where it is subject to winter injury.

George C. Stephenson

Purple cones, dripping with silvery resin, stand upright near the treetops on twigs of the previous year's growth

Devereux Butcher

The hard, flinty, ashy gray bark has the resin-filled blisters characteristic of all balsams

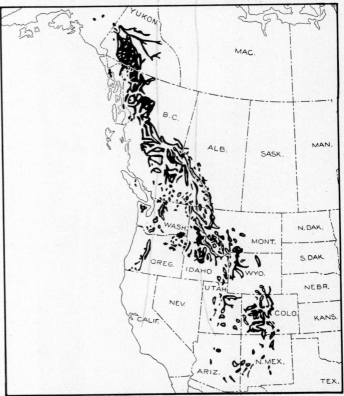

Natural range of Alpine Fir

CORKBARK FIR

Abies lasiocarpa var. *arizonica* (Merriam) Lemm

CORKBARK FIR is a variety of alpine fir, A. *lasiocarpa* (see preceding two pages), which it closely resembles and with which it associates, together with trembling aspen and Engelmann spruce, in the Canadian and Hudsonian zones at between 8,000 and 10,000 feet above sea level. Its scattered range occurs on a number of the highest peaks in southwestern Colorado, northern New Mexico, the Mogollon Mountains in southwestern New Mexico, the Santa Catalina Mountains near Tucson, Arizona, the San Francisco Mountains in eastern Arizona and on Lukachukai Mountain in northeastern Apache County, Arizona, where it was discovered. Dr. C. Hart Merriam, while making a biological survey there in 1889, found the variety and reported it at the time.

Characteristics that distinguish corkbark from alpine fir are the highly elastic, soft, fine-grained, corklike bark which is marked by irregular sinuous ridges; the pale gray bark on upper trunk and branches; and the longer and more slender dark purple cones. As with the cones of all the true firs, the cones of corkbark fir stand erect on the topmost twigs and, when the seeds ripen in spring, the cone scales fall away with the seeds, leaving the cone's central core standing on the twig. The seeds germinate in the moisture resulting from snowmelt, but the shallow-rooted seedlings soon are subjected to the dry spring season, which causes high mortality among them.

The ranges of the two varieties differ widely in that the corkbark occurs over a much smaller area. Whereas the northern limit of the latter, so far as known, is in southwestern Colorado, alpine fir extends on northward in a broad belt to Yukon, Canada, and slightly westward into Alaska.

Preferred sites are the high, cool, open meadows at timberline, where the tree grows singly or in clumps or groups and develops the graceful, spirelike form, the whorled branches being retained almost to ground level in trees of all ages, and having the blue-green foliage typical of that of the alpine variety. Under closed-forest conditions, such as that in the Santa Catalina Mountains, lower branches die out as a result of insufficient light, while the tree attains greater heights. In general, too, corkbark fir tends to be somewhat smaller than alpine fir.

The leaves or needles of the lower branches are longer and more slender than those of the upper, conebearing branches, and are longer also than those of the lower branches of the alpine. The needles grow singly and are arranged alternately on all sides of the corkbark twigs as they are on the alpine.

Where the ranges of the two varieties overlap, they sometimes hybridize, making accurate varietal identification difficult if not impossible. Because of its comparative rarity and its widely broken, limited range, the wood of corkbark fir is of little commercial value. Reports indicate that the tree has been used for horticultural and ornamental purposes.

Forest-grown Corkbark Firs develop a short, pyramidal crown and straight tall trunk free of branches for much of the height. Open-grown trees have a narrow, spirelike crown that extends to the ground

Robert C. Barnacastle

118

The slender, slightly tapering, purple cones stand upright on the topmost twigs and are about two and a half to four and a half inches long and an inch to an inch and a quarter in diameter when mature

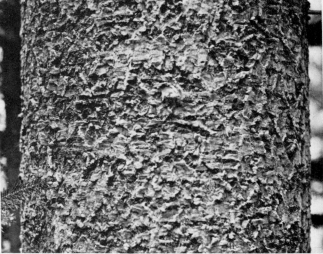

Bark on mature trunks is soft, yielding to the touch, fine-grained and marked by irregular ridges, while on upper stems and branches it is smooth and pale gray

The blue-green needles grow singly on all sides of the twigs, and when young, have a silvery cast. Those on lower branches are about two inches long and on the upper and cone-bearing branches shorter, thicker and blunt tipped

Seeds mature in spring or early summer, and are released when the cone scales drop from the central core, which remains attached and upright on the twig

Natural range of Corkbark Fir

119

BRISTLECONE FIR
Santa Lucia fir, Fringecone Fir
Abies bracteata D. Don

THE dark, extremely slender spires of this rare, unique tree tower above the vegetation on the ocean-facing ridges and in the ravines that open toward the ocean near the summits of the Santa Lucia Mountains in the Ventana Primitive Area of the northern unit of the Los Padres National Forest, Monterey County, California. Reaching heights of sixty to a hundred feet, with trunk diameters of one to two feet, the lower branches have a downward sweep, and the twigs and side branches on the entire tree are long and pendent, giving the tree a weeping form.

Growing on the rocky, gravelly soils on westward slopes at elevations of 2200 to 5000 feet, overlooking the Pacific Ocean, there may be fewer than twenty scattered groups or groves of this tree—the total world population of the species.

In appearance, bristlecone fir differs noticeably from all other firs native to the North American continent, and authors have described it as the most remarkable fir; the most curious fir; unique in almost all characteristics, and as having distinct features. Little wonder that it is recognizeable at long distances from among the shrubs and trees with which it associates.

Young stems and upper trunks of older trees have smooth, thin, gray bark conspicuously marked with horizontal blisters. On the bases of older trunks the bark is less than an inch thick, light red-brown on the surface and red within, irregularly fissured into flat, hard, firm scales.

The branches are stout and grow in irregular whorls. Twigs are red-brown and coated with a bloom, while the large, sharply pointed, ovoid winter buds at their terminals are protected by bright chestnut, papery scales and are lacking in resin.

Flat, stiff, sharp, taperingly tipped, the needles are dense, bright lustrous green, varying from one and a half to two inches in length, are centrally grooved above and marked by rows of silvery white stomata on their under sides. Those on the upper crown are shorter and grow along the upper surface of the twigs, while those on the lower branches are twisted at the base and appear to grow horizontally from opposite sides of the twig. When the needles fall, they leave disk-like scars on the twigs—a characteristic of all the firs.

Flowers appear in May, the male or pollen-producing ones in the form of small yellow catkins, and the female or seed-producing ones cylindrical and yellow-green. The cones, borne on short, stout stems, are plump and oval, and from two and three quarters to three and a half inches tall. They stand erect on the tree's highest branches, as do those of all the true firs. Ripening and turning slightly purple-brown in late August, they dis-

Devereux Butcher

Reaching heights of sixty to 100 feet and trunk diameters up to two feet, Bristlecone Fir, in native habitat, acquires a slender spire of drooping branches and pendent twigs

120

perse their dark, shiny, chestnut-brown, winged seeds in September, dropping their fan-shaped scales soon after, leaving only the woody core of the cone standing on the branch. Seed crops are meager and infrequent, vitality brief and germination low, which may partly account for the small range and comparatively few trees.

An outstanding feature of the bristlecone cones is the slender extension of the bracts, which protrude from beneath the cone scales. These bracts often are two inches long, are flexible and give the cone a bristly appearance, suggesting the common names bristlecone and fringecone fir, as well as the scientific name, *bracteata*.

The light yellow-brown wood, heavier than that of other firs, is coarse-grained and firm. Because of the rarity of this species, the wood is not used, but the roots are important in helping to protect and hold the soil in the ravines and on the slopes where it grows.

This tree has not done well under cultivation in our country, but it is reported to have succeeded better in Europe. Whatever its response to cultivation, this beautiful tree deserves utmost protection from fire and vandalism within its native habitat.

Flowers appear in May, the male or pollen-producing ones in the form of small yellow catkins growing with the needles toward the tips of the twigs

Sharp, lustrous, grooved above and marked by rows of white stomata beneath, the needles are one and a half to two inches long, the shortest on the highest branches

Cylindrical, yellow-green female flowers on the tree's highest branches, develop erect, oval, slightly purple cones unique among fir cones because of the long bracts that protrude as far as two inches beyond the cone scales

Bark on young trees and upper trunks of older ones is smooth and gray, with horizontal blisters, and on old trunks it is broken into hard, flat scales

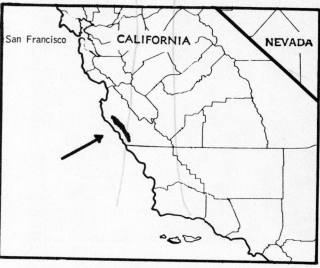

Natural range of Bristlecone Fir

121

GIANT SEQUOIA
Sierra redwood, Bigtree
Sequoiadendron gigantium (Lindley) Buchholz

Leland J. Prater

A Giant Sequoia, more than a thousand years old, lifts its rounded crown above a massive trunk, and shows its size in contrast to neighboring pines and firs

GIANT SEQUOIA or bigtree, largest and almost the oldest of living things, links our civilization with the dim records of the past. John Muir called it "king of all the conifers of the world, 'the noblest of a noble race.'" Flourishing trees now standing in the California groves were swaying in the Sierra Nevada winds when Christ walked the earth. These trees of the *Sequoia* group are remnants of an ancient race, which flourished as far north as the Arctic zone during Tertiary, and Cretaceous times. All but two species, giant sequoia, *Sequoia gigantea,* and the redwood, *Sequoia sempervirens,* have disappeared since the Glacial Period. These two continue growing in the California coast mountains and on the western slopes of the Sierra Nevada, at elevations of 4,000 to 8,500 feet above sea level. The older trees grow on high land from which the glacial ice apparently melted long before it did in the intervening canyons. Here the snow gathers six feet deep for three to six months each year, and the temperature may drop below zero. In contrast to the redwood, the giant sequoia grows at higher elevations and on cooler sites farther from the coast, out of the fog belt. It is found in some seventy groves of five to 1,000 trees in an area extending from the North Calaveras Grove, east to Lake Tahoe in the Tahoe National Forest, southward for 260 miles to the Deer Creek Grove, east of Porterville in the Sequoia National Forest. The largest concentration of trees is in Sequoia and Kings Canyon national parks. The annual precipitation in this area varies from forty-five to sixty inches.

The nearest relative of the *Sequoia* on this continent is the baldcypress, *Taxodium distichum,* of the southern states; but the scientific name of the two western species perpetuates the name of Sequoyah, a talented Cherokee Indian chieftain, who, between 1770 and 1843, invented the Cherokee alphabet.

Giant sequoia thrives in shallow grassy basins, where the soil is deep and sandy to gravelly, and in draws near the headwaters of streams, where soil moisture is abundant. While occasional pure stands of giant sequoias are found, they usually tower amid a forest of sugar pine, incense-cedar, white fir, Douglasfir, or ponderosa pine. The trunk may rise eighty to 225 feet before the first limb, and be surrounded by a crown rounded at the summit, or much broken, depending upon the age of the tree.

Trees attain heights of 300 to 330 feet, and one in the Calaveras Grove is estimated to have once been 400 feet high. This grove of about one hundred trees was first reported in 1841. Ten feet from the ground and above the stump-swell, trees may be twenty-seven to thirty feet in diameter, but more frequently they are twelve to seventeen feet in diameter, 200 to 280 feet high, and from 1,200 to 2,000 years old. The stump of one tree recorded 3,400 rings of annual growth, and John Muir counted the rings on another which he believed to be over 4,000 years old.

Giant sequoia has bright, deep green foliage in the form of scale-like, sharp-pointed leaves closely overlapping one another on the twigs, after the manner of cedars. They are "evergreen" and remain on the branches three to four years.

Tiny flowers of both sexes, borne singly at the tips of different twigs on the same tree, appear in February and

March, when snow is on the ground. The pollen-bearing flowers are about a quarter of an inch long, scaly, and occur in large numbers over the tree. Clouds of pollen from these fertilize the small, pale green seed-producing flowers, which mature in two seasons into woody, yellowish brown, egg-shaped cones varying from two to three inches long. Under each thick cone-scale are five to seven brown, flat, wing-margined seeds, with a kernel about the size of a pinhead. The seeds are released in the late autumn, when the wind carries them relatively short distances from the parent tree, but the empty cones may remain on the tree. Unlike the redwood, the giant sequoia does not produce sprouts, but depends entirely upon seeds for reproduction.

The red-brown bark is twelve to twenty-four inches thick, spongy and in two layers. The outer is composed of fibrous scales, while the inner is thin, close and firm. Vertical breaks extending the length of the trunk give it a fluted appearance.

The heartwood is dull purplish red-brown, lighter and more brittle than that of redwood. The straight grain varies from very fine in the later growth of old trees to coarse in the wood produced during the first 400 to 500 years while growth is rapid. The wood contains much tannin and when freshly cut the heartwood is a brilliant rose-purple surrounded by a thin layer of white sapwood. As with redwood, its uses are many, but the loss in felling is so great, the logs so difficult to handle, and the wood so brittle, that it is now practically off the market.

Between the Kings and Kern rivers are many trees twenty-five feet in diameter containing upwards of 500,000 board feet, and that are 3,000 years old. The largest probably weighs more than a thousand tons.

Giant sequoia owes its long life in no small measure to its freedom from destructive fungus and insect enemies. This may be due to the high tannin content of the wood, and also because there are no pitch tubes, as in the case of the pines, through which fungi may progress through the wood. Most destructive are the results of fire or other more or less natural causes that result in undermining the roots and tipping the tree over.

Giant sequoia seeds germinate best on bare exposed soil in sunny places and, in spite of the small amount of stored food within the seed, seedlings are fairly common on favorable sites. The seedlings will not grow in the shade of the forest where deep litter cause plants to die before becoming rooted in soil. Favorable conditions for natural reproduction frequently follow fires, floods, or where the ground has been disturbed by logging or road building operations. While ground fires help prepare the soil for seedlings to start, subsequent fires are disastrous to the young trees.

Seedlings are successfully grown in nurseries and can be transplanted. Giant sequoia has been extensively planted in California. It will grow in parts of the eastern United States, in the British Isles and in Central Europe.

National Park Service

Sharp-pointed, scale-like evergreen leaves overlap one another. The dull yellow-brown cones are two to three inches long

National Park Service

Deep fissures in the thick, red-brown bark give the Giant Sequoia trunk a fluted appearance

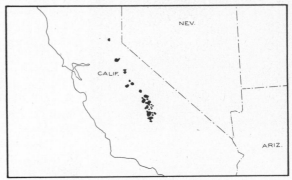

The natural range of Giant Sequoia

REDWOOD
California redwood, Coast redwood
Sequoia sempervirens (Lambert) Endlicher

THE REDWOOD, whose family covered most of the northern hemisphere before the glacial periods, is now confined to an area of less than 1,500,000 acres. It grows in an irregular strip scarcely thirty-five miles wide and 500 miles long, extending along the west slope of the Pacific Coast from the Chetco River in southwestern Oregon to Salmon Creek Canyon, about one hundred miles south of San Francisco in Monterey County, California. The trees grow from sea level to approximately 3,000 feet above the sea, on flats, in canyons and on seaward slopes where rain and fog are plentiful.

The redwood and its close Sierra relative, the giant sequoia, *Sequoia gigantea*, are the largest, and almost the oldest, life forms in North America, if not in the world. Lambert, of London, published the first description of redwood in 1803, under the name *Taxodium sempervirens*, in the belief that it was related to the southern cypress. In 1847, believing it to be a distinct genus, the name *Sequoia* was given by a German botanist, Endlicher, to honor the half-breed Cherokee chief Sequoyah, who formulated an alphabet for his tribe, and *sempervirens* is from the Latin, meaning "ever living."

Although not as long-lived as the bigtree nor as great in girth, redwood grows to a greater height than any other American tree. On flats under good conditions, it grows to be 350 feet high and from twenty to twenty-seven feet in diameter. The oldest redwood found during investigations by the Forest Service was twenty-one feet in diameter and 1,373 years old. Another tree fifteen feet in diameter and 270 feet high, described by Prof. W. R. Dudley, was 2,171 years old. Accurate ring counts cannot be secured without destroying the tree, but it is assumed that redwoods 300 feet high and twenty feet or more in diameter may approach an age of 2,000 years. Most of the redwoods cut in commercial operations are from 400 to 800 years old. These are from three to ten feet in diameter, and 200 to 275 feet tall. The tallest measured tree is 359 feet. It is in Humboldt Redwoods State Park. The Founders' Tree on Dyerville Flat, until it lost some of its top, was even taller—364 feet.

The larger trees have a straight, slightly tapered, heavily buttressed trunk, clear for more than one hundred feet, with an open round-topped crown of relatively short horizontal branches spreading with a downward tendency. The crowns may occupy a third to a half of the total length. Those of young trees ten to fifteen inches in diameter are narrowly conical and may extend to the ground.

The sharply pointed, flat, bright, deep yellow-green leaves of the lower branches and saplings stand out stiffly on opposite sides of the twigs and vary from one-third of an inch to an inch in length, while on the main stem of the branches they may occur as several overlapping lines of closely pressed scale-like forms. The leaves of each season's growth may remain on the tree for four or five years.

Tiny male and female flowers are on different branches of the same tree. The flower buds form in the autumn near the ends of the previous year's shoots. In the late winter or early spring the staminate flowers develop as small greenish yellow bodies in the axils of the leaves, while the more broadly egg-shaped ovulate flowers are terminal.

By early September of the same year the ovulate flowers mature into dull, purplish brown, egg-shaped cones about an inch long, and half as broad. Closely packed under each cone scale are four or five small russet brown, wing-margined seeds, which are shed slowly, and carried comparatively short distances by the wind. They are about one-sixteenth of

Rearing its crown to heights of more than 300 feet, the coast Redwood of California is the taller and more graceful of the two species of *Sequoia*

an inch in diameter and, when clean, require about 123,-000 to the pound. The cones remain on the trees several months after losing their seeds.

The dull red-brown bark of old trees has a grayish hue and is longitudinally fissured. It is very dense and tight, may be a foot thick, and is highly resistant to fire.

Redwood is named for the soft, straight-grained, moderately strong heartwood, which varies in color from a light cherry to a dark mahogany, and also for the color of the bark. The narrow sapwood is almost white. Air-dry heartwood weighs twenty-four to twenty-six pounds to the cubic foot. This is approximately the same as the weight of the wood of eastern white pine, to which it compares favorably in strength and stiffness. The wood is several pounds heavier than that of the giant sequoia and is stronger. It is easy to work, shrinks and swells but little, takes paint well, and resists decay and insects. Railroad ties, bridge timbers, tanks, flumes, silos, bee keepers' supplies, posts, grape stakes, shingles, siding, ceiling, doors, general mill work, caskets and furniture are among its many uses. In addition, the redwood tree has high esthetic value.

Although many seeds are produced nearly every year, only fifteen to twenty-five percent are perfect and germination is low. Even so, millions of seeds germinate and supplement the many vigorous sprouts which are produced from the stumps and root collar.

None of the ordinary wood-rotting fungi grow in redwood timber, and the tree is singularly free from fungus diseases. A so-called brown rot takes heavy toll of the standing timber. This causes parts of the butt to assume the properties of charcoal and to crumble into a fine powder. There also is a stringy type of fungus that does some damage. Few insects cause material harm and the wood is highly resistant to attacks of termites. Fire does relatively little damage to trees that have acquired a thick bark, but the young growth is killed or seriously injured.

Redwood requires a moist, cool climate of high humidity, as shown by its dependence upon the Pacific Coast fogs. It seldom thrives in a dry or warm climate, but will stand temperatures ranging from fifteen to 110 degrees Fahrenheit. The best stands are on protected flats along streams or on moderate west slopes opening toward the sea, where thirty to sixty inches of rain falls in the autumn and winter and sea fogs bathe the region in summer. Redwood grows in mixture with Douglasfir, tanoak, Sitka spruce, Port Orford whitecedar, western redcedar, white fir, and western hemlock. Where conditions are favorable the redwood leads all of these in the struggle for growing space.

To preserve some of the largest and more spectacular redwood groves for the enjoyment of future generations, the Save-the-Redwoods League, since 1918, has carried on a nation-wide campaign to arouse public attention and support. As a result, and with the cooperation of the California Division of Beaches and Parks, a number of outstanding areas have been established as state parks. Muir Woods National Monument, another fine area, is in National Park Service care. But the effort to save the redwoods continues, for what has been saved is little enough, and even this is threatened by highway building and other activities.

The bright yellow-green leaves of the lower branches stand out stiffly on opposite sides of the twigs and remain on the tree three or four years. Those on the main branches are scale-like. The cones are scarcely an inch long, and mature in a season

Redwood bark is reddish gray in color, fibrous in texture and gives a fluted appearance to the tree

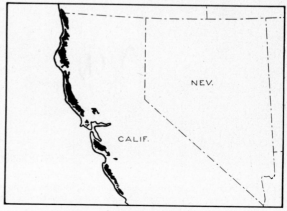

The natural range of Redwood

BALDCYPRESS

Common baldcypress, Gulf cypress, Southern cypress, Tidewater
red cypress, White cypress
Taxodium distichum (Linnaeus) Richard

THE BALDCYPRESS is equally at home on land or in the water. It is the only representative remaining of an ancient race of a number of similar tree species that were distributed over North America and northern Europe. It is making its last stand in the southeastern states, where it grows along the Atlantic coast from southern Delaware to southern Florida, westward along the Gulf of Mexico into Texas, and northward up the river valleys through Oklahoma and Arkansas to southern Illinois and southwestern Indiana. Usually it occurs along low bottomlands in saturated, or seasonally submerged soil. Thousand-year-old trees may become 150 feet tall and twelve feet in diameter, but more often they approach 120 feet in height and three to five feet in diameter. The trunks of older trees are massive, tapering and, particularly when growing in swamps, are broadly buttressed at the base. Especially in the humid coastal areas, crowns are heavily and picturesquely draped in curtains and streamers of gray Spanish moss. In youth the crown is narrow and pyramidal, but with age the branches spread to form a broad irregular crown.

Although a conifer, baldcypress is not an evergreen, for its leaves and small immature twigs are shed each fall. The only other deciduous conifers are the larches.

The scientific name *Taxodium* refers to the resemblance of the foliage to the yew or *Taxus*, while *distichum* is derived from two Greek words meaning twice or double ranked, and refers to the two-ranked arrangement on the twigs of the long, narrow, rather flat leaves. These are one-half to three-quarters of an inch long, light yellow-green, arranged spirally on the twigs, and are feathery in appearance. They turn yellow or brown and drop in the fall.

In the spring each tree may carry male and female flowers which develop on twigs of the preceding year's growth. The male flowers are in slender, purplish, tassel-like clusters, three to six inches long, while the female or ovulate flowers are scattered near the ends of the branchlets. These develop in a single season into spherical, purplish cones about an inch in diameter. Thick rhomboid scales fit closely together and under each

<small>U. S. Forest Service</small>

The massive, buttressed trunk of the Baldcypress supports a broad irregular crown of light green feathery foliage

126

may be two light brown, winged, horny seeds. Cypress also sprouts freely from the tree stumps during the first fifty to one hundred years.

Small, brown and more or less egg-shaped leaf buds appear on light green, slender twigs, which by winter become light red-brown and lustrous.

The reddish brown, fibrous ridged bark of old trees peels off in long strips, and is one to two inches thick. On younger trees the bark is light brown, less deeply ridged and thinner.

Shallow serpentine roots spread out from the buttressed base of the tree. Where water stands during part of the year these develop sharp, elongated cones or "knees" which rise a few inches to five or six feet above the mud surface, corresponding to the high water level of the locality. They are covered with thin bark, are hollow, and usually die when water is permanently drained or when the parent tree is cut. They help anchor the tree. In spite of the unstable soils in which cypress thrives, even the tallest trees are seldom thrown by the wind.

The soft, narrow-ringed, pale brown to reddish wood weighs twenty-two to thirty-seven pounds to the cubic foot when air dry, averaging about twenty-eight pounds. It is easily worked, has no resin ducts, feels slightly greasy or waxy, and has a peculiarly rancid odor. The heartwood is so durable in contact with the soil, or when exposed to the weather, as to be known as "the wood eternal." Cypress is used for structural purposes, for flooring, water tanks, ships, cross-ties, shingles, coffins, laundry appliances and greenhouse equipment.

Baldcypress trees may grow in relatively pure stands in swampy areas or on drier ground in mixture with tupelo gum, green ash, willow, overcup oak, red gum, the soft maples and elms. Single acres with over 100,000 board feet have been measured, while forty-acre tracts have yielded 1,500,000 board feet. Usually, however, stands do not exceed 8,000 to 10,000 board feet to the acre.

This last representative of an ancient race resists most insect enemies, but is subject to a heart-rot fungus which fills the wood with holes. Such wood is known as "pecky" cypress. This has many uses where strength or ability to hold water are not es-

Purplish, woody, spherical cones about an inch in diameter are borne on the twigs of the previous year's growth. Each cone may yield eighteen to thirty light brown, winged seeds

The fluted, buttressed trunk and the "knees," which often protrude above the mud and water, are covered with fibrous, reddish brown bark. The "knees" are hollow and are part of the shallow roots

sential. The thin bark offers little protection against fire and, during years of drought, when swamps are dry, great quantities of timber are burned.

Cypress is successfully planted throughout its range for ornamental and roadside purposes, and individual specimens are proving hardy in central New York and over much of Indiana and Illinois.

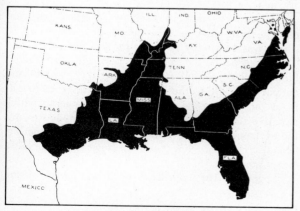

Natural range of Baldcypress

127

INCENSECEDAR

Libocedrus decurrens Torrey

U. S. Forest Service

Incensecedar attains height of 150 feet in the coast ranges of Oregon and California

THE TALL, compactly columnar crown of incensecedar, consisting of flattened frond-like branches, and reared on a rapidly tapering cinnamon-red trunk is frequently seen growing singly or in small groves over the western slopes of the mountain ranges from northern Oregon to Lower California. Confined largely to elevations of 4,000 to 8,000 feet above sea level, it ranges for a thousand miles from the basin of the Santiam River in Oregon, southward along the Cascade Mountains and the western slopes of the Sierra Nevada, over the California coast ranges to the mountains of southern California and Lower California. Eastward it is found in a few scattered mountain areas in Nevada.

Mature trees vary from seventy-five to 110 feet in height and from two and a half to four feet in diameter. Trees 150 feet in height occur throughout the Sierra Nevada and one tree 186 feet high has been recorded. The younger trees, with trunks up to twelve inches in diameter, maintain a narrow, columnar form with branches reaching to the ground. The larger branches have a distinct upward turn. With age and maturity, the crown flattens out and becomes more open. Incensecedar is a relatively slow-growing evergreen that reaches an average diameter of about thirteen inches in 100 years and frequently attains an age of 300 to 500 years. One tree measuring fifty-one inches in diameter at stump height was 542 years old, and trees may reach ages ranging from 800 to 1,000 years.

The yellowish green foliage consists of small, pointed scale-like leaves adhering closely to slender branchlets and capable of remaining on the trees from three to five years. They form flat sprays. Each leaf extends from one-eighth to one-half inch along the branch and has a characteristically long base to which the technical name *decurrens* refers. A small resin gland on each leaf is responsible for the pungent, aromatic odor so apparent when the leaf is crushed.

Libocedrus is derived from two Greek words and may be translated as "the cedar tree, the wood of which was burnt for perfume or to scent ointment."

Libocedrus is the name of a widely distributed family of trees closely related to the true cypress and not far distantly to the *Thuja*. *Libocedrus decurrens* is the only one of the nine species of the genus which is native to North America. Eight other species are found from Chile to Patagonia in South America, China, Formosa, New Guinea, New Zealand, and New Caledonia.

Flowers of the two sexes occur on parts of the

Light brown cones develop in one season and they hang from the ends of the branchlets.

to an increasing extent for pencil slats, cedar chests, so-called moth proof linings for the interiors of wardrobes, and for door and window frames. It is sometimes used for cigar boxes.

Most often incensecedar grows in association with ponderosa and sugar pines, giant sequoia, California black oak, Jeffrey pine, and occasionally with white fir, lodgepole pine, and limber pine. Best development is found on the west slope of the Sierra Nevada at elevations of 5,000 to 6,000 feet above sea level.

The thick, fire-resistant bark makes mature incensecedar trees relatively immune to fire damage, but heavy losses are sustained when fire runs through young growth. The tree has no insect enemies of any importance, but practically one-half of all incensecedar trees, as they stand in the woods, are defective, and most of the loss is due to a dry rot fungus which attacks the heartwood.

Incensecedar has been extensively planted for ornamental purposes in the eastern states where it prospers as far north as Massachusetts. The tree lends itself to unusual landscape effects, does well on well-drained, loamy soils, and is highly tolerant of shade.

The deeply furrowed, shreddy, cinnamon-red bark is two to three inches thick, or even heavier at the base of old trees

same tree, or occasionally on different trees. In January the quarter-inch long, golden-yellow, pollen-bearing male, or staminate flowers shower the tree with gold and coat the snow as it lies on the branches. The female flowers develop on the ends of the past year's growth as small, light yellow-green cones with two to six pairs of leaf-like scales.

By late summer, following the appearance of the blossoms, small urn-shaped cones, from three-quarters to one and one-half inches long, develop and hang on the extreme ends of the branchlets. These cones somewhat resemble those of *Thuja*, or whiteceder, but they have only six leaf-like scales arranged in pairs, and they enclose one or two tiny, winged seeds. By September the cones open and great numbers of seeds drift down on the wind in such quantities as to form a red-brown carpet beneath the parent trees. The dry, yellow-brown cones cling to the trees for several months thereafter.

The widely buttressed bases of mature incensecedar trees are clothed in thick, shreddy, cinnamon-red bark which is deeply grooved and ridged. On young trees the bark is purplish red, flaky, and has a silver sheen on the loosened scales. Later it takes on a reddish brown hue which glows in the sunlight. The upper bark of old trees is two or three inches thick, while along the base it may be six or eight inches thick.

The soft, light brown wood is frequently tinged with red, although the sapwood is cream color. It has a compact, fine, straight grain, splits readily and evenly, and does not check or warp in seasoning. The wood weighs, when air dry, about twenty-five pounds to the cubic foot, is aromatic, takes a good polish and is extremely durable when seasoned. It is widely used for fence posts, railroad ties, shingles, and

Natural range of Incensecedar

NORTHERN WHITECEDAR

Eastern whitecedar, Eastern arborvitae

Thuja occidentalis Linnaeus

IN COOL swamps, or beside streams or lakes from Nova Scotia and New Brunswick west to southeastern Manitoba, and from New England and New York west to northern Minnesota, the narrow, pyramidal crowns of northern whitecedar, or arborvitae, make a familiar sight. Sometimes growing in pure, almost impenetrable stands, this species also flourishes in company with black and red spruce, red maple, larch, alder, and balsam fir. In moist fields and shallow, rocky pastures, it may grow in scattered picturesque clumps, the taller trees thrusting their conical crowns above the center of the group, while smaller trees crowd close around the outer edge.

Devereux Butcher

Northern Whitecedar has a shapely pyramidal crown of feathery dark green foliage

Under favorable conditions in the North, this tree occasionally attains seventy feet in height and three to six feet in diameter. Ordinarily, however, northern whitecedar trees are considered large when they are fifty to sixty feet tall, and have diameters of two to three feet. Southward, the tree becomes less abundant and smaller, so that in the mountains of western North Carolina and eastern Tennessee it is found only at high elevations where it is reduced to a shrub.

A slow growing tree, most of its wood is acquired during early years. It may reach ages of 250 to 300 years.

The smaller twigs and branchlets are so densely covered by scale-like leaves that they appear to be the leaves themselves. Actually, each leaf is scarcely a quarter of an inch long, and with its fellows is arranged in overlapping rows of alternating pairs on the flattened branchlets. The leaves are dark green above and light beneath.

In April or May small liver-colored flowers are borne on the ends of the branchlets, the two sexes being separate and distinct from one another. The solitary elongated staminate cones are about one-sixteenth of an inch long, entire, and composed of three to six pairs of stamens, while the purplish ovulate cones are similar in size and consist of four to six pairs of thin, elongated scales. By late summer the fertilized cones mature. They are a light yellow to cinnamon-red, from one-third to one-half inch long, stand erect on the twigs, and are extremely fragrant when broken. The seeds which form beneath the scales are light brown, about an eighth of an inch long and nearly encircled by thin wings. These help carry the seeds considerable distances.

The trunk may be lobed and buttressed at the base, tapering and often divided into two or more secondary stems. It is frequently distorted and twisted; similarly, the thin, fibrous, light brown bark may seem to spiral around the trunk. It is a quarter to a third of an inch thick. On the larger branches the bark is dark orange marked with shallow fissures.

The wood of northern whitecedar, or arborvitae, is pale yellow-brown, aromatic, soft, brittle, coarse-grained, and durable in contact with the soil. A cubic foot when air dry weighs about nineteen pounds. Surrounding the heartwood is a thin layer of nearly white sapwood. The wood is easy to work and has little tendency to shrink or warp. It splits easily, and the annual growth rings will separate from one another when the wood is pounded. This quality permitted the Indians to separate thin splints for use as canoe ribs. The same feature, however, reduces the value of this wood for many modern purposes and is characterized in many trees as "ring shake" or "wind shake." Because of its durability in contact with the soil and moisture, it is used for shingles, railroad ties, poles, fence posts, buckets, stave cooperage, tanks, cisterns, boats, and canoe frames. Because of its light weight, as well as its durability, it is also used for fish net floats and imitation minnows for fishermen. An aromatic oil is distilled from the leaves and twigs, which is sometimes used to relieve chest colds and for other medicinal purposes.

Thuja occidentalis is not a true cedar, but is more strictly speaking an arborvitae. *Thuja* is a Latin name for a conifer tree, while *occidentalis* refers to the fact that it is native to the western hemisphere and thereby distinct from the oriental cedar. American Indians referred to this tree as Oo-soo-ha-tah, meaning, "feather leaf."

Northern whitecedar once was of great importance in the Great Lakes region. In 1899 there was a lumber cut

The small scale-like leaves are in overlapping rows on the branchlets. The cones are urn-shaped and grow erect near the ends of the leafy twigs.

of 95,000,000 board feet, ninety percent of which came from the lake states.

This tree begins to bear seed when it is ten to fifteen years old. Seed-producing years follow frequently thereafter. The seeds germinate readily and may take root wherever the moist soil is exposed. Because of its trim, somewhat artificial appearance, northern whitecedar is frequently used for hedges and windbreaks. It also is planted as an ornamental tree on lawns and in parks, for which purpose it is ideally suited. Nurserymen recognize some forty-five varieties of northern whitecedar, all of which are propagated by means of cuttings rather than from seed.

Except as protected naturally by its moist environment, this cedar is easily injured by ground fires, but fortunately it has few serious insect or fungus enemies.

Deep fissures break the thin, orange-brown bark into narrow, interlacing ridges

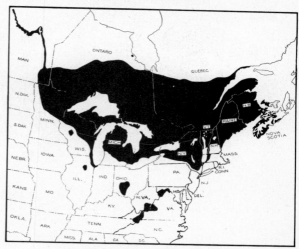

Natural range of Northern Whitecedar

WESTERN REDCEDAR

Giant arborvitae, Canoe cedar, Pacific redcedar, Shinglewood

Thuja plicata Donn

WESTERN REDCEDAR ranks among the large trees of the Pacific coast and is found from southern Alaska to northern California, on sites where the soil is moist. It grows at elevations ranging from sea level in the far

north to 7,000 feet in the northern Rocky Mountains. Those along the rainy, humid Pacific coast attain magnificent proportions, while those at high elevations in the Rockies are wind-blown and are reduced to the proportions of a shrub. Heavily buttressed trees 150 to 175 feet high and five to eight feet in diameter are fairly common, while exceptional trees attain heights of 190 to 200 feet, with occasional diameters of ten to sixteen feet. The centers of large trees usually are hollow.

In densely crowded stands the trees have long, clear trunks, frequently with branches below the main crown. The narrow conical crown of young trees reaches to the ground, and even in dense stands the lower branches are retained until the tree reaches heights of fifty to eighty feet. In old trees the crown extends in width, becoming short and blunt. On young trees the slender limbs curve upward, but with age they swing downward in a long graceful curve. While diameters of twenty-four to forty inches are reached in 200 to 500 years, some of the largest trees are believed to be 800 to 1,000 years old.

Small, scale-like, bright green, pleasantly fragrant leaves form flat, lacy sprays after the manner of the northern whitecedar, *Thuja occidentalis*. They are glossy above, distinctly darker and with white, triangular spots beneath, remain on the tree about three years.

The scientific name, *Thuja plicata*, is derived from Greek and Latin, and refers to a tree having sweet smelling wood whose leaves are plaited or folded.

In April, small, inconspicuous flowers of the two sexes appear, usually on different branches of the same tree. The flowers are about one-twelfth of an inch long and develop singly at the ends of the twigs. The staminate ones are yellowish and the ovulate are pinkish at the time of pollination. From the latter, leathery brown cones about one-half inch

Devereux Butcher

When Western Redcedar grows in densely crowded stands it reaches heights of 175 feet and more

Flat, lacy sprays of scale-like, bright green leaves and up-turned leathery brown cones characterize this tree

long comprised of six fertile scales, mature by the end of August. Each fertile scale may bear two tiny double-winged seeds which are shed in the fall of the same year. The upturned empty cones remain on the tree until the following summer. The cinnamon-red, stringy, fibrous bark is seldom over seven-eighths of an inch thick and so tough that the Indians peel strips twenty to thirty feet long from young trees for making baskets and even for rope or fish line. The strongly aromatic wood is reddish brown when freshly cut, but becomes dull brown with exposure. It is free from pitch, of medium to coarse grain, very soft and brittle, weighs twenty-four to thirty pounds to the cubic foot when air dry, and is unusually resistant to decay and insect attack. About half of all western redcedar goes into shingles of which it forms the bulk of our supply. Other uses include lumber, poles, posts, piling, boats, pattern stock, laundry machinery, cigar boxes, and greenhouse equipment. Paints, varnishes, and lacquers adhere to it well and it glues readily. Because it works easily and warps or shrinks but little, it is favored for the exterior of houses. The Indians of the Pacific Northwest used it for totem poles, canoes, and lodges.

Western redcedar does not grow in pure forests, but forms three to twelve percent of the total growth in company with Douglasfir and western hemlock.

The moist character of the sites where western redcedar grows is an important factor in protecting the tree against fire. The thin bark offers little fire resistance, so that when fires do occur the trees are usually fatally injured. In contrast, however, neither insects nor fungi are major sources of damage.

Although few efforts have been made to use this species for reforestation, it is recognized as a conifer of unusual promise for ornamental planting on the west coast, as well as in the eastern states as far north as Massachusetts. It assumes a graceful pyramidal outline and prospers in fertile well drained soil.

The cinnamon-red, fibrous bark is less than an inch thick

Natural range of Western Redcedar

133

MONTEREY CYPRESS

Cupressus macrocarpa Hartweg

MONTEREY CYPRESS, in its natural habitat, occupies the smallest area of any American conifer. South of Monterey Bay on the coast of California, it occurs in a narrow strip just two miles long, from Cypress Point to the south shores of Carmel Bay and on Point Lobos. Scattered, gnarled and twisted trees, constantly buffeted by the wind, cling to rocky sea cliffs. Elsewhere they form very dense stands. On the east of this limited area they mingle with Monterey pine and occasionally with Gowen cypress.

In youth, the tree has a form entirely different from its mature shape. The trunk is sharply conical when the tree is young, and the crown rigidly straight. Slender branches trend upward in a wide, sharp-pointed pyramid. Such trees may be from forty to fifty feet high and eighteen to twenty inches in diameter. Later, the height growth—rarely more than sixty-feet—ceases, and, if the trees have room enough, the branches develop into long, massive limbs, eventually reaching up to the height of the leader and spreading out into a very wide, flat-topped or umbrella-shaped crown.

The crown of crowded old trees is similar, but not so broad. Exposed to the sea winds, some trunks and their enormously developed limps sprawl on the ground and are grotesquely bent and gnarled.

The stout twigs are at first completely covered with the scale-like, closely overlapping leaves. These fall at the end of three or four years and expose the thin, light or dark reddish brown bark, which separates into small, papery scales. The minute, dark yellow-green leaves are closely attached to the branchlets, their sharp points sometimes standing out slightly from the twigs. In late February or early March, the tiny yellow flowers appear, the male and female at the ends of different twigs on the same tree.

Clustered on short, stout stems, the oblong cones, one to one and a half inches long, and two-thirds of an inch in diameter, are composed of four or six pairs of scales with broadly ovate, thickened projections. The scales of the upper and lower pairs are sterile and smaller than the others. The cones mature by August of the second season, when they are ashy brown. They open slowly, shedding their russet-brown seeds during autumn, after which they remain on the tree for several or many seasons. From eighteen to twenty angled seeds, about one-sixteenth of an inch long, are borne under each fertile cone scale. They are rather heavy and usually lodge near the parent tree.

Point Lobos, within Point Lobos Reserve State Park, contains a small, natural grove of the trees. This well may be the finest existing natural stand of the species. Reproduction of the tree in the area has been extremely low—a fact that has concerned authorities. The area is popular, and trampling by visitors may have had some effect on this in the past. Since the early 1950's, however, the California Division of Beaches and Parks has made a determined and quite successful effort to remedy this by encouraging visitors to walk only on the carefully laid out trail that encircles the grove.

The bark of mature Monterey cypress trunks is about seven-eighths of an inch thick. On the surface, it is weathered to an ashy white, but beneath, it is a deep red-brown, the same color as that of the protected bark of limbs and young trees. Old bark is firm and narrowly seamed with a network of narrow, vertical ridges and smaller diagonal ones.

Ralph D. Cornell

Exposed to sea winds, Monterey Cypress often takes on a grotesque appearance with its gnarled, massive limbs sprawling along the ground. In height, it seldom exceeds sixty feet

Weathered to an ashy white on the surface, old bark is red-brown beneath, and is less than an inch thick

Ashy brown, oblong cones, clustered on stout stems, mature by August. Branchlets are covered with minute, sharp-pointed, yellow-green leaves

Monterey Cypress occupies the smallest area of any American conifer, occurring south of Monterey Bay in California

The fine-grained wood is heavy, hard, strong and very durable. It is clear yellow-brown, with streaks of rose-red and dull yellow, and it has a faint, aromatic, "cedar-like" odor.

The poor timber form of the tree, along with its very limited available supply, prevent the wood from becoming commercially important. It is important, however, as one of the rare forest trees capable of forming a cover on the wind-swept coast, even down to the water's edge. The few trees on the shore of Monterey Bay appear to be the last remnant of a species which once was more extensive.

Apparently the tree's former range was principally on land now swallowed up by the encroaching ocean. There is no danger of its becoming extinct, however, because it is extensively cultivated. It is widely planted in this and other countries and, when grown under favorable conditions, it is graceful and symmetrical. Used extensively in California for windbreaks, its vigorous, rather rapid growth in early life makes it exceedingly useful for this purpose. The trees also serve as hedges and for ornamental purposes, and are very valuable for protective planting in dry situations. Occasionally grown in the southeastern states, Monterey cypress has been much planted in western and southern Europe, temperate South America, and in Australia and New Zealand. The seeds, which are produced in large quantities every year, have a high rate of germination, and the seedlings grow very rapidly. It also grows from cuttings.

While Monterey cypress makes rather rapid growth in early life, it grows slowly after its usual height is reached. Trees from fourteen to nineteen inches in diameter are from sixty to eighty-five years old. Although little is known of its longevity, some of the larger trees in its native habitat are believed to be more than 200 years old. The bark is too thin to protect the tree from severe fires, but it seems to be quite free from any serious fungus diseases or insect attacks.

135

ARIZONA CYPRESS

Arizona smooth cypress
Cupressus arizonica Greene

ARIZONA CYPRESS belongs to the genus of the true cypresses. *Cupressus* is an ancient genus, representatives of which, now extinct, once grew in Greenland and western Europe. The twelve species known today are confined to western North America, Mexico, southeastern Europe, southwestern Asia, the Himalayas and China. About eight species have been described as growing within the United States.

Arizona cypress is readily distinguished from other trees in its range by its conspicuous blue-green foliage. The species has been found to comprise two varieties because of differences in the bark. The more northerly, *Cupressus arizonica* var. *glabra* (Sudw.) Little, commonly referred to as Arizona smooth cypress, inhabits a number of sites in the mountains of central Arizona. The other, *C. arizonica* var. *arizonica*, sometimes called Arizona rough cypress, occurs at several sites in southeastern Arizona and southward in Chichuahua, Coahuila, Durango and Zacatecas, Mexico. Both varieties prefer moist, protected, gravelly north slopes and canyon bottoms at 4500 to 8000 feet elevation. On exposed, dry, sterile, rocky mountain slopes and canyons, the trees are often stunted. They usually grow in dense, pure stands, but occasionally associate with live oak and Arizona ponderosa pine, *Pinus ponderosa* var. *arizonica*.

Trees growing in the most favorable locations are characterized by straight, rather rapidly tapering trunks which are clothed for half their length in narrow, dense, conical crowns composed of large, horizontal branches and long, slender leaders. This feature distinguishes the species, even at a distance, from its associated trees. Such trees are from fifty to eighty feet high and two to four feet in diameter. Young trees of this type are particularly straight, with very sharp-pointed crowns and horizontal branches. In unfavorable locations they develop broad, rounded or flat crowns, seldom reach a height of more than twenty-five or thirty feet, and have very little clear stem. Arizona cypress is of considerable importance in assisting to form a protective cover for the prevention of soil erosion on mountain slopes and on the steep sides of canyons.

The minute, overlapping, scale-like, sharp-pointed leaves, about one-sixteenth of an inch long, are pale green with a silvery hue that is especially pronounced in young trees. They are very finely toothed on the margins and the branchlets are arranged in four ranks and irregularly disposed, although rarely they may occur in flattened sprays. When bruised, the foliage has a strong odor. Indeed, the trees themselves give off an odor which often can be detected for a considerable distance.

The tiny yellow flowers, which appear in early spring at the ends of twigs, are very inconspicuous. Male and female flowers are borne on the same tree. The male flowers are oblong, about a fourth of an inch in length, blunt at the apex, and their six or eight stamens have broad yellow connections.

The dark reddish brown cones are from seven-eighths of an inch to one inch long when mature, are somewhat longer than broad and are attached to the twig by a short, stout stalk one-quarter to one-half inch in length. They have six or occasionally eight scales, each with a central, prickle-like projection. Ripening in September

George D. Russell

Arizona Cypress, with a straight, rapidly tapering trunk, may be fifty to eighty feet tall in favorable locations

at the end of the second season, they remain on the trees for many years, becoming ashy gray with age. There are from six to twenty oblong to nearly triangular, purplish brown seeds to each cone scale. They usually are about an eighth inch long and have narrow, thin wings.

After the leaves fall, the red-brown, stout twigs are smooth and covered with a blue-white bloom. On young branches and trunks, the bark of var. *glabra*—smooth cypress—has irregular, narrow, thin, curling scales that peel; while that of var. *arizonica* is thinly shredded and on older trunks furrowed into long, narrow, flat ridges that separate into persistent shreds. On both varieties, the bark on old trunks becomes an inch and a quarter thick.

The wood, of little value, is soft and light weight, the heartwood a light brown-yellow and the sapwood pale yellow. It is durable in contact with the soil, serving local demands for posts, stakes and corral poles.

Arizona cypress was introduced in England, France and Germany in the late 1800's, and cultivated. It is also a valuable ornamental in northern United States. Several horticultural varieties include one with intensely silver-gray foliage.

W. A. Jackson

Unlike the furrowed bark of **C. arizonica** var. **arizonica,** with its narrow, flat, continuous ridges, that of var. **glabra,** shown here, peels in thin curling plates

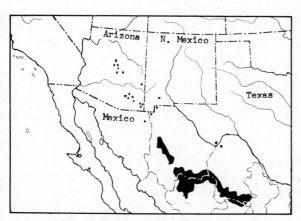

The natural range of var. **glabra** is in central Arizona; that of var. **arizonica** to the southeast

Charles F. Steiger

The sharp-pointed, overlapping pale green leaves have a silvery hue and are finely toothed on the margins

Growth is slow, especially on poor soils. Trees twelve inches and more in diameter may be from 100 to 300 or as much as 400 years old.

Although abundant crops of seed are produced every year, reproduction is often scanty. This is because many of the seeds fall on steep, rocky slopes where there is little or no soil, or where they may be washed away. Seedlings are produced in large numbers, however, when the seeds land on moist, comparatively rich soil in protected places.

In some parts of its range, repeated forest fires have destroyed the stand of Arizona cypress over large areas, so that the tree occurs chiefly in patches and in rather small isolated groups.

Charles F. Steiger

Dark reddish brown cones are somewhat longer than broad, and have six or eight scales

137

ATLANTIC WHITECEDAR

Swamp cedar, Southern white-cedar

Chamaecyparis thyoides (L.)

Britton, Stearns and Poggenberg

H. S. Graves

In the South the Atlantic Whitecedar attains a height of from 70 to 100 feet, but is somewhat smaller in the North

OF ALL the names given to trees and woods probably the term "cedar" is the most confusing. Originally applied to the genus *Cedrus*, it has been used for many kinds of trees. For example, the Spanish cedar (*Cedrela odorata*) is so called because of the aromatic odor of the wood. "Whitecedar" is used as one word to indicate that it is not a true cedar.

Atlantic whitecedar is a tree of the eastern coastal region, although it is also found on the eastern Gulf coast. From southern Maine to southeastern Mississippi it grows almost entirely in fresh water swamps, on lands subject to frequent overflow, and along small streams. Few forest trees grow in denser stands. It often occupies extensive areas to the exclusion of all other trees.

In the most favorable locations this graceful and symmetrical tree extends its spire-like head to a height of 100 feet or more. The crown is composed of slender horizontal limbs with somewhat drooping branchlets. Trees in the forest have long straight trunks and short narrow crowns. In open-grown trees, the crown is longer and has more taper and the trunk is much more limby. The average height is seventy to eighty feet, with a trunk diameter of two to three or four feet. In its northern range the tree is much smaller.

The slender twigs, arranged in fan-shaped sprays, are bluish green at first, becoming light reddish brown during their first winter and eventually, dark brown.

The minute, scale-like, closely overlapping leaves, one-sixteenth to one-eighth of an inch long, are closely appressed and clothe the twigs to the extreme end, making flattened sprays. On vigorous shoots the leaves spread somewhat toward the ends of the twigs. The buds are without scales, are small, and inconspicuous, and are protected by the scale-like leaves.

The flowers, which appear in early spring, are very small, inconspicuous bodies at the ends of the twigs, the male and female being borne on different branches of the same tree. The staminate are dark brown below the middle and nearly black toward the apex, oblong, four-sided, and about one-fourth of an inch long. The pistillate flowers are nearly spherical, pale liver-colored, about one-eighth of an inch in diameter and consist of three pairs of ovate, acute, spreading scales set at right angles, with minute, black ovules on their inner sides.

Standing erect on short leafy branchlets, the spherical cones, about one-fourth of an inch in diameter, are light green when fully grown, changing to bluish purple and finally dark reddish brown when ripe. They mature at the end of the first season, opening in September and October, and remain on the tree for two or three years. The cone scales end in sharp points and each fertile scale bears from one to three rounded, slightly compressed, gray-brown seeds about one-eighth of an inch long, with wings about as broad as the seed and darker in color.

Large crops of seed are produced nearly every year, some trees beginning to bear at the age of four or five years. The small seeds are widely distributed by wind.

The reddish brown bark is quite smooth and thin on small branches and young trees. On the trunks of old mature trees, however, it is divided irregularly into narrow, flat, connected ridges, gray on the surface and separating into long, loose, plate-like scales, which peel off into tough fibrous strips.

The wood is generally straight-grained, with a fine and uniform texture. It is light in weight, a cubic foot of air-dried wood weighing about twenty-three pounds, moderately soft, weak, and low in shock-resisting ability. It shrinks and warps very little in drying, holds paint well, and is easy to work with tools. The heartwood is light brown tinged with red or pink, the thin sapwood lighter. The wood has a slightly spicy, aromatic odor when freshly cut. In resistance to decay the heartwood ranks with the most durable woods, and because of its durability, much of it is used for siding, porch lumber, shingles, poles, small boats, tanks, and pails and tubs, especially ice cream packing tubs, where its light weight is an additional advantage. It is very suitable for telephone poles because the trunk is straight with a uniform and moderate taper and is usually free from limbs for the greater part of its length, and because the wood is durable and light.

There were formerly large stands of Atlantic whitecedar in the swamps of southern New Jersey and in the Dismal Swamp region of Virginia.

Because of its thin bark and highly inflammable foliage, the tree is very susceptible to damage by fire. It is nearly free from insect attack, however, and only slightly susceptible to fungi. It is occasionally planted as an ornamental tree, and will grow under cultivation on almost any soil. There are several horticultural varieties.

L. W. Brownell

Minute, scale-like, closely overlapping leaves clothe the twigs to the extreme ends, making flattened sprays

L. W. Brownell

Small and inconspicuous, male and female flowers appear at the ends of different branches on the same tree

L. W. Brownell

The short, spherical cones are light green when fully grown, later bluish purple, and reddish brown when ripe

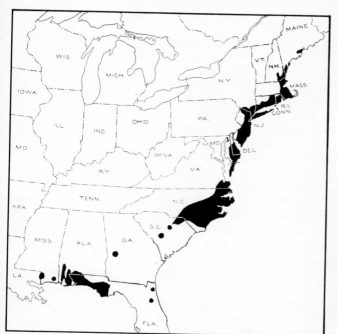

From Maine to Mississippi the Whitecedar is found almost entirely in fresh water swamps and along small streams

U. S. Forest Service

Old mature trunks are shaggy in appearance, the gray bark being divided irregularly into narrow flat ridges

PORT ORFORD WHITECEDAR

Port Orford cedar, Lawson false-cypress, Lawson cypress, Oregon cedar

Chamaecyparis lawsoniana (Murray) Parlatore

A NARROW strip of coast range, from the vicinity of Coos Bay in southwestern Oregon, to the Mad River, south of Eureka in northwestern California, and extending ten to forty miles back from the sea, marks the limited range of Port Orford whitecedar. Here temperatures are moderate, with heavy precipitation, high humidity, and many cloudy days.

This, the largest of three North American members of the genus *Chamaecyparis*, has three other relatives in Japan. Heights of eighty to 175 feet, and occasionally of 200 feet, with diameters of twelve feet, belie the Greek word *"chamai"* meaning "on the ground," which, combined with *"kyparissos"* or "cypress," makes *Chamaecyparis*. The specific name, *lawsoniana*, honors Sir Charles Lawson, a Scottish economist in whose nursery were raised the first seedlings from seeds which William Murray gathered in the canyon of the Sacramento River, in 1854. The larger stands of timber were reported in 1855 from the Coos Bay area.

Diameters of three to seven feet are probably attained in 300 to 350 years, while the largest trees may be 600 years old. Best growth is attained on moist hillsides or canyon bottoms, but the dry, sandy ridges on the western slopes of the coast ranges support trees up to 5,000 feet above sea level. A narrow crown terminating in a nodding, spire-like head, with its main part composed of horizontal or somewhat pendulous branches with fine, flattened, lacy sprays, takes up a quarter to a third of the full height of forest-grown trees. Heavy buttresses mark the base of the larger trees, but these rapidly contract to form round, full stems. The trunks of forest trees may be clear of branches for 150 feet, but the drooping branches of open-grown trees extend to the ground.

Bright green scale-like leaves about one-sixteenth of an inch long, pressed flat, one overlapping another, thickly clothe the branchlets. Each leaf becomes nearly a quarter of an inch long and more loosely spreading near the ends of the leading shoots. Each leaf is glandular on the back, with white stomatiferous lines below. They turn bright red-brown and fall during the third year.

The pollen-bearing catkins are bright red and appear in early spring. Small reddish brown ovulate cones of about seven scales appear at the same time. By early autumn these mature as clear, dark russet-brown, berry-like cones about one-third of an inch in diameter. Each is composed of three pairs of shield-shaped scales overlapping one another to form a series of x-like markings. The erect cones release their two to four small wing-margined seeds late in September or early October.

After about twelve years, trees begin bearing seed crops during alternate years and continue into advanced age. The seeds have a high percentage of germination, but must encounter suitable conditions soon after release. They are

George Grant

Fine lacy sprays droop from the short conical crown of tall forest-grown Port Orford Whitecedar

140

seldom carried far from the parent tree. Seedlings can grow in shade or full sunlight, and so take over available open sites, regardless of whether the areas have been burned. Exceedingly dense cover suppresses the seeds and eventually kills them.

The reddish brown, fibrous bark may become six to ten inches thick, and is divided into broad ridges marked by loose, thin shreds and separated by deep irregular longitudinal fissures.

The even-grained wood of Port Orford whitecedar is moderately soft, durable, and weighs about twenty-nine pounds to the cubic foot when air dry. Its nearly white sapwood is scarcely distinguishable from the yellowish white heartwood. It is easily worked, will take a high polish, holds paint well, and is easy to season. Because of its resistance to the action of acids, one of Port Orford whitecedar's most important uses is for storage battery separators.

Other commercial uses include Venetian blind slats, millwork, deck and boat construction, railway ties, mine timbers, and flooring. An abundance or resin gives an aromatic ginger-like odor which causes the wood to be sought for mothproof box and closet linings. An oil is also distilled from the wood for use in soap.

Devereux Butcher

Three pairs of shield-shaped scales combine to form the small cones which stand erect among the feathery sprays of scale-like foliage

The sawtimber stand of Port Orford whitecedar has been greatly depleted. In 1930 the stand in western Oregon was placed at nearly 1,400,000,000 board feet and, in 1942, only about half of it remained, with a total stand for the United States of approximately 745,000,000 board feet. The most accessible stands have now been cut. The lumber cut in the early 1940's was in excess of 50,000,000 feet.

Limited pure stands of Port Orford whitecedar occur in the vicinity of Coos Bay, Oregon. It usually constitutes less than one-fourth of the stand, being associated with Sitka spruce, western redcedar, Douglasfir, western hemlock and grand fir. In the southern part of its range, this tree inhabits areas occupied by redwood, red fir, California laurel and occasionally ponderosa pine and sugar pine. Stands of 20,000 board feet to the acre are common, with occasional acres measuring 100,000 board feet.

The thick bark protects mature trees, but heavy losses result when fire runs through young growth. It has few insect enemies and the wood is highly resistant to decay.

In the ornamental trade, this tree is known as Lawson false-cypress. Since its introduction, shortly after 1854, some seventy varieties and forms have been planted in northern Europe, New Zealand, and America, and it is hardy as far north as Massachusetts.

W. J. Allyn

The reddish brown fibrous bark is six to ten inches thick

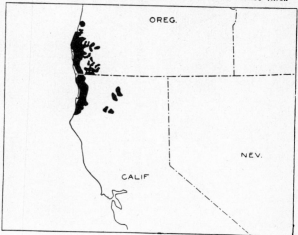

Natural range of Port Orford Whitecedar

ALASKA YELLOW-CEDAR

Nootka false-cypress, Alaska cypress, Sitka cypress, Yellow cypress
Chamaecyparis nootkatensis (D. Don) Spach

LIKE the other western "cedars," Alaska yellow-cedar has a very limited range, occurring in the Pacific coast region from southeastern Alaska southward through British Columbia and Washington, to southern Oregon. In Washington and Oregon it is usually confined to the western side of the Cascade Mountains and is not often found

Alaska Yellow-cedar is a medium-sized tree, usually not over 80 feet in height with a trunk two to three feet in diameter

below an elevation of 2,000 feet. It grows chiefly in moist, rocky or gravelly soils and is commonly found on bottomlands, along streams, in basins, valleys and gulches and on mountain slopes. The principal forests, suitable for commercial timber, are situated in northern Washington, on the west slope of the Cascades and in the Olympic Mountains.

Alaska yellow-cedar is a medium-sized tree, usually not more than eighty feet in height, with a trunk two or three feet in diameter. It takes about 250 years to produce a tree two feet in diameter and the largest trees are between 500 and 600 years old. On high, exposed slopes it assumes a sprawling form, and it may even become prostrate on wholly unprotected sites. In the forest it usually develops a broadly buttressed, often fluted, base and rapidly tapering bole, which is often clear for about one-half its length. The conical crown is composed of numerous drooping branches with long, pendulous, flattened sprays of foliage. While the sprays droop in most of the "cedars," in no other is this drooping as marked and picturesque as in the Alaska yellow-cedar, whose twigs actually look limp as they hang from the branches. The branches themselves, few and distant from each other, have a tendency to droop and the whip-like leader is too weak at its tip to stand erect and bends over gracefully. This "weeping" appearance given by the drooping branches distinguishes the tree from western redcedar, for which it might be mistaken on casual observation. The leaves and the wood of the two trees are also distinctly different.

Alaska yellow-cedar is often called yellow cypress and yellow cedar, from the color of the wood. Sitka cypress is another common name.

The scale-like, blue-green leaves, about one-eighth inch long, are closely appressed, overlapping like tiny shingles. While they closely resemble those of the western redcedar, they can be distinguished from the latter, with which it is often associated, by their distinctive, sharp, spreading points, which make the spray harsh to the touch.

The minute, inconspicuous flowers appear in April, the staminate, or pollen-bearing ones on lateral branchlets of the previous year and the pistillate, or female ones clustered near the ends of the branchlets. The very small, spherical, reddish brown cones, about one-half inch long, stand erect on the branchlets, ripening in September or October, when they open slowly to shed their seeds. Each cone is made up of from four to six scales, each with a blunt, horny point. Under each scale there are from two to four seeds; they measure about one-quarter inch in length and the thin, lateral wings are about twice as wide as the body of the seed.

The fibrous bark is thin, rarely over one-half inch in thickness, even on old trees, and affords poor protection against fire, which, the tree rarely survives. It is ashy brown on the outside, and clear, reddish cinnamon-brown when broken. The surface is irregularly and rather finely

U. S. Forest Service
The blue-green leaves are about one-eighth of an inch long.
The minute, inconspicuous flowers generally appear in April

Asahel Curtis
The reddish brown cones ripen in September or October.
About a half-inch long, they stand erect on the branchlets

broken by shallow seams; the thin, flat ridges have frequent diagonal cross connections, and flake off in long, narrow strips.

The fine and even-textured wood of Alaska yellow-cedar is moderately heavy, moderately strong, moderately hard, is easily worked, shrinks little in drying, and ranks with the most durable species such as baldcypress in resistance to decay. It weighs about thirty-one pounds a cubic foot when air dry. Its bright, clear yellow heartwood is hardly distinguishable from the thin, white to yellowish sapwood. A large part of the cut of Alaska yellow-cedar is used locally for interior finish, furniture, small boat hulls, cabinet work and novelties.

The comparatively limited supply is likely always to confine the usefulness of this wood to a few special but, nevertheless, important purposes, such as small boat construction, for which it is especially well suited, competing with Port Orford whitecedar for that purpose. Other specialty uses are patterns, pyrography, and canoe paddles.

Alaska yellow-cedar generally produces a small amount of seed each year, but large crops are released at irregular and infrequent intervals. The percentage of survival is never very great.

This species is often cultivated as an ornamental, and, when well-grown, makes a handsome, narrow, pyramidal tree with attractive dark-green foliage. The several horticultural varieties of Alaska yellow-cedar have been planted in the Middle Atlantic States, California, and commonly in the countries of western and central Europe. The variety *pendula* has spreading branches and long pendulous-branchlets.

Repeated fires often destroy the young growth and also inflict serious damage on the older trees. Alaska yellow-cedar is quite often free from fungus attacks.

Although long-lived, the tree grows very slowly in height and diameter, requiring 200 years to reach sawtimber size. Trees from fifteen to twenty inches in diameter are from 200 to 275 years old.

Alaska yellow-cedar is very important as an associate of other trees capable of forming protective cover on cold, high slopes, where it grows with mountain hemlock, lodgepole pine, alpine, silver and noble fir, Douglasfir, western larch, western white pine and Engelmann spruce. At lower elevations it occurs with Sitka spruce, western redcedar, western hemlock and grand fir. Sometimes it grows in pure stands of limited extent.

R. L. Putnam
The ashy brown fibrous bark has an irregular surface broken by shallow seams. It is thin — rarely over a half inch thick

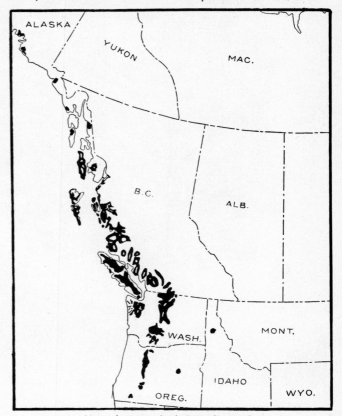
Natural range of Alaska Yellow-cedar

EASTERN REDCEDAR

Red juniper
Juniperus virginiana Linnaeus

Devereux Butcher

The slender columnar form of Eastern Redcedar is most frequently
seen, but with age the crown becomes broader and more open

FENCE ROWS bordering pastures and abandoned fields, dry gravelly slopes, rocky ridges, limestone outcroppings, and even swamps and lake borders over most of the eastern half of the country from the Atlantic seaboard to the Great Plains are frequently accented by the dense evergreen pyramids or columns of eastern redcedar.

Ordinarily a tree twenty to fifty feet tall with a short trunk one to two feet in diameter, on alluvial soils in the southern states, it may attain heights up to 120 feet and produce a deeply fluted trunk four feet in diameter. On poor soil in the North, redcedar may live for years, becoming scarcely larger than a bush. Growing slowly, trees sixteen inches to two feet in diameter may be 130 to 150 years old, but the larger ones live 300 years or more.

A juniper rather than a true cedar, this species of *Juniperus* was distinguished by the name *virginiana* because the first botanical specimens were from the Virginia colony. The family is one of great antiquity, and the early forms of some thirty-five known species are found in glacial deposits throughout the world. None occurs or ever has been found south of the equator. Of the eleven species native to the United States, redcedar is the most widely distributed and most important.

Each tree bears two forms of tiny evergreen leaves. Those on seedlings and vigorous twigs are sharp pointed, blue-green and awl-shaped, while most or all of the twigs of mature trees are covered with closely pressed, overlapping, scale-like leaves that occur in opposite pairs. They remain five or six years on the branches, growing browner with each year.

From February to May, small inconspicuous male and female flowers appear on different trees, and occasionally on the same tree. By autumn, the ovulate flowers develop dark blue, fleshy, highly aromatic, berry-like cones, each containing one or two and rarely three or four tiny, wingless chestnut-brown seeds. The cones are covered with a white powdery bloom that makes them appear to be pale blue-green. Not only do these furnish food for birds and small mammals, but they possess medicinal values and are used to flavor gin. Crops of berries are abundant every two or three years, but only one-third to two-thirds of the seeds are capable of germination. Natural reproduction of redcedar is by seed only, and the seeds often are scattered by birds.

The shreddy, light red-brown bark is scarcely more than one-eighth to a quarter of an inch thick, and it peels off in narrow, fibrous strips. The trunk is often so grooved as to suggest that the tree may have had difficulty in growing. It was the red of both the bark and the wood that led the French of Canada to call this cedar *baton rouge*, meaning red stick. Finding the same tree in Louisiana, they gave this name to their state capital, Baton Rouge.

The slow-grown, fine-grained, brittle, highly aromatic wood is bright pinkish red to deep reddish brown, surrounded by a thin layer of nearly white sapwood. A cubic foot when air dry weighs only thirty-one to thirty-three pounds and because of its soft texture, easy working qualities, fragrance, ability to take a high polish, and durability, it finds an active demand for lead pencils, lining for clothes chests and closets, cigar boxes, canoes, and a wide variety of wooden-ware. Cedar oil is distilled from the leaves and twigs. The scattered stands of this species prevent any satisfactory estimate of the existing volume of redcedar, and for the same reason the commercial production is largely in the form of small lots of short logs

Ernest Crandall

Dark purplish blue berries grow on the sprays of tiny evergreen leaves of Eastern Redcedar

which farmers haul to local markets.

A few destructive boring insects feed on living and dead trees and bagworms occasionally eat the foliage. The chief enemy, however, is fire, for the thin bark and shallow root system leaves redcedar an easy victim of relatively light surface fires. In mixture with other trees, such as the ashes, maples, oaks, hickories, beech, loblolly pine, black gum, and cypress, it is less seriously affected by fire. Wood rots do considerable damage to southern trees, and as the alternate host of the cedar apple rust, it is considered a menace wherever apple growing is of first importance.

Extensively used for ornamental planting, over thirty horticultural forms of redcedar are recognized. It will grow on almost any soil except that which is distinctly swampy.

The shreddy, light reddish brown bark is from an eighth to a quarter of an inch thick

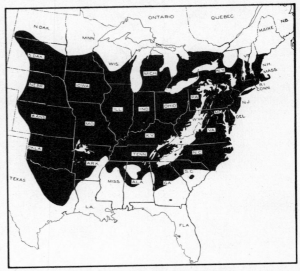

Natural range of Eastern Redcedar

145

ROCKY MOUNTAIN JUNIPER

Rocky Mountain redcedar

Juniperus scopulorum Sargent

FROM THE eastern foothills of the Rocky Mountains in Alberta, southward to New Mexico and westward to the coast of British Columbia and Washington to eastern Oregon, Nevada and nothern Arizona, Rocky Mountain juniper occurs as a scattered tree, often singly, on dry ridges and mountain slopes, and also on rather moist canyon bottoms where the best form occurs. Growing at elevations of 5000 feet in the south, it descends to sea level along the Washington and British Columbia coasts in the north.

In open situations the tree is somewhat shrubby, from fifteen to twenty feet tall, with a short trunk from six to ten inches in diameter, and it has a rather narrow, rounded crown of large, long upward-reaching limbs. The trunk often is divided near the ground into a number of stout, spreading stems. In sheltered canyons, the tree develops a single straight trunk from twenty - five to thirty or more feet high, with trunk diameters from twelve to eighteen inches, supporting a slender, branched crown. In some localities the tree is known as a "weeping juniper," because the ends of the branches and twigs droop.

The slender twigs are at first four-sided, becoming round at the end of three or four years, and are clothed with smooth, pale bark which separates later into thin scales.

The minute, awl-shaped leaves, about an eighth of an inch long, are closely appressed, and occur in four rows of alternately opposite pairs.

A shrubby tree 15 to 20 feet tall, Rocky Mountain Juniper has a short trunk that sometimes is as large in diameter as eighteen inches

Sharp and often taper-pointed, they have smooth margins, are pale to dark green and are covered with a whitish bloom.

The flowers are inconspicuous. The staminate or pollen-bearing ones are oblong and about one-twelfth of an inch in length. The pistillate or seed-bearing flowers have a few sharp or taper-pointed, widely spreading scales.

Ripening at the end of the second season, the nearly spherical fruit, a quarter to a third of an inch in diameter, is smooth and clear blue in color. Like the leaves, it has a whitish bloom which covers the thin, blackish skin. In the sweet resinous pulp, there are two (sometimes one) shiny, brown, sharp-pointed seeds about a sixth of an inch long, with a thick, bony outer coat, conspicuously grooved and angled and marked at the base by a short, two-parted scar.

The tree is quite commonly known as Rocky Mountain redcedar and sometimes as western redcedar, but because this species is not a true cedar, the name juniper, derived from the scientific generic name, is preferred.

The somewhat stringy bark is dark reddish brown or gray, tinged with red on the surface, and is divided by shallow fissures into a network of flat, connected ridges that are broken into persistent, shreddy scales.

The heartwood is dull red or, more often, rather bright rose-red with a thick layer of white sapwood. It is fine grained and durable and although similar in its properties to that of the eastern redcedar, *Juniperus virginiana*, and is suitable for the same uses, it is not likely to be of much economic importance because of the scattered occurrence of the tree and because of its small size. Locally it is used for fence posts because of its resistance to decay and, in some areas, because of the scarcity of other suitable timber.

Rocky Mountain juniper is a slow-growing tree and is rather long-lived. Measurements of individuals with diameters of from six to eight inches show them to be 130 to 175 years old. Because this species thrives on dry sites that are unsuitable for other tree species, it deserves the forester's attention for planting.

U. S. Forest Service

Minute, pointed, appressed leaves cover the twigs. The blue, spherical fruits ripen in their second year

U. S. Forest Service

The stringy, dark reddish brown or gray bark is divided by shallow fissures into a network of flat, confluent ridges

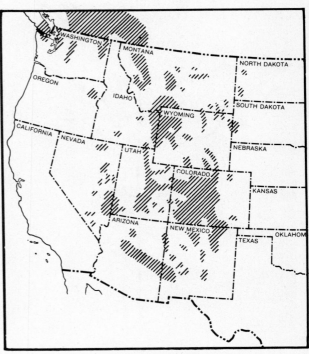

Natural range of Rocky Mountain Juniper

147

UTAH JUNIPER

Bigberry juniper, Sabina
Juniperus osteosperma (Torrey) Little

UTAH, or desert, juniper is the most abundant and widely distributed tree of the Great Basin. Its range extends from southeastern Idaho south through most of Utah, southwestern Wyoming and western Colorado, west through northern Arizona and southern Nevada to the foothills of the Sierra Nevada in California, northwest along these mountains to Lake Tahoe, Nevada, and thence northeast through northeastern Nevada.

Growing extensively on sites which might otherwise be devoid of tree growth, it is found in dry, rocky, gravelly and sandy soils, on desert foothills and mountain slopes, generally from 5,000 to 8,000 feet above sea level. It occurs in rather open and scattered pure stands or mixed with singleleaf pinyon and desert shrubs.

Commonly a low, short-trunked tree, it often assumes a bushy, many-stemmed form with a wide, rounded, rather open crown of numerous upright, crumpled limbs. The largest specimens attain heights of twenty feet and diameters of twelve inches, but they are usually from six to twelve feet high, with base diameters from four to eight inches. Growth is very slow and trees from six to ten inches in diameter are from 145 to 250 years old. The trunk is apt to be one-sided, with conspicuous folds and ridges covered with an ashy gray or light gray bark, which is divided into long, thin, persistent, fibrous scales. The slender, stiff-looking yellow-green branchlets are covered with a thin, light red-brown scaly bark.

The minute, sharp, scale-like, pale yellowish green leaves, about one-eighth of an inch long, are mostly in alternately opposite pairs, and they closely overlap each other in four rows; sometimes they are arranged in six rows, with three leaves at a joint. Leaves of leading shoots are much larger and keenly pointed, while those of seedlings are needle-like. With the aid of a hand lens, minute teeth may be seen on the leaf margins. The leaves of each season's growth persist for ten to twelve years. As in other junipers, the foliage, when crushed, gives off a pungently aromatic odor.

U. S. Forest Service

A short-trunked tree, Utah Juniper often assumes a bushy, many-stemmed form with a rounded, open crown of upright, crumpled limbs. Large specimens attain heights of twenty feet

148

The flowers are minute and inconspicuous. As with junipers generally, the pollen-bearing male flowers are usually borne on different trees from those which bear the fruit-developing female flowers. Occasionally, however, male and female flowers are found on the same tree.

The ripe "berries," which mature in September of the second year, are about one-third of an inch long and are marked by the more or less prominent tips of the flower scales, which are, in fact, similar to the scales of woody cones, but which have become fleshy and have united to form the berry-like fruit. Containing one or rarely two seeds, the berries are covered with a pale bloom which, when rubbed off, exposes a smooth, red-brown, tough skin. The seeds are pointed at the top, are prominently and sharply angled, and marked nearly to the top by what appears to be scale-like basal covering (the seed scar), to which the thin, sweet pulp is attached.

The pulpy flesh of the berries is juicy or mealy, rather sweet and strongly aromatic because of the presence of resin cells. It is eaten fresh by Indians, or is ground and baked into cakes. Birds eat the fruit of junipers, but the hard, bony seeds are entirely unaffected by digestion, except that it is believed to facilitate, in some degree, their germination. Both birds and mammals play a most important part in the dissemination of these seeds. Without their aid, dissemination would be exceedingly slow on level ground, where the heavy berries lie as they fall beneath the mother tree. On slopes, however, they may be carried far by water washing the surface soil.

The light yellowish brown heartwood has a less pungent odor than that of other junipers. The thick sapwood is nearly white. Although the heartwood is very durable, the tree is not adapted to commercial use because it is too small and unsuitably shaped to be converted into lumber. Wherever it is sufficiently abundant, however, it finds important domestic use for fuel and fence posts; but this is because of the scarcity of other trees.

The heavily ridged ashy gray bark is divided into long, thin, persistent fibrous scales

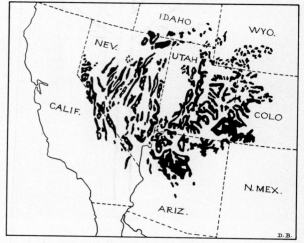

Natural range of the Utah Juniper

149

ALLIGATOR JUNIPER

Checkered-barked juniper, Oak-barked cedar

Juniperus deppeana Steudel

ALLIGATOR JUNIPER differs from the ten or more other species of *Juniperus* native to North America in having a thick bark divided into scaly squares, suggestive of the hide of an alligator; juvenile awl-shaped leaves, usually in whorls of three, while the scale-like mature leaves are usually in pairs; and dark, red-brown berries frequently marked with short tips of the flower scales, about half an inch in diameter, and usually containing four seeds.

It is a low tree, seldom more than fifty or sixty feet high, whose irregular round crown is supported by a short trunk three to five feet in diameter. Whether growing in pure stands or, as more frequently, with nut pine, Emory oak, and Arizona desert oak, the trees are usually rather widely spaced as in an orchard. Individual trees sometimes become weirdly distorted, as they cling to canyon sides or struggle like gnomes along the contours of barren plateaus. Highly resistant to drought, these junipers grow in dry, sterile, rocky soils from 4,000 to 6,000 feet above sea level in the region extending from the mountains of southwestern Texas, across southern New Mexico, southern Arizona, south to the states of Puebla and Vera Cruz, Mexico. The largest trees occur on moist slopes, benches and canyon floors.

Trees of the genus *Juniperus* are found throughout the entire northern hemisphere and below the equator in North Africa. They are perhaps the most widely distributed of all conifers. The name is derived from the Latin words *juvenis*, meaning young, and *parere*, meaning to produce. Presumably, the name refers to the two kinds of leaves produced on each tree—awl-shaped, needle-like young leaves, the points of which stand out, and mature leaves, which are scale-like and pressed close to the stem. The specific name *pachyphloea* is derived from two Greek words meaning thick bark.

The French know the tree as "genièvre," from which are derived the words "Geneva" and "gin." The alcoholic beverage, gin, was originally flavored with a decoction from the berries, while unripe berries are a source of oil of juniper, which is a diuric used in medicine.

The young leaves of alligator juniper are pale blue-green, awl-shaped and often in threes, while the mature, closely overlapping, bluish green scale-like ones, scarcely one-eighth inch long, are usually in opposite pairs.

The young twigs are slender, four-angled and pale blue-green like the leaves. After the leaves fall, the twigs are covered with a

U. S. Forest Service

Seldom more than fifty feet high, the Alligator Juniper has a short trunk, irregularly rounded crown and stout branches

thin, light reddish brown, close bark, which is smooth or occasionally broken into large thin scales.

G. B. Sudworth

The compact foliage is pale blue-green. The berry-like cone is rusty red, pulpy, and is about one half-inch in diameter

The flowers are inconspicuous, being only about one - eighth of an inch long. They open in February and March. The stamens and pistils are in separate flowers, but both sexes grow on the same tree.

The globular, berry-like fruit, about one-half inch in diameter, ripening in the autumn of its second season, is a true cone formed by the coalescence of the flower scales. It is dark red-brown and more or less covered with a whitish bloom during the first season. The thin skin closely covers the thick, dry, mealy flesh, which contains four-pointed seeds. The southwestern Indians grind the berries into a meal from which they prepare a sunbaked cake reported to be resinous in taste, but not too unpalatable. Each thick-shelled seed is markedly swollen at the back and has two lobed scars at the base. Birds eat the berries and scatter the undigested seeds, which germinate in two or three years.

The deeply fissured dark red-brown bark is a scant one to four inches thick with mosaic-like patterns of square, flat-topped plates, one to two inches across. These plates suggest such names as checkered-bark juniper and oak-barked cedar. Mountain cedar and thick-barked cedar are other names sometimes applied to this species.

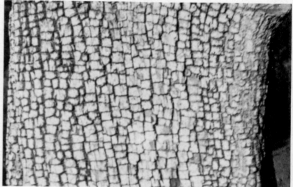

U. S. Forest Service

Dark red-brown bark is fissured with patterns of square, flat-topped plates

Like the wood of other junipers, that of alligator juniper is durable in contact with the soil. It is close-grained, soft, brittle, clear light yellow, often streaked with red, and it is aromatic. The nearly white sapwood is thin. Alligator juniper wood has a dry weight of thirty-six pounds a cubic foot, which is heavier than that commercially used for pencil stock. Were many trunks sufficiently long to produce satisfactory logs or bolts, it would be useful for pencil slats or for furniture. Actually, its relative scarcity and inaccessibility preclude its being used commercially, except locally for fuel and fence posts. It helps to protect soil from wind and water erosion, for it grows where few other trees will grow. Nevertheless, few successful efforts have been made to reproduce it by planting. Natural reproduction by seed is plentiful, and it also often produces vigorous shoots from the base of the trunk or from the stumps of felled trees.

It is one of the handsomest American junipers, remarkable for its checkered bark, slow growth and very long life. It probably reaches an age of 500 to 800 years.

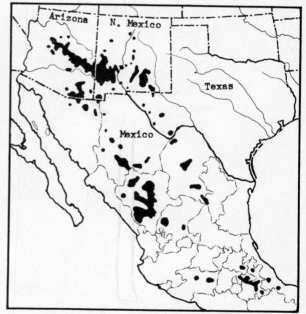

Natural range of Alligator Juniper

151

SIERRA JUNIPER

Western juniper
Juniperus occidentalis Hooker

THE BURLY, time-enduring sierra juniper occupies exposed slopes and canyon sides in dry, gravelly, or rocky soils of high mountain regions from southeastern Washington and western Idaho, through Oregon, western Nevada, eastern and southern California, and in small, scattered stands in Idaho, Montana, Utah, Arizona, and New Mexico. It is widely distributed from 2,000 to nearly 10,000 feet above sea level. The open, round-topped, stocky crown extends to within a few feet of the ground, and trees twenty to thirty feet tall are common, but more frequently sierra juniper is little more than a shrub. Under favorable conditions the tree attains heights of sixty to eighty feet, but the short, abruptly tapering trunk is seldom clear for more than four to eight feet. Huge lower branches often rise from the base and middle of the trunk to extend horizontally, and the trunk often divides into two or more thick forks to form a low, broad crown. Many trees reach diameters of sixteen to thirty inches at breast height.

Enormously large surface roots spread into the dry, rocky soil and rock crevices to anchor the tree against the fierce winds. On sheltered flats the crowns may be symmetrical with densely conical, round tops.

This is a true juniper. There is no record of its earliest discovery, although without doubt members of the Lewis and Clark Expedition saw it sometime between 1804 and 1806. The name *occidentalis* was given it by Sir William Jackson Hooker, in 1839, to indicate that the tree belongs to the western hemisphere.

Two kinds of pale, ashy green foliage are borne on each tree. One of these, the more abundant, consists of scale-like leaves, about one-eighth of an inch long, which overlap one another in groups of three as they closely clasp the stiff twigs to form a rounded stem with six longitudinal rows of leaves. The other, usually occurring on young growth, consists of longer, more needle-like leaves whose points stand out and make the twig rough to the touch. A glandular pit, pale with resin, marks the back of each leaf and, when viewed against the light with a strong lens, shows minute teeth on the leaf margins. The twigs of the Rocky

U. S. Forest Service

The broad open crown of Sierra Juniper, supported on a short chunky trunk, stands firm against the high mountain winds

Mountain juniper, *Juniperus scopulorum*, are four-sided, with leaves arranged alternately in pairs. When crushed, the foliage gives off a pungent, aromatic odor, and a decoction is sometimes used as a remedy for malaria, kidney trouble, boils, headaches, and coughs. The leaves begin to die during the second year and are gradually forced off by the growth to expose smooth, red new bark. There are no distinct or definite winter buds.

George C. Stephenson

Pale, ashy green, scale-like leaves press close against the twigs, near whose ends are borne the bluish black berry-like fruits

The tiny, pollen-bearing male flowers are usually borne on different trees from those which bear the fruit-developing female flowers. In September of the second year, the latter produce bluish black berries about one-fourth to one-third of an inch long. A whitish bloom covers their rough skin, and the outer ends are slightly marked by the tips of the female flower scales, indicating that they are not true berries but modified cones whose scales have become fleshy and united. The two or three pitted or deeply grooved bony seeds are thinly surrounded by dry flesh, and they have large resin cells that give the berry a rather sweet, pungently aromatic flavor. They are relished by birds and by the Indians. The tree reproduces scatteringly in pure mineral soil.

The firm, stringy bark is a clear cinnamon-brown, and is a half inch to an inch and a quarter thick. Wide, shallow furrows extend vertically over the trunk.

The fine-grained wood is pale brown, tinged with red, and is surrounded by a thin, nearly white outer layer of sapwood. It is slightly aromatic, and of great durability when exposed to weather or soil. It is soft and brittle, splits easily, and is one of the heaviest of all the cedars, a cubic foot weighing about forty pounds when air dry. Because of its close similarity to the wood of the eastern cedars, there is some demand for it as a pencil wood. Usually, however, the trunks are short and knotty, so the distinctly local uses are for fence posts, railroad ties, fuel, and novelties.

A slow, persistently growing tree, sierra juniper is recognized principally for its ability to thrive where few other trees can exist. Frequently in pure, open stands, sierra juniper sometimes occurs in association with such trees as lodgepole, Jeffrey and ponderosa pine and the nut pines.

Devereux Butcher

Wide shallow fissures divide the fibrous clear cinnamon bark, which is half an inch to an inch thick

Natural range of Sierra Juniper

PACIFIC YEW

Western yew
Taxus brevifolia Nuttall

THE YEWS are world-renowned trees. The genus *Taxus* contains six species which are widely distributed through the northern hemisphere, being found in North America, Europe, northern Africa, western and southern Asia, China and Japan. Three species are native to the United States and adjacent parts of Canada. The yew is closely associated with folklore and history. Because of the excellence of its wood for bows, it has been highly im-

Oliver V. Matthews

A rounded, often unsymmetrical crown and drooping branches, from which hang slender branchlets, are characteristics of Pacific Yew

portant in archery, its use for this purpose going back to prehistoric times. The European yew (species *baccata*) has been the most popular of all woods for bows, which was one of the principal weapons used in ancient warfare.

The yew has long been considered to have a religious significance. It has been looked upon as a sacred tree, and its association with churches and burial grounds has given rise to many curious legends. Its somber, melancholy appearance is thought to be symbolic of sorrow, sadness and death, while the great age which is attains and its evergreen character are signs of immortality and the resurrection. In Britain the greater number of the oldest yews are to be found in churchyards, but it is the general opinion that the yews were not planted in the churchyards but that the churches were built near the yews, which were already of great age. It is claimed that many of these trees are from 1,000 to 2,000 years old.

The Pacific yew occurs along the coast from the southern tip of Alaska southward through British Columbia, Washington, Oregon and northern Califorina. It occurs also in the Sierra Nevada of eastern California; and farther inland from the Selkirk Mountains of southeastern British Columbia to the western slopes of the Rockies in Montana and Idaho and in eastern Washington and Oregon. The tree is found, for the most part, near mountain streams, on moist flats and benches, and in deep ravines and coves in rich, rocky, or gravelly soils. It grows in small groups or singly, scattered sparingly with Douglasfir, grand fir, western redcedar, western larch, lodgepole pine, western white pine and Engelmann spruce. It attains its largest size in the Pacific coast region. With a usual height of twenty to forty feet and a diameter of twelve to fifteen inches, Pacific yew occasionally attains a height of sixty to seventy-five feet and a diameter of eighteen to thirty inches.

The trunk is straight and conical, but conspicuously ridged and fluted by an apparent infolding of the surface. Except in larger old trees, an open, conical crown extends nearly to the ground and the slender branches stand out straight, often somewhat drooping, while from their sides and extremities very slender branchlets hang down to give a weeping appearance. This habit is strongly marked in trees growing partly or wholly in the open, where the leafy branchlets are much more numerous and dense than those on trees growing in deep shade. The crowns of old trees are usually rounded and often unsymmetrical.

The deep yellow-green leaves of Pacific yew are from one-half to three-fourths of an inch long and one-sixteenth of an inch wide. They are soft to the touch, much paler on their under sides than above, and terminate in a short, bristly point. Attached to the twig by a slender, yellow stem about one-sixteenth of an inch long, they are borne spirally, but by a twist at their base, they stand out horizontally on opposite sides making a flat spray. The leaves stay green for about five years and sometimes longer.

The male and female flowers are borne on different

154

trees. The small, yellowish, bud-like, male or pollen-bearing flowers are borne singly and rather abundantly on the under sides of the branches. The small, greenish female flowers occur similarly but are less numerous. Each of the latter develops into a bright coral-red, berry-like fruit which ripens in September and begins to fall in October. It is often eaten by birds for the rather sweet, mucilaginous pulp which contains an oblong, egg-shaped seed about a third of an inch long. The hard shell of the seed is unaffected by digestion, and the attractiveness of the fruit to birds serves as an important means of its dissemination, otherwise the seed would not be carried far from the mother tree.

Pacific yew has a purplish bark which is conspicuously thin, rarely more than a fourth of an inch, and is composed of thin, papery, easily detached scales, beneath which the newer, unexposed bark is a clear rose or purple-red. The fine-grained wood is very heavy, hard, and strong in bending and is highly decay-resistant. A cubic foot, when thoroughly air dry, weighs about forty-three pounds. The heartwood is a clear rose-red, becoming gradually duller with exposure to light. The thin sapwood is light yellow. In addition to its use for archery bows, it is used also for canoe paddles and small cabinet work, but is of little other commercial importance because of its scarcity.

The Pacific yew produces some seed every year, with large crops at irregular intervals. Seedlings, which are only occasional and often rare, occur mostly in deep shade. Growth proceeds very slowly in such locations, but is very persistent. Trees six inches in diameter are from seventy-five to ninety years old, while those from twelve to twenty inches in diameter are from 140 to 245 years old. The largest specimens are believed to be at least 350 years old.

Pacific yew is a desirable ornamental because of its dense, dark foliage and the showy red fruits of the female tree in the autumn. The yew is the darkest of all evergreen trees and the foliage contrasts well with the lighter greens of other trees.

Charles A. Wellner

The leaves are deep yellow-green and terminate in a short, bristly point. The coral-red, berry-like fruit ripens in September

U. S. Forest Service

Thin purplish bark, composed of papery, easily-detached scales, rarely is more than a quarter of an inch thick

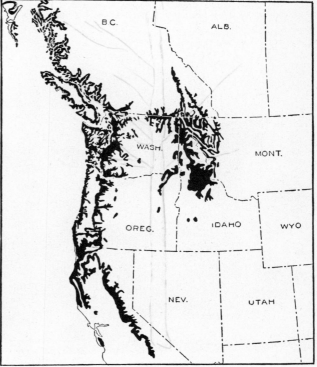

Natural range of Pacific Yew

155

BLACK WILLOW

Swamp willow
Salix nigra Marshall

L. W. Brownell

The bark is dark brown to nearly black and is divided by deep fissures into thick, connected ridges

L. W. Brownell

Quick growth and slender, graceful branches make black willow a good ornamental

THE WILLOWS are probably the most widely distributed woody plants in the northern hemisphere. While they are found to a limited extent south of the Equator, they occur abundantly in the far north, even beyond the arctic circle to the northern limits of tree growth where they take on a stunted form. There are more than 200 species of willow of which about half grow in the United States and Canada.

Of the thirty or more willow species native to the United States that can be classed as trees, only the black willow grows to a size suitable for the manufacture of lumber in commercial quantities. Preferring the banks of streams and lakes, it occurs in every state east of the Rocky Mountains except the Dakotas. It attains its best growth in the bottom lands of the lower Mississippi Valley, where it reaches diameters of three to four feet and a height of more than 100 feet in close stands, with a clear length of twenty to forty feet or more. Willows are usually no taller than thirty to forty feet, with diameters not over eighteen inches. Frequently there are several crooked or inclined trunks growing from a common base. When grown in the open the trunk is short, much branched and crooked, and the crown broad and irregular.

The slender, brittle twigs are bright reddish brown to pale orange color. Buds are red-brown, about one-eighth of an inch long, are narrow, pointed, pressed against the twig and covered by a single cap-like scale.

The alternate, thin, narrow, short-stemmed leaves, three to six inches long and three-eighths to three-quarters of an inch wide, taper gradually to a point and are often curved like the blades of a scythe. They are light green, shining above and smooth below, except for fine hairs along the veins, and the edges are finely toothed. They turn light yellow before falling in the autumn.

The flowers appear in April or May, with the unfolding leaves, in small, erect, spreading catkins, borne at the ends of short leafy twigs, the male and female occurring on separate trees. By midsummer each fertilized female flower has developed into a short-stalked, smooth, light reddish brown capsule about one-fourth of an inch long. It is egg-shaped, tapering gradually above the middle, and contains many minute seeds which are clothed with long, silky hairs. The hairs enable the seeds to be carried long distances by the wind, and large areas can thus be reforested in a comparatively short time. The seeds of black willow are said to germinate more quickly than those of any other species, seedlings having been known to come up in thirty-six hours. The seeds must, however, find lodgment in moist soil as they lose their vitality in a short time.

The dark brown to nearly black bark is divided by deep fissures into thick, closely connected, often interlacing ridges, separating freely into plate-like scales and becoming shaggy on old trunks.

The wood of black willow is quite uniform in texture, light in weight, exceedingly weak when used structurally, moderately soft and moderately high in shock resistance. It is not durable when used under conditions favorable to decay. The average weight of a cubic foot of the air-dry wood is twenty-six pounds. The heartwood is light brown to pale reddish brown or brown, frequently with darker streaks along the grain, and the sapwood is white to creamy yellow. The chief uses are shipping boxes, fruit packages, furniture and kitchen cabinets. Because of its light weight, uniform texture and ability to withstand blows without splintering, it is well suited for special uses, such as artificial limbs and polo balls. Willow plantations are widely used to protect stream banks from erosion and as a binder for shifting sand. River banks are frequently protected by "mattresses" made from small willow trees, so bound together as to form mats about a foot thick and often 1000 feet long by 250 feet wide. These mats are sunk into the mud and sand at the shore line by weighting them with rocks. Willow tree flowers have long been recognized as a source of honey, and many bee keepers have planted willows for this purpose.

L. W. Brownell

The leaves are alternate, thin, narrow, short-stemmed and are from three to six inches long

L. W. Brownell

The slender, brittle twigs are bright reddish brown to pale orange in color

L. W. Brownell

The fruit is egg-shaped, tapering gradually above the middle. It contains many minute seeds

L. W. Brownell

The flowers appear in April or May with the unfolding leaves in small, erect, spreading catkins

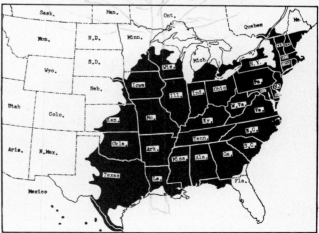

Natural range of Black Willow

157

QUAKING ASPEN

Trembling aspen, Trembling poplar, Golden aspen

Populus tremuloides Michaux

QUAKING ASPEN has a remarkably wide range. It occurs in Labrador and around the shores of James Bay, south to the mountains of Kentucky, and northwest to the valley of the Yukon River, within the arctic circle in Alaska, south through the mountains into northern Mexico and Lower California. It is scattered also across the northern plains states, and is abundant in New England, New York and around the Great Lakes. Quaking aspen thrives on moist, sandy soils and gravelly hillsides from sea level to elevations higher than 10,000 feet in the California mountains.

Quaking aspen frequently reaches forty or fifty feet in height and eighteen to twenty inches in diameter, but in the southern Rockies it attains one hundred feet with diameters up to three feet. It matures at sixty or seventy years, and seldom lives beyond eighty years. Inability to withstand heavy shade causes rapid thinning of dense young stands, but except as man interferes, quaking as-

pen usually maintains its ground against all coniferous competition.

It is a true poplar of the willow family, *Salicaceae*, and it belongs to the genus *Populus*. It is one of eleven members of the poplar or cottonwood group native to

Jay Higgins

In winter, Quaking Aspen makes a colorful picture with its central stem of blotched white supporting innumerable slender, reddish brown twigs

U. S. Forest Service

Aspen lifts its narrow, round-topped crown
of shimmering leaves forty feet or higher

the United States. The fluttering of the leaves, even in the gentlest breeze, is characteristic. The leaves, their slender stems pinched flat from the sides, are small, broadly egg-shaped, and are two to three inches wide. Ending in an abrupt, short point, they are edged with small, regular teeth. The upper surface is shiny green,

George J. Baetzhold

Staminate and pistillate flowers appear before the leaves, and they occur on different trees

Charles F. Steiger

The one-and-a-half to two-inch, dark green leaves are attached by narrow, ribbon-like stems

and the lower a pale, dull green. In autumn, they turn brilliant yellow, or rarely orange, contributing greatly to the color display.

Staminate and pistillate flowers appear in drooping gray catkins, the two sexes occurring on different trees. The seeds mature before the leaves are fully formed. The fruit, about four inches long, is composed of many light green capsules resembling quarter-inch-long Indian clubs. Packed within each capsule, the tiny brown seeds are so small that two million hardly make a pound. They travel long distances on the wind, germinate quickly in moist soil bared by fire, and the small plants, which grow rapidly in exposed situations, help prevent soil erosion.

The pale yellow-green or nearly white powdery bark of young trunks and branches is often marked with dark scars. Bark near the base of old trees is nearly black, one or two inches thick, roughened by bands of wart-like growths, and divided into flat ridges. Branchlets are shiny red-brown, roughened by large elevated leaf scars. They gradually turn dark gray.

The soft, closed-grained light brown heartwood merges into a broad band of nearly white sapwood. A cubic foot when air dry weighs about twenty-five pounds. Aspen wood is used for boxes, furniture and excelsior, and stands located principally in the lake states and the Northeast, consist mainly of cordwood too small to be sawed into lumber, but are suitable as pulpwood for paper manufacture.

Aspen is so subject to heart rot that many trees are useless before reaching fifty years. It is easily killed by fire, but its vigorous sprouting permits a quick return. Fungus often enters through fire scars, as well as in tunnels cut by aspen borers.

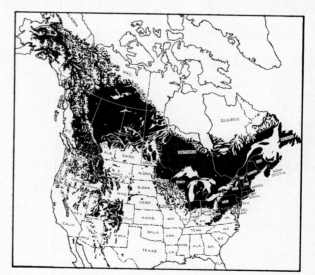

Natural range of Quaking Aspen

159

BIGTOOTH ASPEN

Largetooth aspen

Populus grandidentata Michaux

Bigtooth Aspen usually attains a height of thirty or fifty feet and a trunk diameter of 12 inches

BIGTOOTH ASPEN is also commonly called largetooth aspen, and the name *grandidentata* still further emphasizes the outstanding characteristic of this tree—the coarsely-toothed leaves—which distinguishes it from the quaking aspen. The names aspen, poplar, popple and white poplar are applied to both species.

Bigtooth aspen has a much more limited range than quaking aspen, being confined to the southeastern part of Canada and the northeastern part of the United States, where it prefers moist, sandy soil near the borders of swamps and streams from Nova Scotia and southern Quebec through New England westward to Minnesota and central Iowa south to Kentucky and the mountains of eastern Tennessee, western Virginia and North Carolina.

Usually a tree thirty to fifty feet tall, with a trunk diameter of about a foot, it occasionally attains a height of eighty feet and a diameter of two feet. The straight, gradually tapering trunk usually extends to the extreme top of the tree, and the stout, rather rigid branches form a somewhat narrow round-topped head. Trees grown in the open are characterized by a more oval crown.

The leaves are nearly round or broadly oval in outline and short-pointed at the tip, the margin coarsely toothed above the smooth base, with blunt, stout teeth. They are from three to four inches long and two to three inches wide, thin and firm in texture, dark green above and paler on the lower surface. Their slender stems, one and a half to two and a half inches long, are flattened along the sides, which causes them to flutter like those of the quaking aspen in any slight breeze. They turn a clear bright yellow in the autumn.

Male and female flowers appear in March and April on separate trees in hairy catkins from one and a half to two and a half inches in length. The female catkins ripen in May and June before the leaves are fully grown, when they measure four to five inches long, and contain many

light green, thin-walled, cone-shaped capsules about an eighth of an inch long. Each capsule holds many minute dark brown seeds.

The stout twigs, downy at first, are reddish or orange brown during their first year, and later brownish gray. They are much roughened by the large, elevated, three-lobed leaf scars. The ovate, pointed buds have light chestnut-brown scales and are covered during the winter with fine, gray wool, especially on the margins of the scales. The leaf buds are about an eighth of an inch long and are not more than half the size of the flower buds.

The bark on large branches and on trunks of young trees is thin, smooth and light gray, tinged with green. On old trees it is three quarters to one inch thick, dark brown, often tinged with red, irregularly fissured and divided into broad, flat ridges, and roughened on the surface by small, thick, closely appressed scales.

The grayish white to light grayish heartwood merges into the slightly lighter colored sapwood without any sharp demarcation. The straight grained, fine and uniform textured wood is light in weight, weak, soft, moderately stiff, moderately low in resistance to shock and shrinks on drying. A cubic foot of the air dry wood weighs twenty-seven pounds. Its principal uses are paper pulp, boxes and crates, excelsior, matches and laundry appliances. Bigtooth aspen and quaking aspen wood are cut and used together without discrimination.

The thin bark gives little protection from fire, and the wood is very subject to decay. Aspen borers frequently cut tunnels into the wood through which fungi gain entrance. Many trees are rendered useless from heart rot before they attain maturity. The weak, soft wood is easily broken by the wind. Reproduction frequently takes place through root sprouts. However, bigtooth aspen is a prolific seeder and the hardy seeds are scattered long distances by the wind. They germinate well in moist soil. Although the tree is short-lived, it grows rapidly, especially during its first twenty to thirty years, and can renew quickly the forest cover when it has been burned or logged. Not only does the species build up impoverished soils, but serves to protect the seedlings of other tree species.

The oval leaves are coarsely toothed, and their stems are flattened on the sides, making them flutter in a breeze

Hairy male catkins (upper) are about two and a half inches long. The seed capsules (lower) mature on the female catkins and contain numerous minute seeds

The dark brown bark of old trees may be irregularly fissured, but on young trunks it is smooth and pale gray

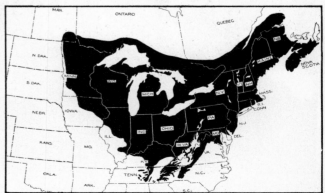

Natural range of Bigtooth Aspen

BALSAM POPLAR

Tacamahac poplar, Balm-of-Gilead, Cottonwood
Populus balsamifera Linnaeus

ITS RANGE of growth extending across the entire continent from the western shores of Alaska to the eastern coast of Labrador, balsam poplar is strictly a northern tree and attains its best development in far northwestern Canada under the arctic circle in a climate too severe for the existence of most other trees. In this region it is the largest tree species and is found chiefly on low river bottomlands, the banks of streams and the borders of lakes and swamps. Sometimes forming pure stands, it more often grows in mixture with willows, alder, birches, black spruce and white spruce. Under the most favorable conditions the tree grows to a height of 100 feet with a

tall trunk six to seven feet in diameter.

In the southern part of its range, which includes, in the United States, the region from northern New England to central Minnesota and from central Colorado to western Montana and northern Idaho, it is smaller—up to seventy feet in height and thirty inches in trunk diameter—and is commonly found in small, widely separated colonies, remnants, perhaps, of more extensive stands which developed in post-glacial times. The long straight trunk is usually clear of branches up to thirty or forty feet and bears a narrow, irregular, open crown which takes on a pyramidal form in open-grown trees and is

Devereux Butcher

L. W. Brownell

Balsam Poplar is generally found in small, widely separated colonies. Growing from 70 to 100 feet in height, it has a long, straight trunk and a narrow, irregular open crown with few large limbs

made up of a comparatively few large limbs with a strong upward trend.

The clear, shining, reddish brown twigs are marked by oblong, bright orange-colored lenticels and much roughened by thick leaf-scars. The terminal buds are about one inch long and the lateral buds smaller, from five-eighths to three-quarters of an inch in length; they are taper-pointed and are covered by five scales and saturated with a pungently fragrant, amber-colored balsam which is called "Balm-of-Gilead" in the drug trade and is used medicinally as a constituent of cough medicine. The name tacamahac, meaning balsam, is applied to this tree. Other names occasionally used are cottonwood and rough-barked poplar.

The leaves are egg-shaped with long tapering points and fine, regular, rather blunt teeth on their margins. Three to six inches long and two to four inches broad, they are smooth and shining dark green above, pale green and more or less rusty colored below with a conspicuous network of veins. The slender leaf stems are one and a half to two inches long and are round in cross-section in contrast to the flattened leaf stems of quaking aspen and eastern cottonwood.

In March or April before the leaves open, the flowers appear in long-stalked catkins, the male and female on separate trees. The male or staminate are from three to four inches long and the loose-flowered female or pistillate ones measure from four to five inches in length before the fruit ripens. The light brown, hairy seeds mature in May, and are contained in two-valved, short-stalked capsules, one-fourth of an inch long.

On the limbs and trunks of young trees, the bark is smooth and reddish brown, often with a greenish shade. On older trunks it is gray, tinged with red, eventually becoming dark gray, three-quarters of an inch to one inch thick, and separated by narrow, deep, regular furrows into broad ridges, scaly or shaggy on the surface.

The soft, uniform-textured wood is light in weight, weak, easily worked with tools and not durable in exposed situations, decaying quickly in contact with the soil. A cubic foot of the air-dry wood weighs twenty-three pounds. The heartwood is light brown and the thick sapwood nearly white. Because it has little tendency to split in nailing, the wood is much used for boxes and crates. Another important use is paper pulp, into which it is readily converted by the chemical process. Some of the largest logs are cut into veneer for the manufacture of fruit baskets.

The principal supply of balsam poplar in the United States is located in the lake states and the Northeast. In lumber statistics the cut of balsam poplar is included under the name "cottonwood" with the cottonwoods and aspens. The tree is planted to some extent for shade. It grows rapidly in early life and attains diameters of fourteen to seventeen inches in forty to fifty years. The dark green, glossy leaves and bright reddish brown twigs enhance its value as an ornamental. The variety Hairy Balm-of-Gilead (*Populus balsamea candicans* (Ait.) Gray) is especially desirable for city and landscape planting.

Warren D. Brush

Staminate catkin, upper left, and pistillate, upper right. Seeds with cotton, lower left, and leaf, lower right

U. S. Forest Service

On young trees, the bark is smooth and reddish brown, but on older trees it has a grayish red tinge, eventually becoming dark gray

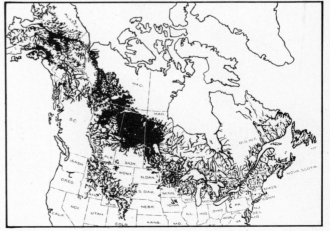

Natural range of Balsam Poplar

EASTERN COTTONWOOD

Eastern poplar, Southern cottonwood, Carolina poplar

Populus deltoides Bartram

THE BROAD spreading crown of eastern cottonwood is common from Quebec to northern Florida and west along the upper streams leading into the Great Plains. Most frequently found along water courses, it often forms extensive groves in the North and West.

Developing first a narrow, conical crown, with maturity it becomes broad and open, supported by a massive

U. S. Forest Service

Winter reveals the short trunk and vigorous growth of limbs and branches

W. G. Baxter

The bright green, leathery, broadly triangular leaves, together with the stems, are four to seven inches long

trunk. Under forest conditions the bole may reach fifty to sixty feet to the main limbs. Ordinarily, eighty to 100 feet tall with a trunk three to four feet in diameter, under favorable conditions west of the Mississippi, trees attain heights of 150 feet and diameters of seven to eight feet.

The poplars are of ancient origin and the name *Populus* may refer to an early Roman expression *arbor populi*, the people's tree. Of some twenty-five species recognized throughout the world, eleven are found in North America. Of these, *deltoides* is the most important eastern representative.

The glossy, leathery leaves are broad and triangular, with coarse, rounded, marginal teeth, and have a flattened stem or petiole about as long as the leaf blade. The shiny brown terminal buds are resin-covered and, like the crushed leaves, have a pleasant balsamic odor.

Flowers of each sex are borne separately on different trees and appear in March or April, before the leaves unfold, in three- to five-inch drooping catkins. By May the more loosely flowered pistillate catkins are six to eleven inches long, with scattered, pointed capsules, which expel the tiny, fragile seeds whose attached fibers of fluffy white down carry them long distances. A few hours must bring them to some place of exposed mineral soil, such as that on recently flooded river banks and islands, or their vitality is lost. Cottonwood also reproduces from stumps and root sprouts, and it may be readily grown from cuttings. The deeply fissured bark of mature trees is a dull gray or brown, two to three inches thick, with rather wide

W. G. Baxter

164

ridges. On young trunks and branches it is smooth, thin, and grayish yellow tinged with green.

The wood is of varied shades of brown with a thick white margin of sapwood. It is close grained and porous, with a dull luster, soft, weak, usually easy to work, but it warps badly in seasoning. A cubic foot when air dry weighs about twenty-four pounds. It is used mostly for boxes, crates, packing cases, excelsior, as a core for veneers, paper pulp, and locally for poles, posts and fuel.

Timber stands of eastern cottonwood are mainly in the Mississippi Valley, particularly the lower part. The most important cottonwood lumber producing states are Mississippi, Arkansas, Louisiana and Missouri.

Cottonwood is remarkable for rapid growth during its first forty years. Thereafter trees may remain sound and vigorous, growing slowly for 100 years or more. Trees have been observed to grow four to five feet in height each year, with diameters increasing two-thirds of an inch for each of the first twenty-five years. Some reach 100 feet in height in fifteen years.

Frequently planted for shelter and ornament in the treeless plains and prairies west of the Mississippi, the widespread, shallow root system which helps make the tree wind-firm, often upheaves sidewalks. Moreover, the tiny rootlets fill drain pipes in their search for water. Accordingly, many towns prohibit the planting of cottonwood within their boundaries.

Fire is destructive until after the trees are fifteen or twenty years old and the bark thick enough to resist the heat. The river overflow lands on which most cottonwoods grow is their chief source of protection from fire. Fungus diseases are more to be feared, and, during the first few years, the young shoots are eagerly eaten by field mice, rabbits, and cattle.

U. S. Forest Service

The densely flowered, pollen-bearing staminate catkins are three to five inches long

W. G. Baxter

The mature bark is dark gray to brown with deep fissures and rounded ridges

Warren D. Brush

Long strands of capsule fruits suggest the name "necklace" poplar

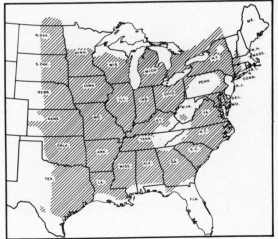

Natural range of Eastern Cottonwood

BLACK COTTONWOOD

California poplar, Balsam cottonwood, Western balsam poplar
Populus trichocarpa Torrey and Gray

BLACK COTTONWOOD attains the greatest proportions of any American poplar, and is the largest broad-leafed tree in the forests of the Pacific Northwest. Its range extends from the coast ranges of southern Alaska eastward and southward through much of British Columbia, into Washington, Oregon, western Montana and Idaho to southern California. It grows to largest size on river bottoms, sandbars and banks in sandy, humus rich soils; at higher elevations in canyon bottoms and gulches, in moist, sandy and gravelly soil it is much smaller. The species forms belts and limited forests of pure growth, or in the north, occurs in association with willows, grand fir and Douglasfir, and southward, at higher levels, with incensecedar and others. The climate in the region of best growth is marked by great humidity and precipitation and by moderate temperatures. Where

Charles A. Wellner

Oliver V. Matthews

Under good conditions, Black Cottonwood grows to a height of 125 feet. Over much of its range, however, it is under 50 feet and from 12 to 18 inches in diameter. It is the largest American poplar

subjected to low humidity, growth is smaller.

Under optimum conditions the tree makes rapid growth, attaining heights of eighty to 125 feet and diameters of three to four feet. It may reach diameters of two to three feet in about 100 years. In the Puget Sound basin and adjacent areas trees 175 to 225 feet high and seven to eight feet in diameter have been found. Over much of its range, however, black cottonwood is under fifty feet and from twelve to eighteen inches in diameter.

The young twigs are indistinctly angled, later becoming round, shiny and reddish yellow. The similarly colored buds, from five-eighths to three-fourths of an inch long, are often curved, as if bent, and covered with a fragrant, yellowish brown gum.

The broadly ovate leaves, gradually narrowed and usually short-pointed or rarely acute at the apex, have a fine-toothed, wavy margin. Mature leaves are thick, leathery, smooth, dark green and shiny above and silvery white beneath, with rusty areas and conspicuous veins. The smaller veins and their branches, as well as the slender, round leaf stems are sometimes minutely hairy. In autumn the leaves become a dull yellowish brown.

The male and female flowers are borne on separate trees. The staminate are in densely-flowered catkins, one and a half to two inches long and one-third of an inch thick, with slender, smooth stems. The pistillate catkins are loosely flowered, are two and a half to three inches long and have stout, fine hairy stems which become four to five inches long before the fruit ripens. Fertilization is accomplished by insects and wind. By the time the leaves are fully grown, the pistillate or seed-bearing flowers develop bud-like capsules arranged on a pendant, thread-like stem. Soon afterwards these thick-walled three-valved capsules liberate many minute light brown, cottony seeds. These are provided with exceedingly fine, silky, white hairs which permit them to be carried long distances by the wind. Large crops of seeds are produced yearly.

The pale gray to dark gray bark, about two inches in thickness, is divided by deep furrows, into flat-topped ridges. The wood is light in weight, soft, brittle and low in resistance to decay. A cubic foot of the air-dry wood weighs about twenty-four pounds. The heartwood is pale gray to light brown, while the nearly white sapwood is not clearly defined and merges more or less gradually into the heartwood. It is much used in the Northwest for barrels and boxes, and is one of the principal fuelwoods of the Pacific coast. Large logs obtainable from the best trees give clear, wide lumber.

K. D. Swan

The broadly ovate dark green leaves are shiny above and silvery white with rust colored areas beneath

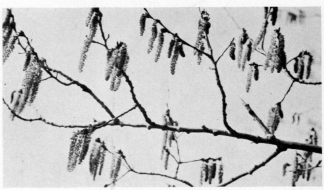
C. L. Broley

Male and female flowers are borne on separate trees. Fertilization is accomplished by insects and wind

The bark ranges in color from pale to dark gray, is about two inches thick and is divided by deep furrows

Devereux Butcher

Natural range of Black Cottonwood

167

LOMBARDY POPLAR

Populus nigra var. *italica* **Muenchhausen**

LOMBARDY POPLAR has long been a puzzle to botanists and many theories have been advanced as to its origin. It has been classified as a variety of the Italian poplar, *Populus nigra*, because the leaves and flowers closely resemble those of *nigra*; moreover it was introduced, probably during the 18th Century, into other European countries from Lombardy, Italy, which accounts for the name. It is claimed, however, that this variety is not native to northern Italy, although it had been grown there for a considerable length of time, but was brought from Asia by Arabs or European travellers.

Lombardy poplar is distinctly different from other poplars in its habit of growth, the closely ascending branches forming a narrow, columnar crown. Because of this difference, it is believed by some botanists to be a "sport" or mutant, which theory seems to be substantiated by the fact that this variety exists only as a male tree and therefore has to be propagated entirely by vegetative cuttings.

U. S. Forest Service

The tree often marks boundary lines and is an
efficient windbreak when planted close together

Devereux Butcher

Closely ascending branches give Lombardy
Poplar a spire-like or candle-like form

The countless specimens now planted all over the world may, therefore, have originated from a single tree. Lombardy poplar differs from the Italian poplar not only in its fastigiate or columnar habit, but as regards the new shoots, which are smooth in the former and pubescent in the latter. Some botanists believe, therefore, that it originated from some variety of the Italian poplar, particularly the variety *typica*, which it also resembles closely.

Probably no other introduced tree has been so widely planted for ornamental purposes as the Lombardy poplar. Its tall, spire-like top is a familiar object in almost every populated region from the Atlantic to the Pacific and from the Canadian frontier to the Mexican boundary. In some European countries it is much more abundant than in our own country. Sometimes attaining a height of 100 feet, the trunk is almost completely covered from the ground upward with suckerlike vertical branches. The young twigs are olive green, later becoming gray, and the pointed winter buds are small, measuring from one-fourth to one-third of an inch long. The bark on the trunks of old trees is grey to brown and deeply furrowed.

The triangularly-shaped, pointed leaves, one to two and a half inches long, have finely-toothed margins. They are rather thin but firm, smooth on both sides, of a rich yellow-green color when they first appear, bright green above and paler at maturity. The slender leafstalks are as long as the blades or somewhat shorter and flattened along their sides. As with our native quaking aspen, they allow the leaf blades to move freely from side to side in the wind. The male, staminate catkins, one and a half to two and a half inches long, appear very early in the spring before the leaves. Female flowers are entirely lacking, no seed, therefore, being produced. Fortunately the tree is easily propagated by cuttings of the branches, and it occasionally spreads by sending up shoots from its roots. The tree grows rapidly but is short-lived.

Lombardy poplar is one of the most interesting of our cultivated trees and, while it cannot be included as a member of our wild arborescent flora, it has been so much planted for ornament and as a curiosity that it is as familiar in many places as any native species. Because it infringes but slightly, even by its shade, on an adjoining property, its stately rows mark many boundary lines of farm and village properties. Although of little value for shade, because the branches have so little spread, the trees are well adapted for city planting, where streets and sidewalks are narrow. They also are often planted close to buildings or bridges or walls, where their candle-like form shows to excellent advantage.

In garden landscaping, Lombardy poplar is of considerable value. It has been called the exclamation point in landscape architecture, and a single tree may be very effective when properly placed. Although the species has an air of rigid sternness about it, a tall, graceful tree may impress one much as does a beautiful church spire. It serves well in relieving low, monotonous lines of vegetation and, by contrast, adds to the attractiveness of other and different kinds of growth, such as when effectively distributed among groups of round-topped trees.

When grown close together, Lombardys make an effi-
cient windbreak. Many of them were planted for this purpose by the pioneers in the prairie regions.

The short life of the tree is a disadvantage, whether planted as a street tree or for ornament. The early dying of the limbs, which it retains, gives the tree an unkempt appearance, and the wide-spreading roots, which grow close to the surface, are often objectionable.

L. W. Brownell

The triangularly-shaped leaves have finely-toothed margins and slender leafstalks

Devereux Butcher

The bark on the trunks of old trees is grey to brown in color and deeply furrowed

169

BLACK WALNUT

Juglans nigra Linnaeus

BLACK WALNUT is common to the eastern half of the United States, and southern Ontario. In the deep alluvial soils from Maryland, Pennsylvania, and Virginia, west into eastern Nebraska and Texas, trees have grown 150 feet high and six feet in diameter, with clear lengths of fifty or sixty feet, while trees with a breast high diameter of three feet and 100 feet high are fairly common.

Juglans is a contraction of *Jovis glans*, a Latin name designating the nut or acorn of Jupiter, while *nigra* may refer to the black bark, the rich brown wood, or the dark outer shell of the nut.

Closely related to the butternut or white walnut, *Juglans cinerea*, it has two relatives in California and the southwest, and belongs to the same genus as the Persian walnut, whose nut is marketed as English walnut, and lumber as Circassian walnut.

The compound leaves are one or two feet long with fifteen to twenty-three lance-shaped, sharply-toothed leaflets attached to a slightly hairy stem.

Each tree bears staminate or pollen-bearing catkins on

Devereux Butcher

The leaves begin to drop in the early fall exposing a divided trunk and a framework of heavy alternate branches. The dark brown or occasionally black bark is broken into rounded ridges, becoming two to three inches thick on older trees

Devereux Butcher

Black Walnut forms a round-headed tree with relatively scant foliage that reveals the sturdy branches. The map shows the natural range of Black Walnut

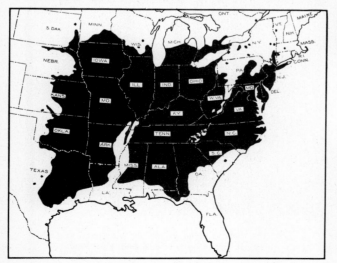

the previous year's growth, and pistillate flowers in groups of two to five at the ends of the new growth, during April or May.

The globular, light green fruits are an inch and a half to three inches in diameter, and consist of a thick pulpy hull surrounding a single nut whose hard, deeply grooved shell protects a kernel of unusual flavor. They mature in September and October, and frequently remain on the trees a week or two after the leaves have fallen. They are prized by squirrels. The kernels are used by confectioners, bakers and makers of ice cream, because the distinctive flavor and texture are not lost in cooking.

In winter, walnut trees may be distinguished by the sturdy crown, dark, deeply grooved bark, stout twigs, and the large gray, downy, terminal buds. The smaller, downy lateral buds are alternate, and above a heart-shaped, three-lobed leaf scar, with three V-shaped bundle scars. The diaphragms of the chambered pith of black walnut are thin and pale buff, while those of butternut are dark and coarse.

The soft, brown, coarse-grained, easily worked wood weighs about thirty-nine pounds to the cubic foot, when air dry. For many purposes it is stronger than white oak, and has been used since earliest American

Two walnuts in their green husks mature at the end of the current year's leafy twig, above. At left, two pistillate blooms, among the new leaves, will each produce a nut by autumn. Staminate catkins, below, left, grow at the end of the previous year's twig

Warren D. Brush

Warren D. Brush

The nut or seed, in its natural size, is shown here without its husk. Its hard, deeply chiseled shell contains a flavorful kernel used by confectioners

history for fine furniture and interior panels. It ranks as America's foremost cabinet wood. The ability of walnut to stay in place after seasoning, its good machining properties, slight coarseness and uniformity of texture, and its strength and shock-resisting ability, without excessive weight, explain its wide acceptance for gun stocks and, during World War I, for airplane propellers. It also is used for veneer. The heartwood is highly resistant to decay.

The nuts may be husked and stored in a cool cellar, embedded in sand or in a pit a foot or more underground, preparatory to being planted in early spring. They do best when spaced twenty-five to thirty feet apart, and prove satisfactory along roadsides and on lawns, because the comparatively light shade cast by the leaves interferes little with the growth of grass. Black walnut trees prosper best in deep, rich, well drained soil where moisture is plentiful. They grow readily from seed and for two or three years are easily transplanted so that trees have been set out in almost every state.

Walnut is relatively resistant to fungus and insect attacks. Tent and walnut caterpillars are sometimes disfiguring, but they rarely kill the trees. The leaves are subject to leaf spot diseases which are unsightly but not harmful.

BUTTERNUT
Oil nut, White walnut
Juglans cinerea Linnaeus

BUTTERNUT, or white walnut, grows from southern New Brunswick and Maine west through the lower peninsula of Michigan to eastern Minnesota, thence southward into northeastern Arkansas and the mountains of North Carolina. It is usually a short-trunked spreading tree seldom more than thirty to fifty feet high and one to three feet in diameter. Occasionally when grown in the forest it attains a height of eighty to one hundred feet and diameters of three to four feet. Butternut closely resembles its relative, the black walnut, but the general form of the tree is lower and more spreading. Furthermore, it prefers greater moisture, adapts itself more readily to poor shallow soils and will grow under greater extremes of temperature. The name *cinerea* is derived from the Latin word *cinerarius* meaning "of ashes" and probably refers to the ashen color of the bark. The entire scientific name as given by Linnaeus might be translated as "ashen walnut."

The alternate compound leaves are fifteen to thirty inches long and have eleven to seventeen leaflets. These leaflets have unequally rounded bases, are pointed, have small marginal teeth and are covered with fine sticky hairs. The leaves and fruit drop early, revealing large, conspicuous, three-lobed leaf scars on the twigs, each of which is surmounted by a pale gray, raised, downy pad, or "eyebrow." This feature, together with the long downy terminal bud and the sticky leaflets, the sticky leaf stalk and the elon-

U. S. Forest Service

Butternut trees are frequently found in old pastures where they take on the spreading, many-branched form of a short-trunked orchard tree. The large compound leaves are lighter green than those of black walnut, have fewer leaflets, and are sticky to the touch. The crown appears thin and lacking in vigor

Mrs. J. G. M. Glessner

Leaves and nuts fall almost simultaneously in the late autumn, revealing the characteristic "Y"-like branching of the smaller twigs. The tree is seldom symmetrical because of the tendency of side limbs to break during the wind and snow storms. The tendency to develop the under buds on each twig gives the limbs a horizontal rather than upright trend

gated nut, help distinguish the butternut from the black walnut.

Inconspicuous flowers of both sexes appear on the same trees at the same time as the new leaves, in May or early June. Long, drooping, yellow-green, pollen-bearing catkins hang from the previous year's growth, while the globular pistillate flowers are in groups of three or five on the new growth. These develop into pear-shaped sticky fruits whose pulpy covering or husk encloses a deeply ridged, oblong nut with a rich, sweet, oily kernel that ripens in October. It is the oily kernel for which the tree is named. Butternut kernels are widely recognized as a food, and the immature nuts are occasionally pickled.

The light brown, soft, coarse-grained wood may be polished to a satiny lustre. It weighs only twenty-seven pounds to the cubic foot, and is lighter in color and not as strong or durable as walnut. Small amounts are used for cabinet work, interior finish, boat trimming and furniture.

Butternut is more valuable for its nuts than for lumber or for use as a shade tree. The annual litter from the nuts, the heavy fall of leaves, the low crown and the brittle limb-wood discourage its use as a shade tree, but it is a pleasing addition to a spacious lawn. The species is short-lived and seldom attains an age of more than seventy-five or one hundred years. The large spreading limbs are frequently broken by wind or snow and few trees reach maturity without serious injury from insects or fungus diseases.

Several strains of rapid-growing trees capable of producing large quantities of easily cracked nuts have been reported, so that butternut may find a real place among food crop trees.

Above: The yellow-green compound highly aromatic leaves are fifteen to thirty inches long, with eleven to seventeen taper-pointed leaflets. The pear-shaped nuts are covered with a sticky green husk and mature in the autumn after one year's growth. The oily, highly flavored kernel is used in cooking, and the immature nuts are often pickled in vinegar, sugar and spice

Right: The gray to black bark with broad flat pale gray ridges and narrow criss-cross furrows may become three-quarters of an inch to an inch thick. The yellow inner bark is bitter, has mild cathartic properties and furnishes a brown dye once used to color cloth

Lower Right: Natural range of Butternut in the United States and Canada

Left: A greenish gray winter twig revealing the chambered pith, typical of the walnut family, the alternately arranged, triangular, three-lobed leaf scars, the downy side buds with the elongated terminal bud, and the raised, downy pad or "eyebrow" between the leaf scar and the bud—these are all characteristic of the Butternut

Chicago Natural History Museum

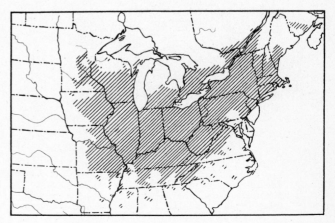

SHAGBARK HICKORY

Carolina hickory, Scalybark hickory, Upland hickory

Carya ovata (Miller) K. Koch

SHAGBARK HICKORY is a distinctly American tree. Only one hickory species exists beyond our continent, and this in eastern China. During pre-glacial periods, however, hickories covered Europe and the Mediterranean countries. Of all the hickories, none is so important or widespread as shagbark.

Its irregular, round-topped crown reaches heights of 120 to 140 feet, and the trunk, which frequently is divided, attains diameters of twenty to thirty inches. It is a common feature of bottomlands and pastures of all the eastern states from southern Maine to southeastern Minnesota, south to Georgia and eastern Texas. It occurs in western Florida, but not on the coastal plain in Georgia and South Carolina. Pure stands are rare and best growth is achieved in mixture with oaks and other broadleafed trees in the Cumberland Mountains and Mississippi River bottoms. Under forest conditions the straight trunk may be clear of branches for fifty to sixty feet.

The compound leaves arranged alternately on the stem have five or seven leaflets whose narrow base is attached directly to the leaf stalk. The three outer leaflets are four to six inches long while the lower ones are smaller. Narrow at the base, wide at the top, the margin of each leaflet is toothed and the shape described as obovate.

In May or June, while the leaves are developing, separate male and female blossoms appear at the base of new shoots. The drooping catkins of staminate flowers are four to six inches long, while the two- to five-flowered pistillate ones—one-third of an inch long—are covered with a rusty wooly growth. Those which are fertilized develop during the summer into green semispherical fruits one to two and a half inches in diameter. This is described as ovate and is responsible for the name *ovata* to distinguish this *Carya* from other hickories. The thick outer husk splits into four sections when ripe and reveals a single, white, thin-shelled nut whose sweet kernel is edible.

Devereux Butcher

E. S. Shipp

Regardless of season, Shagbark Hickory is a rugged, picturesque tree with a strong, frequently divided trunk. Heights of 120 to 140 feet are attained, with trunk diameters of twenty to thirty inches

174

When the leaves drop, conspicuous, slightly elevated, roughly heart-shaped leaf scars are left on the twig to persist two or more years. At the base of the leaf stalk and in the curve of the leaf scar a blunt-pointed, broadly ovate bud is completely formed before fall. The terminal bud is one-half to three-fourths of an inch long, blunt-pointed, and covered with downy, dark brown scales.

The long, flat plates of gray bark of mature trees, loose at one or both ends, gives the name "shagbark." On young trunks, the bark is smooth, firm and light gray.

The reddish brown heartwood was long considered inferior in strength and toughness to the surrounding two to four inches of white sapwood, but laboratory tests show no material difference. No other commercial wood has the combination of strength, toughness, and elasticity, and no other American hardwood could adequately substitute for hickory in case of shortage of supply. Not durable in contact with the soil, it is attacked by borers.

Hickory lumber having no more than twenty rings to the inch is generally the strongest, and is used for handles of axes, picks, hammers, and hatchets. Until recently, large amounts were used in making spokes and rims of wheels, singletrees, and buggy shafts. Increasing quantities are used in athletic equipment. Hickory wood weighs about sixty-three pounds to the cubic foot when air dry and is excellent for fuel.

Hickory is reproduced from seeds and sprouts. Two to three bushels of shelled nuts may be produced by thrifty open-grown trees. Trees of seedling origin grow slowly, but may reach ages of 150 to 200 years. The hickories are attacked by various insects, but suffer greatest harm from the hickory bark beetle.

George J. Baetzhold

Drooping catkins of staminate flowers

Charles F. Steiger

Above—Hickory nut enclosed in husk. Below—The compound leaf has five and rarely seven leaflets

U. S. Forest Service

Long, loose plates of gray bark give Shagbark Hickory its name

U. S. Forest Service

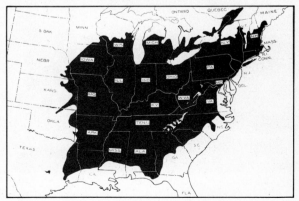

Natural range of Shagbark Hickory

SHELLBARK HICKORY

Bigleaf shagbark hickory, Kingnut, Big shellbark

Carya laciniosa (Michaux f.) Loudon

SHELLBARK HICKORY resembles shagbark hickory, but there are distinct differences in leaves, fruit, twigs and bark by which it can be identified. It grows in a much more restricted range than that occupied by shagbark, extending from central New York west through southern Michigan to southeastern Nebraska, Kansas, northeastern Oklahoma and locally in southern Louisiana and Alabama. Distinctly a tree of the bottomlands, it is sometimes called bottom shellbark. It often occurs in nearly pure groves, or mixed with other bottomland hardwoods on areas which are inundated during high water. It is also known as bigleaf shagbark and kingnut.

Occasionally attaining a height of 120 feet, its straight slender trunk rarely exceeds three feet in diameter and is often free of branches for more than half its height. The spreading branches form a narrow, oblong head. When grown in the open it develops a more or less egg-shaped crown with drooping lower branches.

The stout, orange-brown twigs are at first covered with fine hairs but later become nearly smooth. The large terminal buds, three-fourths to one inch long, are covered with six to eight dark brown, loosely-fitting scales.

The compound leaves are fifteen to twenty-two inches long with five to nine (usually seven) finely-toothed leaflets. The terminal leaflet, five to nine inches long and three to five inches wide, is usually larger than the others. Dark green and lustrous on the upper surface, they are pale yellow-green to yellowish brown and velvety below. A striking feature of shellbark hickory is the presence of old leaf stalks on the twigs of the previous summer's growth.

In May, the pollen-bearing flowers appear in catkins five to eight inches long and the pistillate in two- to five-flowered spikes. The fruit is one and three-fourths to two and a half inches long and is borne solitary or in pairs. The orange to chestnut-brown husk, one-fourth to one-half inch thick, completely separates into four sections. A distinguishing feature is the large nut which is usually oblong and much flattened, one and a fourth to two and a fourth inches long, and one and a half to one and three-fourths of an inch wide, with four or sometimes six prominent ridges and a stout, long point at the base. The thick-shelled nut contains a sweet edible kernel.

The trunk is covered with shaggy gray bark much like that of shagbark hickory, but the long, thick plates usually are less curved. The wood is similar to that of

W. J. Beal

L. W. Brownell

Occasionally attaining a height of 120 feet, the slender trunk of Shellbark Hickory rarely exceeds three feet in diameter. Open-grown trees develop more or less egg-shaped crowns with drooping lower branches

the other commercially important hickories (except the pecans), but is not quite so heavy, a cubic foot of air-dry wood weighing forty-eight pounds. The heartwood is reddish brown and the sapwood white. The wood is very strong, hard and stiff and exceedingly high in shock resistance. These properties adapt it for handles of striking tools; about eighty percent of the hickory used in manufacture goes into these products. Ladder rungs, scythe snaths, gymnastic bars, and skis are commonly made of hickory because they require a wood with a high degree of strength, stiffness and toughness. Hickory is one of the best woods for fuel and for smoking meats.

Hickory timber has been so greatly cut over in the Northeast that west of the Alleghenies and north of the Ohio River only a few scattered remnants of the original stands are left. The falling off in the cut from more than 300,000,000 board feet in 1909 is due not only to diminished supplies, but also to the substitution of steel, particularly in vehicles. In addition to lumber, large quantities of logs are shipped directly to factories where handles and other hickory products are made.

Shellbark hickory, like other hickories, is slow-growing; it reproduces readily, however, both from seed and sprout. Seed crops are fairly abundant, and although much is appropriated by rodents and man, many of the

L. W. Brownell

The compound leaves, 15 to 20 inches long, are dark green above, yellow to brownish and velvety below

nuts are overlooked and serve to reproduce the species. Hickory is difficult to transplant because of its long taproot. Growing on bottomlands and along streams, its moist location protects it from serious fire injury. The tree is often seriously injured by insects, particularly the hickory bark beetle. The logs are subject to attack by a number of wood-boring beetles, and the sapwood, even after it has been seasoned and manufactured into various products, is still subject to damage from powder post beetles.

L. W. Brownell

Orange-brown twigs bear large terminal buds, often an inch long

L. W. Brownell

An orange to chestnut-brown husk, one-fourth to one-half inch thick, covers the thick-shelled nut

Penn. Dept. Forests and Waters

The trunk is covered with shaggy gray bark similar to shagbark hickory, but the plates are less curved

L. W. Brownell

Pollen-bearing catkins, five to eight inches long, and short pistillate flower spikes appear in May

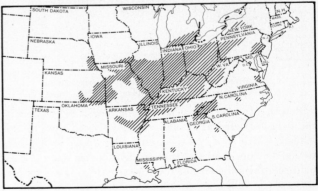

Natural range of Shellbark Hickory

MOCKERNUT HICKORY
Whiteheart hickory, Bullnut, White hickory
Carya tomentosa Nuttall

MOCKERNUT HICKORY, with its coarse leaves and twigs, grows from central New Hampshire across southern Ontario to southeastern Iowa and from northern Florida to eastern Texas. It is found on dry slopes and ridges, but attains best development on rich uplands and deep fertile soil in the lower Ohio basin and in Missouri and Arkansas. Mockernut is the most abundant of the hickories in the South and is the only one found in the southern coastal pine-belt.

Attaining maturity at 250 to 300 years, mockernut hickory sometimes reaches a height of ninety or a hundred feet with a trunk three feet in diameter, but usually it is much smaller, with upright rigid upper branches and gracefully pendulous lower ones.

The fragrant leaves, eight to twelve inches long, have

The strong, rigid branches and dull green coarse foliage form a wide, irregular, rounded crown

flattened, grooved hairy stems and occur alternately on the twigs. Each leaf is composed of five to nine toothed leaflets which taper to the base. The upper leaflets, five to eight inches long and three to five inches wide, are two or three times the size of the lowest pair. The leaves are shiny dark yellow-green above, pale green and more or less finely hairy beneath, with a stout softly hairy midrib

below. They turn yellow in autumn.

The dark reddish brown, hairy winter buds at the ends of the twigs are broadly egg-shaped and nearly three-quarters of an inch long. The side buds are similar in shape and color, but are only one-half or one-third as large. The stout angular twigs are brown, with conspicuous lenticels, and are thickly covered with pale hairs in the first year, becoming nearly smooth and dark gray in the second year. The wooly hairiness of leaf under sur-

In winter the large, stout twigs, the ascending upper branches and drooping lower ones are characteristic

faces, twigs and buds is recognized in the specific name *tomentosa*.

The flowers appear in May when the leaves are half grown. The long-stalked slender, green, hairy staminate catkins are at the base of the new growth and the pistillate ones, in two to five crowded spikes, are narrowly bell-shaped.

The nearly round reddish brown nut is smooth, slightly flattened, usually four-ridged, with a pointed tip and a slightly rounded base. It is enclosed in a thick, red-brown husk which is one and a half to two inches long and readily splits nearly to the base. The name mockernut is given this tree because the sweet kernel is small

U. S. Forest Service

The hairy terminal buds are a half to three-quarters of an inch long, while the lateral buds, though similar in color and shape, are much smaller

and difficult to extract.

Never scaly, the dark gray bark of the mockernut hickory is about one-half to three-quarters of an inch thick and furrowed into flat ridges.

The close-grained wood is heavy, a cubic foot weighing over fifty-one pounds when dry. The brown heartwood is surrounded by nearly white sapwood which is often three inches wide. The strength, hardness, toughness, and flexibility of hickory have made it the foremost wood for shock resisting handles of such tools as axes. Nearly three-fourths of all hickory lumber goes for this purpose. It is also used for vehicle parts and furniture, and it makes an excellent fuelwood.

Mockernut hickory is subject to injury by frost and fire, but young hickory is persistent and will come up in spite of repeated burning and cutting.

U. S. Forest Service

The dark, shiny leaves turn clear or rusty yellow in autumn, and the smooth reddish brown nut is enclosed in a thick, usually hairy, red-brown husk

U. S. Forest Service

The hard, irregularly furrowed bark is broken into broad, close ridges

U. S. Forest Service

The flowers appear in May, and the pollen-bearing ones shown here are hairy catkins borne in stalked clusters, while the seed-producing ones are in crowded spikes

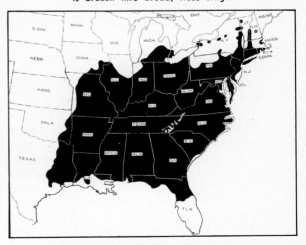

Natural range of Mockernut Hickory

179

PIGNUT HICKORY
Oval pignut hickory, Red hickory, Redheart hickory
Carya glabra (Miller) Sweet

ON DRY ridges and open pastures in woodlands and fertile coves from New Hampshire to Michigan, south through Illinois, Missouri and Arkansas, and from Florida to Louisiana, pignut hickory trees rear their compact, narrow oblong crowns and scatter disappointing nuts. With advancing age the crown becomes increasingly broad and round. The slender, more or less contorted branches droop slightly at the ends, and the trunk

In summer the dark yellow-green foliage fills in the oblong to broadly oval crown of Pignut Hickory

is usually short. Normally, pignut hickory is a tree fifty to 100 feet high, with a trunk two or three feet in diameter, but sheltered trees in secluded fertile coves of the Appalachian Mountains may reach a height of 120 feet and a trunk diameter of five feet. While pignut hickory normally matures at 200 to 300 years, the largest trees live 350 to 400 years.

Five to seven (usually five) dark yellow-green leaflets arranged pinnately along a common stem or petiole, comprise the compound leaf of this hickory. Each lance-shaped leaflet is three to six

inches long and grows directly on the leaf petiole. The entire leaf may be eight to twelve inches long. Leaves are arranged alternately on slender gray to reddish brown twigs. At the base of each leaf stem is a small blunt, red-brown bud which becomes fully formed by late summer. The oval terminal bud, although larger than the side buds, is scarcely three-eighths of an inch long, and like the lateral ones, is protected by several smooth or finely downy scales.

The scientific name, *Carya*, comes from the Greek word, "karua," which means walnut tree, while *glabra* refers to the smooth twigs and buds.

With maturity the dark gray, narrow, flattened bark ridges form irregular diamond-shaped areas. The hard, tough bark is one-half to three-quarters of an inch thick, and usually tight to the trunk.

In May, drooping clusters, or aments, of staminate flowers appear with the limp new leaves, and hidden near the end of the previous year's growth

Gnarled, up-reaching branches, with drooping ends are revealed in the fall and winter

are small pistillate blooms. By early autumn these develop into brown, pear-shaped fruits the hard shell of which splits back along four sutures to reveal a smooth, brown, slightly angled nut. The kernel is generally very difficult to extract from he shell, and the flavor varies from bitter, or astringent, to insipidly sweet.

The close-grained, light brown to creamy white wood, like that of shagbark hickory, is very hard, tough, and resilient. It is the heaviest of all the commercial hickories, weighing about fifty-three pounds to the cubic foot when air dry. As a shock-resisting wood, hickory is without equal, and is widely used for tool handles and athletic equipment where strength and toughness are required. The best hickory shows an oily or glossy side-grain surface when smoothly finished, and gives a clear ringing tone when dropped on end on a hard surface. Wide-ringed, fast growing, heavy hickory, having about six to ten growth rings to the inch, is generally strongest. Buyers are frequently prejudiced in favor of the white sapwood over the darker colored heartwood. This results in giving special value to the wide-ringed white wood from second growth stump sprouts. Careful studies, however, reveal that weight for weight, sound hickory has the same strength, toughness, and resistance to shock, regardless of whether it is red heartwood, white sapwood, or a mixture of the two. Pignut hickory is marketed with the wood of the other true hickories, and timber from this tree contributes substantially to the annual hickory lumber cut.

The wood of all the hickories is admirable for fuel, and for years green hickory has been singled

J. Horace McFarland Co.

Thin-shelled pear-shaped nuts borne on the ends of the previous season's growth are shown with the large compound leaves whose five to seven (usually five) leaflets are dark green and narrowly lance-shaped

out as best for smoking meats. It is the standard against which all other woods are compared when fuel values are considered—a cord of hickory being approximately equal to a ton of coal.

The deep taproots cause this and other hickories to be exceedingly windfirm, but surface fires frequently burn through the thin bark to cause serious injury and open the way for subsequent attacks by wood destroying fungi. Leaf-eating insects are common sources of damage, but of all its enemies the hickory bark beetle is undoubtedly most destructive. They can be discouraged by keeping the trees in a state of healthy vigor.

Pignut, in company with other hickories, is slow growing, and not to be recommended for street or roadside planting, but it is an admirable addition to parks and broad landscapes. It grows naturally in mixture with other trees, and has unusual sprouting ability.

G. B. Sudworth

The dark gray bark with flattened interlacing ridges surrounds the trunk with a tight covering

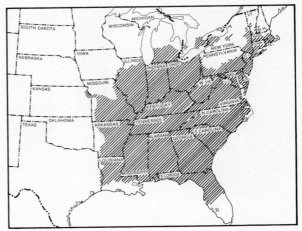

Natural range of Pignut Hickory

181

PECAN

Carya illinoensis (Wangenheim) K. Koch

ALTHOUGH belonging to the hickory genus and known for its excellent wood, pecan lays claim to commercial importance through its delicately flavored nuts. The name is of Indian origin and refers to the nuts which have since been developed to form an important article of commerce. The tree is large and has a massive trunk and stout, spreading branches which, under forest conditions, form a narrow, symmetrical, inverse, pyramidal crown, and in open-grown trees form a broad, rounded crown. Occasional trees have heights of 160 or 170 feet, and trunk diameters of six or seven feet, but usually the pecan is ninety to a hundred feet high with diameters of two and a half to four feet.

The range of pecan has been greatly widened by cultivation. Its natural range extends south from southern Illinois and southern Indiana to western Kentucky, western Tennessee and western Mississippi west through Missouri, Arkansas and Louisiana to southeastern Kansas, eastern Oklahoma and eastern Texas. It is native also as far south as Oaxaca, Mexico. It is a tree of bottomlands, demanding the rich moist soils along streams and rivers.

W. G. Baxter

W. F. Jacobs

Ripening in September or October, the thin-shelled, clustered nuts have tasty kernels which are high in food value

F. W. Besley

Largest member of the hickory group, the stout spreading branches of open-grown Pecan trees form broad rounded crowns

It reaches its greatest size in the Ohio basin. Never found in dry locations, it will thrive, however, when planted on drier sites.

Pecan is the largest of the hickories, as well as the longest lived, and trees 350 years of age or more have been known. In its early life pecan grows rapidly, and faster than any other hickory.

Twigs are rather slender. When young they are somewhat tinged with red and loosely covered with hair, later occasionally becoming smooth and marked with lenticels or pores. The sharply pointed, hairy terminal winter buds measure a half inch in length, while those growing along the twigs are smaller, less pointed, and are sometimes borne on stalks.

Leaves are pinnately compound, measuring twelve to twenty inches in length. They are arranged alternately on the twig, and have nine to fifteen short-stalked, finely toothed, sharply pointed leaflets varying from four to seven inches in length. Appearing in April or May, the slender, pendulous staminate or pollen-bearing catkins are about five inches long, and are borne near the ends of twigs of the preceding year, or occasionally on the young shoots of the current year. The small, inconspicuous, greenish pistillate flowers occur in spikes at the ends of twigs.

Ripening in September or October, the dark brown nuts, which measure from one to two and a half inches in length, are borne in clusters of three to eleven, and are covered with thin husks that break into four sections to release the nut.

Pecan is the most important nut tree native to North America, and several varieties have been developed which produce nuts of larger size and improved quality. Although grown in commercial plantations, large quantities of the nuts on the market come from wild trees. Pecan nuts are remarkable for their high food value.

Wood of pecan weighs forty-six pounds to the cubic foot when air dry and is strong, stiff, very hard and very high in shock resistance. The sapwood is white, sometimes tinged with brown, and the heartwood pale brown to reddish brown. Principal uses are flooring, furniture, small handles and fuel.

Stands of pecan sawtimber, located in the lower Mississippi Valley region were at one time estimated to contain about 500,000,000 board feet.

Pecan reproduces by seed and by sprouts from younger stumps. Never forming pure stands, it occurs in groups or singly in mixture with gum, oak, and ash. Because of its moist habitat, it is seldom damaged by fire. It is, however, subject to attack by the hickory bark beetle and to injury by frost. It is frequently used as an ornamental and shade tree in the coastal areas south from Maryland.

Another name for this tree is "pecanier" given to it by the Acadians. The scientific name Carya comes from the Greek word "karua" which means walnut tree.

Bureau of Plant Industry

Pollen-bearing flowers appear in early June on the twigs of the preceding year. The leaves resemble

W. G. Baxter

The thick bark of mature trunks is light brown or gray, and is divided into interlacing ridges broken on the surface into thick, appressed scales

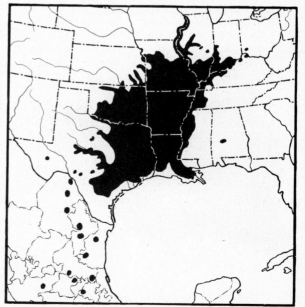

Natural range of Pecan

BITTERNUT HICKORY

Bitternut, Swamp-hickory
Carya cordiformis (Wangenheim) K. Koch

THE tall, sturdy, straight-trunked bitternut hickory, with its well-rounded top, grows from southern New Hampshire and Quebec to Minnesota and southward in all the states to western Florida and eastern Texas.

Bitternut, sometimes called swamp hickory, thrives best in low moist soil near the borders of streams and swamps, but it is also found on the drier uplands.

Ordinarily a stout-branched tree reaching a height of one hundred feet with a trunk diameter of two or three feet, it attains its largest size in bottomlands of the lower Ohio River, where occasionally it develops a trunk diameter of four feet and a height of 120 feet.

There are several species of hickory. Four of them, the true hickories, furnish a very large proportion of the high-grade hickory found on the market. The pecan hickories comprise a large number of species, and it is to this group that bitternut belongs. All the hickories are members of the walnut family, *Juglandaceae*, and all are slow-growing trees, but bitternut grows more rapidly than the rest. It is also the shortest lived of the hickories, reaching maturity at about two hundred years.

George J. Baetzhold

The crown of dark green foliage is usually well-rounded and is broadest at the top. The trunk is straight and column-like

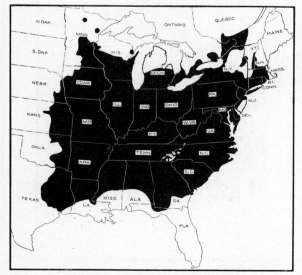

Natural range of Bitternut Hickory

George J. Baetzhold

The stout spreading branches with slender branchlets form a broad handsome head when Bitternut grows in the open

The most striking characteristic of the bitternut hickory is its bright yellow winter buds, which offer a means of identification. Those at the ends of the branchlets are one-third to three-fourths of an inch long, obliquely blunt-pointed, and enclosed in two pairs of rough scales. Buds at the sides of the branchlets are only one-eighth to three-quarters of an inch long, somewhat four-angled, sharp-pointed, nearly egg-shaped, and are often stalked.

The compound leaves are six to ten inches long, alternate on the branchlets and smallest of all hickory leaves.

Each slender hairy stalk carries seven to eleven leaflets shaped like lance heads and margined with coarse, thick-pointed teeth. The leaflets, four to six inches long and three-fourths to an inch and a quarter wide, grow directly from the stalk, and usually have an uneven base. They are dark yellow-green, shiny on the upper side and paler and hairy beneath, and turn yellow in the autumn.

The green staminate or pollen-bearing flowers appears in May or June. They are in three- to four-inch catkins borne on the twigs of the preceding season in clusters of three and hang from a common stem about an inch in length. The pistillate or nut-producing flowers, one or two to a stalk, are a half inch long, slightly four-angled, and covered with a yellow, scaly wool.

The nut, ripening in October, is almost round, abruptly contracting into a point at the end, and is enclosed in a thin scaly husk which splits about halfway down in four lines of division. It is smooth and gray with a reddish brown, very bitter kernel from which the tree gets its common name, bitternut.

Early settlers pressed oil from the kernel, which some used as a remedy against rheumatism, while others used it to feed the flame of crude lamps.

Bark on the lower trunk of mature trees is one-third to three-quarters of an inch thick, and is shallowly fissured into close, flat ridges so interwoven as to give it a net-like appearance. The slender twigs, bright green and somewhat hairy at first, soon become smooth or nearly so, and finally turn pale gray. They are marked by many small, pale, corky growths and small leaf-scars.

The dark brown wood is hard, strong, tough, and close-grained. It is heavy, a cubic foot of air-dry wood weighing forty-seven pounds. Although somewhat inferior to the wood of the true hickories in strength and shock-resisting qualities, it is used for tool handles, agricultural implements, hoops, and vehicle parts. It also makes excellent fuel.

In common with other hickories, the bitternut is susceptible to attack by a number of insects and diseases. The insect responsible for killing many trees is the hickory bark beetle. After the trees have been cut, the green wood is often seriously damaged by pinhole borers. Unless carefully stored, powder-post insects attack the seasoned sapwood of all kinds of hickory products.

Young bitternut hickory in the open is readily injured by frost. It is capable of enduring fairly dense shade for a number of years without losing vitality, and when freed by an opening in the forest, will recover and develop rapidly. This and its persistent sprouting ability when young enable it to survive many unfavorable conditions, but repeated burning or constant pasturing reduces the growth, causes the trees to become stag-headed, lowers resistance to insect attack, and ultimately the tree dies.

Hickory smoke has long been considered best for cur-

George J. Baetzhold

The thin husk of the inch-long nut is four-winged and coated with yellow, scurfy hairiness. The compound leaves of seven to eleven leaflets are relatively small

U. S. Forest Service

The light brown bark is tinged with red, scarcely three quarters of an inch thick, and is broken into thin interlacing ridges which never become shaggy

ing hams and bacon. Even now thousands of cords of wood are burned in farm smoke houses. The wood is also sought by those who enjoy an open fireplace because it forms firm glowing embers and relatively little ash.

The total sawtimber stand of bitternut hickory once was estimated to be about 1,000,000,000 board feet. It is located principally north of the range of the other pecan hickories and is frequently cut and sold in mixture with the true hickories.

SWEET BIRCH

Black birch, Cherry birch

Betula lenta Linnaeus

L. W. Brownell

In the open the trunk is short, and the branches long and spreading, but in the forest, Sweet Birch is tall and slender and clear of limbs for a great height

THE gracefully symmetrical round-topped sweet or black birch, with its nearly black bark, slender branches, and dark green foliage, is found on rich well-drained uplands from southern Maine through New York to eastern Ohio, southward to Maryland and in a narrowing area along the Appalachian Mountains to northern Georgia and Alabama. It is a common forest tree in the north, but reaches its largest size in eastern Tennessee on the western slopes of the southern Appalachians.

Sweet birch belongs to the birch group of the family *Betulaceae*, which also includes the hornbeams, the alders, and the shrubby hazel. *Betula* is the Latin name for birch. The word is supposed to have come from the old Gallic name for these trees, the wood of which the Gauls carbonized to obtain birch tar. *Lenta* means tough, pliant, bending, and applies well to the slender whip-like branches. The name "sweet birch" derives from the fragrant wintergreen flavor of the inner bark.

Sweet birch reaches a height of seventy or eighty feet with a trunk diameter of two to five feet. The bark on old trunks is one-half to three-quarters of an inch thick, dark red-brown or almost black, furrowed, and broken into thick irregular plates. On young stems and branches it is smooth and shiny, marked with long, horizontal, narrow, corky, lenticels or pores. The twigs, pale green at first, change to dark red-brown. As with all the trees in this family, there are no terminal buds. The branches grow from the uppermost lateral buds.

The leaves, growing alternately, often in pairs on the sides of the twigs, are more or less oval with an uneven, rounded or heart-shaped base, a tapering tip, and numerous sharp, slender, incurved teeth on the margin. They are two and a half to six inches long and one and a half to three inches wide. The upper surface is dark dull green and the under surface pale yellow-green, with conspicuous hairy primary veins and yellow midrib. Supported by stout, hairy stems, approximately an inch long and grooved on top, the leaves turn bright yellow in autumn.

The staminate catkins, about three-fourths of an inch long, form in the late summer, and remain on the tree through the winter. In April, before the leaves come out, these

L. W. Brownell

The lower branches are horizontal and the upper ones steeply ascending to form a wide-spreading crown in open-grown trees

catkins open to three or four inches in length, are bright yellow and, later, when the pollen develops, greenish yellow. The pistillate catkins are green and little more than half an inch long, maturing into erect small-scaled cones, one to one and a half inches long.

The wood of sweet birch is strong, hard, heavy, close-grained, has high shock-resistance, and a cubic foot when dry weighs forty-eight pounds. The dark red-brown heartwood is enclosed in pale yellow sapwood that is several inches thick. Its principal uses include general millwork, boxes, crates, spools, bobbins, novelties, woodenware, fuel, motor vehicle parts, pulp, and, because it takes a fine polish, it is used for furniture. Sweet birch is used for distillation in the production of wood alcohol. Distillation of the wood, bark and twigs also produces oil of birch, a substitute for oil of wintergreen used for flavoring, while birch beer is made from the sap.

The worst enemy of sweet birch is the bronze birch borer which tunnels between wood and bark. This pest

Devereux Butcher

The leaves grow in alternate pairs along the sides of the twigs or singly near the tips, and the cone-like fruits grow from the base of the leaf stems

is usually not prevalent in healthy stands of forest-grown sweet birch, but prefers old trees, trees on poor sites, and open-grown trees. Young trees are sometimes attacked by fungus.

Devereux Butcher

Bark on the lower trunk of old trees is cracked into irregular scales, and on young trunks and limbs it is smooth, and has horizontal pores

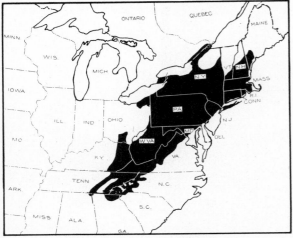

Natural range of Sweet or Black Birch

Devereux Butcher

Seed-producing catkins are pale green and grow erect from the sides of the twigs, while the pollen-bearing staminate ones shown at the right, are yellow and hang from the tips of twigs

YELLOW BIRCH

Silver birch, Swamp birch

Betula alleghaniensis Britton

A LUSTROUS, silvery yellow bark on limbs and young trunks makes yellow birch easy to identify. Except on very young trees, the bark peels into thin, papery strips that give a ragged appearance. Marked by horizontal red and white pine, spruce and balsam fir. Second growth forests sometimes contain limited areas of pure yellow birch, with straight, gleaming trunks.

In the open, trunks are usually short and divide into numerous large ascending limbs with slender, somewhat pendulous branchlets that form a broad open head. Under forest conditions trunks are tall and clear of limbs. Mature trees average sixty to seventy feet in height with trunks two or three feet in diameter. On preferred sites trees reach ninety or a hundred feet with trunk diameters of four feet.

The range of yellow birch extends from Newfoundland, Nova Scotia and the north shore of the St. Lawrence River west to Minnesota and northeastern Wisconsin, and southward along the mountains to Georgia. A tree of

Often attaining large size, the straight, slender trunk and oval crown are characteristic of the forest-grown Yellow Birch

lenticels or pores, the bark on old trunks is gray or blackish, deeply grooved and about a half inch thick.

Yellow birch grows in mixture with beech, maple, ash,

Each scale of the cone-like fruit contains three winged seeds. Seeds and scales drop away in autumn leaving a central, erect core on the twig

During the winter, before developing into pendent catkins, the staminate aments are shiny chestnut-brown, and about three-quarters of an inch long

rich, moist woodlands, its preferred sites are valleys and stream banks, although it adapts itself to higher ground, as in the mountains of New England, where it reaches elevations of 3,000 feet.

The twigs resemble those of sweet birch, but lack the strong wintergreen flavor of the latter. They are green and hairy at first, turning light orange-brown during the first summer, later becoming smooth and dark. Covered with three to eight scales, which are downy on the margins, the winter buds are found only along the sides of the twigs, a terminal bud being absent. At the tips of the twigs the pendent staminate or pollen-bearing catkins are borne in clusters of two to four. At the sides of the twigs the solitary, stemless pistillate or seed-producing flowers appear, and by autumn develop into scaly, seed-bearing cones about an inch in length.

Attached by short, grooved stems, the leaves are pointed, with sharply double-toothed margins. Dull dark green above, they are yellow-green beneath, with hairs on the veins, and measure three to four inches long and one and a half to two inches wide.

Yellow birch wood weighs forty pounds to the cubic foot when dry. It is hard, strong, and takes a satiny polish. Heartwood is light brown tinged with red, and the sapwood nearly white. Most abundant of all our native birches, yellow birch makes up from two-thirds to three-fourths of the stand of birch in the United States. It is used for furniture, packing boxes, button molds, wheel hubs, flooring, veneer, interior finish, woodenware, agricultural implements and many other purposes. Areas of greatest commercial abundance are Wisconsin, northern Michigan, New England, and New York.

The lustrous, silvery yellow bark on limbs and young trunks peels into thin papery curls

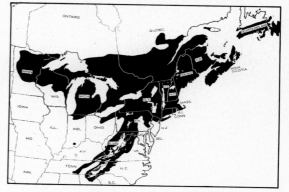

Natural range of Yellow Birch

189

PAPER BIRCH
Canoe birch, White birch
Betula papyrifera Marshall

SINGLY or in clusters, the creamy white stemmed, open-crowned paper birch—bright green in summer and lacy in winter—prefers moist, rich soil, but grows on a variety of sites from Newfoundland, Nova Scotia, New England, Pennsylvania, northwestward across Canada to Alaska, south to western Montana, northern Idaho and Washington. It is the most widely distributed of the world's thirty varieties of birch. Trees reach sixty to eighty feet in height, with diameters of two to three feet, but are usually smaller. Paper birch seldom lives longer than 150 years. With age the crown becomes broad and open with few large limbs, many horizontal branches and flexible twigs.

The simple, irregularly double-toothed, abruptly pointed, oval leaves with broad bases grow alternately from smooth reddish brown twigs. They are two to

A. H. Ballantine

Devereux Butcher

Gleaming white bark and an open crown with small branches and many flexible twigs distinguish Paper Birch throughout the seasons

three inches long, one and a half to two inches wide, bright green above and lighter beneath with warty glands along the main veins.

Slender, brown, tassel-like male catkins three to four inches long hang in twos and threes from the twig ends in April or May. Back from these and nearly erect are short greenish female cones. By autumn,

The irregularly toothed leaves are two to three inches long, while the seed cone, erect at first, later becoming pendant, is an inch or more long

In early spring twigs bear long dangling staminate catkins with shorter nearly erect pistillate cones

these ripen into cylindrical, short-stalked, loose, cone-like fruits packed with thin heart-shaped discs to which tiny, oval seeds are attached. Millions of seeds are released annually to germinate on exposed mineral soil, such as old burns. Thus many available openings are reforested and paper birch may cover more land today than when America was discovered.

On young trees and older branches the chalky, lustrous white bark peels and may be separated into paper-thin layers marked with horizontal lenticels or breathing pores. On the copper-colored inner bark, these pores are bright orange. With age the outer bark rolls back in irregular, frayed, horizontal sheets and the blotchy, blackened lower trunk develops increasingly deep fissures. Early explorers adopted the craft of the northern Indians by using this bark for canoes, as well as for receptacles in which to store or carry food. The modern tendency to strip it is often fatal to the trees and always disfiguring.

The scientific term *papyrifera* describes the paper-like bark, while *Betula* is the Latin name for birch. It closely resembles European birch, *Betula alba*, with its pendulous variety. This species was adopted as the "Mothers' Tree" in 1923.

The close-grained, hard, fairly tough heartwood of paper birch is light brown tinged with red, while the thick sapwood is nearly white. When air dry a cubic foot weighs about thirty-seven pounds. It works readily but is not durable in contact with the soil. It is used for spools, clothespins, toothpicks, shoe pegs, shoe lasts, novelties, turnery, and for pulp and fuel.

Supplies of paper birch, much of which is of cord-wood size, are located mostly in the Northeast and to a less extent, in the lake states. "Red heart" frequently reduces the usefulness of one-sixth the mature stand. Trees may reach sixty to eighty feet with diameters of nine or ten inches in sixty-five years, but seldom live beyond 150 years. Occasionally in pure stands, paper birch associates with white pine, red pine, red spruce, aspen and yellow birch.

Paper birch is especially attractive when planted in combination with evergreens. Trees grown south of the natural range are usually killed by borers.

Horizontal lenticels and dark blotched scars mark the fraying white bark with under layers of orange

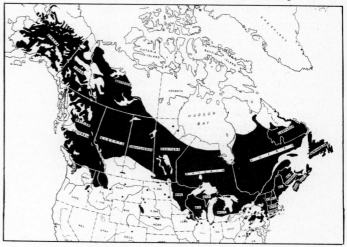

Natural range of Paper Birch

RIVER BIRCH
Water birch, Red birch
Betula nigra Linnaeus

Devereux Butcher

River Birch attains heights of eighty or ninety feet, with trunk sometimes five feet in diameter

growing in drier sites, the bark on branches may be smooth, shiny, and gray. On mature trunks it may be an inch thick, dark red-brown or dark gray with thick irregular scales.

The slender, lustrous, chestnut-brown twigs are hairy and covered with lenticels. The winter buds are pointed, smooth, or slightly hairy and encased by three to seven red-brown scales.

Throughout the world there are thirty species of birch, and, of these, twelve are native to North America with their distribution reaching from the arctic circle south to Texas and Florida.

River birch is also called red birch, water birch, blue birch, and black birch. The scientific name, *Betula nigra*, was given this tree by Linnaeus. While this means black birch, it is in some degree a misnomer. The Latin word *nigra* probably refers to the blackish bark on the lower trunk of mature trees, but since the bark on upper trunk and branches is pale cinnamon to even a silvery gray, the name does not strictly apply. *Betula lenta* is more truly a black birch.

The alternate, angularly ovate leaves of river birch are borne on short, slender, hairy, slight-

Two or three slightly diverging limbs divide into many branches and branchlets to form an irregular crown

Devereux Butcher

STREAM and river banks, the shores of ponds, and swampy forest land in the eastern third of the United States are the natural habitat of the river or red birch. A mature tree usually has a short trunk that divides into several large ascending limbs which compose an open, irregular crown of slender drooping branchlets. Under favorable conditions, particularly in the bayous of the lower Mississippi Valley, river birch attains a height of a hundred feet with a trunk diameter of five feet, but normally it is fifty to eighty feet tall, with trunk diameters of two to three feet. River birch grows as far north as New Hamphire and Massachusetts, but principally from Pennsylvania and southern Kentucky to western Florida and the Gulf of Mexico, and from Iowa to eastern Texas.

Like other birch species, this one is graceful in form, but its chief distinguishing characteristic is the cinnamon-colored bark with its somewhat metallic sheen which separates into ragged, papery scales. On young trunks and the upper limbs and branches of old trees, it is marked by narrow, longitudinal lenticels, or breathing pores. On older trees, epecially those

ly flattened stems, and measure one and a half to three inches in length. They are unevenly double-toothed, pointed at the outer end, and are distinguished by their broad, wedge-shaped base. The newly opened, light yellow-green leaves are hairy on both sides and are accompanied at the base of their stems by pale green stipules, or leaf-like appendages. These drop off after the leaves are fully developed. The mature leaves are thin and tough, deep green and lustrous above, paler beneath, and smooth except on the midrib and primary veins. In autumn they add to the color of the woods by turning dull yellow before falling.

The pollen-bearing staminate catkins form during the preceding season and are clustered at the ends of twigs. By April or May they are two or three inches long. The pistillate or seed-producing catkins appear when the leaf buds begin to open and they are borne singly and erect on the short, two-leaved lateral twigs. Unlike the fall-ripened seeds of other birches, those of the river birch mature in late spring or early summer. The small, winged, nut-like seeds are driven by the wind or carried by water. They germinate readily in the moist, deep, rich, alluvial soils of bottomlands, which are the natural habitat of this tree. Though a fast growing tree when young, river birch is comparatively short-lived, and will tolerate little shade at any stage of its life. Young stumps produce vigorous sprouts.

A cubic foot of the air-dry wood weighs about thirty-five pounds. It is strong, close-grained, rather hard, and more durable in contact with the soil than other birch woods. The heartwood is light brown and the sapwood pale buff in color. It is of relatively small commercial importance because of its scattered distribution and is used largely in the locality where it is grown. When cut, the wood may be marketed with beech and maple, as well as with other birch species. It is used locally in the manufacture of cheap furniture, turned articles, shoe lasts, wooden shoes, yokes, berry baskets, and wagon hubs. Hoops for peach baskets in Maryland and for rice casks farther south are made from the branches. There are no estimates concerning the volume of merchantable river birch lumber available, and no record is kept of the lumber manufactured and sold from this single species. The tree is well able to reproduce itself, and the supply is not being heavily drawn upon.

River birch is not particularly susceptible to disease or to attack by insects, but it is frequently severely injured and even killed by the action of heavy cakes of ice which are carried downstream with the flood during early spring thaws. On such occasions, young trees may be pushed down and stripped of their bark as the ice passes over them.

Because of its graceful form, this tree is well suited for ornamental purposes. In the Northeast it is often planted in parks and on estates, preferring soil which is relatively deep, moist, and well drained.

George J. Baetzhold

Cone-like cylindrical fruits mature in May and June while the undersides of the deep green double-toothed leaves are still coated with fine hairs

Devereux Butcher

The bark on old trunks is dark, red-brown and nearly an inch thick, deeply furrowed, and broken into closely pressed scales

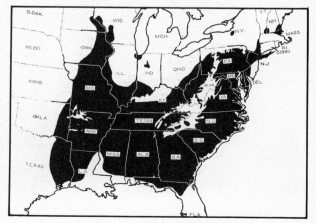

Natural range of River or Red Birch

GRAY BIRCH

Oldfield birch, Poplar birch, Wire birch
Betula populifolia Marshall

THIS is the smallest of our northeastern tree birches. Although it resembles rather closely the paper birch in form of tree and white bark, there are distinct differences which can be easily recognized. Gray birch grows throughout Nova Scotia and Prince Edward Island. Also New Brunswick and Maine except their northern areas. Thence from extreme southern Quebec, it is found southward in New England, eastern New York, Pennsylvania and most of New Jersey. Occurrence is sporadic west to Indiana and south to North Carolina.

It is commonly found on moist soil along streams, ponds and lakes; sometimes also in swamps and along their borders, as well as on dry, sandy or gravelly soil. Because, like paper birch and aspen, gray birch springs up quickly on impoverished soil, it grows on large areas of burned-over and abandoned land and performs a real service in covering the ground and affording an opportunity for the growth of other more valuable species to take over.

The tree commonly attains a height of only twenty to thirty feet and a diameter of fifteen inches or less; it is seldom more than forty feet high and eighteen inches in

Devereux Butcher

Short slender branches and delicate foliage clothe the Gray Birch nearly to the ground, giving it a narrow crown

W. H. Balla

After the leaves have fallen, the graceful, often pendulous. and more or less contorted branches come into prominence

diameter. The short, slender, often pendulous and more or less contorted branches clothe the stem nearly to the ground and form a narrow, pyramidal crown.

The alternate leaves, which occur singly or in pairs on the bright red-brown or gray twigs, are thin and firm, dark green above and paler beneath, turning pale yellow in the autumn. They are nearly triangular in outline and bear a resemblance to those of eastern cottonwood *Populus deltoides*, hence the specific name *populifolia*, which is sometimes translated into the common name "poplar-leaved birch." However, in gray birch the leaves are long-pointed and the margins are double-toothed. Measuring two to three inches long and one and a half to two and a half inches wide, they have long slender stems and, like the quaking aspen, they flutter in the slightest breeze.

In April or May, as the leaves unfold, the male flowers appear in slender, yellowish catkins which, as in all the birches, were formed during the previous growing season. During the winter they are one and a quarter to one and a half inches long and in the spring increase to from two to four inches. They hang from the twigs singly or occasionally in pairs. The greenish female catkins, one-half to one inch in length, stand nearly erect on stems one-half inch long. In the fall they develop into small, cylindrical, erect or drooping, slender-stalked cones with deciduous scales and many small, nut-like, winged seeds. The wings, slightly broader than the seeds, enable them to be carried far by the wind. This accounts for the tree quickly taking possession of burned-over, cutover and abandoned land, which has given the tree the name "oldfield birch." Abundant seed crops are produced nearly every year and the seed germinates readily. Gray birch also reproduces by sprouts from the stump when it is cut.

On young trunks and branches the bark is red-brown or gray, soon becoming white with a reddish yellow inner surface, and on older trunks darker and rough, and irregularly broken by shallow fissures. While resembling that of paper-birch, the bark of gray birch is not quite as clear white, is rougher, peels much less, and has rough, black, triangular patches below the junctions of the branches with the trunk.

The heartwood is light brown and the thick sapwood nearly white. A cubic foot of the air-dry wood weighs about thirty-five pounds. It is close-grained, soft, not strong and has low resistance to decay. Like paper birch, it is easily worked with tools and because of its fine, soft, even texture it is an excellent wood for turning. While the uses are similar to those for paper birch, including small woodenware such as spools, clothespins, and turned novelties, gray birch is of much less value for these products because of the small size of the tree and the consequent waste in manufacture. It is good for fuel, and stands can be cut over for firewood at comparatively frequent intervals because of the tree's ability to renew itself.

A short-lived tree, gray birch grows rapidly and is free from disease and insect injury, except for a leaf miner, although it is often seriously injured by ice and snow. The pleasing form, white bark, graceful, slender branches and delicate foliage combine to make gray birch an attractive tree for ornamental purposes. Its desirability is lessened only by its short life and liability to storm injury.

The cylindrical cones are packed with small, nut-like, winged seeds which are carried by the wind. The thin leaves are triangular and double-toothed

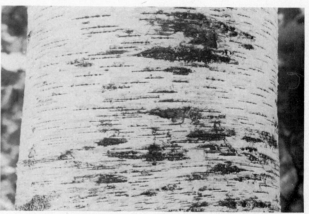

On young trunks and branches the bark is red-brown or gray, soon becoming white with a reddish yellow inner surface. Older trunks are dark and rough

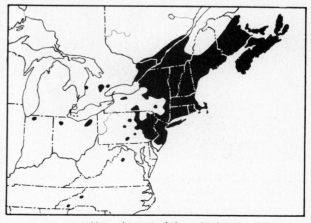

Natural range of Gray Birch

RED ALDER

Oregon alder, Western alder

Alnus rubra Bong.

VISITORS to the Pacific coast sometimes mistake the smoothly rounded trunk and mottled pale bark of red alder for that of birch. Like the birch it is gregarious, loving the company of other trees, particularly those of the same species. Red alder typically occurs in groups or in dense groves along water courses and in sheltered coves where soils are moist and fertile and where rains

are frequent. Usually three or four shallowly rooted stems are close together, the tapering boles inclining outward to present their narrow, pyramidal crowns to the light. Groves may occupy several acres of stream bottoms or moist slopes. Even in mixture with conifers and other hardwoods—as is often the case—it occurs characteristically in groups and seldom singly.

Red alder is the most important of six alders found in the United States and neighboring territory. Four of these occupy the Pacific region. Many other species existed during earlier geological periods.

Wherever soil and moisture are adequate, alder seeds in promptly after old growth forests are removed by logging, fire, or other causes. Being relatively short-lived it gives way to more enduring cone-bearing trees. Meanwhile, it serves to enrich those areas and provides a nurse crop, under the protection of which more

John Woods

Red Alder characteristically occurs in groups or in dense groves along water courses and in sheltered coves. Winter (right) reveals a tapering bole inclining outward to present a narrow, pyramidal crown to the light. Under favorable conditions Red Alder often attains heights of from 100 to 130 feet

valuable trees get started. Accordingly, it is a useful silvicultural tool and, being comparatively fire-resistant, is sometimes planted for firebreaks where new crops of Douglasfir, hemlock, cedar, or spruce are desired.

A common practice is to drill alder seed (with hand drill) or set year-old seedlings along the margins of gravelled truck and rail logging roads. Such roads are built through the forest area for logging use and later abandoned. Usually moisture along the road margins is sufficient to assure rapid growth. Within a few years the little trees spread laterally by sprouting as well as by seeding and eventually fire lines ten to twenty yards in width are established. By the time they are no longer needed as protection the older individuals yield merchantable logs.

Red alders planted for roadside shade and home beautification develop broad, roundly pyramidal crowns quite unlike those of forest-grown specimens. In dense stands, on favorable sites, as in the Puget Sound region, adult red alders attain heights of 100 to 130 feet and are one to three feet in diameter at breast height. Ordinarily they mature in about fifty years when they are eighty to one hundred feet tall and fourteen to eighteen inches in diameter. Trees seldom live more than eighty years.

The leaves are smooth and deep yellow-green on the upper surfaces, paler beneath and coated with short rusty hairs. They are three to six inches long, one and one-half to three inches wide, conspicuously straight veined, and the doubly toothed borders are slightly curved toward the under surface. They are shed in the autumn while still green.

The catkins of both male and female flowers are in clusters, the male four to six inches long; the female smaller with red scales. The latter mature into brown-orange cones containing fifty to a hundred small, flattened, nut-like seeds.

The slender to moderately stout, bright red to red-brown twigs are marked with pale pores. The winter buds are a third of an inch long.

The bark is smooth and mottled light gray to almost white. On large trees it cracks into square-cornered segments. Trunks and larger limbs often are spotted with moss.

Red alder is the most plentiful of the few hardwoods of the Pacific slope. Its range extends from southeastern Alaska, along the coast of British Columbia, Washington, Oregon and California.

The pale yellow wood is generally close textured and straight grained. It is fairly soft and workable, moderately strong, but lacks durability when in contact with the soil. It holds paint or enamel and will glue satisfactorily.

The thick, dark green leaves, four to six inches long, are slightly curved on the edges. The catkins are in clusters, the male (1) four to six inches long, the female (2) about a half-inch long. Cones (3) are borne on orange-colored stems

Bark is gray and mottled

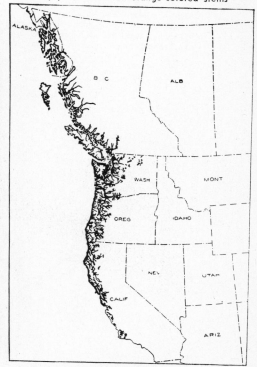

Natural range of Red Alder

197

AMERICAN HORNBEAM

Blue beech, Water beech, Ironwood
Carpinus caroliniana Walter

AMERICAN hornbeam is a small bushy tree with long, slender, tough, more or less zigzag branches, forming a wide-spreading, flat or round-topped crown. The usual height is from ten to thirty feet, with a trunk diameter of one and a half to two feet, but it sometimes attains a height of sixty feet and a diameter of three feet. The short trunk and larger branches are characteristically furrowed and ridged, often irregularly, and are covered with a thin, tight, smooth, bluish gray bark, which has given it the name "blue beech," common in some localities. It is also called "water beech" because it frequently grows near the water. Another name applied to it is "ironwood" because of the extreme hardiness of the wood. Like the hophornbeam, it is found over nearly all the eastern United States from Maine westward to Minnesota, and south to Florida and eastern Texas. It is most abundant and attains its largest size in the south Atlantic states and in Texas. The tree prefers low moist bottomlands and is often seen along the banks of streams where the shade is deep and the moisture plentiful. Frequently it forms an understory in forests of mixed hardwoods.

The leaves, like those of the hophornbeam, are more or less egg-shaped in outline, with long-pointed tips and doubly saw-toothed margins. They are somewhat smaller than those of hophornbeam, however, measuring from two to four inches in length and one to one and three-quarters inches wide. They are thin and firm, pale dull blue-green above, light yellow-green below and are borne on slender, hairy stems about one-half inch long. The slender yellow midrib and numerous slender hairy veins are conspicuous. In the fall they turn scarlet and orange.

Hornbeam, *Carpinus*, differs from other members of the birch family in that the pollen-bearing catkins are not formed until the spring of the year in which they mature. They measure from one to one-and-a-half inches in length when fully grown and hang near the ends of short lateral branches of the preceding season. Slender-stalked, semi-erect female or pistillate catkins are borne at the ends of the twigs. The fruit consists of a small nut about a third of an inch long borne at the base of a leaf-like, coarsely saw-toothed, short-stalked bract from one to one and a quarter inches long and nearly one inch wide, crowded on slender, hairy, red-brown stems five to six inches long.

The small, narrowly egg-shaped to oblong, pointed winter buds are about one-eighth inch long. They are chestnut-brown to reddish brown and

L. W. Brownell

American Hornbeam is a small tree with long branches that form a wide-spreading or round-topped crown. Its usual height is ten to thirty feet, but it sometimes reaches sixty feet. Many of the branches have a zigzag form, most noticeable in the winter

L. W. Brownell

are more or less hairy, especially the staminate flower buds. Lateral buds take the place of terminal buds which are absent. The twigs are slender, dark red and shining, smooth or often somewhat hairy.

The tough, close-grained wood is very hard and strong. When thoroughly air-dry a cubic foot weighs forty-nine pounds. The heartwood is light brown and the thick sapwood pale white. Because the bole of the tree is short, and often crooked, it is rarely converted into sawed products.

Seed is produced abundantly almost every year and is easily distributed by the wind. The tree also reproduces by sprouts from the stump. It is very resistant to wind, insects and fungi.

L. W. Brownell

The leaves are thin and firm with long pointed tips and doubly saw-toothed edges

L. W. Brownell

Somewhat similar to that of beech, the blue-gray bark is thin, tight and smooth

L. W. Brownell

The fruit is a small nut borne at the base of a leaf-like bract

L. W. Brownell

The staminate flowers, borne in catkins, hang from short stems.

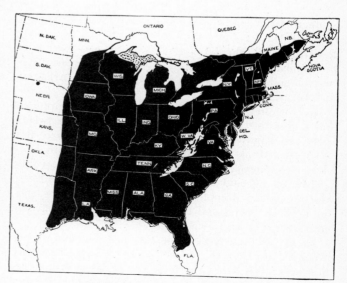

Natural range of American Hornbeam

199

EASTERN HOPHORNBEAM

American hophornbeam

Ostrya virginiana (Miller) Koch

THE eastern hophornbeam is a small, shapely tree with bark of narrow scales and a broad head of slender branches. It seldom occurs in large groups but usually grows scattered singly on well-drained gravelly ridges

Eastern Hophornbeam is a small tree with long, spreading branches that form an irregular, broad crown, often as broad as high

and slopes in the shade of oaks, maples, and other larger trees. It is found from Nova Scotia westward through southern Canada to the lower slopes of the Black Hills of South Dakota and southward in all the eastern states to northern Florida and eastern Texas. It also extends to the highlands of southern Mexico and Guatemala. It is most abundant and reaches its largest size in Arkansas and Texas.

The eastern hophornbeam tree usually is not more than thirty feet tall with a short trunk eighteen or twenty inches in diameter, but occasionally is fifty or sixty feet tall with a trunk nearly two feet in diameter. In most cases it develops a broad top, sometimes as much as fifty feet across, of many small spreading branches, the lower ones sometimes drooping, but with the branchlets tending upward. Twigs and branches are so tough that they are rarely injured by wind.

Though easily mistaken for a young elm, this species is one of four belonging to the *Ostrya* group of the family *Betulaceae*. It is the more widely known of two species native to North America. The other, Knowlton's hophorn-

beam, is rare. It grows in Arizona at Grand Canyon National Park, in the San Francisco Mountains, in northern Yavapai County, and in the Guadelupe and Sacramento mountains of New Mexico, and is reported from southeastern Utah and southeastern Texas. The common name, hophornbeam, is suggested by the fruit, which resembles that of the hop-vine, and by its wood, which has a horny texture. *Ostrya*, the classical name, is from the Greek meaning a tree with hard wood.

The alternate leaves, three to five inches long and one and a half to two inches wide, have short, slender, hairy stems. They are egg-shaped in general, with more or less rounded or slightly heart-shaped bases, tapering tips, and saw-toothed margins. When full grown the leaves are thin and tough, with the upper surface dark yellow-green and the lower surface pale yellow-green. Prominent on the under side are the light yellow, slender, hairy midrib and the numerous parallel, slender, primary veins. In autumn the leaves turn yellow.

During most of the year the twigs are tipped with slender, cylindrical buds of the staminate or pollen-bearing catkins, which are about one-half inch in length. These develop in April and May at the same time as the leaves,

The Davey Tree Expert Co.

Eastern Hophornbeam is a tree of high, dry ridges. It has scaly bark, long slender branches, and tough, upturned branchlets

200

The leaves are thin, papery and tough, turning pale yellow in autumn, and the bladder-like scales of the fruit are pale green or reddish

L. W. Brownell

L. W. Brownell

Pendent staminate catkins, green, tinged with red, and about two inches long, develop in April or May to fertilize the pistillate catkins growing from the sides of the twigs

Bark of Eastern Hophornbeam is thin, flaky and grayish brown broken into flat scales that are loose at the ends

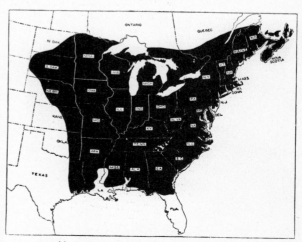

Natural range of Eastern Hophornbeam

becoming about two inches long. The pistillate flowers are in slender, pendant catkins about one-quarter inch long with thin hairy stems and pale green or reddish, leaf-like scales. The hop-like fruit is one to two inches long, two-thirds of an inch to one inch wide and borne on a short, slender, hairy stem. It consists of a number of small sacs each containing a flat nut about a third of an inch long.

The light chestnut-brown winter buds are a quarter inch long and slightly hairy. No terminal buds are formed and the branches lengthen from upper lateral buds. The slender, light green twigs turn a shiny light orange by midsummer. Retaining their luster, they become red-brown during the first winter and gradually grow darker brown with age.

The bark is a quarter inch thick, grayish brown, and rough, with narrow, elongated plate-like scales.

The strong, hard wood is light brown, tinged with red, with an outer layer of nearly white sapwood a few inches wide. It is tough, close-grained, and heavy, a cubic foot weighing fifty-two pounds when dry, is durable in contact with the soil but, while it is capable of taking a fine polish, it commands no special attention in commerce because the trees are small and scattered. It is used for fence posts, tool handles, mallets and other articles.

The eastern hophornbeam is a slow-growing tree that can easily be raised from seed. The seeds usually take two years to germinate. A very hardy tree, it is not seriously injured by disease, rots, or insect enemies.

BEECH

Fagus grandifolia Ehrhart

BEECH is native to a broad area from southern Canada, northern Michigan and eastern Wisconsin to the Atlantic, and south to eastern Texas and northern Florida. Preferring deep, rich, well-drained soils, it grows wherever moisture is in the upper layers. It attains largest size, however, in the alluvial bottomlands of the Ohio and lower Mississippi river valleys, and along the western slopes of the southern Appalachians. Here trees with trunks more than four feet in diameter reach heights of 120 feet.

The glossy, blue-green, straight-veined leaves are simple and alternate on the twigs. They are three to five inches long and rather coarsely serrate with a vein terminating in each tooth.

Male and female flowers, which occur on the same tree, appear in early spring when the leaves are half grown; the yellow-green staminate ones being about an inch in diameter, hanging from long stems, while the

Devereux Butcher

Open-grown Beech trees have a low, wide, spreading crown comprised of many long horizontal branches. The smooth, tight-fitting bark is silvery gray touched with irregular dark blotches and bands

W. R. Mattoon

Devereux Butcher

202

pistillate ones are usually in pairs covered with many pointed bracts and supported on a short hairy stem.

By early autumn the short-stalked bur is ripe. Within, surrounded by a downy lining, there are two or three small triangular, highly polished, brown, sweet-meated edible nuts. These are responsible for the classical Latin name *Fagus*, from the Greek, *phagus*, to eat; while *grandifolia* refers to the leaves. This tree reproduces by root sprouts, as well as by seeds.

The smooth, close-fitting, gray bark covers the trunk and branches like a skin. Seldom more than half an inch thick, it is frequently mottled with dark blotches and bands.

Beech wood is light red in color, heavy, hard, strong, close-grained, and difficult to split. A cubic foot when air dry weighs about forty-five pounds. It shrinks considerably in drying, is not durable when left in contact with the soil, but takes a high polish and wears well when subjected to friction under water. The wood is used for chairs and other furniture, flooring, railroad ties, woodenware, handles, novelties, and, because of its clean odor, for barrels and boxes built to contain foods.

The largest stands of beech are in the southern part of the tree's range.

As an ornamental on large lawns and estates, the beech is exceptionally fine because of its smooth, gray bark, which is especially noticeable in winter, and in summer, its rich, often dense head of foliage, which is strikingly beautiful and effective.

Of relatively slow growth, it may attain ages of 300 to 400 years. It is subject to several injurious insects and fungi, and the thin bark makes it an easy victim of ground fires.

The yellow-green staminate blooms appear when the leaves are nearly grown. Each leaf is three to five inches long with parallel veins terminating at the marginal teeth. The tapering bud is an inch long and polished brown

Triangular nuts are encased in a small prickly bur

Natural range of Beech

AMERICAN CHESTNUT

Castanea dentata (Marshall) Borkhausen

THE American chestnut, which once gave joy to many people, has vanished from the American scene, except for rather widespread sprouting from the old roots. Before the chestnut blight had caused its destruction, chestnut was found from southern Maine throughout the northern states to the foothills of the southern Appalachian Mountains and west as far as southern Michigan through Indiana to northern Mississippi. Suited to a variety of soils, chestnut attained its greatest size on well drained slopes in western North Carolina and eastern Tennessee. Here trees a hundred feet high with trunks five and six feet in diameter were found, and trees sixty to eighty feet high were not uncommon. The tapering trunk divided into several horizontal or ascending branches to form a broad, somewhat pyramidal head.

Commonly called American chestnut, and sometimes sweet chestnut because of the nut, the Indians of central New York called it "O-heh-yah-tah," or prickly bur. *Castanea dentata*, the scientific name, includes the Latin name for chestnut and refers to the conspicuous incurved teeth on the margins of the leaves.

On sprouts, the long catkins of male flowers appear during late June

U. S. Forest Service

Open-grown American Chestnut developed a broad, somewhat pyramidal crown, supported on a short thick trunk

The trunk divided into several sturdy, horizontal or ascending branches to form a broad, somewhat pyramidal head

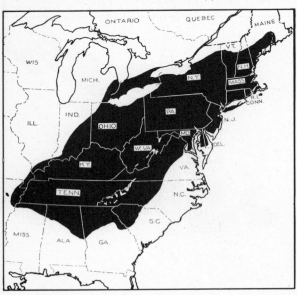

Natural range of American Chestnut

and early July. Less conspicuous fruit-bearing flowers develop simultaneously on the new wood of the same trees, and in a few weeks prickly burs appear. These become two to two and one-half inches in diameter by the end of August, and ripen during October and November, when the prickly covering splits open and reveals one to five dark brown sweet-meated nuts within a velvet-lined case.

The dark grayish brown bark of mature trees was one to two inches thick, hard and deeply cleft to form broad flat ridges. That of young trees was smooth, often shining, and of a purplish brown color. It was an important source of tannin for the leather industry.

The buds are bluntly pointed, chestnut-brown, alternate on the branches, and are borne singly at the ends of the twigs rather than clustered, as with the oaks. The leaves are simple, five to ten inches long, narrow, toothed, and smooth on both sides. A cross-section of a twig reveals a star-shaped pith.

Chestnut reproduces from sprouts, as well as from seeds. When cut or killed by fire or blight, chestnut trees sprouted vigorously from the stump, which resulted in groups of two or more sprouts. In the blight-infested range, the roots and stumps of dead or felled trees annually produce sprouts which live for a year or more before they in turn are struck down by the disease.

The wood was reddish brown with light colored sapwood. Although coarse, light, and relatively weak, it was useful for structural purposes, for interior trim, for fence posts, ties, pulpwood and fuel, as well as for furniture, packing cases, and crates. Superficially resembling oak, but without prominent medullary rays, a cubic foot air dry weighed only thirty pounds. Similarly it lacked the strength of oak. The ability of chestnut wood to resist attacks of wood-destroying fungi encouraged its wide use for fence posts, fence rails and railway ties.

Had it not been for the chestnut blight, this tree would still rank among the more important commercial and horticultural trees of the eastern states. But the commercial supply has disappeared. The chestnuts had long been used for food, while tannic acid, used for tanning leather, was secured from the wood.

The chestnut blight, a fungus disease accidentally brought to North America from Asia before we had enacted plant quarantine laws, was first recognized in New York City, in 1904. From there it spread rapidly, until, by the late 1930's, the entire natural range had been affected.

There are other enemies of the chestnut, but by comparison with the blight, they are of secondary importance. No adequate method of controlling the blight has been found; but scientists still are trying to develop a blight-resistant hybrid with European chestnut. Others still are seeking, through various means, to find or develop a blight-resistant strain. None so far has been found.

Warren D. Brush

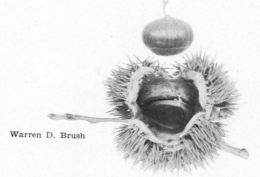

Warren D. Brush

(Upper right) Long catkins of male flowers deck the larger sprouts in June and July, nearly two months after the leaves have appeared
(Center right) Before the leaves have fallen in October, the prickly burs occurring on older sprouts have turned brown, and the sweet-meated chestnuts have burst from their velvet-lined case
(Lower right) The gray-brown bark of old trees was deeply fissured to form broad smooth plates
(Lower left) The winter buds on sprouts are alternate on the twig, bluntly pointed and smooth

205

TANOAK

Tanbark oak

Lithocarpus densiflorus (Hooker and Arnold) Rehder

TANOAK holds a unique position in that, of about 100 species of evergreen trees included in the genus *Lithocarpus*, it is the only one native to the western hemisphere, the other species growing in southeastern Asia and the Indian Archipelago. Moreover, this genus is considered a connecting link between the oaks and the chestnuts; its flowers are nearly identical with those of the chestnut while its fruit resembles that of the oaks. This species was formerly classed as an oak and was called "tan oak" and "tanbark oak" because of the extensive use of its bark for tanning on the Pacific coast. Spelling the name as one word, "tanoak," indicates that it is not a true oak species.

W. A. Eliot

The mature Tanoak attains a usual height of from 50 to 75 feet, with a diameter of from one to two feet

From the Umpqua River in southwestern Oregon southward through the coast ranges to the Santa Ynez Mountains (Santa Barbara County), and also in the northern Sierra Nevada of California, tanoak generally occurs from sea level to 4,000 and 5,000 feet elevation in valleys and on low slopes, the borders of low mountains and foothill streams, coves and ravines. It sometimes grows in nearly pure, small stands, but chiefly in mixture with redwood and Douglasfir, and occasionally with California live oak. It attains its largest size along the coast.

Tanoak is a moderately large tree with a usual height of fifty to seventy-five feet and a diameter of one to two feet. Some trees attain a height of eighty to eighty-five feet or more, with a diameter of three to four feet. Much larger trees were probably once common, but they are now rare. At high elevations it is often reduced to a shrub less than ten feet in height with slender, upright branches.

In close stands the long, clear trunk, which is rarely straight, supports a narrow, pyramidal crown of ascending branches; in the open the trunk is short and thick and often disappears in a mass of large, horizontally spreading limbs which form a broad, dense, symmetrical, round-topped crown.

Young twigs are densely woolly, but the wool disappears after the first year, when the branchlets become deep brown, tinged with red, and are often covered with a whitish bloom. The egg-shaped, obtuse winter buds, one-fourth to one-third of an inch long, are covered with densely hairy, loosely overlapping scales.

The oblong leaves measure from three to five inches long and three-fourths to three inches wide. They are slightly scalloped and toothed on the margins. Fully grown leaves are light green, smooth and shiny, occasionally with woolly areas on the upper surface, and densely woolly, with reddish brown hairs beneath. In late summer they become thick and leathery and the woolliness disappears except for a few hairs on the lower surface, which is then whitish with a very pale blue tint. The leaves of one year's growth persist for three or four seasons.

Male and female flowers are borne separately on shoots of the current season's growth, rarely from buds at the base of leaves of the previous year's growth as in the oaks. The cylindrical male clusters, three to four inches long, are thick and erect, instead of being thread-like and pendulous as in the oaks. The female flowers are usually borne at the base of the uppermost male flower clusters; the male flowers are arranged three in a minute cluster, many of them covering the erect flowering stems. The blossoms appear in early spring and sometimes during the autumn.

The fruit is a bitter acorn, three-fourths to one inch long and one half to one inch broad, occurring singly or in pairs on stout hairy stems one-half to one inch long. The acorns mature in the fall of the second season. The nut is pale yellowish brown, usually smooth and shining, but frequently more or less downy. It is embraced at the base by a shallow, pale yellow-brown cup which is lined with lustrous red-brown hairs on the inner surface and covered on the outside with finely hairy, bristly scales, which are sometimes very woolly at the base.

On the trunks of large trees the bark is three-fourths to one and a half inches thick, pale brown, tinged with red, often with grayish areas, and is broken by deep, narrow seams into wide, somewhat rectangular plates. On young trunks and large branches the bark is smooth and unbroken. It contains appreciable amounts of tannin and has been the principal commercial source of this material on the Pacific coast for many years.

The wood of tanoak is light brown, faintly tinged with red, very hard, heavy, strong and fine-grained. It is of sufficiently high quality to be used for agricultural implements and as finishing and furniture lumber, but is employed more generally for firewood. Economically tanoak is a tree of considerable importance in the Pacific coast forests, both for its valuable tanbark and for its timber in a region particularly lacking in hardwoods. Unfortunately, the tree is often cut for its bark without utilizing the wood.

Tanoak is a rather slow-growing species. Trees fourteen to eighteen inches in diameter are from eighty to 130 years old; trees twenty to sixty inches in diameter are from 150 to 250 years old. Although apparently quite free from insect and fungus diseases, the tree is very susceptible to injury from fire and many of the older trees show fire scars. Tanoak produces large crops of seeds, and seedlings are often abundant in partial shade. It also reproduces by means of sprouts, which grow vigorously from the stumps and become permanent stems.

Devereux Butcher

Appearing in the early spring, and sometimes in the fall, clusters of pollen-bearing flowers are thick and erect

Devereux Butcher

Thick leathery leaves are light green, smooth and shiny. Small acorns occur singly or in pairs on stout hairy stems

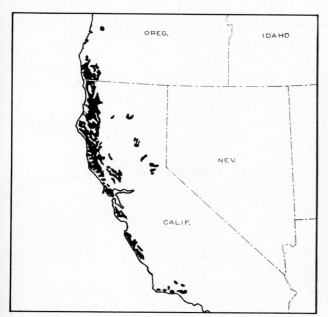

Within its narrow range, Tanoak occurs from sea level to about 5,000 feet elevation in valleys and on low slopes

Devereux Butcher

On old trees the bark is pale brown tinged with red and broken by deep seams. Young bark is smooth and unbroken

207

NORTHERN RED OAK

Red oak, Eastern red oak, Gray oak
Quercus rubra Linnaeus

THE OAKS are naturally divided into two groups —white oaks and red or black oaks. The latter make up a little more than half of the total stand

George J. Baetzhold

The broad, symmetrical crown of dark green foliage and thick, short trunk combine grace and strength in Northern Red Oak

trunks of open-grown trees often separate at fifteen or twenty feet from the ground into several stout branches. In the forest, the trunk assumes greater length and carries a narrow, round-topped crown. Some trees in the Ohio Valley and the mountains of West Virginia, Kentucky, Tennessee, and North Carolina reach 150 feet in height and six feet in diameter, but more often it is seventy to ninety feet high and two to three and a half feet in diameter.

This description combines the two more important and frequently confused red oaks of the North — *Quercus borealis* and the larger *Quercus borealis maxima*. *Borealis*, meaning northern, refers to the range of the species, while *maxima*, or largest, distinguishes this particular variety of oak, whose tree, as well as acorn, is the biggest of all the black oak group. *Quercus* is an ancient Latin name, probably of Celtic origin, meaning "beautiful tree."

The simple alternate leaves

Louis Boeglin

of the oaks, while the quantity of northern red oak is about fifteen percent of the total for the red oak group.

The broad, symmetrically spreading crown of dense dark green foliage of northern red oak is conspicuous throughout the entire Northeast from Nova Scotia, west across New England, southern Quebec, southern Ontario, northern Michigan and northern Minnesota, south to eastern Nebraska, Kansas, Oklahoma, and east to northern Mississippi, southern Alabama, central Georgia, the Middle Atlantic States and the Carolinas. The

The trunk of open-grown trees is relatively short, dividing into several stout branches which grow longer with increasing age

Warren D. Brush

Slender, pendulous catkins of pollen-bearing flowers
are borne late in the spring with the unfolding leaves

have five to eleven unequal bristle-tipped lobes tapering from broad bases. They are five to nine inches long, four to six inches broad, dark green above, and paler green beneath. Appearing late in spring, by autumn they turn deep red or orange to hang on until late fall or winter.

Flowers of each sex develop on different parts of the same tree in May or June with the unfolding leaves, when the long, hairy staminate catkins seem to veil the entire crown. The less conspicuous, greenish pistillate blooms are fertilized by wind-borne pollen from the staminate catkins of the neighboring trees, and take two years to mature singly or in pairs, into broadly oblong, reddish brown acorns, an inch or more long with a diameter only a little less. Each acorn rests in a flat saucer-shaped cup whose narrow border is covered with small closely fitting scales. The dark gray to reddish brown bark of mature trees is a half to three-quarters of an inch thick, and has a light reddish or flesh-colored inner bark.

The strong, close-grained wood is light reddish brown, with a thin layer of lighter colored sapwood. A cubic foot weighs about forty-five pounds when air dry. It is used for general construction, flooring, interior finish, furniture, railroad ties, posts, poles, and fuel. Ranking second in quantity of sawtimber among the red oaks, West Virginia, North Carolina and Tennessee probably contain the largest stands.

Red oak reproduces itself by stump sprouts or coppice, as well as from seeds. It grows in company with other oaks, sugar maples, elm, white pine, and the hickories, and grows more rapidly than all the other oaks.

Warren D. Brush

The dark green leaves are five to nine inches long
with unequal bristle-tipped lobes, while the shallow-
cupped, reddish brown acorns are broadly ovate

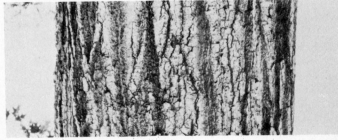

U. S. Forest Service

The dark gray to reddish brown bark
is broken into broad, flat-topped ridges

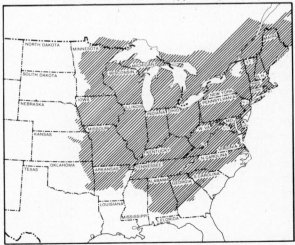

Natural range of Northern Red Oak

BLACK OAK

Smooth-bark oak, Quercitron, Yellow oak, Yellowbark oak
Quercus velutina Lamark

Devereux Butcher

An open-grown Black Oak develops an irregular and wide-spreading crown of large ascending branches

southern Michigan to southeastern Minnesota, and south to northern Florida and eastern Texas, eastern Oklahoma, eastern Kansas, southeastern Nebraska and Iowa. In upland cutover forest areas it is the most abundant species, and although it prefers rich, well-drained, gravelly soils, black oak is not usually found in great abundance in the better soils because it is very intolerant of shade, and unable to compete with other species. It is most often found on the poorer soils of slopes and ridges, the young trees developing long taproots that enable them to survive where many species would suffer for want of water. The most common associates of this tree are the other oaks, occasionally ash and tuliptree.

Bark on the mature trunk is dark gray or almost black, often paler gray in the coastal regions, three quarters to one and a quarter inches thick. Bark on young trunks and on branches is warm gray and smooth; inner bark is deep orange, very bitter to taste, is rich in tannin and is used for tanning leather.

Devereux Butcher

ONE of the commonest and largest of the eastern oaks is black oak, which varies greatly as to form in different localities. Average height is from sixty to eighty feet, with trunk diameters from two to three feet, and under favorable conditions, particularly in the lower Ohio basin, sometimes a hundred and fifty feet, with a trunk diameter of four or five feet. In general habit black oak is similar to scarlet oak, but the limbs are usually somewhat stouter. On good sites the bole is long with little taper, occasionally free of limbs for forty feet, while on less favorable soils the trunk tapers excessively and limbs grow closer to the ground.

The name, *Quercus*, is Latin for oak and means "beautiful tree"; *velutina* comes from the word *vellus* which means fleece and refers to the surfaces of the leaves, which are velvety when young; also, perhaps, to the downy winter buds.

The range of black oak extends from southern Maine and northern Vermont westward through southern Ontario,

Acorns measure one-half to three-quarters of an inch long, and are held by deep, thin-scaled cups

Black Oak leaves vary considerably. They usually have five to seven lobes

From the deep orange inner bark a yellow dye commercially known as quercitron is made.

The stout, smooth, or slightly hairy twigs of black oak are dull red-brown, later turning dark brown, and have large lenticels or pores. The lateral buds are alternate, those near the ends of twigs clustered about the terminal bud; they are yellowish gray, measuring one quarter to one half inch, are sharply pointed, and usually five-sided. The down with which they are covered offers a means of identifying this oak from others in the black oak group.

The alternate leaves average five to six inches in length and three to four inches in width. They are bristle-tipped, as are the leaves of all in the black oak group. Their indentations are deep, rounded and wide, extending at least halfway to the midrib. The mature leaf is thick, tough, smooth, dark green, and very shiny above, paler and somewhat hairy or smooth beneath, with brown hairs at the connections of the main veins. The yellow stout stems are two to six inches long.

In May or June, when the new leaves are half grown, the flowers appear. Borne on the growth of the preceding season, the pollen-bearing ones occur in hairy catkins, four to six inches long, while the seed-producing ones, growing at the bases of the leaf-stems of the season, are reddish and are borne on short, hairy stems. Ripening from October to November of the second season, the acorns are either stemless or on short stalks. The yellow, bitter kernel is not edible. Crops of acorns are produced every two or three years. Black oak is fairly prolific and germination is frequently eighty percent or more. The approximate maximum age of black oak ranges from 150 to 200 years.

Black oak wood is heavy, hard, strong, not tough, coarse-grained, checks in drying, and has fewer and smaller medullary rays than the wood of most other oaks. Heartwood is reddish brown, the sapwood narrow and pale. A cubic foot when seasoned weighs forty-three pounds. Most important of the black or red oaks, it makes up about one-fourth of the stand of this group. The largest supplies are in Tennessee, Arkansas, Kentucky and Missouri. It is used for furniture, flooring and many other products.

The healthy tree is not usually severely attacked by insects or borers. Black oak is seldom planted as an ornamental tree.

Bark on large trunks is broken by deep furrows into ridges that are transversely cut into block-like strips

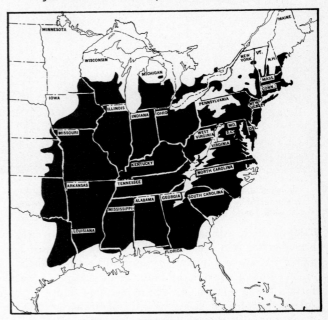

Natural range of Black Oak

SHUMARD OAK

Schenck oak, Shumard red oak
Quercus shumardii Buckley

SHUMARD OAK is said to grow to a greater height than any other American oak. Trees 200 feet high and eight feet in trunk diameter have been found and not infrequently heights of 100 to 125 and diameters of four to five feet are attained. In the forest this species develops

Daniel O. Todd

Shumard oak sometimes reaches a height of 200 feet with a diameter of eight feet. Open-grown trees have broad crowns, while forest-grown ones have narrow, pyramidal crowns.

a long, clear, symmetrical bole which is often clear of branches for fifty feet above the slightly buttressed base, and a narrow pyramidal or rounded crown. When not crowded by other trees the stout, wide-spreading branches form a broad open head. The moderately stout twigs are smooth and bright green or reddish brown at first, becoming grayish brown in their second year. Winter buds

are about one-fourth of an inch long and are covered by gray to gray-brown, smooth or slightly downy, closely overlapping scales.

The range of Shumard oak includes the Piedmont region in the Carolinas to northern Florida, west through the Gulf states to central Texas and in the Mississippi basin as far north as southern Missouri and western Ohio. It is a bottomland species and prefers the borders of streams and swamps and hillsides where the soil is rich, deep and moist but well drained. Shumard oak does not grow in pure stands, but as a single tree or as a group of trees in association with other hardwoods, including willow oak, swamp red oak, swamp chestnut oak, white ash, black tupelo and hickories. It is quite common in the Mississippi basin and makes its best growth on the

Byron L. Groesbeck

212

rich alluvial lands of the lower Mississippi. Farther east it is much less abundant.

The leaves are obovate or oval in outline, with seven to nine bristle-tipped lobes which are divided by broad rounded sinuses that extend half-way or more to the midrib. Six to eight inches long and four to five inches wide they are dark green, smooth and shiny above, pale and smooth below except for tufts of whitish hairs in the axils of the veins. The slender, smooth leaf stems are about two inches in length.

Male and female flowers are borne separately, the pollen-bearing in slender smooth catkins six to seven inches long and the acorn-producing ones on short hairy stalks. Occurring singly or in pairs, the acorns are stemless or on very short stalks. The oblong-oval, light brown nut, up to one and a quarter inches in length and slightly tapering toward the apex, is enclosed only at the base in a thick, saucer-shaped cup which is covered with thin, closely appressed light brown scales.

On young stems and branches the bark is smooth, thin and light gray; on old trunks it is from one to one and a half inches thick and is broken into whitish scaly ridges, which are separated by deep fissures that are considerably darker.

The wood is heavy, hard and strong, the heartwood light reddish brown and the sapwood nearly white. It has the reputation of being superior to that of the other red oaks, but is usually mixed with them in commerce and utilized for the same products. It is used principally for furniture, cabinet work, flooring and interior trim.

The tree makes quite rapid growth and is exceptionally free from insect attack and fungous diseases. Acorns are produced in large quantities, but germination is low and it reproduces itself slowly—seedlings being comparatively rare.

Staminate flowers are six to seven inches long and the pistillate ones are on short, hairy stalks (note end of twig). Light brown acorns are held by thick cups

On old trunks the inch-thick bark is broken by dark fissures into pale, scaly ridges. Leaves have seven to nine bristle-tipped lobes

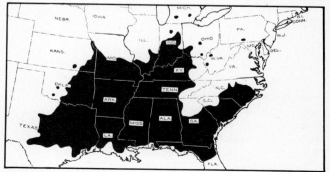

The natural range of Shumard oak

213

SOUTHERN RED OAK

Spanish oak

Quercus falcata Michaux

L. W. Brownell

Forest-grown Southern Red Oak is medium-sized with a long straight trunk, while in the open the trunk is shorter, and the branches wide-spreading

SOUTHERN RED OAK grows as far north as southern New Jersey and southeastern Pennsylvania, but is more common in the south Atlantic and gulf states. Reaching into central Florida, it extends westward to the valley of the Brazos in Texas and northward into Missouri and the southern parts of Illinois and Indiana. The tree is also found in isolated parts of southern Ohio and western West Virginia.

Locally called Spanish oak, Spanish water oak, spotted oak, turkey oak and red hill oak, the confusion of names entered the field of botanists and dendrologists, some of whom followed Marshall and Sudworth in calling it Spanish oak, *Quercus digitata*, while others followed Linnaeus in calling it southern red oak, *Quercus rubra*. Later Sargent revealed

that Linnaeus' type specimen was the same as Michaux had earlier described as *Quercus falcata*. Accordingly, this is the name dendrologists decided upon.

Usually a medium-sized tree, this species, when growing under forest conditions, has a long, straight trunk and upward-reaching limbs that form a high, rounded crown. In the open it develops a short trunk with wide-spreading limbs to form a broad, open, round-topped crown. Heights are usually from seventy to eighty feet, with trunk diameters of two to three feet, but trees one hundred feet high with diameters up to five feet have been recorded.

The dark gray bark on mature trunks is rough, with shallow fissures, and broad ridges. It may be three-quarters to one inch thick, but on limbs and on young trunks it is relatively smooth and lighter in color. Although rich in tannin, it has not been used extensively by tanneries.

The angular twigs are first dark reddish brown, covered with thick rusty down, and in

Maryland State Department of Forestry

214

Opening in April with the leaves, the staminate
flowers are arranged in pendent, hairy catkins

Varying in shape more than those
of other oaks, the leaves are of
two types. Acorns are about one-
half inch long held by a stemless
or short-stalked saucer-shaped cup

their second year become dark red-brown or gray. Winter buds are an eighth to a quarter inch long and covered with chestnut-brown, hairy scales. This oak belongs
to the black oak group. Its leaves are firm, dark green
and glossy above, paler and downy beneath, and occur
in a greater variety of shapes than do the leaves of most
other oaks. In general there are two types. Both have
a taperingly wedge-shaped or rounded base, but the
finger-shaped one has slender, pointed or tooth-tipped
lobes, with the terminal lobe more or less curved after
the manner of a scythe blade. This is referred to in the
scientific name *falcata*, which comes from the Latin
word *falcatus*, meaning scythe. The other shape resembles the outline of a bell, is less deeply cut, and the
broader lobes are distinctly tooth-tipped. Both shapes
and numerous variations of them may occur on the same
or different trees—the finger-like leaves filling the bulk
of the crown, and the broad-lobed, tooth-tipped, bell-
shaped ones on the lower branches. In autumn they
turn dull orange or brown.

Flowers of both sexes appear on the same tree in
April when the leaves unfold. The staminate or pollen-
bearing ones are in clusters of drooping, hairy catkins,
three to five inches long. The pistillate or acorn-producing flowers occur in pairs or singly on stout, hairy
stems. Measuring about half an inch long, and maturing the second year, the rounded, bitter acorns occur
singly or in pairs. They are about one-third covered by
scaly, saucer-shaped cups.

Weighing about forty-three pounds to the cubic foot
when air dry, the coarse-grained, light red wood of
southern red oak is hard and strong, checks badly when
drying, and is not durable in contact with the soil. It is
used for general construction, slack cooperage, crates,
furniture and fuel.

The dark brown or gray bark is broken by
shallow fissures into broad ridges

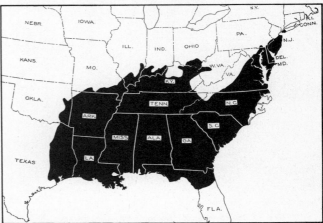

Natural range of Southern Red Oak

215

CHERRYBARK OAK

Bottomland red oak, Elliott oak, Swamp Spanish oak

Quercus falcata var. *pagodaefolia* Elliott

ALTHOUGH swamp red oak occurs in nearly the same region as the type species, southern red oak, there are a number of characteristic differences between the two. Swamp red oak attains larger size, grows on more moist sites, has more nearly uniform leaves and a flaky or scaly bark which superficially resembles that of large trunks of black cherry trees.

It is not, strictly speaking, a tree of the swamps, but commonly grows on bottomlands and flats along streams. It is not restricted to such localities, however, and some of the largest trees are frequently found on moist ridges and old fields. Its range includes the coastal plain region from Virginia to northern Florida and through the gulf states and Arkansas to southern Missouri, western Tennessee and Kentucky and southern Illinois and Indiana. It is especially plentiful in the lower Mississippi Valley, attaining its best growth on rich, moist, well-drained

soils. Commonly associated with it are sweetgum, water oak and swamp chestnut oak.

One of the largest of the southern oaks, swamp red oak often reaches heights of 100 to 130 feet and diameters of three to five feet. In the forest it has a long straight trunk, the massive branches at the top forming a short, narrow crown; when grown in the open the wide-spreading limbs form a great open head. Covered at first with a fine down, the slender twigs become dark reddish brown in their second year. The winter buds, often prominently four-angled, are about one-fourth of an inch long and have light red-brown scales, covered with fine hairs at the apex.

The elliptic to oblong leaves measure five to ten inches long, four to five inches wide, and are rather deeply divided into from five to eleven narrow-pointed lobes. They are coated with fine pale hairs and are dark red on the

One of the largest of the southern oaks, Swamp Red Oak often reaches heights of 100 to 130 feet and diameters of three to five feet. It is not, strictly speaking, a tree of the swamps but commonly grows on bottomlands and flats

upper surface when they unfold. At maturity they are dark green and very lustrous above, and pale and downy beneath. They are borne on stout hairy stems one and a half to two inches in length. They turn a bright clear yellow in the autumn. The flowers are similar to those of southern red oak—the male in pendent hairy catkins and the female on stout hairy stems. The stemless or short-stalked acorns occur singly or in pairs and the nut, about five-eighths of an inch in diameter, is nearly half enclosed by the flat saucer-shaped cup, which is covered by small, thin, reddish, fine-hairy scales.

On the trunks of young trees the bark is smooth, but is later separated by fissures into rather narrow ridges covered with small, closely appressed, gray-brown to dark brown scales. Because of the resemblance of the bark to that of black cherry, swamp red oak is often known as cherry-bark oak.

The wood of swamp red oak resembles that of southern red oak in its properties but is heavier, weighing about forty-eight pounds per cubic foot when air dry, and is stronger. Because the trees grow to larger sizes, swamp red oak also produces a larger proportion of high-grade lumber. The heartwood is light reddish brown and the thin sapwood nearly white. It is largely manufactured into lumber for furniture and interior finish and is considered one of the best timbers of the red oak group.

The available supply of swamp red oak is much less than that of southern red oak and is estimated at five percent of the total for all the red oaks. Although the stand is comparatively small, it is an important tree from the standpoint of timber production because, particularly in the lower Mississippi Valley on the best sites, it grows rapidly and has a long straight bole clear of branches, which yields high quality logs. Some of the largest stands are in Arkansas and Louisiana.

Swamp red oak has been described by some dendrologists as a species under the scientific names *Quercus pagoda* and *Quercus pagodaefolia*. Others recognize another variety of *falcata*, namely *leucophylla*, which occurs in the same region. It is claimed that this variety, which is also called cherry-bark oak, has leaves that are more variable than those of swamp red oaks, some shallowly and some deeply lobed, the two types occurring on the same tree. Otherwise there seems to be no distinction between the two varieties.

Swamp red oak produces large crops of acorns every three or four years and reproduction is good in moderately dry soils. Young growth is especially abundant in scattered and open stands, giving rise to considerable areas of second growth timber. The tree also reproduces by means of stump sprouts.

Like the type species, *Quercus falcata*, swamp red oak is valuable as an ornamental and shade tree because it grows rapidly and thrives in fairly dry localities. When isolated from other trees, so that it has room for full development, the large branches give it a wide rounded top, and the large leaves, displaying alternately their dark green and silvery white surfaces when agitated by the wind, present an attractive appearance. The tree should not be planted outside its natural range, however, because of its susceptibility to injury by frost.

Photos from Textbook of Dendrology, Harlow and Harrar, courtesy of McGraw-Hill Book Co., Inc.

The oblong leaves are divided into from five to eleven narrow-pointed lobes. The stemless acorns have a saucer-shaped cup

W. R. Mattoon

On young trees the bark is smooth but is later separated by fissures into ridges covered with dark brown scales

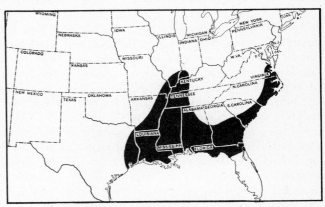

Natural range of Swamp Red Oak

SCARLET OAK

Quercus coccinea Muenchhausen

Devereux Butcher

Scarlet Oak usually reaches heights of from sixty to eighty feet, with a trunk diameter of two or three feet, and it has an open crown

diameter of four feet. The crown is open and narrow with slender lateral branches which droop slightly at the ends. Intolerant of shade, the lower crown is often marked with dead branches.

The thin, five- to nine-lobed, bristly pointed leaves occur alternately, are three to six inches long, three to five inches wide, and broadly oval in general outline. The sinuses between the lobes are deeper than those of the black oak, extending more than halfway to the mid-rib and are rounded at their bases. The mid-ribs and primary veins are yellow. The slender leaf stems are one and one-half to two and one-half inches long and circular in cross section. Though members of the black oak group, to which scarlet oak belongs, usu-

SCARLET OAK occurs naturally from southern New England through southern New York to Indiana, and south to southeastern Missouri, and central Alabama and Georgia. Never forming pure stands, it frequently appears in the North with white pine, white oak and red oak, and in the South with short-leaf pine, post oak and white oak. Its best development is in the Ohio basin.

Favoring light sandy or gravelly soils, it grows well on various sites. Its large spreading lateral roots run so close below the ground level that they often break through the surface and become exposed. Generally sixty to eighty feet tall with a trunk diameter of two or three feet, the rapidly tapering trunk occasionally towers one hundred and fifty feet and reaches a

Maryland State Department of Forestry

The staminate flowers appearing in May or June, occur in clusters of catkins three or four inches long

Broadly oval in outline, the leaves are smooth and have yellow primary veins, while the short-stalked acorns are often striped

ally have hairy leaves, only occasional tufts of reddish pubescence appear in the axils of the veins of scarlet oak leaves. First appearing bright red and finely matted with pale hairs, the leaves turn to a rich bright green. Again in the autumn, they turn bright scarlet and persist late into the season. The specific name *coccinea* comes from the Latin *coccum*, and refers to an oak gall used in making red dyes. It is applied to scarlet oak because of the striking leaf coloration.

Appearing in May or June, both male and female flowers occur on the same tree. The short-stalked, oval acorns ripen in September and October of the second season. They occur singly or in pairs, and are one-half to one inch long, with reddish brown surfaces often lined with thin light stripes. The mildly bitter kernel is nearly white, while that of black oak is deep yellow.

The broadly ovate, blunt-pointed buds are one-eighth to one-quarter inch long, dark reddish brown, and covered with pale, fine hairs. As compared with those of red oak they are broader in proportion to length.

The rough, nearly black bark is almost an inch thick, divided into irregular scaly ridges, and may be mottled with gray. On young stems and branches it is thin, smooth and grayish brown to light brown.

The heartwood is pinkish to light reddish brown, heavy, hard, strong and a cubic foot weighs about forty-seven pounds when air dry. Much of the wood is inferior. Good quality lumber, however, is suitable for the same uses as that of other red oaks.

Reasonably rapid growing, scarlet oak has been planted widely in the United States and Europe as a tree for parks and streets.

Bark on the mature trunk is rough, dark gray or nearly black divided into scaly ridges, and is almost one inch thick

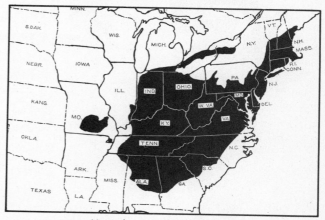

Natural range of Scarlet Oak

PIN OAK

Quercus palustris Muenchhausen

PIN OAK is more widely known as a street or orna-mental tree than for lumber purposes. It grows natu-rally from southwestern New England to northern North Carolina, and from Ohio to Kentucky and western Ten-nessee. Its distribution extends westward to southeastern Iowa, eastern Kansas, northeastern Oklahoma and north-ern Arkansas. Pin oak usually occupies poorly drained flats, low clay ridges, edges of swamps, and occasionally very moist upland sites. One common name, swamp oak, corresponding with the scientific name *palustris*, is de-rived from the Latin word *palus* meaning swamp. *Quer-cus* is reported in *Tree Ancestors* by Berry, to be derived from the Celtic *quer* or fine, and *cuez* or tree. So it may be said that this is the fine tree of the swamp.

Pin oak is a tree of moderate size, rarely exceeding eighty-five or ninety-five feet in height, and three feet in diameter. Occasional forest-grown specimens reach a height of 120 feet with a trunk four or five feet in diame-ter. Its straight trunk extends well up into a symmetrical, pyramidal crown whose tough drooping branches fre-

Devereux Butcher

Devereux Butcher

Open-grown Pin Oaks have a wide head of upward-reaching limbs, while in the forest, the main stem is taller with fewer branches. The glossy leaves have five to seven lobes, and the acorns, set in shallow cups, grow on the wood of the previous year

Devereux Butcher

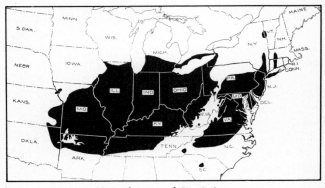

Natural range of Pin Oak

220

quently sweep the ground. With increasing age the crown loses its original pyramidal shape and becomes broad and open.

The bark is light to dark grayish brown, hard, so close as to appear tight, from three-fourths of an inch to one and one-fourth inches thick, and divided by narrow, shallow fissures into broad ridges.

The five- to nine-lobed narrow leaves are three to six inches long, thin, firm, dark green and lustrous above, paler beneath, and perfectly smooth except for tufts of pale hairs in the axils of the larger veins. They have slender stems or petioles, one-half inch to two inches long, and the irregularly toothed lobes taper to narrow, pointed ends.

Male and female blossoms are borne separately on the new wood of the same tree. The male or staminate flowers appear with the leaves in early spring as brown tassels, while the less conspicuous pistillate flowers may be found at the angle where the new leaf joins with the main stem. The reddish brown acorns are broader than long and set close on the main stem in flat, saucer-shaped cups. They take two years to mature, and are set singly or in clusters on the two-year-old branches.

Pin oak has no special commercial importance, but, although generally inferior, is cut and marketed as red oak wherever found in ordinary logging operations. The numerous small adherent limbs cause excessively knotty logs, and the wood has the reputation of being difficult to season. Accordingly, only the best trees are used for lumber. Much of it is utilized for fuel and in wood distillation. About five percent of the stand of the red oaks is of this species.

The upright pyramidal crown, lack of heavy side branches, clean trunk and rich glossy leaves make it one of the most desirable oaks for street and ornamental planting. A fibrous root system without a distinct taproot makes transplanting easy. When planted in well drained moist soils it grows rapidly, produces a dense shade, and with relatively little pruning does not interfere with street traffic. Best results are secured when the trees are planted about forty feet apart.

Aside from attacks by the obscure scale, which resembles the San Jose scale, pin oak is especially free from injury by disease or insects; but fire frequently damages trees growing in the woods or on large estates. The obscure scale can be controlled by spraying with lime-sulphur or miscible-oil solutions in the early spring before the leaves appear and again in midsummer.

Devereux Butcher

Before the spring leaves have reached full size, the tree is decked with tassels of pollen-bearing staminate flowers. The inconspicuous pistillate flowers are hidden within the axils of the leaves

Devereux Butcher

Low, scaly ridges and an appearance of tightness help characterize the dark gray bark of mature Pin Oak trees

WILLOW OAK

Peach-leaf oak, Peach oak
Quercus phellos Linnaeus

Willow Oak has a strong central trunk supporting numerous side branches from which grow many small spur-like branchlets, resembling those of the pin oak

WILLOW OAK lays no claim to size or majesty, but its round-topped symmetrical crown, rapid growth and long life place it among the most attractive of the red oak or black oak group. Occasionally, in the moist fertile portions of its southern range it attains heights of 100 to 120 feet and diameters at breast height of three to five feet. Over most of its range, however, it is usually forty to fifty feet high with a full clear trunk fourteen to twenty inches in diameter, frequently rising intact through the crown. The side branches are slender like those of the pin oak and the lower branches droop or dip down at the ends. The side branches persist except in dense shady stands.

Under forest conditions it develops a tall, straight trunk and a full symmetrical crown.

The trunk prunes itself slowly, leaving many small live and dead branches which form knots in the wood and greatly reduce the clear merchantable length.

It thrives on poorly drained bottomlands that are normally covered each winter with shallow water, occurs in rich moist soil along the margins of streams and swamps, and also on higher land. It grows from southern Long Island and Staten Island in southeastern New York chiefly along the maritime plain to northwestern Florida, through the Gulf region to the Sabine River Valley in eastern Texas and north through eastern Oklahoma, Arkansas, southeastern Missouri to central Tennessee, southern Illinois and eastern Kentucky. Reaching its largest size and greatest abundance in the lower Mississippi Valley, it grows in company with other oaks, hickory, tulip-

The full, round, slightly conical crown of Willow Oak is frequently forty to fifty feet high and may attain a height of one hundred feet or more

tree, maple and elm. It is so frequently found along wet margins of streams and swamps as to be erroneously known as swamp oak, or water oak. The abundant short spur-like branchlets on the lower branches have led to wide use of the name pin oak.

Willow oak gets its name from the long, narrow lance-shaped or occasionally scythe-shaped vivid light green leaves, which, in shape as well as in color, resemble those of a willow more than an oak. In texture, however, they are thicker and more leathery. They are pointed at both ends, two and a half to five inches long, a fourth to an inch wide, with a short stem or petiole and a slender yellow midrib. The shiny light green of the upper side is mildly contrasted by a lighter green below. In the South the tree is nearly evergreen, and the leaves never attain the bright autumnal colors of the red, pin and scarlet oaks but turn a pale yellow before falling. The long, narrow, entire leaf leads occasionally to the common name, peach-leaf oak. Willow oak may be confused with water oak, *Quercus nigra*, laurel oak *Quercus laurifolia*, and shingle oak, *Quercus imbricaria*, because the leaves are rather alike. Willow oak leaves are smaller, narrower, and of almost uniform width, and the acorns are greenish brown; while those of the other species are dark brown or nearly black.

The flowers are each of a single sex and are found on all parts of the tree—the male catkins on last season's growth and the female flowers in the axils of the new leaves. They appear in late March in the South. Farther north they appear in April or May, and they continue in evidence for two or three weeks. The pollen from the staminate blooms, which are like yellow-green knots along the two- to three-inch stems, is carried by the wind to fertilize the pistillate flowers. The latter stand on short, slender, smooth stalks or peduncles at the base of the leaves. As is characteristic of the black oak group, the acorns of the willow oak mature in the fall of the second season, becoming hemispherical, light yellow-brown and about a half inch long, set in a thin saucer-shaped cup. This in turn is covered with thin elongated scales, and is lined with a mat of fine, white hairs. The acorn is held to the twig by a short stalk, and the meat is bitter with tannin.

Dark, chestnut-brown, narrowly conical winter buds about an eighth of an inch long and without angles are borne alternately on smooth, slender, reddish brown twigs marked with dark lenticles or breathing pores. Each of the numerous, well defined bud scales is edged with pale gray or white.

The red-brown to steel gray bark is a half to three quarters of an inch thick, generally smooth and very hard. On large mature trees it is nearly black, broken by narrow fissures into rough, hard ridges and irregular plates. *Phellos* comes from a Greek word that relates to cork and was used to refer to the oak long before the name was accepted by Linnaeus. It has no reference to any special corky quality of the bark of this species.

The wood is heavy and hard. It weighs about forty-nine pounds to the cubic foot when air dry and is used for the same purposes as the other red oaks.

Willow oak is hardy as far north as Massachusetts and in the south Atlantic and gulf states is recognized as one of the best of the quick growing trees for street, and ornamental planting. The comparatively shallow root system helps make it easy to transplant. Trees twelve to fifteen feet high may be dug from the woods and successfully grown, but well rooted nursery-grown stock is more satisfactory for ornamental planting. Although willow oak has few enemies, trees are occasionally seriously retarded by scale insects which feed on the tender bark of twigs and small branches.

The narrow leaves, pointed at each end, resemble those of a willow, and the acorns, about a half inch long, have a shallow saucer-shaped cup

The relatively smooth brown to dark gray bark is one-half to three quarters of an inch thick

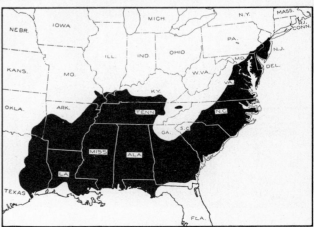

Natural range of Willow Oak

LAUREL OAK

Laurel-leaved oak, Darlington oak, Swamp laurel oak

Quercus laurifolia Michaux

NAMED for its lustrous leaves, which resemble those of the laurel, this large and stately tree is found in the Atlantic and Gulf coastal plain from southeastern Virginia to Florida and west to eastern Texas. It prefers wet localities, occurring mostly along the margins of streams and swamps in association with water tupelo, Atlantic whitecedar, baldcypress and sweetbay. Nowhere abundant, it usually occurs as a scattered species, but it is quite common in eastern Florida where it attains its largest size. When grown among other trees in favorable localities, laurel oak may reach a height of 100 feet with a straight, columnar trunk three to four feet in diameter. Usually it is much smaller. The trunk is tall with comparatively slender branches which spread gradually into a broad, dense, round-topped symmetrical head.

Except for its wider leaves and deeper cup in which the acorn is held, it resembles willow oak, *Q. phellos*, closely. The smooth, slender branchlets are dark red when they first appear and dark red-brown during their first winter, becoming reddish brown or dark gray in their second season. The winter buds, about one-eighth

of an inch long, are ovoid or oval, abruptly narrowed and acute at the apex and are covered with numerous thin, closely overlapping bright red-brown scales, the margins of which are fringed with hairs.

The elliptical to oblong egg-shaped leaves, two and a half to four inches long and one-half to an inch wide, usually have smooth margins but are sometimes irregularly lobed. They are wedge-shaped at the base and pointed at the apex. At maturity they are thin, dark green and smooth above, paler beneath, with a conspicuous, raised, yellow midrib. Each leaf is borne on a short, stout, yellow stalk.

Laurel oak is semi-evergreen, the leaves remaining on the tree during the winter and falling in early spring. The branches are partly bare for only a few weeks before new leaves develop.

Usually in March or April, when the leaves are about one-third unfolded, the pollen-bearing flowers appear in clustered, red-stemmed, hairy catkins from two to three inches long. The acorn-producing flowers are borne on short, stout, smooth stalks.

Though a large and stately tree, Laurel Oak has slender branches that spread gradually into a broad, dense, symmetrical crown. Under favorable conditions it may attain a height of 100 feet

The pointed leaves, wedge-shaped at the
base, are sometimes irregularly lobed

Pollen-bearing flowers appear in clustered, red-stemmed,
hairy catkins, and are two to three inches long

Ripening in the autumn of the second year, the stalk-less or extremely short-stalked acorns occur singly. The dark brown or nearly black nut, about half an inch long, is egg-shaped to hemispherical, hairy at the rounded apex. It is enclosed for one-fourth or less of its length in a thin, saucer-shaped cup. The cup has fine, silky, red-brown hairs on the inner surface and is covered by thin, ovate, closely overlapping, light red-brown scales which are pale, except on their darker colored margins. A large crop of acorns usually is produced every year.

The bark on the trunks of young trees is dark brown, more or less tinged with red and from one-half to one inch thick; it is roughened by small, closely-appressed scales. On old trunks the bark is from one to two inches thick, nearly black, and divided by shallow fissures into broad flat ridges.

The wood is heavy, hard, strong and difficult to season. A cubic foot weighs about forty-four pounds in the air-dry condition. Laurel oak is not utilized commercially to any great extent, its chief uses being for fuel and as distillation wood. One of the less important members of the red oak group, the total quantity of the standing timber is less than five percent of the total of all the red oaks.

Shallow fissures divide the bark into irregular ridges

Enclosed in a thin cup, the dark brown or nearly
black egg-shaped acorn is about one-half inch long

Natural range of Laurel Oak

SHINGLE OAK

Quercus imbricaria Michaux

SHINGLE OAK belongs to the group of willow oaks, so named because their leaves resemble those of the willow. Early pioneers used its wood for the production of split shingles, and this use was recognized by the explorer-botanist Michaux when he gave it the scientific name

the lower Ohio River basin where, on moist soils of fertile hillsides and the bottomlands of streams, it attains maximum height.

The trunk is straight, often free of branches for half its length. When the tree is young it is usually pyramidal

Shingle Oak sometimes attains a height of ninety feet. Its rounded crown is made up of numerous horizontal branches

Terminal buds are egg-shaped and sharp-pointed

A tree of fertile hillsides and bottomlands, it achieves its best form in the lower Ohio River basin

imbricaria, implying an overlapping as in shingles. Northern laurel oak is another name applied to shingle oak because of its resemblance to the laurel oak of the south Atlantic and Gulf coastal region.

It does not have a wide distribution, growing from Pennsylvania to southeastern Iowa, south to Arkansas and Georgia, exclusive of the southern Mississippi Valley region. However, it is one of the most abundant oaks of

in form, the lower branches drooping or spreading and often touching the ground. In the forest, under favorable conditions of growth, shingle oak sometimes attains a height of ninety feet with a straight columnar trunk three to four feet in diameter, and slender, tough, horizontal or somewhat pendulous branches forming a narrow, round-topped, picturesque head. Its usual height, however, is only fifty to sixty feet with a trunk diameter of two to three feet. In the open it develops an oblong top of numerous branches.

The smooth, slender twigs are dark green when they first appear, light reddish brown or light brown during their first winter, and dark brown in their second year.

The oblong lanceolate leaves are longer and wider than those of either the willow or laurel oak, which they resemble in form. From four to six inches long and one to two inches wide, they are bright red when they unfold, soon becoming yellowish green. At maturity, they are smooth, shining and dark green above, paler or brownish and pubescent below with yellowish midribs and numerous, slender, yellow veins. The margins are smooth or slightly wavy and the leaf stems are short, stout and hairy. Before falling late in the autumn they turn dark red on the upper surface.

Male and female flowers, appearing in April or May, are borne in separate catkins on the same tree. The male or staminate catkins, two to three inches long, are densely hairy and the female or pistillate ones have short, slender, hairy stems.

The dark chestnut-brown acorns occur singly or in pairs on stout stems nearly one-half inch long. The nearly spherical nut is one-half to two-thirds of an inch in diameter, and is enclosed for one-third of its length in a thin, bowl-like cup. The nut is often marked with parallel stripes, and the thin, red-brown scales of the cup are pressed flat and covered by fine hairs, except on their darker colored margins.

The egg-shaped, sharp-pointed terminal buds are about one-eighth of an inch long and covered with light chestnut-brown, somewhat hairy scales. The lateral buds are similar but smaller.

On young stems and branches the bark is light brown, smooth and shining. On old trunks it is three-fourths to one and a half inches thick, divided by irregular shallow fissures into broad low ridges, covered by close, slightly appressed, light brown scales tinged with red.

The wood is similar to that of other species of the red oak group. It is heavy, hard, stiff and strong, and has high shock-resisting ability and when dry weighs forty-eight pounds. The heartwood is light brown tinged with red, with thin, lighter-colored sapwood.

Shingle oak is not of any considerable commercial importance because of its limited distribution. The timber is marketed as red oak and is used in building construction, for shingles, railway ties and many other products.

Its symmetrical form and dark green leaves make shingle oak an attractive ornamental tree, and it is occasionally planted in the northern states for this purpose. It is hardy as far north as Massachusetts.

J. Horace McFarland Co.
Bright red when they first unfold, the oblong leaves turn dark green. The acorn is often marked with parallel stripes

Fred Shulley
The bark on old trunks is divided by irregular shallow fissures. Its light brown scales are tinged with red

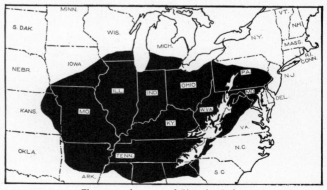
The natural range of Shingle Oak

WATER OAK

Possum oak, Spotted oak

Quercus nigra Linnaeus

Warren D. Brush

When open-grown, the many branches of
Water Oak form a wide, rounded top

Chicago Natural History Museum

Water Oak is a medium-sized tree, sometimes attaining a height of eighty feet

WATER OAK inhabits wet bottomlands along the borders of ponds and streams on the coastal plains of southeastern United States. It grows from Delaware to central Florida, ranging inland through the south Atlantic states to the base of the Appalachian Mountains and west in the Gulf states to eastern Texas and north to eastern Oklahoma and southeastern Missouri. Water oak is not usually found on permanently submerged land as the name seems to imply. On low, moist, cutover land it often occurs in large numbers in the form of second growth. In such locations in the lower Mississippi Valley, water oak and swamp red oak, *Quercus falcata* var. *pagodaefolia*, often make up nearly the entire timber stand.

Water oak is a medium-sized tree, attaining a height of seventy to eighty feet and a trunk diameter of from two to three and a half feet. In the forest the bole is tall and straight and the symmetrical, rounded crown is made up of slender, ascending branches. When grown in the open, the trunk is usually short, with many branches forming a wide, rounded top. The smooth slender twigs are light or dull red, becoming brown in the second season. The winter buds, less than one-fourth of an inch long, are egg-shaped in outline, sharp-pointed, and have dark red-brown, loosely overlapping scales which are covered with short, fine hairs.

The leaves, usually two to four inches long and one to two inches wide, are commonly oblong-obovate or spatulate, gradually narrowed and wedge-shaped at the base. They are often three-lobed at the apex, sometimes with an additional lobe on either side, or they may be long and narrow like those of willow oak, *Quercus phellos*. Leaves of all these shapes may occur on the same tree. Dull bluish green above and paler below, they are smooth and shiny on both surfaces, except for tufts of hairs in the axils of the veins beneath. Attached to the twig by a short, flattened stem, an eighth to a half inch long, many of them remain green and do not fall until late winter.

The pollen-bearing flowers are in red, hairy-stemmed catkins two to three inches long, and the acorn-producing ones are on short, hairy stalks. The acorns, stalkless or with a short stalk, occur singly or in pairs. The hemispherical, yellow-brown nut, about a half inch long, sets in a thin, saucer-shaped cup which is covered by closely appressed light red-brown scales.

The bark, from one-half to three-fourths of an inch thick, is light red-brown at first and covered by smooth, thin scales. On large, mature trees it becomes nearly black with rough, wide, scaly ridges.

The wood of water oak is heavy, hard, stiff and strong and has high shock-resisting ability. When air dry it weighs forty-four pounds to the cubic foot. The heartwood is light brown with thick, lighter colored sapwood. It is usually cut and sold as red oak and is used for most of the same purposes as red oak, such as flooring, furniture, boxes and railroad ties.

228

On large and mature trees the bark becomes nearly black with rough scaly ridges

R. K. Winters

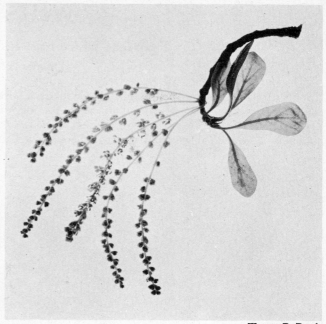

The male, pollen-bearing flowers
are borne in hairy-stemmed catkins

Warren D. Brush

Water oak is probably the most important of the willow oak group, and it comprises between five and ten percent of the total stand of the red oaks. The total saw-timber stand of the willow oaks is about one-fifth that of the red oaks and the quality of the wood is generally inferior. Much of the wood of water oak is of poor quality and is difficult to season. The principal supply is located in the lower Mississippi Valley, where there is much second growth timber.

Spotted oak, possum oak and duck oak are local names sometimes applied to this tree. It is commonly planted for shade in the streets and parks of cities and villages of the southern states. Because of its graceful form and bright green leaves, water oak is a favorite ornamental in many southern cities. It is also desirable from the forester's standpoint as it grows rapidly, particularly on moist sites, and trees may be large enough to be con-verted into lumber in from fifty to seventy years. Be-cause of its ability to take possession of large areas, wa-ter oak may become one of the most important hard-woods of the South, although the quality of the timber is inferior to that of many of the other oak species.

The oblong or spatulate leaves are
often three-lobed at their apex

Warren D. Brush

Warren D. Brush

The nut is held in a saucer-shaped cup

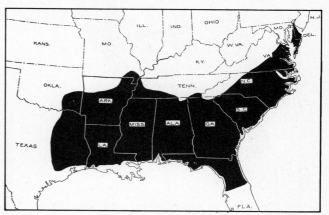

Natural range of Water Oak

WHITE OAK

Fork-leaf white oak, Ridge white oak, Stave oak

Quercus alba Linnaeus

CHIEF of all the oaks and outstanding among trees is the white oak, *Quercus alba*. *Quercus* is the Latin name for oak, while *alba* possibly refers to the light colored bark. It is easily recognized and it is a favorite throughout most of the eastern half of the country from central Maine to northern Florida, west from southern Quebec through southern Ontario and southern Michigan, through Wisconsin, southeastern Minnesota, most of Iowa, eastern Kansas, eastern Oklahoma to eastern Texas, excluding a narrow belt along the Gulf of Mexico. Preferring rich well drained soil, it attains its greatest size in the valleys of the western slopes of the Allegheny Mountains and in the bottom lands of the lower Ohio Basin. There it attains a height of 150 feet and occasionally six or eight feet in diameter, but is more commonly sixty to eighty feet high. Individuals have been known to be 800 years old.

While trees grown in the deep woods are tall and narrow-crowned, as compared with the broad round heads of open-grown trees, the pale gray bark with shallow fissures and scaly ridges is usually characteristic. The bark on old trees may be two inches thick.

The leaves are alternate, from five to nine inches long, narrowed toward the stem, somewhat oblong in outline but usually with the broader end forward, and with seven to nine lobes. They turn russet in the fall. The buds are round and smooth, clustered at the tips of the twigs so as to give the effect of a clenched

U. S. Forest Service

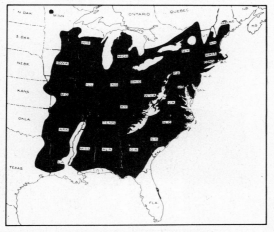

G. H. Collingwood

The wide-spreading branches of the open-grown White Oak are attractive in winter as well as in summer. They form a massive low crown which becomes increasingly broad with age

Natural range of White Oak

fist. In cross-section a twig reveals a five-pointed star-like pith.

In May, when the new rose-colored leaves are scarcely one-third grown the fringed catkins of the stiminate flowers and tiny, close-fitting clusters of pistillate flowers appear. The acorns mature during the early autumn of the same season. Accordingly, white oak carries no acorns through the winter. The shiny, brown nut is three-fourths of an inch to an inch long, with about one-fourth its length in a shallow cup, which is attached directly to the twig or by a very short stem. Squirrels and other mammals, as well as birds, enjoy the sweet-flavored nut so that comparatively few sprout into seedlings.

The light brown wood weighs about forty-eight pounds to the cubic foot when air dry, which is nearly twice the weight of white pine. Its uniform strength, narrow growth rings, durability and attractive color encourage a wide variety of uses, ranging from fine cabinet work and interior trim to flooring, railroad ties, piling, barrels, veneers, bridges, ships and building construction. Originally desired for its strength and durability, its beauty for furniture, floors and interior trim is now of first importance. Quarter-sawed oak reveals large numbers of "mirrors," which are the split medullary or pith rays. These form a pattern prized for many purposes. Tannic acid in the wood protects it from some fungi and insects, but results in unsightly discoloring when iron nails are used.

Of the total amount of oak cut annually, the white oak group probably furnishes less than one-third, and this species less than one-fifth.

White oak has few natural enemies, the worst of which is fire. The oak timber worm or pin worm is destructive to timber values, a twig pruner causes owners of shade trees to be alarmed, but it is seldom fatal. The gypsy moth may prove serious within its range. Several fungi cause heart rot. Fire and gypsy moth may be controlled, and injuries caused by these enemies are often responsible for other difficulties.

Although white oak grows slowly, and a strong taproot makes transplanting difficult, the tree is splendidly adapted for city streets, home lawns and parks. The broadly spreading branches form a round top more than eighty feet high and fully as broad. For best development the young trees should be planted about forty feet apart, and eventually thinned to about eighty feet.

The acorn is the principal means by which the white oak tree reproduces itself, but under favorable conditions it will sprout from the stump. Seedlings may be grown in nurseries and transplanted, or the acorn may be planted.

Pollen-bearing staminate blossoms appear in May when the first leaves unfurl. Inconspicuous pistillate blossoms from which the acorns develop are at the base of the new leaves

Light ash-gray bark with scaly plates and shallow fissures help distinguish the older white oak trees

Glossy leaves with five to nine rounded lobes and sweet-meated acorns, whose shallow cup covers a fourth of the nut, are typical

231

BUR OAK
Mossycup oak
Quercus macrocarpa Michaux

Devereux Butcher

ports a moderately broad, open crown of stout branches. In contrast to these splendid dimensions it may, on unfavorable sites, live for years in thickets without attaining heights of more than six to eight feet.

The lobed leaves, wedge-shaped at the base, are the largest of all the oak leaves, being six to twelve inches long and three to six inches broad at the upper half. Two unusually deep, wide bays or sinuses dip in near the middle of the leaf toward the stout, pale midrib, which is occasionally hairy on the upper side. The five to seven rounded lobes are irregular, and the terminal one occupying more than a third of the entire leaf has irregularly crenate margins. Crowded toward the ends of the twigs, the thick, firm leaves are lustrous dark green above and silvery green and downy below. They turn dull yellow in the autumn.

With its characteristically irregular, broadly rounded crown and gnarled branches, the Bur Oak is one of the largest and most majestic of the American oaks. It never grows in dense stands, but individually or in groups

Devereux Butcher

BUR OAK is one of the largest and, next to the white oak, the most majestic of American oaks. It is characteristic of the Middle West, but grows with surprising adaptability over much of the eastern half of the United States. Its range extends from New Brunswick to central Maine and western New England to southeastern Saskatchewan, south through the Dakotas to a belt roughly bounded by the Nueces and Colorado rivers in Texas, and from Ohio, Kentucky, northern Tennessee to northern Arkansas. It attains greatest size and highest commercial importance in the Wabash River basin of Indiana and Illinois. Typical of the "oak openings" of the lake states, it is the most common oak of Kansas and the prairie states.

Open-grown trees develop an irregular broadly rounded crown with stiff, gnarled branches and stout, frequently crooked, corky winged branchlets. Seldom more than eighty feet high or three feet in diameter, trees 170 to 180 feet high and six or seven feet in diameter have been reported. Under forest conditions bur oak develops a tall, massive, clear trunk, which sup-

232

In May or June the blossoms of both sexes appear, as the leaves unfold. The staminate blossoms are four- to six-inch slender, yellow-green catkins. The reddish, hairy, pistillate flowers grow on the same tree, and frequently on the same branches.

Being of the white oak group, the fertilized pistillate flowers develop by autumn of the first year into short-stalked acorns, three quarters to two inches long, more than half surrounded by a cup. The conspicuous fringe, or "awns," on the cup scales suggest the common names bur oak and mossycup oak. Prolific crops of highly fertile acorns occur frequently.

The scientific name, *macrocarpa*, meaning large fruited, refers to the large, edible nut. Acorns of southern grown trees are usually larger than those of the North. *Quercus* is Latin for oak, and is said to derive from the Celtic *quer*, meaning fine, and *cuez*, meaning tree.

The flaky, grayish to reddish brown bark of old trees is one or two inches thick, broken into vertical ridges. Resembling that of white oak, the bark is firmer and the ridges usually more prominent. First year branchlets have greenish gray bark, turning to a light orange, covered for a short time with fine hairs. Later the twigs become dark brown and develop corky ridges one to one and a half inches wide. As the limbs mature, sections of bark drop off.

The light brown, close-grained, tough heartwood with medullary rays so resembles that of white oak that it is frequently marketed with that species. When air dry, a cubic foot weighs forty-five pounds. It is used for furniture, interior finish, flooring, structural material and for railroad ties because of its durability.

Bur oak never grows in dense stands, but as individuals or in groups associated with other bottomland trees. It grows well on rich, moist bottomlands and on lower slopes, and because of the damp sites, fire damage is rare. It is seldom injured by either insects or fungus.

Of relatively slow growth, it reaches great age and is not considered mature before 200 to 300 years.

The beauty of bur oak, its ability to withstand city smoke, its freedom from insect and fungus injuries, its adaptability to soils and climates, and the comparative ease with which it may be raised and transplanted, recommend it for city streets and lawns.

George J. Baetzhold

The lobed leaves of the Bur Oak, wedge-shaped at the base, are the largest of all the oak leaves, being from six to twelve inches long and three to six inches broad at the upper half. The acorns are short-stalked, and broadly egg-shaped

The flaky, gray to red-brown bark of older trees is from one to two inches thick. Resembling that of the white oak, the bark of the Bur Oak is firmer and the ridges are usually more prominent

Warren D. Brush

The yellow-green male catkins, which appear as the woolly young leaves unfold, are from four to six inches long

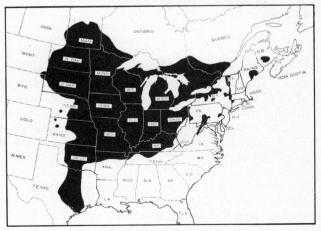

Natural range of Bur Oak

BLACKJACK OAK

Barren oak, Jack oak
Quercus marilandica Muenchhausen

BLACKJACK OAK is a small tree, sometimes as much as forty or fifty feet tall, but the usual height is from twenty to thirty feet, with a trunk diameter of six to twelve inches. The short, stout, spreading branches form a narrow, compact, round-topped crown. Trees grown in the open have a more irregular head and somewhat pendulous branches.

The twigs are stout, woolly at first, becoming reddish

Blackjack Oak usually does not reach heights over forty or fifty feet, and it has stout branches that form a compact crown

brown and ultimately smooth or nearly so and dark brown or gray. The oval winter buds, about one-fourth of an inch long, are prominently angled and pointed and densely brown-hairy. They are similar to those of black oak, *Q. velutina*, but are usually more reddish brown. Those near the tip of the twig are clustered above the terminal bud.

From Long Island, New Jersey, Delaware, eastern Maryland south to northern Florida and eastern Texas, and west across southern Indiana and Illinois to southeastern Iowa, Kansas and Oklahoma, this tree is found on poor, dry soils where conditions are generally unfavor-

able for forest growth. It is not common in the north where it is usually only a shrub or very small tree, but is very abundant southward, particularly west of the Mississippi River, where it often constitutes a large part of the forest growth. It reaches its largest size in southern Arkansas and eastern Texas.

Blackjack oak leaves vary greatly in form. Broadly ovate in outline, they are three- or rarely five-lobed toward the broad apex and the lobes may be short or long, broad or narrow, rounded or acute with smooth or toothed margins. Mature leaves are thick and firm, dark green, smooth and shiny above, and brownish hairy below with a thick, broad, orange-colored midrib. They usually measure from three to seven inches long and two

The tree is most abundant and finds its best growing conditions in eastern Texas and southern Arkansas

to five inches wide. Each leaf is borne on a short, stout, yellowish stem or stalk from one-half to three-fourths of an inch in length.

The flowers appear when the leaves are about half unfolded—the staminate or pollen-bearing in slender, hairy catkins two to four inches long, which are borne on the growth of the preceding season or from the axils of the inner scales of the terminal bud, and the pistillate or acorn-producing flowers on short, stout, hairy stalks from the axils of the leaves of the same season.

The acorns, solitary or in pairs on a short stout stalk, mature in the autumn of the second year. The oblong or somewhat egg-shaped nut is light brown in color and often marked by parallel lines. It measures about three-fourths of an inch long and is enclosed for about half its length in the thick bowl-shaped cup. The inside of the cup is light brown and more or less woolly coated; the outside is reddish brown, covered with loosely overlapping scales, the smaller upper scales forming a loose rim around the top of the cup.

Blackjack oak is known by several other common names, including particularly barren oak and barrens oak, because it grows on dry, sterile soils and scrub oak because of its usual small size.

The dark brown or black bark of mature trees is from one to one and a half inches thick. It is divided by deep fissures into nearly square plates an inch to three inches long, which are covered by small appressed scales.

The wood is heavy, hard and strong, and a cubic foot weighs forty-six pounds when dry. The heartwood is dark brown, and the thick sapwood is lighter colored. Because of the small size of the tree in the North, it is of no commercial value except for fuel, but in the South it often is converted into railway ties and occasionally into lumber. It also is used in making charcoal. Although small, blackjack oak is desirable for ornamental planting, the wide-spreading branches of open-grown trees giving a pleasing variety to the landscape. It is also of value in providing forest cover for sandy soils where other trees will not grow.

Maryland State Dept. of Forestry

Acorns occur singly or in pairs and they ripen by October of their second year

Maryland State Dept. of Forestry

The three- to five-lobed leaves are thick, dark green and glossy above and brownish hairy beneath, with a broad orange midrib

Maryland State Dept. of Forestry

The brown or black bark is one to one and a half inches thick, divided by deep fissures into nearly square plates

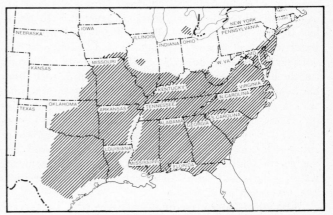

The natural range of Blackjack Oak

OVERCUP OAK

Swamp post oak, Water white oak
Quercus lyrata Walter

OVERCUP OAK is a tree of river swamps and low, moist bottomlands in the Atlantic and Gulf coastal plains and Mississippi River Valley. Its range is from Delaware and Maryland southward to western Florida, and west through the Gulf region to Texas; and in the Mississippi Valley from southern Indiana and Illinois, south through southeastern Missouri and western Kentucky and Tennessee.

In the lower Mississippi River Valley and the low valleys of its tributaries, overcup oak is one of the most

to two and a half feet, overcup oak occasionally grows to a height of 100 feet with a diameter of from three to four feet. A tree of many forms, it more nearly resembles bur oak than any other associated species, because of its deeply cupped acorn and somewhat similar leaves. The trunk is often tall and erect with stout, horizontal lower branches forming a wide and irregular crown. It frequently divides at fifteen or twenty feet above the ground into several principal branches or main stems which are wide-spreading and form a handsome, symmetrical, round-topped head. The branches may be pendulous and sweep the ground with their extremities. Frequently, the trunk forks at narrow angles and the branches spread gradually, forming an oblong head. Or the tree may be of poor form, with a short crooked or twisting trunk and a large open crown featured by crooked branches with relatively few smaller branchlets.

At first, the slender twigs are hairy and green, more or less tinged with red, but they become smooth and orange or gray-brown during their first winter, and ultimately pale gray or light brown. The winter buds are egg-shaped, blunt, about one-eighth of an inch long, with light brown scales covered with loose, fine, pale hairs, especially near their margins.

The leaves are oblong, gradually

Overcup Oak, one of the most common trees in swamps and deep depressions, is seldom more than seventy feet high

common trees in swamps and deep depressions that are usually wet throughout the year. Because it is so prevalent in such locations, it is often called swamp white oak, water white oak, swamp overcup oak and swamp post oak.

Overcup does not occur as extensive forests or in pure stands, but as isolated trees or in small groups with other hardwoods. A comparatively rare tree in the Atlantic and eastern Gulf states, it is most common and reaches its largest size in the valley of the Red River in Louisiana, and the adjacent parts of Texas and Arkansas. Overcup oak is better adapted to withstand frequent and prolonged inundation than many of its associates, including water, willow and laurel oak, water tupelo, water hickory, green ash and sweetbay.

Although usually a medium-sized tree with an average height of seventy feet and a diameter of one and a half

narrowed and wedge-shaped at the base, and divided into five to nine lobes separated by broad, irregular sinuses. The terminal lobe is usually broad, sharp at the apex, and furnished with two small, nearly triangular lateral lobes. The upper lateral lobes are broad and much longer than the acute or rounded lower lobes. Smooth, shining and dark green above, silvery white and light green below and thickly coated with pale hairs, the leaves are from six to ten inches long and one to four inches wide. The leaf stalk, from one-third to one inch long, is stout and grooved.

When the leaves are unfolding the male or staminate flowers appear in long, slender, hairy catkins from four to six inches long. The pistillate flowers, which are hairy throughout, develop into acorns.

The acorns of overcup oak are different from those of any other native oak in that they are enclosed for two-thirds or more of their length in a cup, the margin of which is unfringed. They occur singly or in pairs, are spherical to egg-shaped, light chestnut-brown and about an inch long. Bright reddish brown and hairy on the inside, the deep, thin cup is covered on the outside with thick scales at the base which gradually become thinner toward the margin.

Overcup oak bark is somewhat similar to that of white oak, *Quercus alba*, but is more of a brownish gray. Three-fourths to one inch thick, it sheds in large, thick, irregular plates, the surfaces of which are covered with thin scales.

The wood of overcup oak is heavy, hard, stiff and strong and moderately durable. It is inclined to check and warp during seasoning. The heartwood is brown with thin, lighter colored sapwood. Overcup is used for the same purposes as white oak, and especially for railroad ties. Its region of greatest importance includes northwestern Louisiana, southwestern Arkansas and extreme eastern Texas.

Overcup oak bears acorns abundantly every three or four years, but seedlings are infrequent and the young trees are often destroyed by browsing cattle. Like most specimens of the white oak group, overcup oak is a slow grower and large trees are often 300 to 400 years old. It is very susceptible to attacks by insects.

Acorns, enclosed in cups two-thirds or more of their length, are distinctive. Narrow leaves are dark green

The slender, hairy, male catkins are four to six inches long

The brownish gray bark, three-fourths to an inch thick, sheds in large, thick, irregular plates which are covered with thin scales

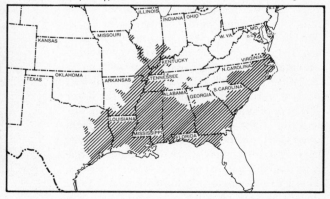

The natural range of the Overcup Oak

POST OAK

Iron oak

Quercus stellata Wangenheim

S. L. Frost

Stout, gnarled branches of the Post Oak form a broad, dense, round-topped head. On open-grown trees the trunk may be short and limby

low oak, water oak, sweetgum, elm, ash, hickory and occasionally loblolly pine.

Post oak is the common oak of central Texas on limestone hills and sandy plains. In the northern part of its range, from southern New England to Kansas, it is rather rare and inclined to be shrubby. It is of comparatively frequent occurrence from the coast of the south Atlantic and the eastern Gulf states to the lower slopes of the Appalachian Mountains. Post oak is the dominant tree species on the beautiful Wichita Mountains National Wildlife Refuge in south central Oklahoma.

Although usually a medium-sized tree not more than fifty or sixty feet tall and from one to two feet in diameter, it sometimes reaches a height of 100 feet and a diameter of three feet. The stout spreading branches, which are characteristically gnarled or somewhat twisted, form a broad, dense, round-topped head. The twigs are covered with yellowish brown, matted, woolly hairs and the buds have chestnut-brown hairy scales, coated toward the margins with scattered pale hairs.

The thick, somewhat leathery leaves, four to six inches long and three to four inches wide, are five-lobed. The two middle lobes,

S. L. Frost

POST OAK grows naturally throughout nearly all the eastern United States, except the lake states, northern New York, northern New England, and southern Florida. Its range is included in the area from southern Connecticut, Long Island, southern New Jersey, Pennsylvania, Ohio, Indiana and Illinois to southeastern Iowa, southwest to west central Texas, and east to Florida.

For the most part, the tree occurs on poor, dry, gravelly or sandy upland soils, and on rocky ridges, being associated in the "barrens" or in sand-plain country with black, blackjack and scrub oaks, pitch pine and eastern redcedar. In the southern Appalachian Mountains post oak grows at altitudes up to 2,500 feet. It attains its largest size and best quality on the higher bottomlands of the lower Mississippi Valley. Because the trees in this location differ so greatly in size and form from those on the drier locations of the same general region, they were described at one time as a separate species, *mississippiensis*. The usual associates of this bottomland form include swamp chestnut oak, white oak, wil-

usually the largest and opposite each other, give the leaves a more or less cruciform appearance. They are dark green on the upper surface, which is roughened by scattered pale hairs. The under surface is covered with short soft hairs which may be gray, light yellow or rarely silvery white.

In the spring when the new leaves are only partly grown, the staminate pollen-bearing catkins appear, together with the pistillate acorn-producing flowers, which are borne on the same tree, frequently on the same branch.

The acorns, which measure from one-half to three-fourths of an inch long, mature in September and October of the first year. They are sometimes covered with fine soft hairs at the tip and at times have dark, longitudinal stripes. They occur singly or in pairs and the nut is enclosed for one-third to one-half its length in a bowl-shaped cup attached to the twig or on a very short stem. The cup is covered by thin reddish brown scales, those toward the rim of the cup having long pale hairs.

The reddish brown bark, one-half to one inch thick, is divided by deep fissures into broad ridges and is covered on the surface with narrow, closely appressed, or rarely, loose scales.

While post oak produces some acorns every year, abundant crops are borne every two or three years. They are a favorite food of the wild turkey, as well as other birds and mammals, particularly the squirrel, whose activity in burying the nuts facilitates the dispersal and propagation of the species.

Borers often render trees unfit for lumber. To a large extent, the trees are converted into railway ties and construction timbers. A cubic foot of the air-dry wood weighs approximately forty-seven pounds, only one pound less than the weight of white oak.

When the leaves are partly grown, long pollen-bearing catkins and short acorn-producing flowers appear on the same tree

Acorns occur singly or in pairs, close to the twig

Reddish brown bark, one half to one inch thick, is divided by deep fissures into broad ridges covered with narrow scales

The thick, somewhat leathery leaves are dark green and rough on the upper surface and covered with soft hairs beneath

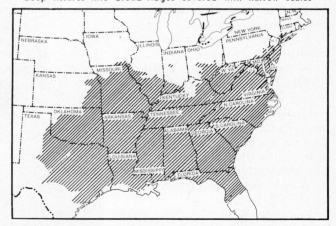

Common on poor soils throughout the East, the Post Oak makes its best growth in the lower Mississippi Valley bottomlands

OREGON WHITE OAK

Garry oak, Oregon oak

Quercus garryana Douglas

ington to the shores of Puget Sound whence it follows the islands to Vancouver Island. On Vancouver it is found on the southeastern tip, and also in two small isolated stands, the farthest of which, on Vancouver Island, is nearly the most northern outpost of oak on this continent, this being slightly out-distanced by bur oak in the southern part of Manitoba. There is also a small stand of Oregon white oak in British Columbia.

Often a gnarled, picturesque tree, Oregon white oak grows in a variety of soils and sites, from deep moist humus to dry, gravelly and rocky situations in the zone between grassland and forest, or on

OREGON WHITE OAK, or Garry oak, as it also is known, was named by the botanical explorer Robert Douglas in honor of Nicholas Garry, secretary of the Hudson Bay Company. Douglas honored Garry thus because of the aid rendered by the latter to botanists studying the flora of the Northwest. This species is a tree of dark green foliage and rugged appearance, which sometimes attains massive proportions.

In lowlands from the Willamette Valley of Oregon northward to Puget Sound this oak reaches its best development with a height of seventy-five to ninety feet and diameters of four or five feet. On mountainsides it is smaller. Southward in the Siskiyou Mountains and in exposed situations along the coast, it is considerably reduced in size.

From the Santa Cruz Mountains of California, its range extends northward through western California, western Oregon, and western Wash-

southwest slopes that are excessively hot and dry in summer. It is rarely found above three thousand feet elevation. Occurring occasionally in pure stands, it is generally in mixture with Douglasfir, California black oak, ponderosa pine, and madrone. In the bottomlands where young stands of Douglasfir crowd close about its base, it is usually tall and without lower limbs.

The light gray-brown bark is broken by shallow narrow grooves, to form scaly plates. The young twigs are hairy, later becoming smooth and bright reddish brown, while red fuzz covers the long pointed buds. Resembling those of *Q. alba*, the leaves grow alternately, are four to six inches long, and two to five inches wide, and have five to nine rounded lobes, whose thickened margins curl under. Smooth, shiny, and dark green above, they are paler with conspicuous veins beneath. A tough, leathery upper surface and hairiness on the under side help to retain moisture during summer droughts.

The staminate flowers are pendent catkins that occur in clusters, and the pistillate ones are erect blooms occurring solitary or in pairs. Oregon white oak is a prolific seeder about every other year, but the rate of germination of acorns is usually very low and therefore seedling trees are scarce. Acorns are one to one and a half inches long and about half as broad. The shallow cups are hairy, covered with thin, loose, pointed scales, and are usually stemless.

This is the only timber oak in the coast country of the Northwest. Pale yellowish brown in color, the wood is hard, fine-grained, tough, strong and durable. It is used in furniture, ship construction, buildings, agricultural implements, vehicles, barrels, cabinet work, fuel and interior finish. Insulator pins for electric lines, saddle trees, stirrups, and baskets are some of its more unusual uses.

A long-lived, slow-growing tree, it attains ages up to 250 and 350 years. In the northern part of its range,

Devereux Butcher

Leaves, growing alternately along the twigs, are shiny above and hairy beneath, while the acorns, which ripen in one season, are sweet and eaten by wildlife

winters are exceedingly wet and favorable, but its growth and reproduction are limited by the excessive drought of summers.

Enemies are a leaf mold and a root rot, neither of which is serious. A twig girdler causes the loss of many small branches; and about once in seven years an epidemic of leaf galls produced by a small wasp reduces the vitality of many trees. The parasite mistletoe is proving to be an enemy of increasing destructiveness.

Devereux Butcher

Bark is light grayish brown. On old trunks scaly ridges are separated by narrow fissures

Natural range of Oregon White Oak

241

CALIFORNIA WHITE OAK

Valley white oak, Valley oak, Weeping oak

Quercus lobata Née

THE BROAD crowned, graceful California white oak with its massive trunk and drooping sprays of branches is peculiar to the state whose name it bears. It is the largest of fourteen oak species native to California, only nine of which attain tree stature. It inhabits low valleys and low rolling plateaus between the Sierra Nevada and the Pacific, from the Trinity River in the north to Tejon Pass in the Tehachapi Mountains on the south.

Trees forty to seventy-five feet tall are common, while a few individuals reach 100 feet or more. The trunks are short and massive, with diameters ranging from two feet to occasionally ten feet. With maturity the broad crown consists of many high, arching branches extending into long slender pendulous branchlets.

Found most abundantly on fairly rich soil, this tree favors hot, moist valleys and avoids those which are open to the ocean. It grows from a little above sea level to 2,700 feet in its northern range and up to 4,500 feet above sea level in its southern range. In the foothills above the valleys it is seldom over thirty feet tall.

The deeply indented, leathery, deciduous leaves have seven to eleven obliquely rounded lobes. They vary in size and form on the same tree, but are usually two and a half to four inches long. A covering of fine hairs on both surfaces helps the leaves resist the drying influence of days of sun and hot wind. The wedge-shaped base leads to a stout, hairy stem or petiole a quarter to a half inch in length.

The staminate flowers are apparent in early spring as yellow, hairy strings two to three inches long. The less conspicuous acorn-bearing pistillate flowers are borne singly, or occasionally with a few others, on elongated spikes. Both sexes grow on different parts of the same tree.

Heavy crops of bright chestnut-brown acorns about one and a quarter to two and a half inches

California White Oak raises a great dome of foliage above the valley or low plateau

With the loss of leaves in winter, long, pendulous, graceful branches are revealed

long usually are produced every other year. They are slender and quite pointed, with a pale woolly or even warty cup which covers about one-third of the nut. Borne singly or in pairs, they have little or no stem and mature at the end of one season. Having a sweet kernel, the acorns were formerly eaten by native Indians, but are now fed only to hogs.

The light brown to ashen gray bark of the main trunk is checked deeply to form rough, irregular cubes one to two inches across. It is one to four and a half inches thick.

The wood is dull brown in color, hard, brittle and close-grained. Lighter than white oak, a cubic foot weighs thirty-nine to forty pounds when air dry. It is perhaps the least valuable of the Pacific coast hardwoods, but early settlers built log cabins with it. In spite of the frequent cross grain, they succeeded in riving shakes and splitting out posts and rails from the trunks. Its chief value is for fuel. Large trees sometimes produce fifty to ninety cords of stove wood, but the soft texture early gave it the name "mush" oak.

Frequently referred to as valley oak, the more inclusive name California white oak is now accepted. *Quercus*, the Latin name of the oak family is derived from the ancient Celtic *quer* or fine and *cuez* for tree. This has been interpreted as "beautiful tree." The rounded lobes of the leaves are probably referred to in *lobata*. Louis Née, an eighteenth century botanist of French birth, but a Spaniard by adoption, is credited with the earliest description of the tree. While rounding the world with a Spaniard named Malaspina, from 1789 to 1794, Née made botanical collections and observations in Mexico and on the Pacific coast.

Between the ages of 125 and 300 years, when the tree has attained a height of fifty to 100 feet, with a form resembling American elm, long pendulous branches develop to produce a weeping stage. The amazing vigor of this species is shown occasionally when old trees, whose branches have been lost by storm or disease, develop a new crown of erect, relatively straight branches.

This white oak grows with reasonable rapidity. One tree is credited with having attained a diameter of twenty-one inches in fifty-seven years. It may live for 400 or more years.

Germination requires that acorns be well covered with fresh litter or soil. In spite of the heavy biennial crops of acorns, reproduction is poor. This is because agriculture and livestock have taken over much of the rich, level valley lands that are the oak's favored habitat, and because quantities of the acorns are eaten by hogs and other creatures. As a result, the large, picturesque old trees that were left standing by ranchers are dying and not being replaced by young trees. It may not be long before many areas will know their graceful forms no more.

Under natural conditions, the species has few enemies, and it resists long periods of drought. Although seldom cultivated outside California, the tree deserves to be planted increasingly for its beauty and shade along highways throughout the Sacramento and San Joaquin valleys, as well as in cities and towns and around homes. To allow for the wide spread of branches in maturity, trees should be planted eighty or 100 feet apart.

Woodbridge Metcalf

Leathery leaves with seven to eleven rounded lobes partly conceal the slender pointed acorns

G. B. Sudworth

The deeply divided bark may be ashen gray to light brown

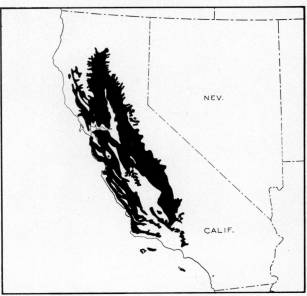

Natural range of California White Oak

GAMBEL OAK

Rocky Mountain white oak, Utah white oak
Quercus gambellii Nuttall, *Quercus utahensis* Rydb

GAMBEL OAK is named for William Gambel, an American naturalist who collected plants in the southern Rocky Mountains in 1844, and was the first to report the species. Because of leaf characteristics, which vary according to location, several naturalists have suggested more than twenty different scientific names. For the sake of simplification, certain authorities have settled for one or two names.

The species inhabits dry foothill slopes, canyons and mountain sides from the Upper Sonoran and Transition zones to 10,000 feet above sea level. In its favored sites, it occurs in two distinct forms: as a shrub in dense thickets at such locations as Raton Pass, 7800 feet above sea level, on the Colorado-New Mexico boundary, and as trees twenty to thirty feet tall in the south rim country of the Grand Canyon, in northern Arizona, where thickets also occur. The scattered range of Gambel oak includes parts of Nevada, Utah, Colorado except the eastern and northern areas of the state, most of New Mexico, the moutains of western Texas, and Arizona except the southwestern quarter. In Mexico, Gambel oak occurs in northeastern Sonora and northwestern Chihuahua.

David Ochsner

Devereux Butcher

Forming shrubby thickets on much of its range, Gambel Oak also reaches tree size, with heights of twenty to thirty feet and more

The deciduous leaves are two and a half to seven inches long and one and a half to three inches wide. They are divided into three to six pairs of round-tipped lateral lobes by sinuses or indentations that sometimes reach almost to the midrib. The tip of the terminal lobe may be entire or two- or three-lobed. Rounded lobes indicate that this tree is a member of the white oak group. Wedge-shaped at the base, the leaves are dark green, except pale green when young, are smooth or nearly so above, and paler and softly hairy beneath, with prominent midrib and primary veins. Petioles or stems two fifths to an inch in length are covered with pale hair when young, becoming smooth or finely hairy before maturity.

Flowers appear in late March or April, the staminate or pollen-bearing ones in clusters of yellow catkins two to two and a half inches long, borne at the ends of the growth of the preceding year, and the pistillate or acorn-producing ones singly or in pairs, born with or without a short stalk at the axils of the leaf petioles. The cup, covered with thick, hairy scales, embraces the lower half of the nut, which is broadly oval and green when young, turning brown and lustrous when ripe in August or September. It measures three fifths to three quarters of an inch in length.

Twigs are stout, pale red-brown and hairy when young, later becoming orange-gray. The winter buds are an eighth to a quarter inch long, brown and hairy. Bark on young stems is gray-brown and smooth, while on large trunks it is thin, light gray and narrowly fissured into long, rather rough ridges.

Gambel oak wood is hard, close-grained, weighs fifty-two and a half pounds to the cubic foot when dry, and has little commercial value except locally.

Unlike other oaks, this one rarely reproduces by acorns. This is particularly true of the ten- to twenty-foot-high thickets (or clumps) of stems. These leafy stems usually spring from roots (rhizomes) that spread along the perimeters of the clumps. According to studies, clumps expand at the rate of about four inches or less a year. Reproduction in the clumps occurs also by layering—by shoots bent down to the soil where they develop roots and send up new stalks. Large, freestanding individual Gambel oaks, such as those in the accompanying illustrations, are perhaps the only instances of this species springing from acorns.

David Ochsner

Two and a half to seven inches long, the dark green deciduous leaves of Gambel Oak have three to six pairs of round-tipped lobes and a wedge-shaped base. The catkins, two to two and a half inches long, are borne at the twig ends of the previous year's growth

David Ochsner

Devereux Butcher

David Ochsner

Gambel Oak bark is pale gray and, on larger trunks, is thin, narrowly fissured into rough ridges. Acorns, sometimes with a short stalk, grow from the axils of the leaf petioles

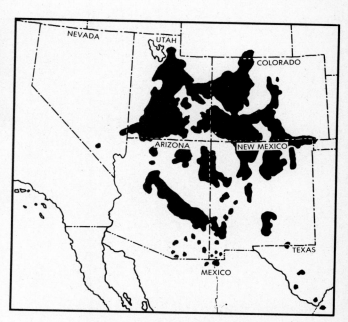

The natural range of Gambel Oak

CHESTNUT OAK
Rock chestnut oak, Rock oak
Quercus prinus Linnaeus

Maryland State Department of Forestry

The trunk of Chestnut Oak may be tall and straight, or divided into large ascending limbs, with spreading branches that form a broad open head

CHESTNUT OAK is found from southern Maine westward through Ohio and southern Indiana and southward through Kentucky and Tennessee to northeastern Mississippi and Georgia. It is most abundant on the Appalachian hills from southern New York to Georgia and Alabama, and reaches its largest size on the lower slopes in the Carolinas and Tennessee. An exceptionally large specimen was the "Washington Oak" on the east bank of the Hudson River near Fishkill, New York, under which Washington used to mount his horse when he went from headquarters on the west bank of the Hudson to the army encamped at Fishkill. This tree was seven feet in diameter and its estimated age was 800 to 1,000 years.

Although chestnut oak is generally associated with dry soil and sandy, rocky ridges, it frequently grows on rich well-drained soil close to the banks of streams. It is usually sixty to seventy feet tall with a trunk two to three feet in diameter, but sometimes reaches a hundred feet in height with a trunk six to seven feet in diameter. On rocky ridges and dry mountain slopes chestnut oak has a scrubby form about twenty or thirty feet tall with a trunk eight to twelve inches in diameter. The trunk usually divides into several large limbs not far from the ground to give the tree an open irregular spreading head.

Sometimes this tree is called rock oak or mountain oak because it grows on high, rocky slopes, but its more common name, chestnut oak, refers to its leaves which are similar to those of the chestnut, except that they are scalloped or wavy on the edge instead of sharp-toothed.

L. W. Brownell

This species makes up about eight percent of the stand of all oaks.

The leaves, five to nine inches long and one and a half to four inches wide, are narrowly oval in outline, with coarsely scalloped margins, wedge-shaped or rounded bases, and tapering tips. They are shiny yellow-green above, pale green and hairy below, and turn dull yellow or yellow-brown in autumn. They have short stems one half to one inch long, stout yellow midribs, and ten to sixteen pairs of conspicuous, straight, primary veins.

The bright, rich brown, edible acorns of chestnut oak are borne singly or in pairs on short, stout stems. They are one to one and a half inches long and five-eighths to one

inch thick. The acorns are enclosed to about half their length by thin, rough, scaly cups. The white, rather sweet kernels are eagerly eaten by squirrels. Large acorn crops occur irregularly and at infrequent intervals, and the acorns prefer deep humus for germination.

The stout twigs, green with a purple or bronze cast when they first appear, are light orange or reddish brown the first winter and turn dark gray or brown the second year. The smaller branches have thin, smooth, purplish brown bark, and the bark on the trunk and large limbs is thick, nearly black, divided into broad ridges, is rich in tannin, and is used to tan leather.

The wood is hard, strong, tough, and close-grained. A

Leaves somewhat resemble those of chestnut, and the acorns, which mature in the first season, are useful as food for wildlife

cubic foot when dry weighs nearly forty-seven pounds. It is marketed as white oak and much of it is used for rough construction and railroad ties. In quantity of standing timber it ranks second among the white oaks, making up from fifteen to twenty percent of the total for the group.

Chestnut oak requires much light, especially as it grows older. Its root system is adaptable, and where the soils are deep the taproot is long. In rocky or shallow soils the lateral roots are strongly developed. Repeated fires reduce sprouting vitality, but the thick bark is a protection against fire.

Bark on mature trunks is deeply fissured into long, continuous, firm ridges

Pollen-bearing flowers, shown here, appear in May or June with the acorn-producing ones which are small, and grow from the base of leaf stems

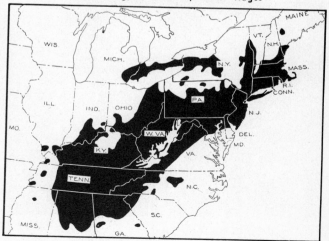

Natural range of Chestnut Oak

SWAMP CHESTNUT OAK

Basket oak, Cow oak
Quercus michauxii Nuttall

ALTHOUGH the leaves of the oaks show considerable variation, each species has a characteristic leaf form by which it can usually be identified. The leaf of swamp chestnut oak resembles that of chestnut oak, but it differs in outline and is toothed rather than scalloped on the margins. The leaves of both these species resemble those of the chestnut, but the latter has sharp, bristle-tipped teeth. The chestnut oaks, belonging to the white oak group, do not have bristle tips on their leaf lobes.

Swamp chestnut oak and chestnut oak are not likely to be found in the same locality. The latter prefers upper slopes and ridges and is most abundant in the Appalachian Mountain region; swamp chestnut oak is usually found in bottomlands and along streams and the borders of swamps in the Atlantic coastal plain and part of the Piedmont region from New Jersey to northern Florida, west in the Gulf states to eastern Texas and north in the Mississippi Valley through central Arkansas and west central Tennessee to southern Indiana and southern Illinois. Swamp chestnut oak occurs usually on moist or wet loamy soils that are inundated for short periods in the fall or winter. It does not form pure stands, but is mixed with other hardwoods including water oak, laurel oak, water hickory, red maple, and blackgum.

One of the most important timber trees of the South, swamp chestnut oak grows to a usual height of sixty to eighty feet and a trunk diameter of two to three feet, but occasionally reaches a height of 120 feet and a diameter of seven feet. The straight, massive trunk is often clear of branches for forty or fifty feet, and the large limbs rise

W. W. Ashe

One of the important timber trees of the South, Swamp Chestnut Oak grows to a usual height of 60 to 80 feet

George J. Baetzhold

Large limbs, rising at a narrow angle from the trunk, produce a typical round-topped, rather narrow crown

at a narrow angle with the trunk to form a round-topped, rather compact crown.

The stout twigs are dark green at first with pale, deciduous hairs. During their first winter they become bright red-brown or light orange-brown and later ashy gray. The oval, pointed buds, about one-fourth of an inch long, have thin, closely and regularly overlapping dark red scales, pale on the margins and covered with fine hairs.

The leaves, from five to eight inches long and three to five inches broad, have bluntly pointed tips and are generally wedge-shaped at the base. The margins have regular rounded teeth, which decrease in size as they reach the tip. Dark green and shining above, pale and downy below, they turn a dark rich crimson in the fall. They are borne on short slender stems one-half to one and a half inches long.

Flowers of both sexes appear on the same tree in the spring when the leaves are only partly grown. The male or pollen-bearing blossoms are in slender, hairy catkins, three to four inches long, and the female or acorn-producing ones are on few-flowered spikes with short, pale reddish, densely haired stems. The bright brown, ovoid-oblong acorns, one to one and a half inches long and three-fourths to one and a fourth inches wide, are borne on short, stout hairy stalks. They are enclosed for about one-third their length in a thick bowl-shaped cup which is covered on the outer surface by regular overlapping, somewhat wedge-shaped scales, the lower ones much thickened and the tips of the upper ones often forming a rigid, fringe-like border to the rim of the cup. The acorns are sweet and edible and are eaten by cattle, hence the name "cow oak" by which the tree is sometimes called. Basket oak is another name applied to the tree because of its local use for baskets made of strips split from the straight-grained wood.

The ashy gray bark is from one-half to one inch thick on mature trees and separates into thin, closely appressed scales. It is similar to that of white oak, but is rougher and has a reddish brown cast, especially on freshly-cut surfaces.

The wood is heavy, hard, stiff and strong and has high shock-resisting ability. A cubic foot of air dried swamp chestnut oak weighs forty-seven pounds, which is only one pound less than the average of white oak. The quality of the wood is considered second only to that of the best white oak and it is utilized for the same purposes. In the form of lumber it is highly valued for flooring, furniture, motor vehicle parts, car construction, house finish, boxes and crates, and building construction in general. In other forms much of it is used for railroad ties, barrels, mine timbers and fuelwood. Although one of the most important hardwoods of the Mississippi River Delta region, the stand of swamp chestnut oak is comparatively small and has been reduced by heavy cutting.

Swamp chestnut oak seems to be quite free from insect and fungus diseases. Its worst enemy is fire to which it is very sensitive while young. Its occurrence in moist locations, however, often serves as a protection. In growth it resembles white oak. It reaches maturity in from 100 to 180 years, and some trees have been known to live to be 350 years old.

Warren D. Brush

Pollen-bearing blossoms occur in long, slender, hairy catkins. Female flowers are on short reddish spikes

George J. Baetzhold

The broad leaves are from five to eight inches long. The acorns are enclosed in thick, bowl-shaped cups

Maryland State Department of Forestry

The ashy gray bark on mature trees is similar to that of the white oak, but it is rougher, with a reddish cast

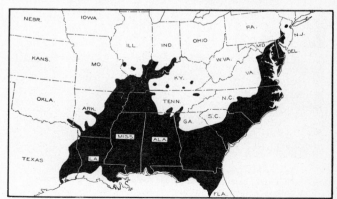

Within its range, Swamp Chestnut Oak occurs in mixed stands in bottomlands, along streams and swamp borders

249

SWAMP WHITE OAK

Quercus bicolor Willdenow

THE range of the swamp white oak is within that of the white oak, but the swamp species does not grow quite so far north and is found in only a small part of the South where the white oak occurs. While the white oak prefers the well-drained soils of coves and upper bottomlands, swamp white oak, as the name indicates, is most often found in more moist localities on the borders of streams and swamps and in low, poorly-drained pastures and meadows. The two species also have many distinct differences in leaf, fruit and bark.

The name *bicolor* refers to the two colors of the leaves —dark green above and pale or often silvery white below. Swamp white oak is usually classed with the so-called "chestnut oaks," so named because the leaves have dentate and wavy margins rather similar to those of chestnut; in swamp white oak they may also be lobed, somewhat resembling other species of the white oak group.

The oaks, generally, show much variation in the form of the leaf, not only those of the same species on differ-ent trees, but often on the same tree. Another cause of confusion in identifying the oaks is that different species and varieties may cross, producing hybrids which have some of the characteristics of each parent. This might conceivably result in the development of a new species and is an indication that the oaks are in a stage of rapid development compared to other groups of closely related trees. Their occurrence in such large quantities over extensive areas is proof that they have been highly successful in their struggle for survival, due perhaps in large measure to their means of reproduction.

Swamp white oak usually occurs in widely scattered small groves and nowhere is it very abundant. Its natural range is from southern Maine south to northern Delaware and Maryland and westward to southeastern Minnesota, and south through eastern Iowa to southeastern Minnesota and western Kentucky. It occurs locally in Kansas, Tennessee and North Carolina. The tree is most common and grows to largest size in western New York, northwestern Pennsylvania and northern Ohio.

Usually a medium-sized tree sixty to seventy feet in height and two to three feet in diameter, it has been known to attain a height of 100 feet when crowded by other trees in the forest. The trunks of isolated trees are

U. S. Forest Service

The rather small, tortuous branches of Swamp White Oak are generally pendulous below and rise above into a narrow, round-topped, open head. The upper trunk is often fringed with short drooping branches

Maryland State Dept. of Forestry

250

sometimes six to eight feet in diameter. The rather small, tortuous branches are generally pendulous below and rise above into a narrow round-topped open head. The upper trunk is often fringed with short, pendulous branchlets.

An outstanding characteristic of the tree is its scaly bark. On young stems and small branches it curls back in ragged, papery scales, displaying the bright green inner bark; on old trunks it is one to two inches thick and is deeply and irregularly divided into broad, flat ridges covered by small, appressed, gray-brown scales, often slightly tinged with red.

The blunt-pointed winter buds, about one-eighth inch in length, have chestnut-brown scales that are usually slightly hairy above the middle. The leaves are from five to six inches long and two to four inches wide, much broader toward the tip and wedge-shaped at the base, irregularly toothed, scalloped, or lobed sometimes half-way to the midrib.

Flowers of both sexes are found on the same tree, appearing in May or June together with the leaves. The male or pollen-bearing ones consist of clusters of hairy catkins three to four inches long, the female or acorn-producing ones are borne on elongated, slender, woolly stems.

The light chestnut-brown acorns, three-fourths to one and a quarter inches long and one-half to three-fourths of an inch thick, usually occur in pairs. They are enclosed for about one-third of their length in the thick, light brown bowl-shaped cup, which is lined on the inside with fine hairs and roughened on the outside by thin scales, which form a short fringe-like border on its rim. The long, slender stalks, one to four inches in length, on which the acorns are borne, are a characteristic feature of this species and help distinguish it from swamp chestnut oak. The nuts ripen in September and October of the first season.

A cubic foot of the air-dry wood weighs fifty pounds, which is two pounds more than the weight of white oak. It is hard, stiff and strong, and has high shock-resisting ability. Because of its resistance to decay, the wood is suitable for railway ties, even without preservative treatment. It is also valuable for tight barrels to hold liquids and for mine timbers, furniture, flooring and other interior finish.

The male or pollen-bearing flowers are in clusters of hairy catkins three or four inches long

The leaves resemble those of chestnut and chestnut oak, but are often irregularly lobed

Old bark is gray-brown, irregularly grooved

The light chestnut-brown acorns, which usually occur in pairs, are supported on stems one to four inches in length—a distinguishing characteristic of this tree

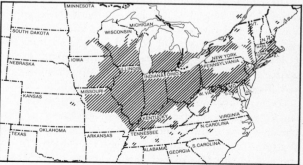

Natural range of Swamp White Oak

CHINQUAPIN OAK

Yellow chestnut oak
Quercus muehlenbergii Engelmann

CHINQUAPIN OAK is one of the less important members of the chestnut oak group, which includes the species chestnut oak, swamp chestnut oak and swamp white oak. They are named chestnut oaks because their leaves suggest those of chestnut. They belong to the larger group of white oaks. Chinquapin is the name in use for several important species of chestnut, *Castanea*.

U. S. Forest Service

Maximum height of the Chinquapin Oak is from eighty to a hundred feet. The crown is wide and well rounded

The range of chinquapin oak extends westward from western New England through southern Michigan and Wisconsin and southeastern Minnesota and south through Iowa, eastern Kansas and central Oklahoma and Texas. It does not inhabit the Atlantic coastal plain or lower piedmont region. It also occurs locally in southeastern New Mexico.

Throughout the Atlantic states it is comparatively rare, usually growing on dry hillsides and rocky ridges, where it makes poor growth and is small in size. Farther west it attains greater commercial importance and is quite common in the Mississippi basin, especially in Missouri, Kentucky, Arkansas, Tennessee, Mississippi and Alabama

where, on rich, deep soils, it attains its largest size. In the lower Ohio basin, including the Wabash River Valley of southern Indiana and Illinois, it grows to large size, trees in the original forests measuring 160 feet in height and five feet in diameter. Ordinarily, its maximum height is eighty to 100 feet, with a diameter of three to four feet. The average size, however, is much smaller than this.

When crowded by other trees, chinquapin oak develops a tall, straight, columnar trunk above the broad and often buttressed base, with comparatively small branches forming a narrow, dense, round-topped crown. Trees grown in the open usually have a short trunk and a wide, rounded top of many branches.

The slender twigs are green, more or less tinged with red and velvety when they first appear, later becoming smooth, reddish brown and eventually brownish gray. The chestnut-brown winter buds are only about an eighth

Chicago Natural History Museum

Open-grown trees have short trunks, many branches
Forest-grown trees are tall with narrow crowns

252

The acorns occur singly or in pairs

of an inch long, and are covered by scales that are white, membranous and slightly hairy on their edges.

The oblong-lanceolate or obovate leaves are usually crowded at the ends of the branches and resemble the chestnut leaf even more than do those of the other chestnut oaks; they taper gradually toward the tip and are coarsely and sharply serrate with pointed and often incurved or broad and rounded teeth. Measuring from four to seven inches long and one to four inches wide, they are thick and firm, the upper surface smooth and yellow-green, and the lower pale downy. The slender stems by which they are attached to the twig are from one-half to one inch long. In the autumn they turn bright orange and scarlet.

In May or June, as the leaves are developing, blossoms of both sexes appear. The pollen-bearing ones occur in pendulous, hairy catkins three to four inches long on the growth of the preceding season and the acorn-producing ones in short, white, woolly clusters from the axils of the new leaves.

The stemless or short-stemmed acorns, usually less than three-fourths of an inch long, occur singly or in pairs. The chestnut-brown acorn is enclosed for one-half or less of its length in a rather shallow bowl-shaped cup. The small pale brown scales of the cup are woolly and slightly thickened and knobby at the base. The acorns ripen in October and November of the first season and they develop a sweet and sometimes edible kernel.

The light gray bark is thin, rarely as much as one-half inch thick, and on old trunks is broken on the surface into thin, loose, silvery white flakes, similar to that of white oak, *Quercus alba*, but sometimes slightly tinged with brown.

The wood is close-grained, heavy, hard, strong and stiff, similar to that of other members of the white oak group; because of its usual small size, however, the tree is of secondary importance and is used mainly for railway ties, construction timbers and bridge planking.

Other names applied to the tree are chestnut oak, dwarf chestnut oak, yellow oak and scrub oak. The tree makes rather rapid growth—more rapid than white oak—but it is shorter-lived. Chinquapin oak is quite free from insect and fungus damage, its chief enemy being fire, which may seriously injure or entirely destroy the young timber. Seed is produced when the trees are quite young and, while some seed is produced every year, heavy crops occur only at intervals. As with all the oaks chinquapin oak can reproduce by sprouts from the stump.

The yellow-green leaves, resembling those of the chestnut, are crowded at the end of the branches

Broken on the surface into thin, loose, silvery white flakes, the bark seldom is more than half an inch thick

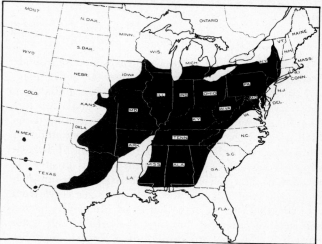

Natural range of Chinquapin Oak

LIVE OAK

Virginia live oak
Quercus virginiana Miller

THE massive live oak is one of the most impressive and majestic of our southern trees. Inhabiting most of Florida, its range extends north to southeastern Virginia in a narrow belt along the coastal plain and on the offshore islands of our southeastern states, around the Gulf of Mexico to western Texas, reaching inland as far as the Red River Valley and south into northern Tamaulipas, Mexico. It also inhabits southern Mexico, Central America and Cuba.

bearing acorns when only a foot high. Westward from the coast of Texas it often forms the principal part of the shrubby growth on low, moist soil.

The name live oak has been given this tree because it retains its leaves throughout the year. They remain about thirteen months on the tree before being pushed aside to make room for new ones. The evergreen leaves are usually elliptical or egg-shaped, and are borne on short, stout stalks. They are two to five inches long, and

R. K. Winters

Live Oak is often much broader than high with long, spreading limbs,
massive trunk and a rounded crown of small evergreen leaves

The live oak in its best known form is a dense, round-headed tree seldom more than fifty feet tall with a massive trunk three or four and rarely seven feet in diameter above its swollen and buttressed base, divided a few feet from the ground into two or more large, spreading limbs fifty to seventy feet in length. Although seldom attaining more than sixty feet in height, the width of branch spread is sometimes as much as three times greater. It reaches its best development and largest size on rich hummocks and ridges a few feet above sea level from the Atlantic to the eastern Gulf coast. In sandy, barren soil near the seacoast and on the shores of salt water bays it attains the proportions of a shrub, sometimes

a half to two and a half inches wide. Most of the leaves have entire margins slightly rolled under, wedge-shaped bases, and rounded tips; but occasionally leaves occur with a few teeth beyond the middle, and a sharp-pointed tip. They are shining dark green above, whitish and downy beneath, and when the new leaves appear toward the end of winter those of the previous season turn brown and drop off. A thick- and a thin-leaved form are recognized, although the thin-leaved form is the most widely distributed, and includes nearly all the large live oak trees. The leaves of this form are only slightly curled on the margins, while those of the thick-leaved form are conspicuously curled on the edges.

O. G. Babcock

Flowers appear in March or April, after the new leaves, which are shiny above and downy beneath with edges turned under

J. R. Dilworth

The shiny, dark brown, egg-shaped acorns are held by light reddish brown scaly cups on long stalks

Flowers appear in March or April, the yellow pollen-bearing ones in hairy catkins two or three inches in length; the acorn-producing ones in spikes on slender, hairy stems.

Acorns of the live oak are egg-shaped, shiny, dark, chestnut-brown, about an inch long and one-third of an inch thick. They are enclosed for about one-fourth of their length in a top-shaped, light reddish brown cup, whose inner surface is matted with fine hairs. Three to five, occasionally one or two, acorns grow on the stout, downy, light brown stalks which are one to five inches long. Because of their sweet meat, live oak acorns were gathered and eaten by the Indians. Today they afford valuable food for hogs.

Bark on the trunk and large limbs is dark brown tinged with red, and is from one-half to an inch thick. It is deeply furrowed, breaking at the surface into small tight scales. The slender rigid branchlets are light gray or brown, and are downy through the first winter, but become darker and smooth the following season.

The wood is light brown or yellow with thin nearly white sapwood, and is hard, strong and tough. It is close-grained and very heavy, a cubic foot weighing nearly sixty pounds. It takes a fine polish, but is difficult to work. Before 1860 when all ships were made of wood, live oak was used extensively in shipbuilding. It was especially important for ships' "knees." These were cut from where the junction of large roots with the base of the trunk forms a natural "knee," so that the interwoven grain makes it far stronger than a similar piece of wood carved from a straight timber.

Live oak bears the distinction of being the first North American tree to be conserved for future use in a forest preserve. The value of its wood for shipbuilding was brought to the attention of Congress because of the need for ships of war to protect American commerce against pirates, and three hundred and fifty acres of live oak timberland was purchased in 1799. By 1845 the government had obtained over a quarter of a million acres of live oak land in five southern states. With the passing of wooden ships most of this land was turned over to the General Land Office and opened for settlement.

The present uses of live oak wood are few, but because the tree is readily transplanted when young, and because it is picturesque, the live oak long has been popular as a shade and ornamental tree in the South.

Bark on mature trunks is dark brown or nearly black and deeply fissured into narrow ridges

Orlando, Florida, Chamber of Commerce

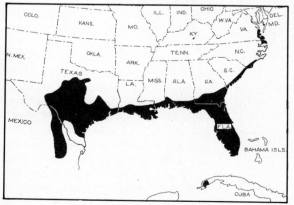

Natural range of Live Oak

CANYON LIVE OAK

California live oak
Quercus chrysolepis Liebmann

TRUE to its name, this evergreen oak is commonly found in narrow canyon bottoms, on steep canyon slopes and in coves and sheltered depressions. In dry sandy and gravelly soils or in broken rock and in crevices, canyon live oak grows from southwestern Oregon south along the California coast ranges and the western slopes of the Sierra Nevada to the San Bernardino and San Jacinto mountains of southern California and into Lower California. Its range extends eastward sporadically, principally to the mountainous areas of central and southeastern Arizona.

It occurs up to 9,000 feet above sea level, sometimes

in small pure clumps or patches, but usually in mixture with California black and live oaks, interior or highland live oak and bigcone spruce.

In sheltered canyons it occasionally reaches a height of 100 feet and a diameter of nine feet. Usually, however, it is not more than sixty to eighty feet high and three to five feet in diameter. As a rule, the trunk is rather short, divided into large, widely spreading or drooping branches which often touch the ground. The tree usually has a broad, round-topped head, but in narrow canyons and on cool, steep canyon walls it grows tall and slender with a slightly tapering trunk clear of branches for fifteen or twenty feet. In open situations it is a wide-spreading tree thirty to forty feet high with huge, horizontal limbs forming a very large spreading crown sometimes 150 feet across. On exposed dry mountain slopes and ridges, between 4,000 and 6,000 feet elevation, it assumes a shrubby habit, often forming dense thickets fifteen to twenty feet high.

One of the larger canyon live oaks on which accurate measurements have been made is the "Old Scotty" tree located in the Hupa Valley, California. In 1910 this tree was reported to be ninety-five feet high and slightly more than six feet in diameter at breast height. It had a crown spread of 125 feet.

Young twigs are densely covered with fine woolly hairs, becoming dark reddish brown and sometimes smooth during their first winter. Ultimately they turn light brown or ashy gray. The broadly oval, pointed winter buds, about one-eighth of an inch long, have closely overlapping, light chestnut-brown scales which are usually covered with fine hairs.

The oblong-ovate or elliptic, short-stemmed leaves, one to four inches long and one-half to two inches wide, are somewhat variable in form. Those of large trees have few or no teeth on their margins while the leaves of young trees, and especially of vigorous shoots, are spiny-bordered. Mature leaves of one season's growth are thick, leathery and light yellowish green. Smooth on the upper surface, they are covered by a yellowish down beneath. Later they lose all

Ralph H. Anderson

In sheltered canyons, this tree occasionally reaches a height of 100 feet. Open-grown trees develop large limbs, a wide-spreading crown

their woolliness and become pale bluish green beneath. Leaves of each season's growth persist from three to four years.

The flowers of both sexes appear in May and June on the same tree. The male or staminate flowers are borne in clustered, slender, hairy catkins two to four inches long; the hairy calyx is five- to seven-lobed and often red-tipped, with smooth, yellow, sharp-pointed anthers. The pistillate or acorn-producing flowers are usually solitary, but sometimes appear in short, few-flowered spikes; the scales enveloping the base of each flower are woolly, and the light red styles are short and broad.

The egg-shaped acorns, which ripen in the autumn of the second season, are usually solitary. They are stemless or have very short stalks, and vary in length from one-half to two inches.

The light chestnut-brown nut, downy at the point, is enclosed only at the base in a thick, shallow cup which is densely covered with a whitish or yellowish short wool that is so dense in some instances as to obsure the cup

Ralph H. Anderson

From one to four inches long, the yellowish green leaves are thick and leathery. Acorns are egg-shaped, stemless

Ralph H. Anderson

The bark, gray-brown tinged with red, is broken into small scales which in old age become flaky and fall off

scales. This yellow coating has given the tree the name of "golden-cup oak" in some parts of its range.

The bark, gray-brown tinged with red, is from three-fourths to one and one-half inches thick, and is broken into numerous small, closely appressed scales, which in old age become flaky and pliable and fall off. It thus resembles in appearance the bark of the white oak.

The wood is heavy, hard, strong and stiff. A cubic foot of the air-dry wood weighs fifty-four pounds. The heartwood is light brown with thick, lighter colored sapwood. It is the best oak timber of the west coast and is well known locally because of its high value for parts of vehicles and agricultural implements, such as wagon tongues, whiffletrees and wheel stock.

Although classed as a red oak because the acorns mature in the second season, the heavy wood of canyon live oak resembles more nearly that of the white oak.

Canyon live oak produces large crops of seeds at infrequent intervals, although a few acorns are borne each

year. Reproduction, while scanty at all times, is apparently as frequent in open as in sheltered sites, the thick leaves protecting the seedlings. The tree often reproduces by sprouts from the stump when it has been killed by fire.

This is a long-lived tree, probably reaching an age of at least 250 to 300 years. Growth is steady but not rapid. In favorable locations, trees 100 to 150 years old measure from ten to eighteen inches in diameter.

The canyon live oak is often known locally as white live oak, California live oak, mountain live oak, canyon oak, hickory oak, blue oak and maul oak.

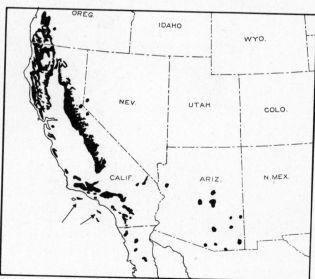

Natural range of Canyon Live Oak

EMORY OAK
Black oak, Blackjack oak
Quercus emoryi Torrey

EMORY OAK, a handsome member of the group of south-western evergreen oaks and one of the most abundant, is a medium size tree from twenty to forty and rarely fifty feet tall, with a trunk diameter of one to two and a half feet. Maximum growth is attained in cool, moist canyons, but on exceptionally hot, dry, southward-facing mountain slopes it may be reduced to much smaller size. The stiff, stout, wide-spreading upper branches, with lower ones slightly drooping, form a broad, rounded head of thick, luxuriant foliage of small, glossy leaves.

In the United States, this species is confined principally to the mountains and, in some localities, grasslands. The range extends from western Texas and southwestern New Mexico, west into Arizona as far as Yavapai County, south to the Baboquiviri Mountains in Pima County, and throughout most of Santa Cruz and Cochise counties, at altitudes of 4000 to 7000 and rarely 8000 feet. The largest part of the range is in Mexico, in the bordering states of Sonora, Chihuahua and Coahuila, extending also into Durango and Sinaloa. In both countries the region is one of brilliant sunshine, high temperatures and low humidity, in which the tree's dense foliage supplies welcome shade to man and wildlife.

The dark gray or nearly black bark is smooth on younger trees and on branches, but on older trunks it is deeply and narrowly furrowed into rectangular, thick plates of closely appressed scales.

The numerous, stiff, slender twigs are pale brown and finely downy at first, becoming smooth with age and turning red-brown or black. Leaf buds are sharply pointed, ovoid, and an eighth of an inch long, covered with brown, hair-tipped scales.

Young leaves, appearing in spring before those of the previous year turn yellow and drop off, are light green, sharply tipped, oblong-lanceolate, with an eighth to a quarter inch stout stem. One to two and a half inches long, finely hairy or downy above and dull and lighter beneath, they become thick, stiff, shiny on both surfaces and

Devereux Butcher

Emory Oak, a southwestern evergreen, is a small to medium size tree with rounded head of dense, dark, shiny foliage

darker above. Their obscurely net-veined undersides usually have tufts of white hair at the base of the midrib. Margins are widely bristle-toothed, occasionally irregularly and sparsely toothed or entire, with truncate, sometimes unequal, heart-shaped or occasionally rounded bases.

The male or staminate pollen-bearing flowers are in two-inch, woolly, yellow-green aments or catkins, and the female or pistillate, acorn-producing flowers are stemless or on short, stout stalks. The acorns are small and borne singly or in pairs on the twig. They are oblong or narrowly ovoid, thin shelled and a half to three quarters of an inch in length, ripening from July to September of the first season. Green when young, they turn dark brown or almost black, and are hairy at the rounded apex when mature. The scaly, light brown, hemispheric cups, stemless or nearly so, are downy inside and embrace a third of the nut.

Because the meat is sweet and edible, these acorns have commercial value as food among Mexicans and Indians, and they are sold in markets. They also are important as food for birds and small mammals.

Emory oak wood is dark brown or nearly black, close-grained, soft, strong but brittle, with thick, bright red-brown sapwood. It is of little value except as fuel.

The scientific name, *emoryi*, honors William H. Emory, 1811-1887, a member of the commission which surveyed the United States-Mexican border in 1857.

Devereux Butcher

The dark, nearly black bark is smooth on young trunks and branches, but deeply and narrowly grooved into thick, rectangular plates on mature stems

Devereux Butcher

In late March or April, when the previous year's leaves are yellowing and falling and new leaves budding out, two-inch-long pollen-producing catkins appear

Devereux Butcher

The small, dark brown acorns, green when young, are thin-shelled, born singly or in pairs, ripening from July to September

Devereux Butcher

The oblong-lanceolate leaves are one to two and a half inches long, leathery, dark above, paler beneath, shiny, with edges entire or irregularly prickle-toothed

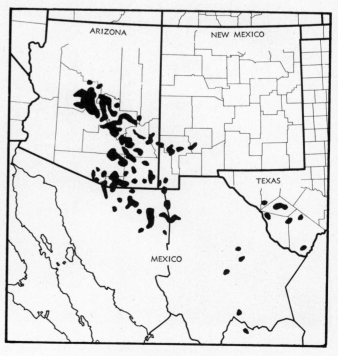

Natural range of Emory Oak

ARIZONA WHITE OAK

Arizona oak
Quercus arizonica Sargent

THIS IS THE LARGEST and one of the more abundant oaks of southern Arizona, New Mexico and northern Mexico. Botanically it belongs to the white oak group. Others in this southwestern group, except Gambel and Arizona white, are referred to as evergreen oaks. Gambel oak loses its leaves in the fall and the tree remains leafless from then until spring; while Arizona white oak misses the appellation "evergreen oak" by an interval of only a few days, because the leaves of the previous year drop off in spring, just before the leaves of the present year appear.

Not only is Arizona white oak abundant, but it is also, some say, the handsomest. Most often thirty to forty feet tall, it sometimes attains heights up to fifty and rarely sixty feet on optimum sites, with trunk diameters of three to four feet. The massive lower limbs spreading almost

horizontally and the upper branches ascending, form a broad, round-topped, symmetrical head of thick foliage. The stout branchlets or twigs when young are covered with dense, dull yellow hair, which persists through the winter, the twigs turning red-brown or pale orange and hairy in their second year, eventually becoming smooth and darker.

The tree inhabits the Upper Sonoran and Transition zones from 5000 to 10,000 feet above sea level, in association with other southwestern oaks, pinyons, junipers, and, in stream valleys, Arizona sycamore.

Leaves, lance-shaped to broadly obovate, are often sharply tipped or are sometimes blunt or rounded, their margins slightly curled under. Frequently they are toothed above the center, or they may be undulating or entire, with bases heartshaped or rounded. One to four

Devereux Butcher

Most often thirty or forty feet tall, Arizona White Oak sometimes attains heights up to fifty feet and more, with trunk diameters of four feet, and massive, spreading limbs that form a broad, symmetrical head of thick foliage

inches long and a half to two inches wide, they are leathery in texture, firm and dull dark blue-green, nearly smooth above and paler and duller on the lower surface, which is covered with yellow down. The yellow midrib is thick and conspicuous on the under surface, the primary veins less so, and the stout, woolly stems are a quarter to a half inch long.

Occurring in clusters of woolly catkins, the pollen-producing flowers are borne at the ends of the previous year's growth; while the seed- or acorn-producing ones are either stemless or borne on short hairy stalks in the axils of the leaves. Ripening from September to November of the same year, the acorn is enclosed for half its length in a hemispherical cup. Three quarters to an inch long and dark lustrous brown, the nut is obtuse and rounded at the minutely downy tip. The cup is covered by closely overlapping, hairy scales with light red, pointed ends.

On young stems and branches the bark is thin and pale gray. On old trunks, it is about the same color, but is an inch or more thick and deeply broken by narrow, vertical fissures into broad, horizontally cracked plates of closely appressed scales. The wood of Arizona white oak is strong, hard, close-grained, dark brown or almost black, with thick, paler colored sapwood and, when dry, weighs sixty-three pounds to the cubic foot. It has little commerical value except locally for fire wood.

The woolly catkins occur at the ends of the previous year's growth, and the acorn producing ones in the axils of the leaves

The acorns, held by a scaly cup, are three-quarters to an inch long and dark lustrous brown, obtuse and rounded at the tip

Pale gray Arizona White Oak bark, an inch or more thick, is broken by narrow fissures into horizontally cracked plates

The leathery leaves, dull blue-green and nearly smooth above, are paler and duller beneath; while margins often are toothed above the center, or are undulating

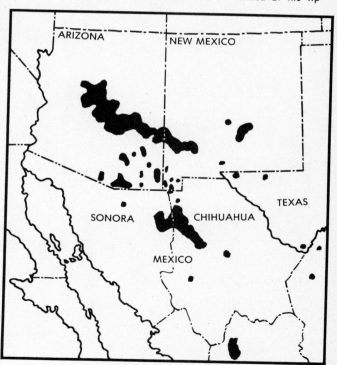

Natural Range of Arizona White Oak

261

MEXICAN BLUE OAK
Quercus oblongifolia Torrey

WESTERN TEXAS, southwestern New Mexico, southeastern Arizona, together with adjacent Mexico—northeastern Sonora, central and southern Chihuahua and extreme northwestern Coahuila—at 4000 to 6000 feet elevation, comprise the natural range of Mexican blue oak. On optimum sites where moisture is sufficient, the tree reaches heights up to thirty feet and more, with diameters of one to two feet, but extremely hot, dry sites, on southward-facing mountain sides may reduce the tree to smaller size, or about ten feet. Good specimens may be seen on the southern slopes of the Huachuca Mountains in and around Coronado National Forest and Coronado National Memorial, and on the southern slopes of the Santa Catalina Mountains near Tucson, Arizona.

The rather unusual blue-green or gray-green coloring of the foliage and the pale, ash-gray of the bark help to distinguish this species from other southwestern evergreen oaks. The bark is narrowly fissured into small, blocky, scaly plates. The many stout, spreading and ascending, winding branches form a broadly rounded crown of dense foliage.

Twigs are numerous, slender, smooth, pliant and light green when very young, turning darker with age and becoming light brown or red-brown to light gray and stiff, the surfaces roughened by leaf scars. Leaf buds, ovoid, brown and sharply tipped, are smooth when first formed.

The oblong or elliptical leaves, one to two and a half inches long, are rounded at the apex, and rounded, heart-shaped or slightly wedge-shaped at the base, usually narrowing toward the base. They are attached to the twig by an eighth to a quarter inch stem. The faintly curled margins are entire, seldom wavy and rarely scalloped. When fully grown in March or April, they are leathery, not shiny, with the midrib minutely raised above the upper surface. The underside is paler and of a more yellow green. The leaves persist through the winter, turning yellow in spring and falling before the new leaves are developed. The oblong shape of the leaves suggested the scientific name *oblongifolia*.

Flowers appear also in March or April, the male or pollen-bearing ones in yellow-green, woolly catkins about an inch to an inch and a half long, two to five growing together from the axils of the leaf stems of the preceding year. The pistillate or acorn-producing ones are

Devereux Butcher

On the best sites, Mexican Blue Oak, a southwestern evergreen tree, may attain heights of thirty feet and more

stemless or on short hairy stalks. The acorns, usually single but occasionally in pairs, are stemless or sometimes borne on a short stalk. The half-round, scaly, brown cup contains a third of the nut, which matures in the fall of the same year, and is. a half to three quarters of an inch long, ovoid or ellipsoid, its thin, smooth shell, green at first, becoming dark red-brown, later turning light brown in color.

The wood of Mexican blue oak is dark brown, hard, strong, brittle and heavy, but is not used commercially, except for fuel, because it is difficult to split and to work, and it cracks or checks when drying.

A few of the other southwestern evergreen oaks to be seen in association with Mexican blue oak are the netleaf, gray, Emory, Arizona white and silverleaf. Manzanita and a number of other shrubs often are present and, in some localities, Mexican pinyon and Arizona cypress.

Certain insects cause galls on the leaves and small canker worms eat the leaves of this oak.

Devereux Butcher

Male or pollen-producing catkins, shown here in bud, are yellow-green, about an inch long appearing in March or April at the same time as the acorn-producing flowers

Devereux Butcher

Bark on mature trunks and branches is broken into small, blocky, scaly plates of a pale gray color, which is a distinguishing characteristic of the species

Devereux Butcher

Acorns occur singly or in pairs, their scaly cups embracing a third of the small, smooth-shelled nut, which is green when young, turning light brown with maturity in the fall

Devereux Butcher

Gray-green and leathery, the leaves are two to two and a half inches long, round-tipped, bases heart-shaped or wedge-shaped and margins entire or wavy

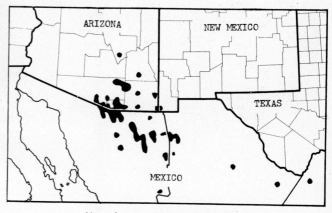

Natural range of Mexican Blue Oak

SILVERLEAF OAK

Whiteleaf Oak
Quercus hypoleucoides A. Camus

THE LEAVES of this southwestern evergreen oak are narrow and lance-shaped resembling more closely those of a willow than of an oak, and for their unique beauty, can hardly be equalled by any other North American oak. Rich, dark lustrous green above, they are conspicuously bright silvery white beneath.

Indigenous to the mountains of northern Chihuahua and northeastern Sonora, Mexico, silverleaf oak thrives also in the mountains of southwestern New Mexico, extreme western Texas and southeastern Arizona, in the Upper Sonoran and Transition zones at elevations from 5000 to 7000 feet above sea level. In moist soils of stream valleys, silverleaf oak attains heights of from twenty to thirty feet and rarely sixty feet, with trunk diameters from ten to fifteen inches and rarely two feet. In drier locations throughout its range it reaches only shrub size.

At elevations from 5000 to about 6000 feet above sea level, silverleaf associates with other evergreen oaks, such as netleaf, Mexican blue and Emory oaks, as well as with Arizona sycamore, alligator juniper and Arizona rough cypress, *C. arizonica* var. *arizonica*. Higher up it mingles with Apache, Chihuahua, Mexican pinyon and ponderosa pines.

When unfolding in the spring, the young leaves are pale red or pink and are covered with white hair above and thickly coated beneath with white, woolly hair. At maturity, they become thick and firm, dark lustrous yellow-green above and thickly coated with silvery white wool below. Two to four inches long and a half to one inch wide, the leaves vary from lanceolate or broadly lanceolate to occasionally falcate—scythe-shaped—acute at the apex or sometimes terminating in an almost hair-like tip. At their base they are wedge-shaped, rounded or heart-shaped, and their margins curling under, are occasionally slightly undulating and toothed above the middle, with minute rigid spines. During the spring, the leaves of the preceding year turn yellow or brown and drop off gradually after the new, young leaves appear.

The male or staminate flowers occur in clusters of about five aments or catkins four to five inches long, borne on the growth of the preceding year, and the female or pistillate ones, usually solitary, stemless or short-stalked, are borne in the axils of the leaf petioles. The acorn, a half to two-thirds of an inch long, ripens in the first year or sometimes in the second, and, although green when young, it turns brown and sometimes is laterally striated or striped toward the apex. The thick cup, which embraces the lower third of the nut, is hairy on its inner surface and covered outside with thin, ovate, light chestnut brown scales.

The slender, ascending branches develop a round head of dense foliage, and

Devereux Butcher

In the moist soils of stream valleys, Silverleaf Oak reaches heights of twenty to thirty feet and occasionally higher, with trunk diameters from ten to fifteen inches, but on drier sites it seldom exceeds shrub size

264

the stout twigs, coated with thick white hair until the first winter, turn light red-brown with a coating of white bloom and later become dark gray or nearly black. Winter buds an eighth inch long, are encased in brown scales.

Bark on mature trunks is three quarters to an inch thick and sometimes more, and is deeply furrowed into broad, flat, gray or almost black ridges horizontally cracked into rectangular blocky plates.

Silverleaf oak heartwood is strong, hard, close-grained and dark brown, with thick, paler sapwood. When dry, a cubic foot weighs fifty pounds. Because of the tree's rarity and scattered range in the United States, it has little commercial value, except locally.

Russell D. Butcher

Dark, shiny green above and coated with thick, silvery white wool beneath, the leaves of Silverleaf Oak are lanceolate, four inches long and from a half inch to an inch wide

Devereux Butcher

Bark on mature trunks is an inch or more thick, broken by furrows into gray or black ridges that are cracked into blocky plates. Acorns, a half to two-thirds of an inch long, turn brown at maturity, their lower third embraced by a scaly cup

Devereux Butcher

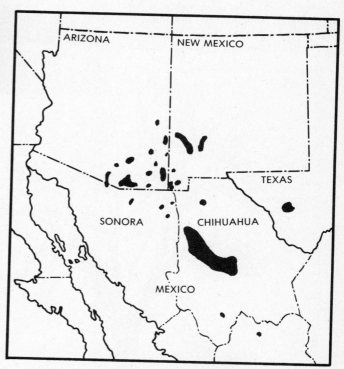

Natural range of Silverleaf Oak

AMERICAN ELM

White elm
Ulmus americana Linnaeus

THE DIGNIFIED and courtly American elm is characteristic of the northeastern landscape and has been planted over most of the United States. Typically vase-shaped, it sometimes develops heavy far-reaching limbs after the manner of the oaks.

Elm belongs to the family *Ulmaceae*, which also includes the hackberries—the family of the nettle. The genus *Ulmus*, which is the ancient Latin name for elm, has sixteen species distributed in the north temperate countries of the world. Six elms are native to eastern North America, with American elm the largest and most important. None is native west of the Rocky Mountains, but they grow successfully in all western states.

American elm is known as white elm, and sometimes as water or soft elm. It grows naturally in river bottoms and on low fertile hills, from southern Newfoundland to central Florida. The range extends west from Nova Scotia and New Brunswick across southern

Devereux Butcher

In summer American Elm combines grace and dignity with exceptional beauty, while in winter it reveals the strength of its limbs and branches above a sturdy trunk

Quebec, southern Ontario and southern Manitoba to eastern Saskatchewan, and south in the Dakotas through Nebraska, central Kansas and Oklahoma to central Texas and the Gulf of Mexico. Its western limits are confined principally to stream banks.

The main trunk of open-grown trees divides at ten or twenty feet to form a broad crown, while in the forest, trunk lengths of thirty to sixty feet are attained. Trees two to four feet in diameter and eighty to one hundred feet high are common, but elms eight to eleven feet in diameter and 120 to 140 feet high have been known.

The lopsided, double-toothed, alternately placed, sharp-pointed leaves are two to five inches long and one to three inches wide. Evenly spaced, parallel veins extend from the midrib to the sawtooth edges.

The upper surface is slightly rough, while the under surface is softly hairy. In early autumn the leaves turn golden yellow, then sere and brown and quickly fall.

At the base of each short petiole or leaf stem is a blunt-pointed, smooth, slightly flattened bud, which appears to be at one side of a semi-circular leaf scar after the leaves drop. Before the leaves are fully open, in May or June, the seeds ripen. They are flat, entirely surrounded by a broad, slightly hairy, papery wing, which measures approximately one-half inch in diameter. If planted immediately, most of the seeds will germinate in a few days, but some may lie dormant until spring. Each seed develops from an inconspicuous light green perfect blossom with red stamens. The flowers hang in clusters and are produced before the leaves.

The wood is light brown, heavy, hard, tough, so cross-grained as to be difficult to split, and weighs thirty-three to thirty-five pounds to the cubic foot when air dry. It has a broad area of lighter colored sapwood. Because of its toughness it is used for the hubs of wheels and for hoops and staves in slack cooperage, for shipbuilding, furniture, flooring, sporting goods, boxes and crates. Relatively easy to season, it works fairly well, and while it can be scoured to a clean whiteness, does not polish easily. The Iroquois Indians of western New York used the bark for canoes and twisted it into ropes.

Much of the total sawtimber stand of all species of elm in the United States is in the lake states.

American elm grows from seed, and it sprouts readily from the stump and from root ends. Horticultural types may be reproduced by cuttings, buds and grafts. Preferring rich, deep, well-drained loam, it will grow in almost any soil. The vigorous, shallow root system permits comparatively easy transplanting while small.

Of its leaf pests, the elm leaf beetle is chief. By eating the leaves this beetle and its larvae occasionally kill trees, but this pest can be controlled.

Much more to be feared is the Dutch elm disease, for which no cure has been discovered. Elms dead and dying of this disease are to be seen today throughout most, if not all, of the tree's natural range—in the forest, along hedgerows and in villages and towns. The only hope of saving this handsome, popular species may be in finding an immune strain.

One side of each leaf is larger than the other. Each seed is surrounded by a broad, papery wing one-half inch in diameter and deeply notched at the apex

Bunches of light green blossoms appear from last year's buds ahead of the new leaves

The dark, ashy gray bark of the main trunk is broken into interlacing flaky ridges

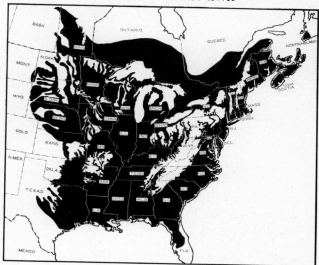

Natural range of American Elm

ROCK ELM

Cork elm
Ulmus thomasii Sargent

ROCK ELM does not have the characteristic vase shape of the American elm, and it differs in form from slippery elm also, in that the stem extends undivided well into the crown with a cylindrical trunk free of branches, sometimes as high as sixty feet when growing in the forest. It has a narrow, round-topped crown with short, stout,

Unlike the vase-shaped American Elm, Rock Elm has a single trunk that may reach a height of 100 feet

spreading limbs and, when grown in the open, it develops drooping lateral branches along the lower trunk, the lower ones often extending to within six or eight feet of the ground. The average height is sixty to seventy feet, with a trunk diameter of two feet or less; but under favorable conditions forest trees may reach a height of 100 feet and a diameter of three to four feet.

The slender, rigid branchlets are light reddish brown when they first appear and are coated with soft, pale pubescence, ultimately becoming smooth, lustrous and dark brown or ashy gray. In their second season the twigs usually develop several irregular, thick, corky wings or ridges from which the tree is often called cork elm.

The terminal bud is absent. The lateral buds are similar to those of American elm, but are longer, about a quarter of an inch, narrower and sharply pointed. The bud scales are chestnut-brown and have soft, white hairs on their margins. On young trunks the bark is more deeply and irregularly furrowed than in the American elm. It is from three-fourths to one inch thick on mature trees, grayish brown and deeply divided by wide, irregular, interrupted fissures into broad, flat ridges broken on the surface into large, irregularly shaped scales.

Rock elm has a much more restricted range than either American or slippery elm, the area extending from western New Hampshire and southern Quebec through southern Ontario and southern Michigan to southern Minnesota south to eastern Nebraska, and locally in Tennesses and Kansas. It is a tree of dry uplands, rocky ridges and steep slopes occurring singly or in groups mixed with such species as sugar maple, basswood, white ash, beech, butternut and hophornbeam. It will thrive under a great variety of soil and moisture conditions, but because of its slow growth and its inability to grow in the shade of other trees, it is often forced onto dry and poor soil. The original stand, which was quite abundant in southern Michigan and southern Wisconsin, has been greatly reduced by excessive cutting.

The leaves are oval in outline, coarsely double-toothed, abruptly pointed at the apex and uneven at the base. They are nearly like those of American and slippery elms, but are smaller, about two and a half to four and a half inches long, and one and a quarter to two and a quarter inches wide, usually more symmetrical at the base, and are smooth on the upper surface. They are hairy above and below when they unfold, but at maturity are thick and firm, dark green and somewhat lustrous above, with prominent midribs and secondary veins, pale beneath and covered with fine hairs as are also the leaf stems, which are about a quarter of an inch long.

The greenish flowers appear in early spring before the leaves. They are borne on slender, drooping stems often a half inch long, with two to four, but usually three, to a cluster. The flat, oval, winged fruit ripens when the leaves are about half grown. They are pubescent all over, densely hairy on the margins and contain a single seed. While they are produced in large numbers, full seed crops occur only once in three or four years. Many of the seeds do not germinate, and their vitality is low under normal conditions.

The name rock elm derives from the quality of the wood, which is extremely hard and tough. It is about equal to white oak in strength and hardness, and superior to it in ability to resist shock. It weighs about forty-four pounds to the cubic foot when air-dry. It is difficult to split, has a large shrinkage in drying and is only moderately resistant to decay. The heartwood is light brown, often tinged with red, and the sapwood, which is from three quarters to one and a half inches wide in mature trees, is nearly white. While rock elm lumber makes up a comparatively small part of the total elm cut, it is much in demand for special uses, such as parts of heavy agricultural implements, vehicles, handles and boats, where hardness and high shock resistance are essential.

The rock elm tree grows slowly, especially in its usual habitat on poor soils. On good soil it grows rather rapidly, but not fast enough to encourage planting. It reaches an age of from 150 to 200 years and sometimes more. As with the American elm, this species is severely injured by defoliating insects, but is quite free from fungus diseases. It is only occasionally planted as a shade and ornamental tree.

Norman F. Smith

The flat, oval-winged fruit ripens when the leaves are about half grown

Arnold Arboretum

Greenish flowers appear in early spring and are borne on slender stems a half inch long

H. E. Troxell

The gray-brown bark is broken into broad, flat ridges

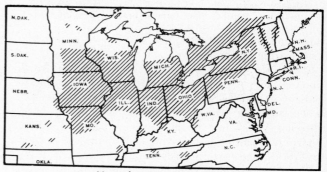

Natural range of Rock Elm

SLIPPERY ELM

Red elm, Gray elm, Soft elm
Ulmus rubra Muhlenberg

SLIPPERY ELM has neither the graceful symmetry nor the large size of the more commonly known American elm. It is usually a tree of medium size averaging from forty to sixty feet in height with a comparatively short trunk one to two feet in diameter. Occasionally trees reach seventy or eighty feet in height and on especially favorable sites specimens 135 feet tall with trunk diameters up to four feet have been found. The large, stout, spreading limbs branch haphazardly from the

The flat, broadly-winged fruit, three-fourths of an inch long, occurs in clusters along the twigs

soils, and is found most frequently along stream banks and on low, fertile, wooded slopes. Sometimes it grows on rocky ridges or limestone outcrops, but in such sites it makes poor growth.

Bark on old trunks of slippery elm is frequently an inch thick, deeply furrowed into large, loose plates, and is ashy gray to dark, reddish brown in color. The inner bark is pale and strongly mucilaginous. It is the latter

Usually slender with short trunk, Slippery Elm has stout, spreading branches that form a broad, open crown

trunk, and form a broad, open, flat-topped crown that is often irregular in outline.

Of the six species of elm native to eastern North America, slippery elm is second to American elm in abundance, and has a natural range almost as extensive as the latter. It grows from Maine and the lower St. Lawrence Valley in Canada, westward across southern Ontario to eastern South Dakota and southward to western Florida and eastern Texas.

Slippery elm prefers rich, moist, alluvial, well-drained

The alternate, wrinkled, thick leaves are coated on the upper surface with rough hairs

A. Varela

quality which gives the tree its common name. Also aromatic, the inner bark is sometimes chewed to allay thirst, and because it has a soothing effect, it is used medicinally, for which purpose many trees are stripped of their bark and killed. In the North the tree is sometimes called moose elm because moose eat both twigs and bark.

Hairy and roughened by pores and leaf scars, the twigs are at first pale gray or grayish brown, later becoming darker. They are stout, tending to turn upward, and have no buds at the tip.

The tawny hairs of winter buds offer a means of distinguishing slippery elm from the American elm, whose winter buds are smooth. Leaf buds are about a quarter-inch long, located toward the outer ends of the twigs, while the stouter, thicker flower buds are farther back. Flowers appear in April or early May before the leaves and are in crowded clusters on short stalks.

Another characteristic of slippery elm is the extreme roughness of the upper surface of its leaves. Growing alternately along the twigs, these leaves are covered with stiff hairs above, and are rough to the touch when rubbed in any direction. Firm, wrinkled and dark green above, paler beneath and coated with soft hairs, especially on the midrib, the leaves of slippery elm measure four to seven inches in length and two to three inches in width, and are doubly-toothed on the margins, pointed at the tip, and rounded and uneven at the base.

Wood of slippery elm is hard, strong, compact, and durable in contact with the soil. A cubic foot weighs forty-three pounds when dry. Heartwood is reddish brown and the sapwood paler. Although slippery elm is not an important timber tree, its wood is used for furniture, wheel hubs, fence posts, railroad ties, sills, shipbuilding and agricultural implements.

Like other elms of this continent it is susceptible to Dutch elm disease and to a virus known as *phloem necrosis.*

The perfect short-stemmed flowers appear in March or April before the leaves

George J. Baetzhold

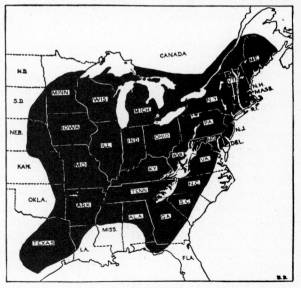

Courtesy Macmillan Co. from "Some American Trees"

The deeply furrowed bark has an under layer that is ruddy brown, and an inner layer that is mucilaginous and nearly white

Natural range of Slippery Elm·

271

HACKBERRY

Sugarberry
Celtis occidentalis Linnaeus

THE RAGGED and often unshapely hackberry grows from southern New England and New York to southeastern North Dakota, south to eastern and central Texas, and from northern Arkansas to central Georgia and South Carolina. Best growth is confined to the rich bottoms of the central Mississippi Valley, where forest trees attain heights of 130 feet and diameters as large as two or three feet. In such cases the trunk is smooth and shapely. Elsewhere the trees are frequently so isolated

Devereux Butcher

Open-grown Hackberry trees branch low and develop ragged, irregularly oval crowns of dense foliage

and so difficult of recognition as to be called the "unknown tree." Early French settlers even called it by the equivalent term *bois inconnu.*

Belonging to the *Ulmaceae* or elm family, it is sometimes mistaken for an elm because of its superficial similarity in appearance. There are marked differences, however, particularly in the flowers and fruit.

The simple, alternate, coarsely toothed, light green leaves are two and a half to four inches long, with long narrow, tapering points. Three conspicuous ribs branch from the lop-sided base. The upper surface is smooth or slightly rough, while below it is smooth and pale. Hackberry leaves are attacked by numerous insects, including the spiny elm caterpillar, but are seldom disastrously defoliated.

Inconspicuous pale greenish flowers of both sexes appear with the young leaves in April or May on the new growth. The staminate flowers grow in clusters at the bases of the new shoots, while the pistillate flowers grow singly or in pairs from the axils of the upper leaves. Both flowers occur on the same tree.

The dark purple, cherry-like fruits hang suspended on slender stems and ripen in September and October. They remain on the tree throughout the winter, and the sweet orange flesh provides food for birds. Seeds are thus carried miles from the parent tree, and this accounts for the tree's wide, scattered range.

On the trunk and larger limbs the bark is an inch to an inch and a half thick, light brown to silvery gray, and is broken into discontinuous ridges. Frequently the bark is

D. E. Ahlers

"Witches brooms" often disfigure the slender twigs. The tendency of branches is to be horizontal to the main trunk

roughened by irregular, corky warts which may occur as ridges. On young trees and secondary branches the bark is smoother. It is rich in tannin and exudes a gum similar to that found on cherry trees. The numerous, slender branches are generally horizontal, and, when grown in the open, divide a few feet from the ground. Thick clusters of twigs resembling mistletoe or birds' nests occur on many trees. These are caused by a fungus and are known as "witches brooms."

The clear, light yellow wood is soft and comparativly heavy, weighing about thirty-seven pounds to the cubic foot when air dry. The annual rings are marked by several rows of large open pores. It takes a good polish, but is not durable in contact with

Pale greenish staminate and pistillate flowers, and also flowers with both stamens and pistils, appear with the unfolding leaves in early spring

the soil, and is frequently badly riddled by wood-boring insects. Hackberry is usually sold with lower grades of ash and elm, which it superficially resembles. It is not strong enough or in sufficient commercial abundance for building construction. Offering considerable resistance to shock, it is used for farm implements, as well as for crates, boxes, furniture, and to some extent for carving.

Because of its wide range and remarkable tolerance of soil and moisture conditions, hackberry is often

The bark of the trunk is often roughened by corky warts and ridges

planted for shade and ornament throughout the region from the Mississippi River to the Rocky Mountains, and to some extent in other parts of the country.

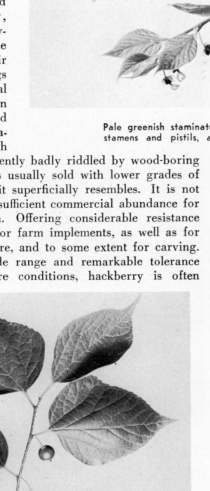

Dark purple, cherry-like fruits hang from the base of simple, alternate, long pointed leaves

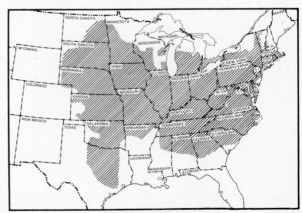

Natural range of Hackberry

273

EASTERN REDBUD

Judas-tree
Cercis canadensis Linnaeus

IN EARLY SPRING the bright pink flowers, which are borne in profusion before the leaves, make this an easily recognized tree in the forest. Later the purplish pods show in pleasing contrast to the glossy green leaves. Redbud, appropriately named from the blossoms, is also called

Eastern Redbud is a small tree with a straight trunk that usually separates into two or more branches a short distance above the base

Judas-tree from an Oriental species of that name on which, it was said, Judas hanged himself, and this caused the blossoms to turn red.

Eastern redbud grows naturally over nearly all of eastern United States from New Jersey to northern Florida, west to Iowa and south to northeastern Texas. It prefers the borders of streams and rich bottomlands, often forming, especially west of the Allegheny Mountains, a thick undergrowth in the forest. There is also a western species *occidentalis* called California redbud.

A small tree with a straight trunk, usually separating

Devereux Butcher

Because of its bright pink blossoms, which appear in April and May, Redbud is widely used as an ornamental

a short distance above the ground into several stout branches, eastern redbud sometimes attains, in the forest, a height of forty or fifty feet, and has an upright head. When grown in the open, it is much shorter, forming a low, wide, flat-topped or rounded head. The slender, smooth, somewhat angled branchlets are brown and lus-

The lustrous, brown, angled branchlets bear small, globular buds. Smooth and heart-shaped, the leaves are from three to five inches long and broad. By May in the South and midsummer in the North, the pink, rose-red or purplish, flat seed pods are fully grown, following the early spring blossoming of the pink, pea-like flowers, which are a half inch long and occur in groups of four or eight

The bark is divided by deep longitudinal fissures into long narrow plates, the surface separating into thin scales

trous during their first season, becoming dull and darker the following year and ultimately dark or grayish brown, with small, brown, globular buds. The trunk, which is rarely more than ten or twelve inches in diameter, has a grayish or reddish brown bark about a half inch thick, divided by deep, longitudinal fissures into long, narrow plates, the surface separating into thin scales.

The smooth, dark green, nearly round and more or less heart-shaped, simple leaves are from three to five inches long and broad. They have from five to seven prominent veins and are attached to the twig by long, slender stems. They are paler beneath, with tufts of white hairs in the axils of the veins. In the autumn, before falling, the leaves turn a bright, clear yellow.

In April and May the pea-like blossoms, a half inch in length, in close, short-stalked clusters of four or eight, appear along the slender branchlets of the preceding year and frequently along the trunk. The flat, bean-like, many-seeded pods are two and a half to three and a half inches long. Oblong or broad-linear in form, they have a straight upper edge and a curved lower edge and taper at each end into a long point. In the South, they are fully grown by the end of May, and in the North, by midsummer, turning pink, rose-red or purplish and lustrous at maturity. They fall late in the autumn or in early winter, or sometimes remain on the tree throughout the winter. Birds often open them for their small, oblong, flattened seeds, which measure about a fourth of an inch in length.

The heavy, hard, close-grained wood weighs about forty pounds per cubic foot when dry. The heartwood is a rich dark brown tinged with red, and the thin, light-colored sapwood is made up of eight to ten layers of annual growth. Because of the small size of the tree, it is of no commercial importance as a source of timber.

Eastern redbud is often cultivated as an ornamental tree in eastern United States and occasionally in western Europe. It is quite hardy and is easily grown, and it is often planted with conifers, especially on lawns, where the bright pink blossoms are most attractive against the dark foliage of the evergreens. When growing wild in the forest, it adds a conspicuous touch of beauty, for it blooms before the forest has come into leaf.

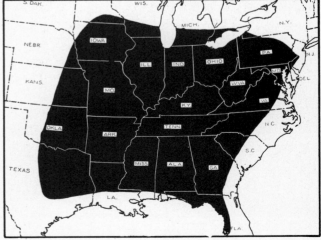

Natural range of Eastern Redbud

RED MULBERRY

Morus rubra Linnaeus

THE mulberry family of *Moraceae* includes about 1,000 species of trees, shrubs and herbs which occur principally in the warmer regions of the world. They are characterized by a milky sap which in some species is a source of rubber. Other important members of this family are the fig, the hop and the hemp, species of which have been naturalized in southern United States. The genus *Morus*, which is the ancient Latin name for mulberry, has about twelve species of trees and shrubs native to the temperate and subtropical regions of the northern hemisphere. White mulberry, *Morus alba*, of China and Formosa is the most valuable species, the leaves constituting the chief food of the silkworm. This tree has been extensively planted in eastern United States, and another species, *nigra*, a native of Persia, has been grown in the southern and Pacific coast states for its large juicy fruit.

The red mulberry is a rather small tree usually from thirty to fifty feet in height with a short trunk from one to one and a half feet in diameter, sometimes attaining a height of seventy feet and a diameter of three to four feet. The trunk often divides near the ground in many stout, spreading branches, forming a compact, broad, round-topped crown. The twigs are slender and somewhat zigzag, dark green with a reddish tinge when they first appear, becoming in their second and third years dark reddish-brown. Terminal buds are absent. The lateral buds are ovate, rounded or bluntly pointed, and about one-fourth of an inch long, with six to seven shining, chestnut-brown scales.

Although not abundant anywhere, occurring as a single tree or in small, scattered stands, its area of distribution is large, covering nearly all of the eastern United States from western Massachusetts and Connecticut through central New York, southern Ontario, southern Michigan and Wisconsin, southeastern Minnesota and southeastern Nebraska, south to eastern Texas and southern Florida. It prefers deep, moist soils such as are found in rich woods and river valleys and on low hillsides, and reaches its largest size and greatest abundance in the basins of the lower Ohio and Mississippi rivers.

The altrnate, simple, abruptly pointed leaves are from three to five inches long and two and a half to four inches broad. Thin and membranous in texture, their margins are singly or occasionally doubly toothed. They are variable in form, some, especially on young shoots, have from three to five lobes or a single lobe on one side. The leaves are dark bluish green and smooth or rough above, pale and soft hairy beneath, borne on stout petioles three-fourths to one and a fourth inches long. The petioles exude a milky juice when broken. The leaves turn a bright yellow in the early autumn.

In May or early June when the leaves are about half grown, the flowers appear, the male and female in separate, narrow catkins either on the same tree or on differ-

The trunk of red mulberry often divides near the ground into many stout, spreading branches forming a compact, broad, round-topped crown

ent trees. The male or pollen-bearing catkins are from two to two and a half inches long and the female or seed-bearing ones are shorter, one inch or less. The berry-like fruit, about one inch long, is red when fully developed, becoming dark purple or nearly black when ripe. It is sweet and juicy and very attractive to birds. The small, oblong, sharp-pointed seeds are light brown.

On young trunks and branches the bark is smooth and brownish, becoming from one-half to three-fourths of an inch thick, dark reddish brown and divided into irregular longitudinal plates, which tend to separate on the surface into long, close scales.

The wood is course-grained, soft, light in weight, weak and decay-resistant. The heartwood is pale orange with thick, lighter colored sapwood. Because of the small size of the tree and its scattered occurrence, the timber is of little commercial importance. It is used for fence posts, boat building and small articles of furniture.

Red mulberry is a tree of rapid growth, but it does not reach great age and is generally mature at 100 years or less. It is frequently planted as an ornamental shade tree and also for its fruit, which is useful for fattening hogs and as food for poultry. It is particularly relished by birds, and the tree is desirable for bird sanctuaries. A number of horticultural varieties have been developed which are valued for ornamental purposes and for their large fruit.

U. S. Forest Service

Alternate, simple, abruptly-pointed leaves are three to five inches long, two and a half to four inches wide

L. W. Brownell

Bark is dark reddish brown, divided into longitudinal plates which tend to separate

E. R. Mosher

The female, or seed-bearing, catkins of the tree are somewhat shorter than the pollen-bearing catkins

L. W. Brownell

The berry-like fruit, about an inch long, is red when fully grown, becoming dark purple to black when ripe

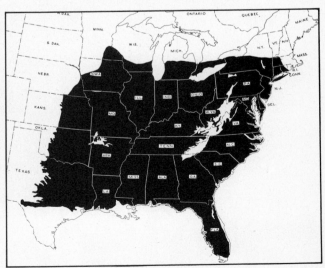

Natural range of Red Mulberry

OSAGE-ORANGE

Bodark, Bois-d'arc, Bowwood
Maclura pomifera (Rafinesque) Schneider

ORIGINALLY confined to the rich bottomlands of the Arkansas and Red River valleys in the region inhabited by the Osage Indians, the hardy, drought-resistant qualities of Osage-orange, its adaptability for hedges and windbreaks, and the varied uses of its wood have so widely encouraged its planting that it is now found growing throughout most of the country. It is usually a small, thorny tree with a crown of irregular, ragged contour. It reaches heights of fifty to sixty feet, with a short, stout, early divided trunk, which is seldom more than two to three feet in diameter.

The glossy green leaves are simple and arranged alternately on the twigs. They have smooth margins, are three to six inches long and two to three inches wide, generally egg-shaped but terminating in a slender point. The slender leaf stem or petiole is one and half to two inches long. When either this or the leaf is broken, a thick juice exudes.

The stout, tough branchlets are centered with a thick orange-colored pith, and the pale bark is marked with pale orange lenticels. Short, stout, straight spines arm the twigs. Greenish clusters of tiny staminate and pistillate flowers develop on separate trees in June. By late summer the pistillate blooms

Above: Gnarled branches spread from a short trunk to form a low, ragged crown

Left: Osage-orange trees are usually small, but may reach heights of fifty or sixty feet with a low, irregular, spreading crown

278

are noticable as yellowish green balls which become three to five inches in diameter before maturing in the autumn. These are compound fruits, like those of other members of the *Moraceae* or mulberry family, of which this and the fig are members. The coarse fibrous texture and sticky, bitter, milky juice makes these fruits unpalatable for man or animal.

The orange-brown, shreddy outer bark is scarcely an inch thick. It is irregularly divided by deep furrows. The dark orange inner bark and the lemon-colored s a p w o o d were used by the Indians

Devereux Butcher

Clusters of greenish staminate flowers ornament the glossy green foliage of early summer. The leaves are three to six inches long with smooth margins and attenuated points

to dye their blankets. More recently it has been a source of yellow, tan and khaki dyes, as well as of tannin in the treatment of leather.

Heartwood, as well as sapwood, is bright yellow, but the former turns brown on exposure. It weighs about forty-eight pounds to the cubic foot when air dry, is stronger than white oak, but not so stiff, and is very hard. Because of its durability in contact with the soil, material of suitable size is used for fence posts, railroad ties, and cabin supports. In the horse and buggy days the hubs and rims of wheels for farm wagons were made of Osage-orange. Pulleyblocks are now made of it, but perhaps its most specialized use is by modern archers, who, like the early Indians, prize the flexible wood of straight clear-grained specimens for the construction of bows. Thus the name *Bois-d' Arc*.

Although seldom used for shade or ornamental purposes, Osage-orange was, before the widespread use of wire fences, so generally planted for hedges as to be commonly known as "hedge plant."

Devereux Butcher

This immature compound fruit will reach three to five inches in diameter. The name Osage-orange recognizes the resemblance of this fruit to an orange and the tree's usefulness to the Osage Indians

George J. Baetzhold

The rough shreddy outer bark is dark orange-brown and scarcely an inch thick

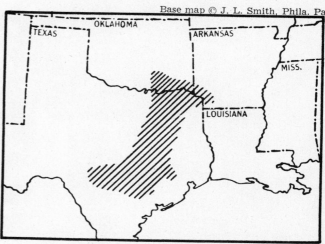

Base map © J. L. Smith, Phila. Pa.

Original range of Osage-orange

SOUTHERN MAGNOLIA

Great-flowered magnolia, Bull-bay
Magnolia grandiflora Linnaeus

NAMED *grandiflora* by Linnaeus because of its large showy flowers, this magnolia has been called by the eminent authority Charles Sprague Sargent, "the most splendid ornamental tree in the American forests." The large creamy-white flowers, the lustrous, leathery leaves and conspicuous egg-shaped fruit, are its outstanding characteristics. Not only is it an ornamental tree, but it grows to large size and is a source of commercial timber.

The size and simple construction of the flower indicate that this and the other magnolias are among the most ancient trees and shrubs in the world—a fact substantiated through the study of fossils. Present day magnolias are only a remnant of a once extensive group of north temperate forest trees which formerly grew in Europe, Siberia, western North America, Canada and Greenland before the Glacial Period. They are believed to be almost as ancient as the ginkgo, and in early times they probably had an equally wide distribution.

The natural range of southern magnolia extends in a broad band a hundred miles wide or less along the Atlantic and Gulf of Mexico coasts, from southeastern North Carolina to Mississippi, southeastern Louisiana, and locally in central Louisiana and eastern Texas. The tree also inhabits a little more than the northern half of the Florida peninsula.

Southern magnolia requires a rich soil and considerable moisture for its best growth. It is most commonly found on moist, well-drained soils along streams, near swamps and on other moist locations in the uplands. Although it is a southern bottomland species, it will not survive long inundations and does not occur on the lower bottoms of the Mississippi River that were overflowed before the levees were built, and seldom on the higher bottoms. In Louisiana and Mississippi it is most abundant in the hills between Vicksburg and Baton Rouge.

The tree does not grow in pure stands but in mixture with other species such as tuliptree, sweetgum, oak and hickory. Forest-grown trees are commonly sixty to eighty feet high and two to three feet in diameter, with a straight bore clear of branches up to forty feet from the ground. They occasionally exceed a height of 100 feet and approach five feet in diameter. The branches are rather small, spreading, or stiffly ascending, forming a pyramidal or conical crown.

Other common names applied to this tree, including evergreen magnolia, laurel-leaved magnolia and laurel bay, refer to the bright green, glossy leaves which measure five to eight inches long and two to three inches wide, and are persistent on the stout woolly, brown stems until the second

The Southern Magnolia commonly attains a height of sixty to eighty feet. It is a source of commercial timber

Fonville Winans

280

spring. They are narrowly oval, have smooth margins, and are bluntly pointed at both ends. Smooth and shiny above, they are usually coated beneath with rust-colored down. The foliage is highly valued for decorative purposes, and branches are commonly shipped to northern cities for the Christmas season.

The large conspicuous, fragrant, creamy-white flowers, contrasting with the lustrous green leaves, appear in the South from April to June, later in the North under cultivation, and are the crowning glory of the tree. Borne singly at the ends of the branchlets, they measure six to eight inches in diameter and can be seen at a distance of a mile. The petals, numbering six to twelve, are wax-like and each one has a spot of color at the base, which gives the flower a purple center.

Each flower lasts from two to four days, according to the weather, when the petals fall and the egg-shaped or oval fruit appears. When young it is dull pink, covered with thick lustrous hair. At maturity both fruit and hair turn rusty brown. Measuring three or four inches in length and one and a half inches thick, it bears many scarlet seeds on its surface. They are more or less flattened in shape, measuring one-half inch in length and, as do the seeds of all magnolias when first released, hang for a while by slender white threads before dropping to the ground.

The woolly winter buds are rusty or pale brown, and terminal buds measure one to one and a half inches in length. The brownish gray bark is one-half to three-quarters of an inch thick and is covered with thin scales.

The light to dark brown heartwood is usually tinged with yellow or green and occasionally contains colorful greenish black or purplish black streaks in contrast to the yellowish white sapwood.

The wood has a close, uniform texture and is generally straight-grained. It is moderately heavy with an average of thirty-five pounds per cubic foot in an air-dry condition. It is moderately low in shrinkage, moderately weak in bending and compression, moderately stiff, hard, and high in shock resistance. It is not durable when subjected to conditions favorable to decay.

The wood of southern magnolia resembles both yellow poplar (tuliptree) and cucumbertree, but is somewhat heavier, hardier and stronger. It was formerly marketed in mixture with yellow poplar and sold as such, but it has been found to be such an excellent wood for certain special uses that it is now sold largely under the name magnolia. Its most exacting use is for venetian blind slats, for which the wood has proved to be well-suited because of its fine, uniform texture, hardness, and ability to remain flat without warping. About two-thirds of the magnolia used in manufacturing wooden products goes into furniture. It also is used in the manufacture of boxes and for inside house finish.

This valuable ornamental tree is planted as far north as New Jersey on the Atlantic coast, and along the Pacific coast northward to British Columbia.

J. Horace McFarland Co.

Creamy - white flowers, six to eight inches across, are borne singly at branchlet ends

The egg-shaped fruit amid lustrous green leaves bears scarlet seeds on its surface

Brownish gray bark, a half inch thick, is covered with thin appressed scales

Natural range of Southern Magnolia

SWEETBAY

Sweetbay magnolia, Swampbay, Southern Sweetbay, White bay
Magnolia virginiana Linnaeus

Warren D. Brush

In the South the tree is tall and straight,
with small, ultimately spreading branches

SWEETBAY is known by several other names, including small magnolia, swamp magnolia, swamp laurel, white bay, laurel magnolia, beaver-tree and swamp sassafras. More of a moisture-loving species than even its larger relative the southern magnolia, *Magnolia grandiflora*, it grows naturally in the low, moist soil of swamps and on the borders of ponds from New Jersey along the coastal plain to Florida and west to Texas. In the south Atlantic and Gulf states the tree attains a height of sixty to seventy feet, and has a tall straight trunk two to three feet in diameter and small, mostly erect but ultimately spreading branches that form a narrow, oblong head. When not crowded by other, trees it tends to form a rounded, shapely crown. In the South sweetbay is associated with loblolly-bay, redbay, holly and red maple; on the borders of pine-barren ponds and shallow swamps it forms, with redbay, low almost impenetrable thickets. Farther north it is a slender tree twenty to thirty feet high with a trunk rarely more than fifteen to twenty inches in diameter. At the extreme northern limit of its range it becomes a many-stemmed shrub.

In the South sweetbay is an evergreen, the leaves remaining on the branches with little change in color until the appearance of the new leaves in the spring. In the North they are shed late in November and in early winter. When the oblong or oval leaves unfold they are covered with long, white, silky, deciduous hairs; at maturity they are thick, smooth, bright green and lustrous on the upper surface, and pale or nearly white and downy underneath. Four to six inches long, they have a conspicuous midrib and primary veins.

In May the creamy-white, fragrant, cup-shaped flowers appear and continue to open during several weeks in spring and early summer. Borne singly on slender, smooth stems one-half to three-fourths of an inch long, at the ends of the branches, they measure two to three inches across and are made up of nine to twelve obovate, concave petals. The dark red, cone-like fruit is oblong in shape, about two inches long and one-half inch thick, smooth and bearing many much-flattened oval seeds about a fourth of an inch long.

The slender twigs, bright green and fine hairy when they first appear, later become smooth and reddish brown. The buds are covered with fine silky hairs and the terminal buds are from one-half to three-fourths of an inch long. The light brown or grayish bark is broken into small, thin scales.

The light brown heartwood is usually tinged with red and the thick, creamy-white sapwood may include as many as 100 layers of annual growth. The wood has a fine, even texture and is usually straight-grained. It is moderately heavy, a cubic foot weighing about thirty-

L. W. Brownell

At the northern limit of its range sweetbay often becomes a many-stemmed shrub

L. W. Brownell

The dark red, smooth, cone-like fruit, oblong in shape, contains many much-flattened oval seeds

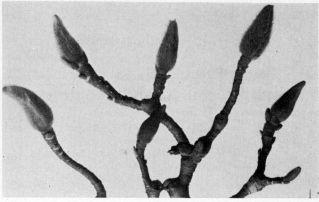

L. W. Brownell

The buds, up to three-fourths of an inch long, are covered with fine silky hairs

L. W. Brownell

The creamy-white, fragrant, cup-shaped flowers are found during the spring and early summer

L. W. Brownell

The leaves are bright green and lustrous above and are pale or nearly white below

L. W. Brownell

The light brown or grayish bark of Sweet-bay is broken up into small, thin scales

four pounds when air-dry, moderately weak, moderately stiff, hard and high in shock resistance. It works well with tools, but is not durable when used in locations favorable to decay.

Practically all the sweetbay trees felled in logging operations are sawed into lumber which is marketed as magnolia, together with southern magnolia, because the wood of the two species is much alike.

It is used mostly for furniture because it keeps its shape well and takes stains and other finishes readily. Because of its light color, good nailing qualities, and suitability for food containers, much of it goes into boxes. A specialty use is venetian blinds because it holds its shape. Sweetbay is occasionally used locally in the southern states in the manufacture of broom handles and other articles of woodenware because it turns well on a lathe and finishes smoothly.

The sweetbay tree is often cultivated as an ornamental on lawns and in gardens and parks in eastern United States and in Europe. Its shining, dark green leaves can be seen in nearly every American city park where the climate will permit; and there the large white flowers fill the air in early summer with their pleasing fragrance.

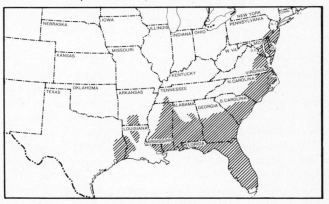

Natural range of Sweetbay

283

CUCUMBERTREE

Cucumbertree magnolia, Cucumber magnolia
Magnolia acuminata Linnaeus

OF seven tree-size magnolias native to the United States, the cucumbertree is most hardy. Never common, but usually scattered throughout the forest, its range extends from western New York, Pennsylvania and eastern Ohio, sporadically southwest to Arkansas, and south along the Appalachians to South Carolina, Georgia and Alabama, thence west to Louisiana. Forest-grown trees are fifty, eighty, or rarely one hundred feet tall, with trunks

George J. Baetzhold

In the forest the Cucumbertree is straight and tall, but in the open, with limbs often sweeping the ground, it develops a conical crown

three to four feet in diameter, which may be clear of branches for fifty feet or more. The trunks of open-grown trees support long, sweeping, ground-touching limbs, while the relatively slender upper branches ascend to form a broad pyramidal outline. It is the largest of the magnolias.

A rapid grower maturing in eighty to 120 years, it does best in loose, moist, fertile soil on low mountain slopes, along the banks of streams and in narrow protected valleys. It attains maximum size and greatest abundance in narrow valleys at the base of the Great

Smoky Mountains of North Carolina and Tennessee. Its companions include the tuliptree, white oak, white ash, sugar maple, and the hickories.

The name *Magnolia* commemorates the work of Pierre Magnol, an early eighteenth century professor of botany at Montpelier, France; *acuminata* refers to the sharp points of the simple alternate leaves whose smooth upper surfaces are dark green, with the undersides pale and slightly hairy along the veins. The leaves are seven to ten inches long, four to six inches wide, papery thin, with prominent midribs and smooth wavy margins. In autumn they turn pale yellow before falling and leave narrow elevated scars on the slender, shiny twigs.

Perfect, bell-shaped, green or pale yellow flowers appear from April to June. Their six petals are pointed, two to three and a half inches long, and so similar to the young leaves which precede them as to be frequently overlooked.

The fleshy fruit resembles a two-or three-inch long

In winter the straight trunk, the drooping lower branches and ascending upper ones serve as an aid in identifying an open-grown tree

George J. Baetzhold

cucumber. Hence the name. First green, then pink, and at maturity a purplish red, it has several scarlet, one-celled seeds which grow on the surface like scattered kernels on a corn cob. When fully ripe the seeds drop away to hang singly by slender white threads. Once on the ground, they may remain in the duff until the second spring before germinating. The many seedlings resulting from a seed crop are so intolerant of shade that few grow large and fewer reach maturity.

The firm grayish brown bark is one-half to three-quarters of an inch thick, broken and covered with small scales. Narrow ridges flow one into the other and are divided by long, vertical grooves.

The yellow-brown heartwood sometimes is streaked with shades of green, and it has narrow white sapwood similar to that of the tuliptree. When air dry it weighs twenty-nine pounds to the cubic foot. The wood is without special strength, and it is soft, durable, close-grained, porous and works easily. The uses of cucumber-trees include crates, boxes, cheap furniture, cabinet work, interior finish and flooring.

The bark gives little protection against light surface fires, and scale insects may attack the branches.

The symmetrical form, the almost tropical foliage and the scarlet late summer fruits encourage its ornamental use in the eastern states and in central Europe. It is readily grown from seed, but the brittle roots demand special care in transplanting. Seedlings are used as root stock on which to graft the several varieties of ornamental magnolia.

The large knobby fruit is first green, then pink, and finally red at maturity when the several scarlet seeds drop

Paul S. Carter

The Cucumbertree is easily identified from other magnolias because it is the only one with deeply furrowed bark

Walter E. Rogers

The flowers of this magnolia are inconspicuous because they are of the same pale green color as the spring foliage which is present when they bloom

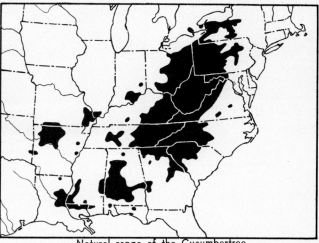

Natural range of the Cucumbertree

TULIPTREE

Yellow poplar
Liriodendron tulipifera Linnaeus

A tall, irregular crown of glossy, dark green leaves in summer, and numerous, upward-reaching branches in winter are characteristic of the tuliptree

ONE of the largest and most valuable trees of the eastern states, the tuliptree, is found in the region bounded by southern New England through New York to southern Michigan and south to west central Louisiana and northern Florida. It reaches its largest size in the deep rich soil of the lower Ohio Valley and in rich sheltered coves and valleys of the southern Appalachian Mountains, where occasionally it attains a height of over one hundred and fifty feet and a diameter of eight or ten feet. Occasionally the trunk of forest grown-trees will be eighty to one hundred feet tall before the first branch. It is always found in mixture with other trees rather than in pure stands, as with some of the pines.

In some regions it is known as white-wood, while the Onondaga Indians of central New York called it the white tree, *Ko-yen-ta-ka-ah-tas.*

It is characterized by the clean-cut, glossy, fiddle-shaped leaves, which the botanist describes as truncate, or ending abruptly, as if cut off. This gives rise to the name "saddle-leaf-tree." The large greenish yellow and orange tulip-like flowers develop into dry cone-like fruits about three inches long, which remain on the tree after the leaves drop, and from which the winged seeds fall and twirl to the ground. In winter when the leaves have fallen, one sees the dark reddish brown buds which are alternate on the branches. The blunt terminal buds are especially noticeable.

The tuliptree belongs to the magnolia family, which is far removed from any of the poplars and cottonwoods, but because of its soft wood it is frequently called yellow poplar. *Liriodendron* is from two Greek words describing a tree with lily-like flowers. *Tulipifera* refers to the tulip-like blossoms. It is a tree of ancient origin and, with its close relatives, is geologically recorded in Europe and Asia.

Devereux Butcher

The wood is light yellow to brown with a creamy white margin of sapwood. It is soft, easily worked and takes paint well. When air dry it weighs only about twenty-six pounds to the cubic foot. It is used in many kinds of construction, for interior finish, in the manufacture of boxes, crates, baskets and woodenware, for excelsior, veneer wood, and also as a core upon which to glue veneers of other wood. Small amounts are cut for pulpwood to make into paper. Occasionally planks sixty inches or wider are produced.

The inner bark of the root and trunk is intensely acrid, bitter and has been used as a tonic and stimulant. It is a source of hydrochlorate of tulipiferine, which is an alkaloid possessing the power of stimulating the heart.

Tuliptree is frequently used as a shade tree and for street planting, for which it is well adapted.

The tree is moderately free from pests, but frequently unsightly brown spots caused by a gall insect cover the leaves. Also the leaves may turn yellow and drop during the summer.

Top: The tulip-like flowers grow on slender branchlets among the early summer leaves. Center right: The conical fruit, which ripens late in September and October, stays on the tree through the winter. The cross-section shows the flat-winged seed cases attached to a central spike. Lower right: A winter twig shows the dark red bud and prominent, alternate leaf scars

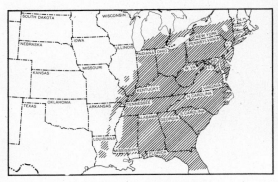

Natural range of the Tuliptree

U. S. Forest Service

The deeply furrowed bark of a mature tree is sometimes two inches thick. Bark of young trees is thin and smooth

CALIFORNIA-LAUREL

Oregon-myrtle, Pacific-myrtle, Pepperwood, Spice-tree
Umbellularia californica (Hooker and Arnott) Nuttall

CALIFORNIA-LAUREL is the only native representative of the laurel family in western North America. It is also popularly called Oregon-myrtle, and sometimes pepperwood. The species is most in evidence on open slopes and bottomlands of the Coos Bay-Coquille River area of southwestern Oregon where, on protected and fertile sites, it reaches heights of 100 to 175 feet and diameters of three to six feet. Elsewhere it is a medium-size tree, forty to eighty feet tall and eighteen to thirty inches in diameter. Its range extends southward along the coastal mountains and lower Sierra Nevada to the southern border of California, between sea level and 1,500 feet

elevation in the north, and from 2,000 to 4,000 feet in the south.

On open sites, particularly where exposed to coastal winds, the tree assumes a protective, umbrella-like shape, spreading a network of matted branches over fence corners and small structures. Myrtle Point, Oregon, presents a characteristic occurrence of myrtle as a village shade tree, where literally hundreds of rounded crowns shield and shade houses and sheds from wind and sun. On bluffs facing the ocean it is often reduced to heavy mats of prostrate stems.

Quite different are the forest-grown specimens, which

On open sites, particularly where exposed to coastal winds, California-laurel assumes a protective, umbrella-like shape—a network of branches

have fairly long boles. However, even in the forest, this species commonly divides near the ground into several nearly upright limbs supporting a broad, dense and rounded top. On dry, shallow, rocky soils it is inclined to be shrubby.

The evergreen leaves are lanceolate to elliptical, three to four inches long. They turn to a beautiful yellow or orange color and fall one by one during their second season, or often remain on the branches for several years. When crushed or bruised, the leaves give off a strong, but pleasant, camphor-like odor. They are sometimes browsed by goats. The flowers, arranged in flat, yellowish green clusters (umbels), appear in January to March before the new spring leaves. The fruit is a greenish yellow plum-like drupe. The bark is dark, reddish brown, with scales that appear as though they had been pressed flat.

The heartwood is varied in color from a light rich brown to a grayish brown, frequently with darker streaks; the sapwood is whitish to light brown. The wood is hard and heavy, fine textured and works well with tools. Turning and quarter-sawing often yield striking figure effects. Air dry, it weighs about thirty-nine pounds a cubic foot.

Forest-grown logs are made into beautiful, interior finish and furniture, albeit on a limited scale. More sought after commercially are the burls, small and large, which often are found on the trunks of older trees. When free of defects, these command high prices. The smaller are turned into innumerable small woodenware novelties, while the larger are sawn into thin veneers.

"Oregon-myrtle" supports a large number of roadside or home industries in southwestern Oregon, making ornamental woodwork, such as paper-weights, desk sets, trays, candlesticks, bookends and the like.

The California-laurel was first observed and collected without any particular notation by Archibald Menzies, the naturalist of Captain Vancouver's ship, *Discovery*, on the voyage of 1790-1792. The next reference to it is found in the journal of David Douglas, who, in 1826, observed that, "This elegant evergreen tree, which attains the height of forty to 120 feet and from two to four feet in the diameter of its stem, forms the connecting link between the gloomy pine forests of northwest America and the tropical-like verdure of California. The foliage, when bruised, gives out a most powerful camphor-like scent, and even during severe hurricanes I have been obliged to remove from under its shade, the odor being so strong as to occasion violent sneezing. The hunters often make use of a decoction of the leaves, which they take without any bad effect; indeed, it stimulates the system, and produces a glow of warmth. . . . I trust that this fine tree will ere long become an inmate of English gardens, and may even be useful in medicine and afford a perfume. It is *Laurus regia*."

In this last statement he was mistaken, as were also Hooker and Arnott, who, in describing the botanical collection of Captain Beechley's voyage of 1827, incorrectly placed it in the genus *Tetranthera*. Sixteen years later, the English botanist, Thomas Nuttall, described it fully as a single species of the genus *Umbellularia*.

The California-laurel is the only North American representative of a genus *Umbellularia* that grows almost entirely in tropical and semi-tropical areas. A horticultural variety, *pendula*, has been developed for ornamental planting.

The evergreen leaves are three to four inches long. The fruit is a small greenish yellow plum-like drupe

Dark, reddish brown bark is covered with scales, appearing as though they had been pressed flat

Natural range of the California-laurel

SASSAFRAS

Sassafras albidum (Nuttall) Nees

FROM southern Maine to Ontario and south over the Mississippi Valley to east Texas and central Florida, sassafras is known by its flat unsymmetrical crown, or twisted branches which spread almost at right angles from the trunk to support many upward reaching branchlets.

Devereux Butcher

The broad, sometimes flat-topped crown of Sassafras is intensified by the side branches which stand out almost at right angles from the main trunk

Little more than a shrub in the north, it reaches heights of forty to ninety feet and trunk diameters of four to seven feet from Pennsylvania on south. The largest trees are reported on the deeper soils of the Great Smoky Mountains of North Carolina and Tennessee. Sassafras grows moderately rapidly, but slows down after attaining a diameter of two to two and a half feet. It may live for 700 to 1,000 years.

Ancestors of this sassafras inhabited much of the northern hemisphere during early geologic periods, and a species almost identical with *Sassafras albidum* grows in China.

The name *Sassafras* appears in explorers' reports as early as 1591 and it evidently was in use from New England to Florida. The Narragansett Indians on Long Island Sound called the wood "sasau-aka-pamuch." The word sassafras probably is of Indian origin.

Three forms of the yellow-green, aromatic, short-stemmed, simple leaves may grow on a single branch. Some are lance-shaped and entire, others are shaped like a mitten with an oblique lobe on one side, while still others have a lobe on each side. All are wedge-shaped at the base and are three to six inches long and two to four inches wide. They are slightly hairy when young, becoming smooth, shiny and rich green above and paler beneath, with net-like veins. In autumn they turn yellow or orange, often tinged with red.

With the unfolding leaves come inconspicuous greenish yellow flowers in two-inch clusters or racemes from the inner bud scale axils at the twig ends. The staminate and pistillate flowers grow on different trees. By September or October the seed-producing pistillate ones develop

U. S. Forest Service

into dark blue, berry-like fruits about half an inch long on the enlarged end of a fleshy, crimson pedicel.

On old trees the red-brown, deeply furrowed bark, with flattened ridges about an inch and a half thick, appears as if washed with ashen gray. On young trees the bark is thin, reddish brown and evenly striated or cracked into buff-colored blocks. The smooth, green, aromatic twigs are mucilaginous when chewed.

Sassafras wood is tinged with red. It has seven or eight rings of light yellow sapwood. The darker shades seldom develop before the trees are fifteen or eighteen inches in diameter. Air dry wood weighs thirty-one to thirty-two pounds to the cubic foot. It is soft, brittle, coarse-grained, and slightly aromatic and is not strong. It is used for cooperage and small boats, and its resistance to rot makes it suitable for fences and house sills.

During early colonial days, the supposed medicinal properties of the roots and bark made sassafras one of America's chief exports. Sassafras tea has long been a spring tonic to "thin the blood and purify the system." Oil of sassafras is distilled from the bark of the roots to perfume soaps and flavor medicines.

Sassafras grows readily from seed, sprouts from the roots and can be reproduced from root cuttings. Insects seldom do serious harm; but fire kills young trees and injures old ones.

Inconspicuous, greenish yellow flowers appear with the new spring leaves. These pistillate blooms grow on trees separate from the staminate ones

The twisted ridges of the red-brown bark often appear as if washed with light gray

A three-lobed leaf with partly mature fruits of Sassafras

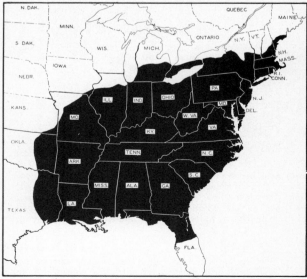

Natural range of Sassafras

291

SWEETGUM

American sweetgum, Redgum, Bilsted
Liquidambar styraciflua Linnaeus

SWEETGUM—commonly called red gum—flourishes from southern Connecticut to Florida and west as far as eastern Texas, Oklahoma, Arkansas and southeastern Missouri, where it prefers rich, moist soil and, while not a swamp tree, grows vigorously on occasionally flooded land. It also grows on high land, but seldom attains as great size as along stream bottoms where it grows in mixture with red maple, elm, ash, cottonwood and several oaks. A closely related variety reappears in the mountains of central and southern Mexico and in the highlands of Guatemala. Sweetgum trees eighty to 120 feet high and eighteen inches to three feet in diameter at breast height are common. Occasionally, however, they attain heights of 150 feet and are five feet in diameter. They are most abundant and attain greatest size in the bottomlands of the lower Mississippi Valley and the southeastern coastal states. In the forest the trunk is straight and clear of side branches for approximately two-thirds of its height, but young open-grown trees have a pyramidal crown with a straight central stem like that of a coniferous tree. With maturity, the side branches become heavier and develop a narrow but more irregular crown.

Sweetgum is frequently confused with the tupelos, but belongs to the witch hazel or *Hammamelidaceae* family. There are three closely related species—one in Mexico,

The Davey Tree Expert Co.

Sweetgum becomes a tall symmetrical tree when grown on rich moist bottomland, but will do well on high, well drained soils. The clean trunk, dense, glossy, green, summer foliage, gorgeous autumn coloring and comparative freedom from pests make it a favorite for street and ornamental planting

The Davey Tree Expert Co.

The slender side branches of the straight central trunk support twigs with corky wings or ridges, from which dry seed balls on long, thread-like stalks, hang through the winter

292

one in central China and a third in parts of Asia Minor, where the liquid storax of commerce is secured. The scientific name, *Liquidambar styraciflua*, was given by the Swedish botanist, Carl von Linne, and refers to the yellowish, fragrant, balsamic liquid which exudes from the bark. This resembles the liquid storax of commerce, for which it is frequently substituted. Trees near the northern limit of its range yield little resin, but the flow is abundant in the South.

The glossy, aromatic, star-shaped, five- to seven-pointed alternate leaves give rise to the common name, "star leafed" gum. The name "red" gum refers to the color of the wood, but applies also to the brilliant autumn foliage, which is comparable to that of the maples.

The flowers of both sexes occur separately on the same tree. In the South they appear as early as March, and in the North during April or May, when the leaves are about half grown. The clusters of hairy, green, pollen-producing flowers are two or three inches long, at the end of the new growth. The seed-producing flowers hang in round clusters on long, thread-like stalks from the base of the upper leaves. These develop into brown seed balls or burs one to one and a half inches in diameter. They remain swinging on the trees through the winter. Each seed ball consists of a number of closely connected woody, horn-tipped capsules in which are enclosed the seeds. With maturity the capsules split apart permitting the half-inch long, winged seeds to escape.

The slender first-year twigs are light orange to reddish brown and have prominent lenticels. After the second year, corky wings or ridges develop. Larger branches have a broken, warty bark which gives the tree the name, "alligator wood." The soft, deeply furrowed, dark gray bark of the main trunk may be over an inch thick.

Sweetgum develops a long, strong taproot in deep bottomlands, which usually prevents loss from windfall and encourages vigorous growth.

Sweetgum wood, because of its interlocking grain, is strong and stiff. It works moderately well with tools. Its air-dry weight is thirty-four to thirty-seven pounds to the cubic foot. The hard, straight, close-grained wood is bright brown, tinged with red, and it has a thin white sapwood. The heartwood has a satiny luster and pleasing, varying figure. Few American woods equal sweetgum in beauty of natural grain but, in deference to the prejudice against "gum" wood, it is frequently marketed as satin walnut, Circassian walnut and hazelwood. Furniture, interior trim, railroad ties, cigar boxes, boxing, crating material, cheap flooring, barrels, woodenware and wood pulps are among its many uses. It is also one of the most important sources of plywood.

To a large extent, sweetgum grows on lands subject to overflow. For this reason, damage by fire tends to be rather slight. Insects and fungi attack felled trees and those which have been injured by fire and wind, but loss from these sources is not serious.

Sweetgum is superb for ornamental planting, ranking with the most beautiful of our eastern broad-leaved trees. It is hardy as far north as Massachusetts, is easily planted and grows fairly rapidly. The splendid fall coloring—gorgeous scarlet, orange and yellow tints, as well as purple, lilac and brown tones—together with its freedom from pests make it especially attractive on streets and lawns.

E. R. Mosher

In early spring clusters of green pollen-bearing and seed-producing flowers, glossy green, aromatic, five-pointed leaves, and dry, horn-tipped seed balls of the previous year are characteristic features of Sweetgum

The soft gray bark is deeply furrowed and usually about an inch thick

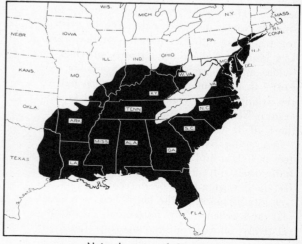

Natural range of Sweetgum

293

AMERICAN SYCAMORE

American planetree, Buttonball-tree, Buttonwood

Platanus occidentalis Linnaeus

George J. Baetzhold

American Sycamore is recognized in winter and summer by its mottled white bark, its thick buttressed trunk and its broadly oval crown

open-grown specimens, large wide-spreading limbs, extend to form a broad, irregular crown occasionally one hundred feet or more across. This form gives way under forest conditions to a slightly tapering trunk whose clear length is sixty feet or more.

The simple, alternate, palmately veined leaves are roughly three- to five-lobed, with occasional coarse teeth. It is the largest single-bladed leaf native to the American forest, being four to ten inches long and equally broad. Bright green on the upper side, paler beneath but without hairs, the leaves have a leathery texture. At the base of the stout, one- to two-inch leaf stem or petiole is a flaring ruffle-like stipule, while the entire stem is finely coated with hairs and the broad hollow base completely caps and encloses a long, smooth, blunt, conical bud of the coming season.

Inconspicuous flowers of both sexes are borne on the same tree but on different stalks. They appear as the leaves unfold in early May. The male flowers are in dark red

AMERICAN SYCAMORE, while not the tallest, attains the most massive proportions of any American hardwood or broad-leaved tree and is of considerable commercial importance. The wide buttressed trunk and smooth, variegated bark extending its glistening whiteness into the branches of the crown is a familiar sight along streams, on river islands, and in rich, moist bottomlands. It grows throughout most of the eastern half of the country from southern Maine to southeastern Nebraska, south into Texas and along the Gulf of Mexico to northern Florida.

Averaging sixty to one hundred and twenty feet in height and two to five feet in diameter, individuals 140 feet tall and up to fourteen feet in diameter have been recorded. As the tree attains maturity the trunk becomes irregular and eccentrically buttressed. From the relatively short, rapidly tapering trunk of

clusters, borne on a short base, while the small, light green, pistillate or female blooms form closely packed, ball-like heads attached to a long, slender, thread-like stem. By October these develop into a dense ball or compound fruit dangling from a long slender stem and, after hanging through the winter, break up into many hairy, one-seeded nutlets. American sycamore has single seed balls, while those of the Oriental sycamore and London plane, *P. orientalis* and *P. acerifolia*, hang in pairs or even fours. These seed balls give rise to the common name buttonwood or buttonball.

While sycamore fruits abundantly nearly every year, the vitality is low and the seeds are slow to germinate. Many seeds are carried by the water of early spring freshets and deposited on muddy flats where they germinate in considerable quantities. Even under upland woods conditions, however, the seeds require exceedingly moist surroundings in which to grow. Sycamore sprouts readily from the stump and reproduces itself by this means, as well as from seeds.

The bark assumes a variety of forms and colors according to the age of the tree and the conditions under which it grows. Most easily recognized is that of young to moderately old trees in which large, thin plates peel off the trunk, exposing conspicuous areas of whitish, yellowish, or greenish inner bark. This is probably caused by the inability of the bark to stretch as the limbs and trunk expand. As the tree grows older, the bark on the lower trunk becomes two to three inches thick, broken by many shallow fissures to give a scaly appearance, and the light colored mottled look gives way to red-brown or dark gray.

Interwoven fibers make the reddish brown, clean appearing, coarse-grained wood tough and difficult to split or work. It is moderately hard and weighs thirty-five to thirty-six pounds to the cubic foot when air dry. Because it is so easily consumed by decay it is not generally used for railroad ties or fences, but its toughness results in use for butchers' blocks, saddletrees, vehicles, tobacco and cigar boxes, as well as for shipping boxes, crates, and slack cooperage. It is also used for musical instruments and when quarter sawn the mottled texture makes it desirable for furniture and interior trim.

American sycamore is scattered through the forests in company with other hardwood trees characteristic of bottomlands. It belongs to the plane-tree family and is the most important of six or seven species native to the United States, Mexico and Central America, and one—*Platanus orientalis*—native to southwestern Asia.

George J. Baetzhold
Single buttonball fruits, composed of many hairy nut-like seeds hang on a slender stem

George J. Baetzhold
The leaves, frequently broader than long, are palmately veined, four to ten inches across, shiny green on the upper surface and pale beneath

G. H. Collingwood
The mottled bark with browns, yellows and greens against a background of white, is the result of inability to stretch with the expanding trunk

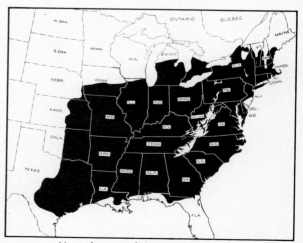

Natural range of American Sycamore

CALIFORNIA SYCAMORE
Planetree, Buttonwood, Buttonball-tree
Platanus racemosa Nutt.

CALIFORNIA SYCAMORE has many characteristics similar to those of the American and Arizona sycamores, differing mostly in the shape of the leaf. The tree belongs to a genus that, world-wide, contains a half dozen species. Of these, the natives *P. racemosa* and *P. wrightii* also are native to northern Mexico, with *P. occidentalis* extending into southern Ontario, Canada. The other species are native to Central and South America, southeastern Europe and southwestern Asia.

The California tree thrives on moist bottomlands and in canyons, its range extending through the southern Sacramento Valley from Tehama County south along the interior valley of the western foothills of the Sierra Nevada, and from Monterey south through the valleys of the coast ranges and the southern canyons of the San Bernardino Mountains to 4000 feet elevation. The range extends also into northern Lower California, as far as the canyons of Sierra San Pedro Martir. It occurs also in valleys along the eastern shore of the Gulf of California south from about Puerto Penasco to approximately Mazatlan.

Frequently growing in groups of three or four or five trees, the trunks in close proximity, one or more of them tipping or even sprawling on the ground, this species, usually not quite as tall as the eastern tree, attains heights of from forty to sixty or, in deep canyons, rarely ninety feet, with diameters of three to six feet. The large, irregular, wide-spreading branches form a broad, irregular, open crown fifty to eighty feet across, often supporting large, dark green clumps of mistletoe noticeable in winter when the tree is leafless.

The flowers appear in early spring with the leaves, both sexes growing separately but on the same tree, the inconspicuous, dark red clusters of male or pollen-bearing blossoms occurring in four or five globular heads about three eighths to a half inch in diameter. They are attached by short stems along a slender, smooth, pliant, pendent stalk about three to seven inches in length, growing from leaf clusters on twigs of the preceding year. The small, light green, closely packed clusters of female or seed-producing flowers develop into two to seven globular heads three quarters of an inch to an inch in diameter, attached by short stems along a similar stalk six to nine inches long, often growing from the tip of a twig of the season. These stalks with their globes are referred to as racemes, hence the scientific name *racemosa*. In late summer or early fall, the female heads develop into balls of numerous, closely packed, elongated, hairy, brown seeds held together by a hard, central, globular cob or core securely attached to the stalk. The seed balls remain on the tree through winter, after which the brown seeds, bristly at the inner end, fall to the ground or often are carried by a stream to new sites where a few may find conditions favorable

M. M. Deaderick

California Sycamore, sometimes occurring singly, but more often in groups of two to four, with an occasional leaning individual, the tree supports a wide, ragged crown

to germination. The tree also reproduces by sprouting from the stump.

The leathery palmate leaves, light green above and considerably lighter beneath, are five to eleven inches long and wide, and are divided into three to five

Devereux Butcher

slender, tapering, pointed lobes with margins coarsely toothed or entire. Their bases are heart-shaped, wedge-shaped or truncate. Young leaves are finely and densely hairy or woolly, more so on the paler underside. The stout petiole or stem also is finely woolly. The swollen base or axil of the petiole, hollow and cup-shaped, fits tightly over the winter bud, which is conical, sharply tipped and nearly a half inch long. The base of the petiole is protected by a small, green, leaf-like formation about three eighths of an inch wide, called a stipule. When the stem falls, the bud is exposed and surrounded by the leaf scar.

Bark at the base of older trunks is two to three inches thick, broken by shallow furrows into small, light brown or gray scaly ridges. Above the base the bark on trunk and branches is very thin, smooth and mottled with scales of varying shades of green, gray and brown. These drop off annually with diameter expansion to reveal the conspicuous, smooth, new inner bark, which is chalk white.

Because the tough, coarse-grained wood quickly decays when in contact with moist soil and weather, it usually is not suited for such uses as fence posts and railroad ties. Although difficult to work, it is used for cigar boxes, butchers' blocks, saddletrees, woodenware, crates and musical instruments. The interlacing roots act to prevent soil erosion, and the tree sometimes is planted on stream and river banks for this purpose.

As with the other native sycamores, the California species is attacked by a fungus disease called anthracnose, which kills the young spring leaves usually before hardly an eighth grown, forcing the tree to put out new leaves. The same disease also attacks the twigs causing a disfiguring dieback.

The European sycamore is widely planted as an ornamental in our country, perhaps particularly in eastern and mid-western city parks and along streets and boulevards; but because its new bark never is gleaming white or pale green or yellow, but tends toward a somber yellow, green or brown, and because the leaves are differently shaped, it is readily distinguished from our native sycamores. The foreign tree, too, has a more symetrical form, making it better suited for ornamental purposes.

Devereux Butcher

Female flower and seed globes, a half to three-fourths of an inch in diameter, are attached by short stems along pendent stalks and the smaller male globes attached to similar but shorter stalks on the same tree, appear in spring with the leaves

Devereux Butcher

The leathery, palmate leaves, five to eleven inches long and wide, have three to five slender, sharply pointed lobes, with entire or coarsely toothed margins

Devereux Butcher

Bark on trunks and branches is patterned with thin scales of brown, green or gray and, where these have dropped, the new, white inner bark is conspicuously revealed

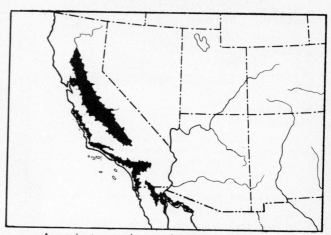

Approximate natural range of California Sycamore

ARIZONA SYCAMORE

Buttonball-tree, Buttonwood, Arizona planetree
Platanus wrightii S. Wats.

IN APPEARANCE, Arizona sycamore resembles the other two sycamores which are native to the United States. Except for its range, the principal differences are in the leaves and in the number of flower heads on a stem.

Habitats of this species, from 2000 to 6000 feet above sea level, are rocky stream beds in mountain canyons and the sandy washes in grassland and desert, particularly in proximity to where streams flow from the mouths of canyons.

Arizona sycamore inhabits most of Yavapai County, Arizona, north to Ashfork and Oak Creek Canyon, south to southwestern Mojave County and southeasterly to the Mexican border, and Catron, Grant and Hidalgo counties, New Mexico. The range south of the border includes northwestern Chihuahua and northeastern Sonora.

In various localities, the tree associates with Mexican walnut, Fremont cottonwood, desert willow, netleaf hackberry, a mulberry—*Morus celtidifolia*—boxelder, western

taining heights of thirty to forty feet, with diameters from one to two feet. On moist, warm, sunny, sandy desert washes at altitudes of about 2300 feet in southern Arizona, it may reach sixty feet and diameters of one and a half to two and a half feet. Occasionally three to a half dozen trees growing close together, will join their trunks in later years to appear as a single trunk of five or six feet in diameter.

The sharply pointed, brown winter buds are covered by a shiny cap-like scale. During the preceding summer, these buds are encased by the swollen, cup-like base of the leaf stem or petiole, and when the leaf falls, the bud is exposed, encircled by the leaf scar. The base of the stem is protected by a stipule—a small, green, collar-like formation.

Bark at the base of older trunks is shallowly furrowed into thin, scaly, light brown or gray ridges. On upper trunks and branches and on the bases of younger trunks as well, the bark is mottled by patches of thin, scaly bark in shades of dark green, brown or gray. These drop off in the spring with the diameter expansion of the wood to expose the conspicuous, new, pale gray, creamy white or chalk white bark that is characteristic of the sycamores.

The alternate, palmate leaves are divided into three to seven tapering, pointed lobes

Devereux Butcher

Walter S. Phillips

On optimum sites, Arizona Sycamore attains heights up to sixty feet and diameters of two feet, their white-barked limbs supporting a large, irregular head

soapberry and four species of ash—Lowell, Gregg, fragrant and velvet.

In cool, rocky canyons at higher elevations, Arizona sycamore is comparatively small, at-

(sinuses deeper than those of *P. racemosa*), are six to eight and sometimes ten inches long and wide, with margins entire or occasionally slightly toothed, and bases heart-shaped, but occasionally truncate or wedge-shaped. They are pale green beneath, darker above, and finely hairy or woolly, densely so when young, with petioles one and a half to three inches long, often cupped at the base, noticeably woolly or downy, as are the young ash-brown twigs, which become smooth and red-brown or gray with age.

Staminate or male flowers and pistillate or female flowers occur on the same tree, but in separate ball-like heads. The male globular flower clusters are about a half inch or less in diameter attached by a short stem along a four- or five-inch long, smooth, pendent, flexible stalk. The female flower heads, three quarters of an inch to an inch in diameter, are attached by short stems to a similar pendent stalk about six inch long. As the female flower head develops its tightly packed, angular, smooth, brown, round-topped seeds, the diameter of the head expands and envelops its stem so that a half inch or so of the adjoining pendent stalk passes into and through the seed head. The seeds which, together with the stem, are fixed to a hard central core or cob, ripen in late winter or early spring.

The wood of Arizona sycamore, like that of our other native sycamores, is tough and coarse-grained, with interwoven fibers, and is difficult to split and work. Although sycamore wood decays rapidly, the drier climate of Arizona and New Mexico may permit uses here which bring it into contact with weather and soil. It is suited also for saddletrees, mine timbers, slack cooperage and musical instruments.

The root system is wide-spreading and helps to hold soil along stream banks. As with the other two native species, this one is subject to the fungus disease, anthracnose.

The scientific name, *wrightii*, honors the botanist Charles Wright, 1811-1885, who traveled through Texas and New Mexico in 1849 and again in 1851-52.

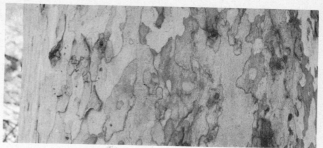

Devereux Butcher

Bark on trunks and branches is mottled by patches of thin scales in shades of green, brown or gray which, when they drop off, expose the new white bark

Walter S. Phillips

The alternate, palmate leaves, pale green beneath and darker above, are divided into five to seven narrow, tapering lobes, their margins entire or slightly toothed

Devereux Butcher

Globular female flower heads, one to seven attached to a pendent stalk, are three fourths of an inch in diameter, while the smaller male clusters are attached to a similar but shorter stalk on the same tree

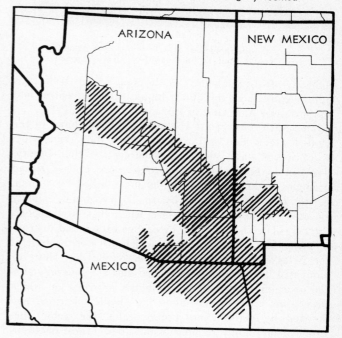

Natural range of Arizona Sycamore

HAWTHORN

Haw, Red haw, Thorn, Thorn-apple
Crataegus spp.

THE HAWTHORNS comprise a large group of small, thorny trees and shrubs widely distributed in this and the Old World, where they are confined mostly to the north temperate zone, with the bulk of the distribution in eastern United States. From the abundance of their keen, often very long, woody thorns they are everywhere known and generally distinguished from other woody plants. There are probably about 150 species in North America—the exact number is not known because of the

The hawthorns are typical of open pasture land where their sharp thorns protect them from grazing animals. Because of their aggressiveness they frequently take possession of abandoned farm or cleared lands. Later their impenetrable thickets gradually may be invaded by forest trees through the agency of wind and animals and finally, under dense shade, the hawthorn succumbs.

The margins of the small, simple, alternate, hawthorn leaves are generally toothed and they are often more or

J. Horace McFarland Co.
Low and wide-spreading, Hawthorn trees are generally less than 25 feet in height with numerous branches

L. W. Brownell
Light green at first, the twigs later become red- or orange-brown

difficulty of distinguishing the different species from each other—and ninety in China, Japan, Siberia, central and southwestern Asia, and in Europe.

There are fewer than 150 species of hawthorn in the United States that grow to tree size. Low and wide-spreading in habit, they are generally less than twenty-five feet in height with numerous, more or less zigzag branches, round in cross-section and marked by oblong, mostly pale lenticels and by small, horizontal, slightly elevated leaf scars. Light green when they first appear, the twigs later become red- or orange-brown and lustrous or gray. The spines or thorns, which grow at the base of the twigs or leaves, may be stout or slender, short or elongated, and simple or branched and are generally similar in color to that of the branches or trunk on which they grow. The winter buds are small, spherical, and covered by many over-lapping scales, the outer ones rounded or bluntly pointed at the apex, bright chestnut-brown and lustrous, and the inner ones green or rose.

The rigid, zigzag branches are round in the cross-section and marked by oblong pale lenticels and small leaf scars

The margins of the small, simple, alternate leaves are generally toothed and are often more or less lobed. These flowers and leaves belong to *Crataegus macrosperma*

The white or rarely rose-colored flowers are similar in appearance and structure to pear and apple blossoms. These blooms are of the species *C. pediculata*

less lobed, especially on vigorous leading branchlets. Attached to the twig by a petiole or stem, the leaves are borne, like those of the apple, on small, dwarf shoots and they fall to the ground in the autumn.

The conspicuous white or rarely rose-colored flowers are similar in appearance and structure to pear and apple blossoms. They are produced in flattish, branched, erect clusters after the leaves are grown. Myriads of insects visit the flowers and assist in their cross-fertilization. The small, spherical or oblong or pear-shaped, apple-like fruits, bright red, yellow or black, generally are open and concave at the apex, and are borne in branched clusters. The flesh is usually rather dry and unpalatable, but in some species it is tart and palatable, and contains from one to five joined, but separable, very hard, bony seeds.

The bark is usually dark gray and scaly. The wood is close-grained, hard, heavy and tough. Although subject to warping and checking, it is occasionally used for small tool handles and other turned articles.

Many of the hawthorns are valuable as ornamentals. Their attractive and abundant flowers and showy fruits make them desirable as ornamentals in parks and gardens and should be more widely used, especially for screens, borders and hedges. As a hedge plant the hawthorn has been used in the Old World for centuries—the word "haw" coming from the Anglo-Saxon and meaning fence or hedge—and many of our native species are equally if not more desirable as such and are well adapted for trimming. Many of the hawthorns are also very desirable for individual lawn plants, for which a number of cultivated forms are especially suitable, some of them with magnificent red flowers, bright red fruit which remains on the trees during the winter, and leaves that change to orange and scarlet in the fall. The fruit is a favorite food of many of our native birds, and that of several southern species is sometimes made into preserves.

Both birds and mammals assist in disseminating the seeds and are responsible for the wide distribution of these trees. Because of their thick shells, the seeds are slow in germinating, often "lying over" for a season.

The small, spherical apple-like fruit is bright red, yellow or black and is borne in branched clusters

The bark is usually dark gray, and scaly. The wood is close-grained, hard and heavy and warps easily

BLACK CHERRY

Prunus serotina Ehrhart

BLACK CHERRY grows from Nova Scotia to Maine and Minnesota south to eastern Texas and east to central Florida. It is also found in eastern and southern Mexico

Devereux Butcher

Open-grown Cherry trees develop a spreading oval crown whose tortuous, more or less horizontal branches are clothed in summer with dark green foliage. Forest-grown trees are frequently characterized by a long symmetrical trunk, usually free of side branches

and Guatemala. Frequently reaching heights of sixty to eighty feet with trunk diameters at breast height of two or three feet, occasional forest trees are 100 feet high and four feet in diameter, with a clean, uniform trunk extending forty to sixty feet. In the open, tortuous more or less horizontal branches form a spreading oval crown. Best development is found

in the southern Appalachians, where extreme ages of 150 to 200 years are attained. Black cherry prefers deep, rich soil with uniform moisture, but thrives under many soil and moisture conditions.

The dark green, simple leaves are oval or pointedly lance-shaped, with fine incurved teeth on the margin. They occur alternately on the twigs, are two to five inches long, one inch to one and a half inches wide, smooth on both sides, pale green below, with fine hairs near the light colored midrib and veins, and one or more red glands near the base. The slender leaf stem, or petiole, one-half to three-quarters of an inch long.

In April or May, when the new leaves are still red, four- to six-inch drooping clusters of perfect, five-petaled white flowers appear. Domestic cherries produce blossoms before the leaves, so the Latin name *serotina*, meaning "appearing late," refers to the belated flowers of this species, while *Prunus* is the scientific name for cherries and plums.

Drooping clusters of pea-sized cherries, so dark red

Devereux Butcher

as to be nearly black, with purple, juicy pulp, develop by late summer. They have a pleasant, slightly bitter taste and are sometimes used in a beverage called "cherry bounce" —hence the name "Rum Cherry." Within each fruit is a thin-walled, slightly egg-shaped pit about a third of an inch long, enclosing the seed. Trees bear seed at intervals of three or four years from early youth to old age. The fruit is eagerly eaten by birds which distribute the seeds over wide areas. The seedlings demand sunlight and grow best in the open.

The dark bark of old trees is broken into irregular, easily peeled, scaly plates and is about three-quarters of an inch thick. On young trees and branches it is satin-smooth, dark red-brown, with conspicuous horizontal, pale lenticels or breathing pores. When wounded, a gum similar to gum arabic exudes from the bark. The twigs are slender, smooth, red-brown, and, like the leaves and inner bark, contain prussic acid which gives an aromatic flavor resembling bitter almonds. This is used in tonics and cough remedies. The same substance may cause severe illness or death to livestock which eat the wilted leaves.

The reddish brown, close-grained wood is hard, relatively light, and when air dry weighs about thirty-six pounds to the cubic foot. The sapwood is yellow and thin. Cherry is extensively used by the printing trade to back electrotypes and zinc etchings. Its beauty, luster, ability to withstand knocks, and ease of working encourage its use for furniture, interior trim, veneers, and tool handles. Like mahogany, the color deepens with age, and the wood ranks close to walnut for cabinet purposes. Consequently it is one of the most valuable forest trees.

Cherry trees are susceptible to many insects and diseases. Tent caterpillars feed on the leaves and sometimes fatally denude the trees, while "black knot," a fungus disease of the twigs and branches, causes severe injury. Surface fires permit the entrance of wood-rotting fungi, causing hollow butts.

Cherry is not a satisfactory street tree, but it can be planted anywhere within its natural range for its showy blossoms, its fruit which attracts birds, and its unconventional form.

Drooping racemes of white flowers, with the principal parts in fives, appear after the leaves

The dark colored bark of mature trees consists of many irregular, easily peeled, scaly plates and may be three-fourths of an inch thick

Drooping clusters of dark red cherries with purple, juicy pulp, ripen in late summer and early fall

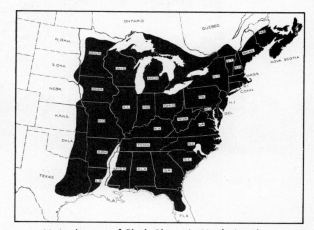

Natural range of Black Cherry in North America

AMERICAN MOUNTAIN-ASH

Mountain sumac, Wine tree, Rowan-berry, Elder-leaved sumac
Sorbus americana Marshall

THE mountain-ashes comprise a group of small trees and shrubs that are valued for their attractive appearance. They are widely distributed through the cooler regions of Europe, Asia and North America. There are three or four species in the United States, two of which reach tree size, and many species in eastern Asia and in Europe. Because of their handsome foliage, showy flower clusters and scarlet berries, they are valued highly for decorative purposes. The most common species in cultivation is the European mountain-ash, *Sorbus aucuparia*, which is called rowan in England, and old superstitions cluster around the rowan tree in all rural sections, which are preserved in the folk-lore and the literature of many countries. The trees were considered effective in exorcising evil spirits and leafy twigs were worn as charms or amulets.

The American mountain-ash is a small tree twenty to thirty feet in height with a trunk four to twelve inches in diameter, or a shrub with numerous stems. Even when it has a single stem the trunk is usually short, and the spreading, slender branches form a narrow round-topped head. The stout twigs, hairy at first, are soon smooth, becoming in their first winter brown, tinged with red, and reddish brown in their second year, when the thin papery outer layer of bark is easily separable from the bright green fragrant inner layers. The stems are marked by large leaf-scars and oblong, pale lenticels or breathing pores. The winter buds, one fourth to three-fourths of an inch long, have dark, wine-red, pointed scales and are covered with a gummy exudation.

The tree grows naturally from Newfoundland, Quebec and Ontario to northeastern Minnesota, northern Wisconsin and northern Michigan, and from the high mountains of eastern Tennessee and western North Carolina through Pennsylvania, New York, New England and New Brunswick, chiefly at the higher elevations. Preferring moist sites, it is found along lake shores, mountain streams, the

Maine Forest Service

Even in winter the Mountain-Ash is a distinctive and decorative tree

Devereux Butcher
The Mountain-Ash is a small tree, 20 to 40 feet in height. Its trunk is 4 to 12 inches in diameter

Six to 8 inches long, leaves are made up of from 13
to 17 lanceolate, acute taper-pointed leaflets. The bright
red, berry-like fruit ripens in September after leaves turn

Appearing in May or June, flowers of the
Mountain-Ash are small and white and grow
on short stems in large flat-topped clusters

borders of swamps and in damp woods. It also thrives in
drier situations on rocky hillsides.

The alternate, odd-pinnately compound, green or reddish stemmed leaves, six to eight inches long are made
up of from thirteen to seventeen lanceolate, acute taper-
pointed leaflets, two to four inches long and one-fourth
to one inch wide. The margins are sharply toothed,
smooth and dark yellow-green above, paler and sometimes hairy below. They turn a bright clear yellow before falling in the autumn.

In May or June after the leaves are fully grown, the
small white flowers appear on short, stout stems in large
flat-topped clusters, three to four inches across, at the
ends of the branchlets. The bright red, berry-like fruit,
about one-fourth of an inch in diameter, ripens in September after the leaves have turned. Unless eaten by
birds, they may remain on the tree until spring. The light
chestnut-brown seeds, rounded at the apex and pointed at
the base, are about an eighth of an inch long.

The bark is about an eighth of an inch thick, even on
mature trees. It is light gray and smooth, but may be
irregularly broken into small, appressed, plate-like scales.
The light, soft, close-grained wood is made up of pale
brown heartwood and lighter colored sapwood. Because
of the small size of the tree, it is of no economic value.

Many names have been applied to this tree, including
mountain sumac, wine tree, life-of-man, rowan-berry,
service-berry, dogberry, elder-leaved sumac and "Miss-
mossey." Its slender, spreading branches, graceful leaves,
attractive flowers and large clusters of showy red fruit,
which hang at the ends of the twigs in autumn and early
winter, make this a handsome and conspicuous tree at
any season of the year. It is often cultivated as an ornamental tree or shrub in the northeastern states and southern Canada, and is commonly transplanted from the forests to the dooryards of country homes. In the mountains of Tennessee and North Carolina, home remedies
are made from the juice of the fruit.

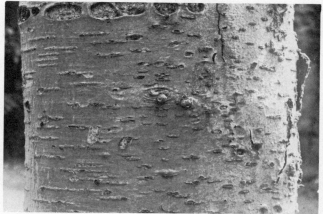

Bark of Mountain-Ash is light gray and
smooth, but may be broken into small,
irregular scales

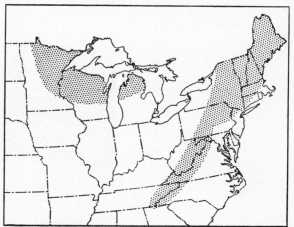

Natural range of the American Mountain-Ash

KENTUCKY COFFEETREE

Gymnocladus dioicus (Linnaeus) Koch

THE Kentucky coffeetree is the sole North American representative of the genus *Gymnocladus*. The only other species is in southern China.

W. R. Lazenby

The thick, blunt-tipped twigs are a characteristic of the winter tree

U. S. Forest Service

Heavy, ascending branches form a high, narrow, irregularly rounded crown

From southern Ontario and western New York to Minnesota and eastern Nebraska, southward through eastern Oklahoma to northern Louisiana, and on rich bottomlands within the Appalachian Mountains to middle Tennessee, the coffeetree grows as a solitary specimen or, rarely, in groups.

It reaches heights of one hundred and ten feet and five feet in diameter, but more usually is forty to eighty feet high with diameters of two to three feet. Open-grown trunks may be ten to twelve feet tall, with three or four heavy ascending branches turning slightly outward to form a high, narrow and irregularly round crown. Under forest conditions, trunks may be clear for seventy feet.

Gymnocladus, meaning "naked branch" is of Greek origin. The leaves break out late in the spring and drop early in the fall. During six months or more the tree shows no signs of life, so that the French of southern Canada refer to it as "Chicot," or "dead tree," and the southern mountaineers as "stump tree."

The minute leaf buds are hidden in hairy cavities of the bark or in the notches of the heart-shaped leaf scars. The large doubly compound leaf is one to three feet long and often two feet wide, with five to nine pinnately compound secondary leaves branching from the main stem. Each of some forty to sixty small, smooth-margined, abruptly pointed leaflets are two to two and a half inches long and arranged opposite one another on a central stem. The secondary leaf stalks often occur in pairs, but seldom in direct opposition. The large leaves, taken as units, grow alternately along the twigs. Their stalks are thickened at the base, while the first or second basal pair of leaflets are usually slightly lobed, and somewhat larger than the others. They are lustrous on the upper side and pale beneath. In early autumn the leaflets turn yellow and fall separately.

For a week or ten days in June, clusters of greenish purple flowers hang inconspicuously among the new leaves. Male and female flowers occur on separate trees, to which the specific name *dioicus* refers. This is derived from Greek words meaning "two-houses." The pollen-bearing clusters are three to four inches long, while the pistillate or seed-producers are six to twelve inches long and slightly hairy.

Belonging to the family *Leguminosae*, coffeetree is a podbearer after the manner of the bean and pea. The purplish brown fruit is one of the largest tree pods of this continent, being six to ten inches long, one to two inches broad, thick and full. They mature in one season and often persist, dry and rattling, into the winter. Each pod encloses six or more hard, round, flat, dark reddish brown seeds about three-quarters of an inch in diameter separated by a thick, dark colored layer of inedible, sticky pulp. The name coffeetree recalls efforts of early settlers to use the heavy bitter seeds as a source of a coffee-like beverage.

The rough, deeply fissured bark is three-quarters to one inch thick and varies from dark gray to brown. A reddish inner bark may often be seen at the bottom of the longitudinal furrows, which are separated by sharp, scaly ridges.

The light red to reddish brown wood is coarse-grained, medium hard and a cubic foot weighs about forty-three pounds when air dry. It polishes well, is durable in contact with the soil, and is used locally for railroad ties, fence posts, poles, and construction material. Too sparsely distributed to be considered commercially important, the lumber is usually sold in combination with miscellaneous hardwoods.

Leaves are three to four feet long with forty to sixty leaflets, are lustrous above, and the flat pods contain six or more seeds

The dark gray or brown bark is deeply fissured, and is three-quarters to one inch thick and often reveals traces of reddish inner bark

From "Some American Trees," courtesy Macmillan Co.

R. Lynn Emerick

George J. Baetzhold

Pistillate flowers occur on long pedicels, and, like the staminate ones, are greenish purple. The two sexes are borne on separate trees

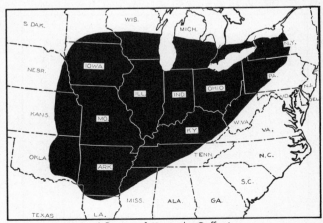

Natural Range of Kentucky Coffeetree

HONEYLOCUST

Common honeylocust, Honey shucks locust, Sweet bean tree

Gleditsia triacanthos Linnaeus

THE honeylocust, with its open plume-like crown of finely divided foliage and its thorny trunk and branches, occupies a great inland region of moist, fertile soils along meadows, stream borders, and lake shores from Western Pennsylvania to southeastern South Dakota south in Nebraska, Kansas and Oklahoma to eastern Texas, east to Alabama and north along the western slopes of the Appalachian Mountains. This species is nowhere abundant and usually grows singly or scattered in groups.

It is a tree of medium size with a short bole often divided near the ground. Ordinarily some seventy-five feet high with trunk diameters of two or three feet, the maximum height is about 140 feet with occasional trunks six feet in diameter. Honeylocust reaches its best growth in the valleys of small streams in southern Indiana and Illinois. Everywhere the slender, spreading, somewhat pendulous branches form an open, flat-topped crown.

While belonging to the *Leguminosae* or pea family, botanists classify it with Kentucky coffeetree and redbud, rather than with the black locust, *Robinia pseudoacacia*, with which it is often confused. Some twelve species of *Gleditsia* are scattered throughout North and South America, southwestern Asia, China, Japan, and west tropical Africa. Two species and a hybrid occur in eastern North America, of which honeylocust, the largest, is a tree of secondary commercial importance. In 1753 Linnaeus named the genus *Gleditsia* in honor of Johann Gottlieb Gleditsch, then professor of botany at Berlin. The forked spines are recognized in *triacanthos*, meaning "three-thorned."

The compound and frequently doubly compound, or bipinnate leaves are six to eight inches long. They are arranged alternately on the branches, but the several

Maryland State Department of Forestry
The crown of Honeylocust is like a great green plume

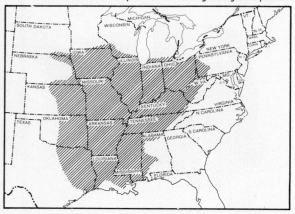

Natural range of Honeylocust

Devereux Butcher
A Honeylocust tree with typical distribution of thorns on the trunk and lower branches. Proper grafting and budding methods produce entirely thornless trees

pinnae or leaf stems, have eighteen to twenty-eight small oval or slightly pointed leaflets in opposite pairs. The leaves are dark green and lustrous above and dull yellow-green below, and they turn pale, clear yellow in the autumn.

From May to July, depending on the location, when the leaves are nearly full grown, flowers of both sexes hang from the axils of the previous season's leaves in short, inconspicuous, greenish yellow clusters. The pollen-bearing blossoms are usually distinct from those which develop seeds. Both sometimes occur on the same tree. They are fragrant and sought by bees for their nectar.

Flat, strap-shaped, dark brown or purplish, twisted pods a foot or more long, mature in autumn and hang on the trees until early winter. The numerous, brown, oval bean-like seeds enclosed within the pods are separated by a sweet and succulent pulp. They are eaten by cattle, deer, rabbits, foxes and squirrels which scatter the hard-shelled seeds over broad areas. Bobwhite and starlings also feed on them. Names like honeylocust, honey shucks locust, or sweet bean tree are derived from the sweet pulp in the young pod. These locust trees begin to bear seed crops at an early age, but large crops are seldom produced more often than every three to five years.

On young trunks and branches the bark is smooth and grayish-brown, while on mature trunks it is a quarter of an inch to three-quarters of an inch thick, divided into narrow ridges by deep, longitudinal fissures. It has a tendency to peel off in strips, and is grayish brown to nearly black. Relatively large, light colored lenticels are noticeable on the smoother areas. The trunk, branches, and even the zigzag branchlets often bristle with long, slender, forked thorns. These grow from deep in the wood and are developments of true buds. Occasionally they put out leaves. A variety, *inermis*, has no thorns.

The thick, fibrous roots are deep and wide-spreading, but unlike most other legumes they are without nitrogen-fixing nodules and do not add this element to the soil.

The bright brown or reddish heartwood, with its thin layer of pale yellow sapwood, is hard, strong coarse-grained, takes a high polish, and is durable in contact with the soil. A cubic foot when air dry weighs about forty-four pounds. Its ability to resist decay encourages its use for fence posts and railroad ties, but the supply is limited. It is also used for rough construction, furniture, interior finish, and turnery.

The ability of honeylocust to adjust to various soils and climates, and the ease with which it may be transplanted, result in its wide use for ornamental, shade, and hedge purposes. The species matures at about 120 years, but may live longer. In general it is sturdy, windfirm, free from diseases, and is not subject to borers.

Buckingham Studios, Inc.

Pale yellow-green, pollen-bearing blossoms grow in drooping racemes among the new foliage

George J. Baetzhold

Long, forked spines grow singly or in clusters from the hard, gray-brown bark

George J. Baetzhold

Twisted, strap-shaped pods a foot or more long show reddish brown among the finely divided compound and doubly compound leaves

AMERICAN YELLOWWOOD
Virgilia
Cladrastis lutea (Michaux f.) K. Koch

A SMALL TREE of very limited range, American yellowwood nevertheless has become well known because of its value as an ornamental tree. It grows naturally only in extreme western North Carolina, on the western slopes of the high mountains of eastern Tennessee, and in central Tennessee and Kentucky, northern Alabama, south-

Dr. E. A. Hubbard

The short trunk usually divides six or seven feet from the ground into two or three large ascending stems

Extension Service

American Yellowwood attains a height of sixty feet and is broad and graceful when not crowded by other trees

ern Missouri and northern Arkansas. It prefers fertile, well-drained soils, and usually occurs in river valleys and on limestone ridges and slopes. It often overhangs the banks of mountain streams. The tree is particularly abundant along the streams that drain the western slopes of the Allegheny Mountains and flow into the Ohio River.

Sometimes American yellowwood attains a height of sixty feet, and develops a short trunk of from one to two and occasionally three feet in diameter. The trunk usually divides six or seven feet from the ground into two or three large, ascending stems. These divide into many slender, wide-spreading and more or less pendulous, brittle branches, to form a graceful, broad, rounded top, when not crowded by other trees.

The twigs, when they first appear, are covered with fine, soft hairs, but soon become smooth. During their

first season they are light brown, tinged more or less with green, are very smooth and lustrous, and are marked with numerous dark-colored lenticels. In their first winter they are bright red-brown, the following year a dark dull brown. The short hairy winter buds are nearly surrounded by leaf scars.

The thin, smooth, grayish bark resembles that of the beech, the lighter inner bark showing in streaks where the outer bark becomes fissured in growth.

The compound leaves are from eight to twelve inches long with five to eleven leaflets, three to four inches in length and one and a half to two inches wide. The terminal leaflet, rather shorter than the others, is from three to three and a half inches wide. Smooth and bright

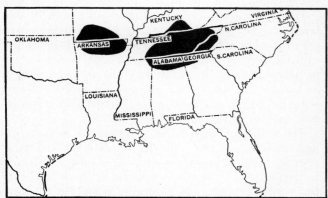

Natural range of American Yellowwood

When the outer bark becomes fissured in growth, the lighter inner bark shows in streaks

The flat, bean-like pods, two to three inches long, are full grown in August, and ripen in September

green above and lighter beneath, the leaflets turn bright yellow late in the autumn.

About the middle of June the delicate, pea-like fragrant white flowers appear in loose clusters twelve to fourteen inches long and five to six inches wide. Hanging from the twig ends on slender stalks, they are very showy against the background of young leaves in various tints of green. The small, flat, bean-like pods, two to four inches long, are fully grown by the middle of August, ripen in September, and soon fall. Each pod contains a few flattened, bony seeds.

As the name of the species implies, the heartwood is a bright, clear yellow. When exposed to the air it changes to light brown, or yellow streaked with brown. The thin sapwood is nearly white. The wood is hard, heavy and fine-textured, a cubic foot weighing about thirty-six pounds in an air dry condition. It is occasionally used for gunstocks, and the heartwood yields a yellow dye. Other names for American yellowwood are gopher wood and virgilia, the latter commonly applied to it by nurserymen. *Cladrastis* is from the Greek meaning fragile branch, referring to the brittle twigs. There are only three other known species of *Cladrastis*—two in western China and one in Japan.

American yellowwood is often planted in the eastern United States as an ornamental tree. It is hardy as far north as northern New York and Ontario. It is easily raised from seed and root cuttings, grows on many different kinds of soil and is very resistant to insect and fungus attack. Its desirability as an ornamental was discovered a century ago, and seeds were sent to Europe where it is now quite widely grown.

Appearing in June, the pea-like, fragrant white flowers form loose clusters 12 to 14 inches long. The compound leaves have 5 to 11 leaflets

BLACK LOCUST

Yellow locust, False acacia
Robinia pseudoacacia Linnaeus

THE BLACK LOCUST, or false acacia, *Robinia pseudoacacia*, sometimes called yellow locust, belongs to the pea or legume family, and has the ability to add nitrogen to the soil. The species originally was native only to the Appalachian Mountains from Pennsylvania to Alabama, and part of Arkansas, eastern Oklahoma and southern Missouri but now has been planted successfully in most states. In its natural range, black locust grows along streams, in mountain coves or on the borders of forests, usually in mixture with other hardwood trees. In many parts of the country it has escaped from cultivation and has so established itself as to be generally accepted as native. It prefers deep, sweet, well-drained fertile loam and soils with a limestone origin having brown or reddish brown subsoils, but will grow almost anywhere except in soils that are poorly drained or very wet, heavy or acid.

Trees may attain heights of forty to eighty feet and trunk diameters of two to four feet, but they seldom live longer than 100 years.

The open branching and frond-like leaves give the crown a feathery appearance. The alternate and pinnately compound yellow green leaves are eight to fourteen inches long and composed of seven to nineteen rounded leaflets, each on a slender stalk.

W. R. Mattoon

Maryland State Dept. of Forestry

Black Locust forks frequently and develops a rather uneven crown which gives a feathery appearance to the tree when in full leaf. The seeds in their bean-like pods, flutter and rattle on the tree all winter

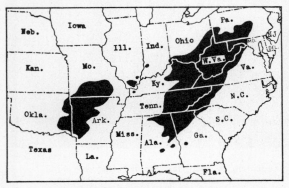

Natural range of Black Locust

The pinnately compound leaves are alternate on the twig, and each of the seven to nineteen oval leaflets, borne opposite each other, form the full leaf

They develop in April or early May. During rainy days and on the approach of evening, the leaflets fold and the entire leaf droops slightly, after the manner of the true acacias. By the end of September or occasionally early October, the leaves turn a pale, clear yellow, before dropping.

The dark, reddish brown, rough, deeply fissured bark is an inch to an inch and a half thick.

The twigs are pale green and silvery in the spring, turning reddish brown in the summer and are marked with scattered, pale lenticels. They bear pairs of short woody spines or thorns like those of a rose.

The new leaves are scarcely formed when clusters of fragrant white pea-like blossoms appear over the entire tree. These are perfect flowers, having a pistil, as well as stamens, and are filled with nectar which attracts bees and other insects. From these come thin, smooth, bean-like pods with four to eight small, dark orange seeds that ripen during September and October and hang on the trees through the winter.

Black locust wood weighs about forty-eight pounds to the cubic foot when air dry, and is stronger and stiffer than white oak. Freshly cut wood is greenish yellow to dark brown, coarse-grained and surrounded by creamy white sapwood.

Black locust is the wood favored for insulator pins used on the cross arms of telephone and power transmission lines. Approximately 18,000 cords of high quality timber were necessary to make the 25,000,000 pins manufactured in a single year for this purpose. Smaller amounts go into the hubs of wagon wheels, treenails to pin ship timber together, fence posts, mine timbers, poles and tool handles.

Black locust was introduced in Europe during the early part of the seventeenth century by Jean and Vespasien Robin, herbalists to the King of France and, bearing their name, is now the most generally accepted American tree in Europe. Because of its wide-spreading fibrous root system, its tendency to send up shoots from the roots, and the ability common to this and most other leguminous plants to develop nitrogen-fixing nodules on its roots, black locust is unusually well adapted to soil erosion control.

Serious injury and disfigurement frequently follow attacks by the locust borer, and in some parts of the East a leaf miner gives the foliage a ragged, burned appearance.

Racemes of fragrant white pea-like flowers appear in May and June. They produce bean-like seed pods with four to eight seeds

The deeply furrowed orange-brown bark of the trunk is an inch or more thick

313

AMERICAN HOLLY

White holly

Ilex opaca Aiton

THE GLOSSY, yellow-green, spiny leaves and red berries of holly are usually associated with the Christmas season. The tree is less well known than the foliage, but is of economic importance in several southern states, where it frequently grows forty to fifty feet high, and occasionally eighty feet. The trunk may be one or two feet in diameter, twenty feet long, and it tapers rapidly. Occasionally specimens four feet in diameter have been reported. The crown is frequently narrowly pyramidal.

Superficially resembling the English holly, *Ilex aquifolium*, Linn., the American holly grows naturally from the coast of Massachusetts, southward to central Florida, west to eastern Texas, north to southeastern Missouri and to central West Virginia. In hardwood bottomlands it grows in association with the oaks, and on the flat, sandy coast lands among the pines. Although capable of growing on poor soil, best growth is achieved on deep, fertile, moist soil, and the largest trees are found on the rich bottomlands of eastern Texas and southern Arkansas. Growth is slow, but trees may reach an age of one hundred years or more.

The spiny-toothed, alternate evergreen leaves are thick, leathery, and firm, from two to four inches long and one to one and a half inches wide. They are dark, shiny green above and paler, tending toward yellow on the lower surface. The midrib and lateral veins are prominent on the lower surface, and the stout stem, or petiole, is half an inch long and grooved. Leaves remain on the tree for three years and are shed in the spring.

Ilex, the classical name of the evergreen oak of southern Europe, with leaves similar to holly, is one of five genera of the large family *Aquifoliacea*, meaning "trees with needles on their leaves." Thus the Latin name of both family and genus refers to the spiny character of the leaves. The name holly may be derived from its early use during the holy week. Of thirteen members of the genus *Ilex*, growing in the United States, *Ilex opaca* is the only one of economic importance.

The inconspicuous four-petaled white flowers appear in small clusters in the axils of the young leaves, or scattered along the shoots of the current year's growth. The flowers of the two sexes are borne on separate trees. The pistillate ones develop into small, red or yellow berry-like fruits and remain on the tree through the winter. The pulpy covering is relished by birds, but the four hard, ribbed nutlets within each berry are not

American Holly frequently grows forty or fifty feet high and develops a dense, pyramidal crown with many short, nearly horizontal branches

314

digested, and new seedlings are frequently the result of distribution by birds. Although attractive to birds, the berries should not be eaten by human beings.

The smooth, light gray bark is approximately a half inch thick and becomes roughened by wart-like excrescences in old trees.

The wood is hard, tough, close-grained, not strong, but moderately heavy, weighing thirty-six to forty pounds to the cubic foot when air dry. The heartwood is creamy or ivory white when first cut, turning brownish with age or exposure, and takes a high polish. The sapwood is wide and whiter than the heartwood. It is used for cabinet work, turnery, small musical instruments, and, because of its similarity to ivory, as keys for pianos and organs. Its fine grain makes it useful for wood engraving.

Holly is tolerant of shade, will recover from suppression after growing years under heavy shade.

A deep taproot supported by numerous spreading laterals makes possible the transplanting of young trees. The best time to move them is in the fall, when the new wood is nearly ripened, or in the spring before new growth starts. When transplanting wild hollies from the woods, the tops should be severely pruned and most of the remaining leaves removed.

Holly berries may be sown in beds and covered with a heavy mulch until the spring of the second year, when the seed will germinate. Thereafter, the mulch should be removed and the seedlings given partial shade. Cuttings of the current year's ripened wood, with a little of the two-year-old wood and three or four leaves, made between August and December, may be rooted under a glass frame, or in a greenhouse. These should be set slanting in about six inches of mixed peat moss and soil, with the leaves lying flat on the surface.

J. Horace McFarland

The spiny-toothed, leathery, alternate evergreen leaves remain three years on the branches and are shed in the spring. The leaves and berries, are widely used for Christmas decorations

The bark is light gray, approximately a half inch thick and becomes roughened on old trees

Warren D. Brush

The inconspicuous, white, four-petaled male and female flowers, quite alike in appearance, are borne in the axils of the young leaves or are scattered along the current year's growth, on separate trees. The staminate flowers occur in clusters of three to nine, while the pistillate are solitary or in twos or threes

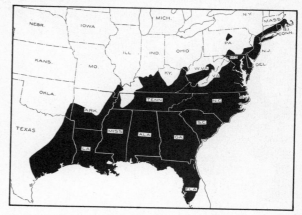

Natural range of American Holly

315

SUGAR MAPLE

Hard maple, Rock maple
Acer saccharum Marsh.

SUGAR MAPLE grows naturally in every state east of the Great Plains except Florida, South Carolina and Delaware, but is most important in the northeast and in the higher elevations of the southern Appalachian Mountains. The name, sugar maple, refers to the spring crop of sugar and syrup that is boiled from its sweet sap. In autumn the leaves change from green to brilliant reds and yellows, and are an outstanding feature of the northern landscape. Open-grown maple trees have a short trunk and a compact, globular crown. In the forest the tree lifts a relatively small rounded crown high upon a long trunk, to attain total heights of from seventy to 130 feet. Forest-grown maples are frequently two or three feet in diameter.

The smooth, silvery bark of young trees becomes darker, more broken and deeply grooved as the tree matures. Quite often conspicuous shreddy flakes are developed.

Distinguishing features of most maples include the five-lobe leaf, the delicate, pointed buds which grow opposite one another, the double-winged fruit or key, and the opposite branching. Large quantities of fertile seeds mature in the early summer from inconspicuous, long-stemmed flowers

In winter the relatively short stem and
brushy effect of many branches is revealed

Devereux Butcher

U. S. Forest Service

The symmetrically rounded head of
an open-grown Sugar Maple tree

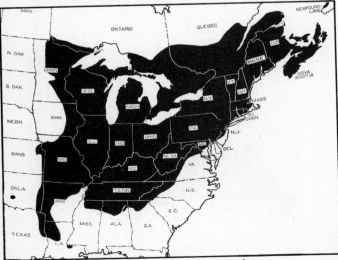

Natural range of Sugar Maple

316

that appear with the news leaves in April or May. Staminate and pistillate flowers are in separate clusters on the same trees, but occasionally a tree may have flowers of only one sex. *Acer*, the scientific name of the maple family, means hard or sharp. The Romans used European maple for pikes and lances, as well as for tables and other furniture. *Saccharum* refers to the sweet sap. Most widely known as sugar maple or hard maple, this species also is known as sugar tree and rock maple, while a quite similar species is known as black maple. Nearly a hundred species of maple are distributed over the northern hemisphere, of which thirteen are native within the United States. Maple trees and shrubs extend across the equator to the mountains of Java, and reach toward South America in the uplands of Central America.

The wood is known to the lumber trade as hard maple, and the bulk of maple lumber is of this species. The wide white sapwood may stain to a pale brown if improperly seasoned. The heartwood is light reddish brown, and the luster of each helps distinguish sugar maple from other maple wood. A cubic foot of air-dry maple weighs forty-four pounds. Although lighter than white oak, the wood is stronger and stiffer, and ranks as one of our more valuable hardwoods. Sugar maple may make up as much as three-fourths of the total stand of maple in the United States, and Michigan has the largest amounts. It is used for flooring, shoe trees, agricultural implements, musical instruments, furniture and a wide variety of materials which need a strong, firm, close-grained wood able to stay in place and capable of taking a polish. Accidental forms, with contorted grain, known as curly maple and bird's eye maple, are prized for cabinet-making.

Maple syrup and sugar are important spring crops on many farms in Vermont, New York, Ohio, Pennsylvania, and Michigan. Ordinarily forty-five to fifty gallons are boiled down to make a gallon of syrup, and fifteen to twenty gallons of sap are secured from most of the trees. The average tree produces two and eight-tenths pounds of sugar, or else twenty-six-hundredths of a gallon of syrup. Eight pounds of sugar are produced from one gallon of syrup.

Capable of thriving under a variety of conditions, sugar maple grows especially well on gravelly, slightly alkaline soils. A few plantations have been established for sugar, as well as lumber production, but the slow growth does not encourage such an investment. It is produced readily from seed and is an important species in the management of many northern forests.

Although not so well adapted to city street conditions as some of the other maples, sugar maple is a favorite along suburban streets and country roads. Seedlings and small trees are easily transplanted.

None of the many insect and fungus pests is serious enough to discourage planting sugar maple for ornamental purposes. The sugar maple borer kills large limbs and occasionally entire trees by boring under the bark and in the outer sapwood. Similar damage is done by the larva of the leopard moth. The white grub of a twig pruner occasionally mars the trees and litters the ground by cutting off twig ends in the early autumn. Tent caterpillars, white-marked tussock moths and a green-striped maple worm may work on the leaves, but seldom consume all of them. Other insidious insect enemies are the scales that attach themselves to the young tender bark.

Warren D. Brush

Typical of most maples are the five-lobed leaf and the double-winged fruit or key. The wings of the Sugar Maple key form an acute angle

The delicate, pointed winter buds of the Sugar Maple grow opposite each other along the twig, and they are tinged with purple

U. S. Forest Service

The ash-gray bark breaks up into hard, flinty flakes

BLACK MAPLE

Black sugar maple

Acer nigrum Michaux f

BLACK MAPLE resembles sugar maple so closely that some botanists consider it a variety of the latter rather than a separate species. As evidence of this, it is pointed out that some trees have characteristics that are inter-

When grown in the open, Black Maple has a tall, dense, compact crown, but in the forest a tall trunk supports a shallow, flat-topped crown

mediate between the two. However, because black maple shows quite distinct characters, it can be considered a separate species.

Black maple does not grow as far north, south or east as sugar maple, its range covering extreme southern Quebec, southern Ontario, southern Michigan and Wisconsin, southern Minnesota and southward, including the greater part of Missouri, eastern Kentucky, eastern Tennessee, extreme western North Carolina and Virginia and all of West Virginia, Pennsylvania and New York, and western New England. Like the sugar maple, it occurs under a wide range of soil and moisture conditions. In

in other localities well within its range it does not occur at all.

Although commonly smaller, it sometimes attains as great a size as the sugar maple. It occasionally reaches a height of eighty to 100 feet and a trunk diameter of three to four feet. Under forest conditions the bole is long and columnar, with a shallow, flat-topped crown; in the open, the stout, spreading or often upright branches form an ovoid top, the branches gradually bending outward in old age to make a broad, round-topped crown.

In winter, the twigs, which are stouter than those of sugar maple, help to identify Black Maple

The twigs are usually stouter than those of sugar maple, and have conspicuous warty lenticels. They are orange-green and hairy when they first appear, becoming orange-brown and smooth during their first year and pale grayish brown the following season. Another characteristic that helps to distinguish black maple from sugar maple in winter is the larger, more hairy buds of the former, which are ovoid, pointed, and an eighth of an inch long, with dark red-brown, acute scales covered with fine white hairs on the outer surface and often slightly hairy on the margins.

Black maple is distinguishable from sugar maple by its thicker, three-, or occasionally five-lobed, more or less drooping leaves which, on the under surface, are fine hairy, as also are the leaf stems. The lobes taper to a slender point and are separated by broad, rounded sinuses. At maturity they are dull dark green and smooth above, yellowish green below and hairy, particularly along the veins. The stout, usually pendent, leaf stems are from three to five inches long.

The flowers are similar to those of sugar maple, but generally open a few days later, when the leaves are about a third grown. They are yellowish green, about a fourth of an inch long, the male and female blossoms occurring in separate clusters or in the same clusters on the same or on different trees.

In the double-winged, U-shaped fruit or samara, the wings, about an inch long, are slightly more divergent than those of sugar maple. A smooth, bright red-brown seed a quarter of an inch long, is enclosed at the base of each wing. While some seed is produced almost every year, abundant crops come only at intervals of from three to five years. Much of the seed is not fertile and its vitality is not high, so that the proportion of seeds that germinate is rather small. Reproduction is mainly by seed, as the species does not sprout well from the stump. Seed should be collected and planted in the fall, because spring is the time of germination.

Black maple, also often called black sugar maple, takes its name from the bark, which on mature trees is deeply furrowed, and sometimes is almost black. On young stems and on branches it is thin, smooth and pale gray. The wood weighs forty-three pounds to the cubic foot when dry. It is similar to that of sugar maple and is used for the same purposes, both woods being sold as hard

Devereux Butcher

Black Maple leaves usually are three-lobed, a characteristic that further helps to distinguish this tree from sugar maple. The wings of the keys or samaras are slightly more divergent than those of sugar maple

maple. The trees of both species are used for the production of maple syrup and sugar.

As with the sugar maple, the growth of black maple is slow, making its best growth on deep, rich, moist, well-drained soils. It is long-lived and reaches an age of from 300 to 400 years.

Fire may cause serious injury to the tree because of its comparatively thin bark. It is subject to attack by numerous insect enemies, the most serious being the maple borer, which works under the bark and may kill the branches or even an entire tree. The branches are not so brittle and easily broken as are those of silver maple.

Like the sugar maple, black maple is a desirable shade tree because of its dense foliage. The fall coloring of the foliage, ranging from bright yellow to scarlet and crimson, makes it especially attractive at that season.

On young trunks and on branches, the bark is thin, smooth and pale grey, while on old trunks, it is deeply furrowed and dark

Devereux Butcher

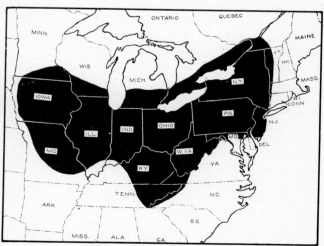

Natural range of Black Maple

SILVER MAPLE
White maple, Soft maple, River maple, Silverleaf maple
Acer saccharinum Linnaeus

Devereux Butcher

Open-grown Silver Maples develop a short trunk that divides into several large ascending limbs with long pendulous branches

rounded crown. Forest-grown trees have trunks that rise clear of limbs for thirty to fifty feet before the branches form a medium broad crown sixty to eighty feet high. It is most abundant in the Ohio basin, where it reaches 125 feet.

During the first mild days of late winter or early spring, when the leaf buds have scarcely begun to swell, the yellowish green flowers appear. Growing in

U. S. Forest Service

Bark on trunk and larger limbs of mature trees is thin, gray, and broken into broad, flaky scales

Devereux Butcher

SILVER MAPLE, sometimes called soft maple, is one of sixty or seventy species of the *Acer* family distributed widely over the northern hemisphere, with one species south of the equator in Java.

It is found as far north as New Brunswick and westward across southern Quebec and southern Ontario to Michigan, Wisconsin and Minnesota, south to eastern Oklahoma and northwestern Florida. It is seldom found on the Atlantic coast or on the high Appalachian Mountains. It never forms pure stands, but grows scattered through the forest in the moist soil of bottomlands, or along the borders of swamps and sluggish streams. It endures moderate shade, tolerating more shade in wet sites than in dry ones. Silver maple seldom lives more than 125 years.

In the open, silver maple develops a short trunk measuring two to four feet in diameter, and dividing into several large ascending limbs that terminate in long pendulous branches to form a broad,

320

short-stalked, thick clusters on the twigs of the preceding year, the staminate and pistillate flowers appear on the same or different trees. Later, leaves appear borne on slender drooping stems. They are pale green and shiny above, smooth and silvery beneath, and measure fuor to six inches long and nearly as broad. They are five-lobed, deeply indented, sharply toothed with an even or heart-shaped base. The fruit, suspended in clusters on slender stalks, is made up of two thin, divergent wings one to two inches long. Some seed is produced every year, but abundant crops occur at irregular intervals. When they fall on moist soil, germination follows shortly and, before the end of the summer, have produced plants with several pairs of leaves. Silver maple sprouts readily from the stump, but trees begin to lose the ability to sprout or coppice after the trunk diameter exceeds a foot.

The thin gray bark on trunk and larger limbs of old trees is broken into broad scales which flake off readily, while on younger trees and on branches of mature ones it is smooth, gray, or slightly tinged with brown. Twigs are green or reddish, and when broken, give out a rank odor. Leaf buds at the ends of the twigs are encased with three or four pairs of red scales and measure about one-quarter inch in length. Buds along the sides of the twigs are borne on short stalks and are usually accompanied by the lustrous flower buds.

The light brown wood weighs thirty-four pounds to the cubic foot when air dry, is strong, brittle, close-grained and rather hard. The sapwood is pale to almost white and, with the heartwood, takes a good polish and is used for cheap furniture, flooring, interior finish, woodenware, veneer and fuel. Considerable quantities are burned for charcoal, wood acetate and other products of distillation. Silver maple is sometimes mixed with the wood of other maples, but is not as strong, hard or heavy.

It is widely planted as an ornamental tree along roadsides and around homes, where its principal attribute is the comparative rapidity with which it grows. The tree, however, is not as well adapted for this purpose as are the sugar and red maples, because its limbs are brittle and are quite subject to injury by wind and ice storms. Large silver maples in cultivation are sometimes pruned as a means of helping them resist such damage.

The cottony maple scale, a sucking insect, is an enemy of the tree; while the wood is attacked by the boring leopard moth. Mature trees often have hollow trunks or show heart rot due to attack by fungus diseases. When growing in the forest, this tendency to become hollow makes the tree valuable to many forms of wildlife such as raccoon, opossum, and owls. Owing to the thinness of its bark, fire is another serious enemy of the species, although the usually moist sites in which the tree grows somewhat reduces the fire danger.

There are several varieties of silver maple known as cutleaf maples. These have twigs and branches that are more drooping than those of silver maple, and leaves that are more deeply cut and decorative. These varieties are used ornamentally in parks and on estates.

Warren D. Brush

Staminate flowers occur on the same or different trees from the pistillate, and are yellowish green

Warren D. Brush

Leaves are green above, and silvery beneath, while the fruit which ripens in spring occurs in pairs or keys

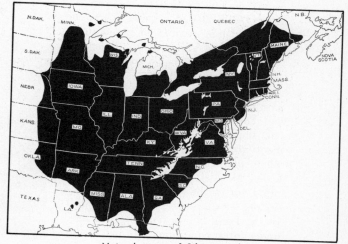

Natural range of Silver Maple

RED MAPLE

Swamp maple, Water maple, Scarlet maple
Acer rubrum Linnaeus

EXTENDING over much of the eastern half of the United States and into Canada is the red maple, one of thirteen or more of the family *Aceraceae*, native to North America, and one of four eastern

The Red Maple is most conspicuous in autumn when its brilliance adds greatly to the coloring of eastern forests

species to attain tree size. Because it occurs on low ground or in swamps, along the banks of streams where it will stand long periods of inundation, and on moist soils, it is frequently known as swamp maple. It thrives in any moist fertile soil.

Usually associated with other lowland trees such as black ash, the gums and cottonwoods, cypress and water oak, the largest sizes and best development are in the lower Ohio Valley, while greatest abundance is in the lower Mississippi Valley. Growth is rapid during the early stages, but trees seldom attain ages greater than 150 years. Long before reaching this age, under forest conditions, a broad, round

crown is developed with a moderately long clear trunk, the whole tree averaging sixty to ninety feet in height and one and a half to two and a half feet in diameter at breast height. Occasionally trees grow to a height of 125 feet and are five feet in diameter.

Red maple is best known by its three- to five-lobed, doubly toothed, simple, bright green leaves which are three to four inches long, nearly as broad, and occur opposite one another on the twigs. While smooth above, the leaves are finely hairy beneath and have slender stems or petioles two to four inches long. Although basically green, the stem may be tinged with red, and in the early autumn the leaves turn to brilliant shades of scarlet, frequently mixed with orange, giving one of many reasons for the Latin name *Acer rubrum* which translated is red maple.

The small but conspicuous clusters of ruby-red flowers open in March or April

Open-grown Red Maple develops a short trunk and a broad oval crown, but in the forest a broad, round crown with moderately long trunk

considerably before the leaves. They occur as distinct male and female blossoms and may be on the same tree or segregated on different trees. By spring or early summer the fertile pistillate blossoms have developed into the characteristic

U. S. Forest Service

In March or April the ruby staminate blossoms appear. Characteristically the stems of the three- to five-lobed leaves often are red on the upper side. Bark on young trunks and branches is smooth, but on old trunks it is dark gray and broken into ridges

U. S. Forest Service

George J. Baetzhold

key, sometimes in large, thick, pink clusters.

Red maple wood resembles that of hard maple, but the heartwood is light brown tinged with red, while the sapwood is lighter colored. It is

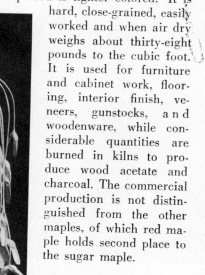

hard, close-grained, easily worked and when air dry weighs about thirty-eight pounds to the cubic foot. It is used for furniture and cabinet work, flooring, interior finish, veneers, gunstocks, and woodenware, while considerable quantities are burned in kilns to produce wood acetate and charcoal. The commercial production is not distinguished from the other maples, of which red maple holds second place to the sugar maple.

U. S. Forest Service

Clusters of newly formed maple keys

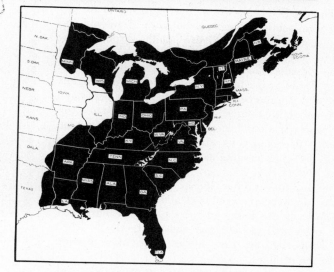

Natural range of Red Maple

MOUNTAIN MAPLE

Acer spicatum Lamarck

THIS is the smallest of the eastern maples. It some-times reaches a height of twenty-five to thirty feet with a short trunk six to eight inches in diameter, but more often is a large shrub. It is found at the higher eleva-tions inland, but it comes down to sea level on the Maine

Devereux Butcher

Although usually a very small tree, Moun-tain Maple sometimes reaches a height of twenty-five or thirty feet. It rarely grows singly

coast. The range extends from Newfoundland to eastern Saskatchewan, south through northeastern Minnesota and Iowa to central Michigan; also south through New Brunswick, Nova Scotia and the northeastern states, and along the Appalachian Mountains to northern Georgia. Mountain maple grows best in moist, rich loam and for-est shade and is quite common on moist, rocky slopes and banks of mountain streams of the northeastern states and Canada, where it often forms the greater part of the un-dergrowth. It reaches its largest size on the western slopes of the high mountains of Tennessee and North Carolina.

The leaves, four to five inches long and broad, are three-lobed or partially five-lobed and sometimes slightly heart-shaped at the base, and the gradually narrowed, pointed lobes are coarsely and sharply toothed. Their slender stems, two to three inches long, often become scarlet in the summer.

In June, after the leaves are fully grown, the small,

greenish yellow flowers, about one-fourth inch across, appear at the terminals of the new growth in erect, many-flowered, long-stemmed spikes three to six inches long. Each flower is on a slender stem one-half to three-fourths of an inch long. Male flowers are borne near the tip of the spike and the female, which grow toward the base, develop into the typical maple key with wings about one-half inch long, which are divergent at an acute or nearly right angle. The fruit is fully grown and bright red or yellow in July, turning brown late in the autumn.

The short trunk of the tree supports an irregular crown of small upright branches and slender branchlets which are light gray and fine hairy at first, becoming smooth during the summer, bright red during their first winter, and gray or pale brown the following season.

The winter buds are pointed, the terminal one an eighth of an inch long with bright red outer scales, the inner

W. H. Ballard

The stout, ascending branches are con-spicuous in winter, with their pale bark. The species often occurs in dense, shrubby clumps

ones becoming at maturity one inch or more in length. The side buds are much smaller.

On the trunk the bark is very thin, reddish brown and smooth or slightly furrowed. The wood is light, soft, close-grained, the heartwood light brown tinged with red, with thick, lighter colored sapwood. When dry, it weighs thirty-three pounds to the cubic foot.

Devereux Butcher

The bark on young stems and on branches is smooth and pale warm gray, while on older trunks it is slightly furrowed, thin, and is brown or reddish brown

Chicago Natural History Museum

The leaves are three-lobed or partially five-lobed; the flowers are in erect, long-stemmed spikes, with the male near the tip and the female near the base

The erect stalks of pale yellow flowers, which develop into red and yellow keys later in the summer, and the light green leaves, which turn in the fall to various shades of orange and scarlet, add to the attractiveness of this little tree. It is occasionally cultivated as an ornamental in parks and in gardens in the northeastern states. Because of its small size and because it requires some shade to be grown successfully, mountain maple fills a niche that few other trees can occupy.

Devereux Butcher

The keys of Mountain Maple, ripening in July, are pale green at first, becoming red, then turning brown in autumn

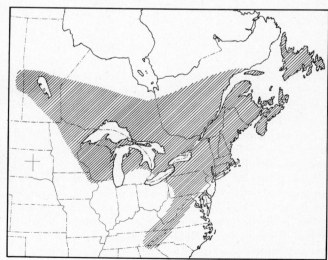

Natural range of Mountain Maple

STRIPED MAPLE

Moosewood, Striped dogwood, Goosefoot maple
Acer pensylvanicum Linnaeus

Devereux Butcher

Striped Maple seldom grows taller than forty feet and often it is much smaller and shrub-like

Scotia and the Gaspé Peninsula of Quebec, along the St. Lawrence River Valley to Ontario in the region north of Lake Superior, south through northern Michigan and eastern Ohio; also south through the northeastern states and along the Appalachian Mountains to northern Georgia.

In the forested areas of northern New England, striped maple often forms a large part of the shrubby undergrowth. It attains its largest size on the slopes of the Great Smoky Mountains of Tennessee and of the Blue Ridge of North Carolina.

The bark on old trunks is an eighth to a quarter of an inch thick, firm, grayish brown, and has rather indistinct darker vertical markings. Stems two to three years old are bright green in summer, with conspicuous, white, lateral markings resulting from growth expansion. Young stems are bright green and smooth at first, turning reddish brown during their first winter.

The winter buds of striped maple are conspicuous—even more so than those of the mountain maple. The terminal buds are stalked, sometimes almost a half inch

The Davey Tree Expert Co.

In winter the tree shows its characteristically ascending branches

ALTHOUGH a larger tree than mountain maple, with which it is often associated, striped maple rarely exceeds a height of forty feet and a trunk diameter of ten inches. The short trunk soon divides into small, upright branches, forming a dense, rounded crown. When not crowded by other trees it has a rather wide top with spreading branches. It often takes on a shrubby form.

Like mountain maple, it prefers the shade of other trees and is often associated with sugar maple, yellow birch, beech, hemlock and red spruce. Inland it usually grows at higher elevations, but on the Maine coast it comes down to sea level. It prefers ample moisture, as along mountain streams. Its range is nearly the same as that of mountain maple. It grows naturally from Nova

long and are covered by two thick, bright red, boat-shaped scales, the inner scales green and leaf-like, becoming a half to two inches long and yellow or rose.

The wood is light, soft, close-grained, pale brown, with thick, lighter colored sapwood made up of as many as thirty to forty layers of annual growth.

Because the young twigs are browsed by deer and moose it is called moosewood; other names are striped dogwood and goosefoot maple.

The leaves are larger than those of mountain maple, five to six inches long and four to five inches wide. They are three-lobed, with each lobe contracted into a tapering point. Smooth, pale green above and paler below, turning in the fall to a pale yellow, the margins are sharply and doubly toothed.

Toward the end of May or early in June, when the leaves are nearly grown, the bright yellow flowers make their appearance. They are borne in slender, drooping, long-stemmed clusters from four to six inches long, the male and female flowers occurring separately on the same tree. The winged seeds or keys, typical of the maples, develop in pairs in pendent clusters. The seeds are a quarter inch long and are dark brown, pitted on one side. Each wing has a nutlet at the base.

Because of its gracefully drooping clusters of yellow flowers, followed by the pendent bunches of dainty keys, the large pale green leaves turning yellow in the fall, and the conspicuous pale stripes on young growth, this tree is sometimes cultivated as an ornamental in the northern states, and occasionally in Europe. Like the mountain maple, it requires ample shade and moisture.

Devereux Butcher

The keys of Striped Maple, upper left, occur in pendent clusters. Upper right is the striped, bright green bark on a young stem a half inch in diameter, from which the tree gets its common name. Bark on a mature trunk, below, is an eighth of an inch thick, firm and grayish brown

Devereux Butcher

Warren D. Brush

The leaves of Striped Maple are three-lobed at the apex, and the bright yellow flowers are in slender, drooping, and long-stemmed clusters

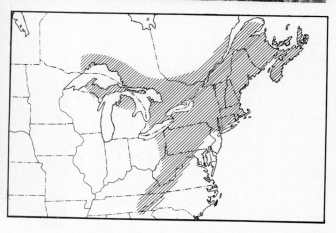

Natural range of Striped Maple

BOXELDER

Boxelder maple, Ash-leaf maple

Acer negundo Linnaeus

THE WINGED seeds of boxelder place this tree, with its compound leaves within the family *Aceraceae*. Because a Malayan tree, *Vitex negundo*, has leaves similar to those of boxelder, this tree has been named *Acer negundo*, which means "a maple with negundo-like leaves."

It inhabits borders of streams and lakes. Its range extends from New England to Florida, west over much of

each of the first fifteen or twenty years. Thereafter growth slows down until sixty or rarely a hundred years is reached. In contrast with other maples, the opposite leaves are compound, composed of three to seven, or rarely nine, short-stalked leaflets. Each leaflet is irregularly toothed, two to five inches long, one to three inches

U. S. Forest Service

Early division of the short trunk gives
Boxelder a low, broad, bushy crown

Devereux Butcher

Clusters of V-shaped keys hang for months from the branches of pistillate trees

Maryland State Department of Forestry

the United States, with small areas in California and the Rocky Mountains, and north to southern Manitoba, Saskatchewan and Alberta. Usually forty to fifty feet high with two- or three-foot diameters, individual trees reach seventy-five feet and four feet in diameter. The short, crooked trunk usually divides into several irregular spreading branches to form a wide bushy crown.

Boxelder is often scattered in company with bottomland hardwoods such as American elm, hackberry, silver maple, and black walnut. It is most abundant in the Mississippi and Ohio valleys, but ability to thrive in dry areas has increased its occurrence in the prairie states. In good soils, diameter growth may equal an inch for

328

wide, pointed at the tips, sometimes three-lobed, and pale on the under surface. The leaves, having a distinctive odor when crushed, turn yellow in autumn before dropping, and a scar remains that nearly surrounds the stem.

In April or early May, before or with the unfolding leaves, tiny yellowish green flowers appear on growth of the preceding year. Drooping clusters of pistillate or female flowers occur on trees separate from those which bear the hairy clusters of staminate blooms.

One- to two-inch V-shaped winged keys or double samara hang from the twigs in six- to eight-inch clusters, from early summer through winter into spring. Their broad membranous wings converge into narrow, pointed nutlets. Heavy crops of moderately fertile seeds are borne each year and are blown far from the parent tree to germinate in moist soils of open lowlands.

The pale gray-brown bark is a quater to a half-inch thick, shallowly broken into narrow, firm, flat-topped ridges which crack horizontally into thick irregular short scales. On young trunks, branches and twigs the bark is smooth, greenish or purplish, with conspicuous raised lenticels or pores, and the twigs are sometimes coated with a powdery white bloom.

The soft close-grained, creamy white wood, lightest of the American maples, weighs about twenty-six pounds to the cubic foot when air dry.

Boxelder trees frequently attain lumber size, but are rarely cut for lumber. The wood is sold with that of soft maple and is used for crates, boxes, slack barrels, handles, paper pulp, charcoal, cheap furniture, woodenware, and fuel.

Until the beginning of the twentieth century, boxelder was widely planted for street and windbreak purposes. These uses are now usually discouraged because of the tree's short life, frequent injury by wind and sleet, tendency to attack by several sucking, defoliating and boring insects, and its susceptibility to heart rot.

Yellow-green pollen-bearing flowers appear with the new leaves on staminate trees

The shallowly fissured gray-brown bark is scarcely half an inch thick

Each pinnately compound leaf has three to seven irregularly margined leaflets

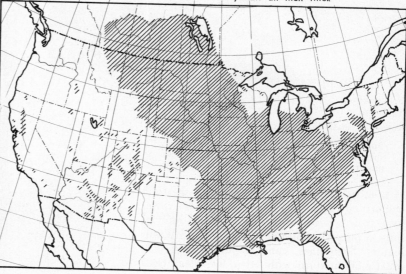

Natural range of Boxelder

329

BIGLEAF MAPLE

Broadleaf maple, California maple, Oregon maple

Acer macrophyllum Pursh

EXTENDING some twenty degrees of latitude along the Pacific coast from Alaska to southern California, bigleaf maple is the sole commercial species of four western maples. Demanding moisture, this tree occurs along the borders of foothills and on low mountains from sea level to elevations of over 3,000 feet in Washington and Oregon, and to 6,000 feet in California.

In the open this maple develops a broad, rounded crown of dense, blue-green foliage and a short trunk. Such trees may be fifty to sixty feet, or occasionally seventy-five feet high, with trunk diameters of two, three, or rarely five feet at breast height. Forest grown trees reach heights of 100 feet with a full, straight bole, clear

George C. Stephenson

Open-grown Bigleaf Maples have broad, dense, round-topped crowns with short trunks. Leaves and fruit frequently hang on into the winter

of branches for one-half to two-thirds the total height and supporting a short, narrow crown. Best growth is in moist, gravelly, rich, alluvial soils in the river bottoms of Oregon and Washington. Sometimes found in pure stands, it is usually in mixture with other broadleaf trees and conifers.

Bigleaf maple seldom lives very much longer than 150 or 200 years. The simple, opposite leaves are the largest of any American maple, being six to twelve inches long and slightly broader, which accounts for the name—*macrophyllum*. They are usually deeply cut into five wavy or subdivided lobes. The leaves vary in size on the same tree, and on trees of different ages, but are always conspicuously large as compared with those of other maples. Deep green and shiny above, and a paler green beneath, they are deciduous. In autumn the clear green of summer becomes a golden yellow, and the leaves hang on into the winter.

No other native maple flowers compare with the four- to six-inch drooping clusters of fragrant yellow blossoms that deck the bigleaf maple in April and May, after the leaves are formed. Flowers of both sexes occur on the same tree.

The winged fruit is longer than that of most other maples, and the seed is covered with short, stiff hairs. They are one and a half to two inches long, tawny or yellowish brown, ripen in the autumn, and hang on into the winter or early spring. Open-grown trees produce abundant quantities of seed nearly every year, but production in the dense forests is sporadic. A large quantity germinate, but

Chicago Natural History Museum

only seedlings whose roots reach mineral soil before dry weather sets in survive. They will live under dense shade, but to attain any size, direct overhead light is required. Supplementing reproduction by seeds are fast growing coppice sprouts from stumps. The ashy to brownish gray bark is seldom more than half an inch thick, and is broken into rough, fairly broad ridges as the tree matures.

The wood is light brown with a pale tint of red. It is firm, fine-grained, takes a high polish, and a cubic foot weighs about thirty-four pounds when air dry. No figures are available on the sawtimber stand or the production of bigleaf maple lumber. Furniture takes the bulk, but considerable quantities go into interior finish, flooring, broom handles, saddles, pulleys, boats, boxes, and baskets. Curly or wavy wood is occasionally found, and fancy-grained burls command high prices for furniture veneer and novelties.

Bigleaf maple is reasonably resistant to insect attack and, as part of the understory of humid forests, seldom suffers from wind or fire. When fire occurs, however, the thin bark offers little resistance. Wood-destroying fungi often reduce the trunk of large trees to scarcely more than a shell. Well suited for ornamental purposes within its natural range, it is a favorite street tree in many western towns. This tree does not prosper under our eastern conditions, but grows well in parts of England and western Europe.

Asahel Curtis

Largest of all American maple leaves are the deeply divided ones of this species. The wings of the fruit may be two inches long

U. S. Forest Service

The ashy gray to reddish brown bark is thin and deeply furrowed

Chicago Natural History Museum

Yellow, fragrant flowers hang in clusters four to six inches long

Natural range of Bigleaf Maple

VINE MAPLE

Acer circinatum **Pursh**

THE towering conifer forests of the Northwest owe what little bright color they have, mostly to this small tree. Vine maple usually takes the form of a tall shrub of many slender, pliant, erect or prone stems twenty to thirty feet long. The tree's range is the rainy, humid coastal fringes of North America from the southern British Columbia coast south to Mendocino County, California.

This is one of the few deciduous trees in the rain forest belt. Highly tolerant of shade beneath the giant forest, it makes splashes of bright green in the understory growth, as it follows the steep shores of the winding British Columbia inlets and the banks of the coastal rivers of Washington, Oregon and northern California. In Washington, it ranges from the rainy, western slopes of the Olympic Mountains, east to the moist valleys and slopes of the Cascades at elevations up to 2000 feet, and south to Mount Rainier, where it occurs at 4500 feet above sea level. Along the Columbia River Valley it is found as far east as Mount Hood where, on western slopes, it climbs to 5000 feet. It finds its way also along the banks of northern California's rivers, invading westward-facing slopes of the coast ranges to mingle with the redwoods.

Although vine maple thrives on many soils from the almost continuously wet, alluvial coastal valley bottoms near sea level to gravelly or rocky, drier, exposed sites on mountain sides, the tree reaches its maximum development in the deep, wet soils of the coast. Here occasionally it attains heights of forty to sixty feet, with trunk diameters

of eight to ten inches when sixty to seventy years of age and older.

In these locations, the vine maple's associates are some of the world's largest and commercially most important trees, among them Sitka spruce, Douglasfir, grand fir, western redcedar, western hemlock, western white pine, Port Orford cedar and coast redwood, together with such deciduous species as bigleaf maple, Pacific dogwood, black cottonwood, red alder, California-laurel and cascara buckthorn.

The gray to gray-green or red-brown bark is smooth except at the base of old trunks, where it is slightly fissured. Twigs are green or red-brown, smooth and frequently coated with bloom. The slender branches form a narrow, open, irregular crown in the forest shade, where often the main stems, borne down by snow, become contorted and sprawl on or close to the ground. Where stems come in contact with the moist soil and are covered with mats of moss or dead leaves, they take root, send up new stems and create impenetrable thickets.

The eighth-inch-long winter buds, protected by a covering of thin, red scales, expand in spring as the young leaves unfurl. Red-tinged and downy at first, the leaves turn bright green, slightly paler beneath, and become smooth except for silvery hairs at the axils of the main veins on the underside. Three to four inches long and slightly broader when fully grown, they are palmate, with five to nine sharply pointed lobes, heart-shaped at the base

British Columbia Forest Service

Vine Maple often is shrub-like in form, with numerous slender, upright or sprawling stems, but sometimes it grows as a single tree of forty to sixty feet in height

and have toothed margins. Borne on one- to two-inch, grooved stems, they occur oppositely along the twig.

With the opening of the leaves, loose clusters or corymbs of ten to twenty monoecious flowers with purple or red sepals and green petals appear, on one- or two-inch stalks, in the axils or bases of the two leaf-stems at the twig terminal. The blossoms, opening from April to June, soon are followed by pendent clusters of samaras or winged pairs of seeds—a distinguishing mark of the maples. The seeds, an eighth inch in diameter, are light yellow-brown and the wings one and a half inches in length, bright rose-red and noticeably more divergent than those of most other maples.

In autumn, the foliage takes on the coloring characteristic of the maples. On sunny sites the leaves vary from scarlet through pink to orange, while in partial shade a branch may contain leaves having two or more of these colors at once. In deep forest shade, they turn pale yellow and in openings on high mountain slopes and canyon sides, where the vine maple sometimes becomes the dominant species, unbroken masses of brilliant red may be visible for long distances.

The heavy, hard, dense, fine-grained wood is light brown to almost white, with thick, lighter colored sapwood. It checks badly on drying, is not strong and finds little use on the market, except in small quantities locally for tool handles and fuel. Vine maple responds well to cultivation and because of its beauty is planted as an ornamental.

Clusters of ten to twenty small flowers with red sepals and green petals appear in April through June, suspended by a short stalk from the twig terminals

Soon after the flowers disappear, they are replaced by pairs of red-winged seeds, which are conspicuous among the bright green, toothed, five-, six- or seven-lobed leaves

Devereux Butcher

Gray-green or red-brown, the bark, often coated with moss and lichens, is smooth except at the base of old trunks, where it may be slightly broken into scales

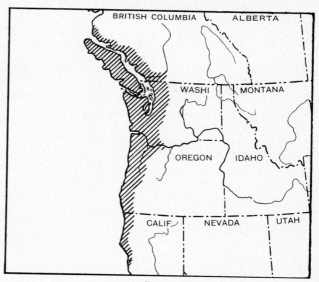

Base map © J. L. Smith, Phila. Pa.

Approximate natural range of Vine Maple

NORWAY MAPLE

Acer platanoides Linnaeus

ALTHOUGH not a native tree, Norway maple is well known in the United States because it has been so extensively planted here. It has proved to be one of our best ornamental trees because of its pleasing form and its hardiness. The wide-spreading branches above the short

Wide-spreading branches of the Norway Maple produce a rounded, compact head thickly covered with leaves

trunk and the rounded, compact head are covered thickly by the bright green leaves. While trees occasionally attain a height of 100 feet, they are usually much less than this, especially when grown in the open.

The leaves bear a close resemblance to those of sugar maple, but they are somewhat thicker in texture and darker in color. They are five- and sometimes seven-lobed and each lobe usually has one or more pointed teeth. One peculiarity of this species is that the leaf stem when broken exudes a milky juice. The bark is close and ridged in contrast to the scaly bark of the sugar and sycamore maples.

In the spring the tree is densely covered with clusters of greenish yellow flowers which are fully developed when the leaves are beginning to unfold. In the same cluster may be found separate staminate (male) and pistillate (female) flowers, but some flowers have both sta-

mens and pistils. The fruit is the most distinctive of any of the maples, consisting of winged seeds in pairs, the wings and seeds or nutlets set opposite each other and meeting in nearly a straight line. They are fully grown in late spring, although the seed does not mature until fall, and throughout the summer the pale green key clusters make a fine appearance among the bright green leaves.

The winter buds are much larger than those of sugar maple. They are oval and reddish brown in color, and, when broken off, a milky juice exudes similar to that from the leaf stems.

As the name implies, the tree is a native of Norway, but its natural range extends as far south as Switzerland. Norway maple is very resistant to insect and fungus at-

While occasional trees may attain a height of 100 feet, they are usually much smaller when open-grown

tack. The tussock moth and the leopard moth frequently injure the leaves, and sometimes the leaves are attacked by plant lice and a blight known as maple wilt. The damage to the tree is usually so slight, however, that spraying is seldom necessary.

Norway maple is fast-growing, attaining maturity at the age of sixty years. It makes satisfactory growth on

The fruit is distinctive—winged seeds in pairs, set opposite each other and meeting in almost a straight line

poor soils and is particularly well-adapted for cities, because it seems to withstand well the smoke, gases and dust. It is much more resistant to disease than the sugar and silver maples and does not grow as large, which makes it more desirable for planting on streets, especially where the houses are close to the street. Norway maple is easily transplanted. The trees should be pruned from time to time so that the lower branches are a sufficient distance from the ground. As a lawn tree the dense foliage provides heavy shade; moreover the leaves appear earlier in the spring and remain later than those of our native maples. They turn a bright yellow before falling.

Clusters of greenish yellow flowers are fully developed before the leaves begin to unfold

The bark is close and ridged in contrast to the scaly bark of the sugar and sycamore maples—an aid to winter identification

Closely resembling those of the sugar maple, the leaves are thicker in texture and darker in color

Not a native tree, the Norway Maple is a favorite for ornamental plantings east of the Missouri River and along the West Coast

SYCAMORE MAPLE

Acer pseudoplatanus Linnaeus

LIKE the Norway maple, sycamore maple is a European species which has been cultivated in the United States for many years. In England it is called "sycamore," while the sycamore, as we know it, is called "planetree"—a name sometimes used for sycamore in the United States.

The yellowish green flowers open in May and hang from long stalks. The double-winged fruits or keys, which mature in August and September, cling to the twigs over winter in long pendulous clusters. Each of the two wide-spreading wings has a small seed or nutlet at its base.

Devereux Butcher

The leaves are smooth, dark green and leathery in texture

Devereux Butcher

Sycamore Maple, also known as "planetree," attains a usual height of 70 feet and has a large spreading head

The name *pseudoplatanus* means false sycamore or false planetree. Sycamore maple attains a usual height of about seventy feet with a large spreading head. When grown in the open, it resembles Norway maple in form, with its short trunk, spreading limbs, and rounded crown, but the top is generally not so compact.

The smooth, dark green, five-lobed leaves resemble those of our native American sycamore. They are three and a half to seven inches across, thick and leathery in texture, and pale underneath, with prominent hairs on the prinicipal veins. The margins of the lobes are wavy and bluntly toothed and the base is heart-shaped.

L. W. Brownell

When grown in the open, it resembles Norway maple in form, with its short trunk, spreading limbs and rounded crown

The bark, which closely resembles that of other maples known in this country, breaks into broad, flaky scales

The flowers are yellowish green in color and hang from long stalks. They generally open sometime in May

The winter buds are green and hence can be distinguished from those of Norway maple which are reddish. The bark resembles that of most of the maples, breaking into broad flaky scales.

Sycamore maple is an important timber tree in Europe, ranking in value with our sugar maple. Figured wood sliced into thin veneer and artificially stained gray is known as harewood and silver greywood and is highly valued in cabinet work. The tree is well liked in Europe as a shade and street tree but it does not seem to thrive as well under our conditions as at home. It grows rapidly, but lacks the hardiness of Norway maple and is more subject to disease and boring insects. When grown in the United States, sycamore maple is likely to be short-lived. In form it is not so attractive as Norway maple because the crown is somewhat too spreading, except when planted along wide avenues. As a street tree, sycamore maple in general is not as satisfactory as the native sugar maple. While it is not cultivated in the United States nearly as much as the Norway maple, it does constitute an unusual and interesting form in the plantings of many cities, particularly in the East.

There are many horticultural varieties desirable for ornamental use on lawns and in gardens. Some of them have purplish red leaves, and others have leaves with white blotches and spots while still others bear attractive bright red fruit.

The winter buds are green

The double-winged fruits or keys, which mature in August and September, cling to the twigs in clusters through winter

YELLOW BUCKEYE

Sweet buckeye, Large buckeye

Aesculus octandra Marshall

THIS IS the largest and most important of the seven native species of buckeye in the United States. (Horse-chestnut. *A. hippocastanum*, is an introduced tree.) Only one other, the Ohio buckeye, is of commercial value. Yellow buckeye usually has a straight trunk with a small crown made up of pendulous branches. It attains heights of from sixty to ninety feet, with diameters of two to three feet.

The species prefers river bottoms and moist mountain slopes from southwestern Pennsylvania and southern Ohio to southern Illinois south to northern Alabama, Georgia and western North Carolina north to West Virginia. In the northern part of its range it grows chiefly

Tennessee and North Carolina, where it occurs in mixture with other hardwoods.

The stout twigs are orange-brown at first, becoming pale brown in their second year. They are marked by numerous lenticels and large leaf scars on which may be seen several bundle scars arranged in a V-shaped pattern. The buds, about two-thirds of an inch long and free of resin, are enclosed in broadly ovate scales, the outer ones pale brown and the inner ones yellow or occasionally scarlet.

The palmately compound leaves are borne on a stem four to six inches long and made up of five, rarely seven, long-pointed, finely toothed leaflets that are narrowed at the base, and are from four to seven inches in length and two to three inches wide. They are dark yellow-green above, duller beneath, smooth on both surfaces when mature, except for a few fine hairs along the stout

L. W. Brownell

Mature Yellow Buckeye trees often attain diameters of two to three feet and heights of sixty to ninety feet

on bottomlands, but farther south it prefers mountain slopes where, in some localities, it may constitute one of the principal species. In dry situations it is usually small and sometimes shrubby. It is most common and makes its best development on fertile soils in the mountains of

midrib on the under surface and in the axils of the principal veins. They turn yellow in autumn.

In April and May, when the leaves are about half grown, the showy yellow flowers appear in five- to seven-inch clusters. Each flower is from one to one and a half inches long and has four petals, the two upper longer and narrower than the lower. The smooth or slightly roughened fruit ripens in September. Nearly spherical, it measures from two to three inches in length and generally contains two pale brown, thin-shelled, nut-like seeds, one and a half to two inches wide. Yellow buckeye often is called sweet buckeye because the fruit is sweet by comparison with that of the Ohio buckeye. It is not sweet enough to be eaten by man, but is eagerly sought by cattle and hogs. Other names for the tree are large buckeye and big buckeye.

The dark brown bark, about three-quarters of an inch thick, is divided by shallow fissures and separates on the surface into small, thin scales. The wood is uniform in texture, generally straight-grained, weighs about twenty-five pounds to the cubic foot when air-dry, weak when used structurally, soft, and low in shock resistance. The heartwood is creamy white or yellowish white. The sapwood also is white, but generally lacks a yellow tinge. Yellow buckeye is used for crates and boxes, particularly food containers, because the wood is odorless and tasteless, is white, and is light in weight. It also is used for hidden parts of furniture, such as drawer bottoms and sides, and for caskets and artificial limbs.

Yellow buckeye grows rapidly, especially when young, but is short-lived, reaching maturity in sixty to eighty years. Seed is produced nearly every year by open-grown trees and frequently by forest trees. The species sometimes is injured by the buckeye stem borer, and because the wood is subject to fungus attack, large trees often have hollow centers.

The tree is used ornamentally, especially the pink or purple-flowered variety, *A. hybrida*, Sargent, in parks and gardens in eastern United States and in western and central Europe.

L. W. Brownell

Stout orange-brown twigs are marked by lenticles and leaf scars, and in winter, are tipped with large buds

L. W. Brownell

Palmately compound leaves have five, rarely seven, finely-toothed leaflets, each four to seven inches long

L. W. Brownell

In April and May, before the leaves are fully grown, loose clusters of yellow flowers appear

L. W. Brownell

The spherical fruits, two to three inches in diameter, ripen in September

L. W. Brownell

Shallow fissures and small, thin scales characterize the dark brown bark

Natural range of Yellow Buckeye

OHIO BUCKEYE

Fetid buckeye

Aesculus glabra Willdenow

George J. Baetzhold

ing from the midrib to the finely toothed margin. The underside is a lighter green, with fine hairs visible on the veins. In the autumn the leaves turn yellow before dropping to uncover a horseshoe-shaped scar on the twig.

In May or early June after the leaves have burst from the large shiny brown buds and have reached full size, stiff, upright clusters of greenish yellow flowers appear at the ends of many of the upturned twigs. While some are perfect with a five-lobed calyx, four petals, a pistil and seven stamens, others on the same tree may have only a pistil, or the seven stamens without a pistil. Their disagreeable, fetid odor has led some to call this the stinking or fetid buckeye.

In spite of the inedible and possibly poisonous nature of the seeds of this and other members of the

IN THE central area west of the Alleghenies, one of the first trees to leaf out is the Ohio buckeye. Resembling its larger and better known European relative, the horsechestnut, it differs in the five, more slender, finger-like leaflets, the smaller and less attractive yellow blossoms, and in other ways. Fertile bottomlands and the borders of streams from Ohio to northern Alabama, and west into eastern Kansas and Oklahoma, are its natural haunts.

It is of medium size, ranging from thirty to seventy feet in height, with a trunk seldom more than two feet in diameter. Except in the deep woods, the stem divides low to form an irregularly broad, rounded crown, with coarse, drooping branches, and reddish brown upcurved twigs.

Both twigs and leaves are arranged oppositely. The yellow-green compound leaves consist of five or occasionally seven lance pointed, oval leaflets, diverging palmately from a common point at the end of the long stem or petiole. Each leaflet is three to six inches long, with parallel veins lead-

George J. Baetzhold

Buckeye is a medium sized tree with a broad, rounded crown. When the yellow-green foliage drops in the autumn, the opposite branching, and the thick, drooping twigs with upcurved ends are revealed

340

family, the name *Aesculus* is derived from *esca*, meaning food, and is the ancient name for a kind of oak tree. The first description was by a German botanist, Willdenow, in 1809, who selected the specific name *glabra*, meaning smooth, with reference to the buds and young leaves.

The ashy gray bark is densely furrowed and broken into large scaly flakes. On old trees it may be three-quarters of an inch thick. When bruised, or when the twigs are broken, these also give off a disagreeable odor. An extract of the bark has been used as an irritant of the cerebro-spinal system.

The white, close-grained wood weighs only twenty-five to twenty-eight pounds to the cubic foot, and, like that of the larger yellow buckeye, resists splitting, but at the same time is easily carved or whittled. It is used largely in the making of artificial limbs, and the early settlers planed straight sections into long fine shavings with which to make summer hats. Ohio buckeye is of so little commercial importance that there are no figures to show its estimated stand. It is sometimes used for woodenware, pulp, veneers, and general construction.

The younger Michaux found so many of these trees along the Ohio River during his travels in 1810 that Ohio is known as the Buckeye State. It is usually associated with beech, sugar maple, and basswood. Because the leaves and fruit are believed poisonous to livestock, the tree is frequently destroyed by landowners.

As with the horsechestnut, Ohio buckeye is subject to a fungus disease that first shows itself as brown spots or blotches on the leaves. By midsummer the entire tree may appear as if scorched by fire. Owners of ornamental trees may check this disease by promptly raking and burning all fallen leaves, leaf stalks, and fruits. Early spraying or

In late summer and fall the five-fingered foliage hides round, prickly fruits which hold the glistening brown buckeye

The densely furrowed, ashy gray bark may be three-quarters of an inch thick

dusting with lime sulphur or Bordeaux mixture is also helpful.

Generally considered a messy tree, because of the flowers, fruit and leaves, which fall throughout the entire growing season, it nevertheless is occasionally planted as an ornamental in the eastern states and in Europe. It is hardy as far north as Massachusetts.

Panicles of yellow, ill smelling blossoms appear among the darker foliage in May or June

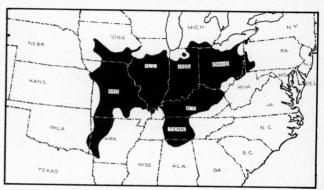

Natural range of the Ohio Buckeye

CALIFORNIA BUCKEYE

Aesculus californica (Spach) Nutt.

CALIFORNIA BUCKEYE is one of seven species of the buckeye genus *Aesculus* native to the United States. This one often assumes the proportions of a large shrub, with a number of main stems three to six inches in diameter and from ten to twenty feet tall, growing from a common root. It sometimes reaches heights of twenty-five to thirty feet with diameters up to one and a half feet. The wide-spreading limbs support a rather flat-topped, rounded, open crown.

The range, confined to California, comprises two separate areas: the valleys of the humid coastal belt in Mendocino and Humboldt counties at elevations from 500 to 2500 feet and higher, south to San Luis Obispo County, and inland in Shasta County along the streams of the Sacramento Valley, east to the comparatively dry western foothills of the Sierra Nevada at elevations up to 2000 feet, south to southern Kern County and northern Los Angeles County at elevations up to 4500 feet. It inhabits moist stream borders, as well as the dry, gravelly soils on canyon

leaves are palmately compound, with four to seven, but more often five finely toothed, finger-like, lanceolate to oblong-lanceolate, sharply tipped leaflets three to seven inches long and one and a half to two inches wide. Bright green and slightly hairy above when young, they become nearly smooth, and are considerably paler beneath, with minute hairs in the angles of the conspicuous veins. Borne on short, slender, grooved stems, they are attached to the terminal of a grooved, four- to five-inch main stem or petiole. Trees in the Sierra Nevada foothills lose their leaves in summer, probably because of the dry, hot climate there at that time of the year.

Soon after the leaves are fully mature in May, showy, erect, densely hairy, five- to ten-inch panicles of white or sometimes pale pink flower clusters begin to bloom at the terminals of the many upturned twigs of the previous year. Each flower has five to seven stamens with long, slender, excerted filaments and short, orange-colored anthers. The flowers on the upper part of the panicle or spike are solely pollen-producing; while those below are bisexual, having both stamens and ovary and produce the fruit or nut.

After the leaves have fallen, the fruit ripens. Conspicuous on the leafless tree, it consists of a smooth, thin, dull green, pear-shaped, leathery, two-valved husk on a slender pendent stalk enclosing one or rarely two hard, glossy brown, thin-shelled, nuts that sometimes are nearly two inches in diameter, bearing a circular, light-colored scar. This scar, together with the surrounding dark color of the shell, suggests an eye, hence the common name.

Wood of California buckeye is soft, light, very pale yellow or white, close-grained, with thin

Devereux Butcher

John Bryan

California Buckeye produces a broadly rounded crown of thick foliage which, in May, puts out many blossoms and, in winter, the abundant branching is visible

sides of the foothills. Maximum development is attained in the canyons of the coast ranges north of San Francisco.

Bark on the short trunk and long, wide-spreading branches is smooth or nearly so, is light gray or sometimes almost white. Young twigs usually are smooth and gray-brown to red-brown. The acutely shaped winter buds are contained within narrow, dark brown scales that are heavily coated with resin.

Growing oppositely along the twigs, the

342

sapwood containing ten or a dozen annual growth rings. It has no commercial value, the tree's principal importance being the provision of cover for wildlife and as an ornamental in parks and gardens in California and Europe. It produces abundant seed, which germinates when well covered with soil. The seedlings tolerate some shade during their early years, and the tree may live more than a hundred years.

Among the associates of California buckeye are live oak, redbud, Digger pine, manzanita, as well as a number of other species belonging to the chaparral forest.

In preparing the nuts for eating, the Indians roasted then soaked them in water to rid them of a poison.

John Bryan

The fruit consists of one or two thin-shelled, glossy brown nuts in a dull green, leathery two- or three-valved husk. Bark is smooth except on old trunks, where it is shallowly cracked into thin scales

Devereux Butcher

The palmately compound leaves, usually with five sharply tipped leaflets, three to seven inches long, are finely toothed, bright green above and paler beneath

Ells Marugg

After the leaves mature in spring, densely hairy, erect, showy panicles of pale pink or white flowers appear at the ends of the many thick twigs of the previous year

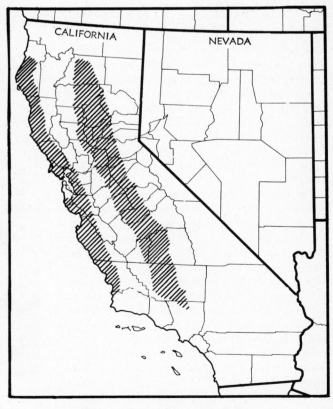

Approximate natural range of California Buckeye

343

HORSECHESTNUT

Aesculus hippocastanum Linnaeus

George J. Baetzhold

In winter the tree is easily recognized by
its symmetrical form and stout twigs which
turn upward at the ends

THE horsechestnut is a member of the buckeye
genus, *Aesculus*. It was introduced from Europe in the eighteenth century, and is a native
of southern Asia, ranging from the Himalayan
Mountains to northern Greece. A favorite
shade tree in the Old World, it has spread in
popularity in America and now appears as a
planted ornamental tree in most states. Its popularity is well justified by its good form and
floral display.

The leaves of the horsechestnut are from six
to fifteen inches in diameter; the leaflets are
four to eight inches long, extending palm-fash-
ion from the end of a stout petiole which swells
abruptly at the base. The slightly wavy margins of the leaflets are irregularly toothed and
their upper surface is faintly wrinkled Broader
at the outer ends and terminating in an abrupt
point, the leaflets taper toward the base, and at
maturity are dark green above and paler beneath. In the fall they turn brown.

Showy, pyramidal flower clusters six to
twelve inches high appear in June and July
when the tree is in full foliage. The five petals
are white, spotted with yellow and purple, and
the long, curved stamens are yellow, extending

far beyond the petals. The only other tree-sized
buckeye bearing white flowers is the California
buckeye, and its natural range is limited to the
slopes of the Sierra Nevada and coast ranges of
California.

The fruit, ripening in September, consists of two
or three reddish brown, smooth nuts, each bearing
a whitish scar, and enclosed in a corky husk two or
three inches in diameter covered with blunt spines.
In the fall the husk turns brown, hard and leathery,
and cracks into three segments to liberate the nuts.
These are without economic importance in this
country and are so bitter as to be inedible without
special treatment. Powdered dried nuts mixed with
two parts of wheat flour and alum-water are said
to make a vermin-repellent bookbinder's paste.

The horsechestnut may have acquired its common name from the legendary use of the fruit as a
source of medicine for horses, or from the shape
of the leaf scars which resemble the print of a
horse's hoof. The name *Aesculus* is from the Latin
for winter oak, and *hippocastanum* is a combination of two Latin words meaning "horse" and
"chestnut."

The twigs are dotted with large lenticels or
breathing pores, while the large reddish brown opposite buds are protected throughout the winter by

Devereux Butcher

Large ascending limbs and spreading branches
form a rounded crown of dense foliage

344

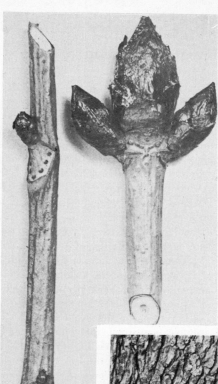

Twigs bear large terminal buds and smaller lateral ones, and have horseshoe-like leaf scars which aid identification

The showy, white flower clusters appear in June or July, and stand erect amid the large palmate leaves

U. S. Forest Service

Devereux Butcher

Bark is thin, and on the lower trunks of old trees it is broken into flat scales by shallow fissures

by the caterpillar of the white-marked tussock moth, while the wood-boring larva of the leopard moth causes the twigs to wilt and break off. The oyster shell scale feeds on the sap. Rarely are any of these attacks fatal.

The bark is dull brown or black, and on old trunks is thin, broken into large scales separated by shallow cracks or fissures.

The wood weighs about thirty-five pounds to the cubic foot when air dry. It is white, soft and close-grained, but is not commercially important. In Europe it is used for box material, veneer, woodenware, and artificial limbs and as a source of charcoal for gunpowder.

a sticky shiny gum. The terminal flower buds are one-half to one inch long and below them on each side is a smaller leaf bud. The bud scales are arranged oppositely in pairs. Beneath each side bud is a large, rounded V-shaped leaf scar marked by seven prominent dark dots.

The lower branches droop slightly, with tips upturned in candelabra fashion; the crown is rounded into a broad cone by ascending limbs with spreading lateral branches. The horsechestnut grows rapidly, often reaching a height of seventy feet and a diameter of three feet. Horticulturists have produced ornamental varieties of horsechestnut with peculiar characteristics such as double flowers and deeply cut leaves.

The flowers of the dwarf, *Aesculus pavia alba*, an ornamental tree, have an apparent toxic effect on the Japanese beetle, while an extract from the seeds of red buckeye, *Aesculus pavia*, will stupefy fish. The horsechestnut flowers and leaves are preferred foods of the Japanese beetle. Its leaves also are attacked

Courtesy Romeyn B. Hough Co.

Ripening in September, the fruit consists of two or three reddish brown nuts borne within a spined husk

345

CASCARA BUCKTHORN

Cascara, Cascara sagrada, Bearberry, Bearwood, Bitterbark, Wahoo

Rhamnus purshiana de Candolle

CASCARA buckthorn occurs from sea level to 3,000 feet most commonly from the Puget Sound region of British Columbia and Washington. It also occurs in northern and eastern Washington and northern Idaho, as well as northern California as far south as the coast ranges north of San Francisco Bay and on the slopes of the Sierra Nevada.

Locally called bearberry, chittim, bearwood, coffee-berry, coffeetree, bitterbark and wahoo, the species was discovered by the Lewis and Clark Expedition in Montana, in 1805-06, and was collected at Kamiah, Idaho, the next year. Frederick Pursh first described it, but duplicated another name by designating it as *Rhamnus cathartica*. In 1825, the French botanist de Candolle corrected this error and recognized Pursh's work in the specific name. In *materia medica* the tree is called cascara sagrada.

Usually a medium sized tree twenty to forty feet high and six to fifteen inches in diameter, it has been observed with diameters of two to three feet. Open-grown trees have a short, stubby trunk and a thick, bushy crown, with numerous large upright limbs. Forest-grown trees have long slender trunks and a light crown, with the stem de-void of branches for fifteen or twenty feet. The species assumes a shrub-like form in the drier parts of its range.

The bark, one-tenth to one-fourth of an inch thick, ranges in color from dark brown to ashy gray, and is broken on the surface into short, thin scales. Young bark frequently resembles that of bigleaf maple, *Acer macrophyllum*. The freshly cut inner bark surface is bright yellow, but darkens rapidly on exposure to air.

The bark has been well-known as a laxative since 1877 and it is collected extensively from trees in western Oregon and Washington, southern British Columbia and northern California. There is an annual harvest that comprises a forest industry of major importance to some rural regions. In accessible areas bark peeling inroads have kept down the average diameter to six inches or less. Such trees provide the major source of harvest.

A great deal of stump sprouting is prevented because trees are not cut down after the bark has been peeled. Actually more than fifty percent of the active material in a mature tree is stored in the woody parts. Stumps sprout vigorously and produce from four to fifteen stems. For this reason there is no dearth of wild bark at present. However, the demand is growing even in competition

Albert Arnst

Albert Arnst

Open-grown trees have a short stubby trunk and a thick bushy crown, with large upright limbs. Usually it is of medium size, 20 to 40 feet high and 6 to 15 inches in diameter

with synthetic products; and each year the bark gatherers must go farther and farther back into the mountains. Plantations have been attempted on a small scale, but so far these have not proved feasible.

Mature twigs are smooth or slightly and minutely downy, usually dull reddish brown. Cascara is the only known deciduous tree on the west coast whose buds are not covered by bud scales. A coat of fine, rusty brown hairs protects the young leaflets. This naked bud serves as a means of winter identification.

The simple leaves are deciduous, except in seedlings, which retain their yellowish leaves through the winter. Leaves are broad elliptical with a broad and prominent midrib and primary veins and a finely serrated margin. One and a half to seven inches long and about two inches wide, they are bluntly pointed at the apex and slightly cordate at the base, with short hairs on the lower surface. They are commonly confused with those of red alder, *Alnus rubra*.

Flowers appear in May or June. They are small, five-petaled, greenish in color and are carried on slender hairy stalks in clusters near the ends of branches.

The fruit, maturing in August or September, is a drupe, one-half to one-third inch in size, smooth and black, with juicy, rather thin, sweetish, pulp, containing two or three hard, smooth, olive-green seeds. It is much relished by birds, and the tree's abundance along fence rows can be attributed to this fact. The fruit matures in one season. The tree is a prolific seeder.

The wood is pale, yellowish brown, with a faint tinge of red, hard and heavy, weighing thirty-six pounds a cubic foot in an air-dry condition. The layer of pale sapwood is thin in forest-grown trees, but thick in open-grown ones. It has no economic use other than for fuel, but could be used for turnery purposes.

Cascara buckthorn occurs commonly as scattered individuals or sprout groups on cutover lands, along rural fence rows and country lanes. In the forest, the tree mixes with Douglasfir, Western redcedar, hemlock and bigleaf and vine maples; in broad river bottoms it is crowded out by the more rapidly growing alder and cottonwood trees. Plenty of moisture and a slightly sandy soil are necessary for the abundant growth and large size of this tree.

Albert Arnst

Extensively collected bitter bark is broken on the surface into short thin scales

Albert Arnst

Simple leaves have prominent veins. The small flowers cluster at branch ends

Albert Arnst

Fine hairs protect the scaleless buds

Albert Arnst

The fruit is a smooth, black drupe with juicy pulp and thin rather sweet juice

Natural range of Cascara Buckthorn. It is often found scattered on cutover land

347

AMERICAN BASSWOOD

American linden
Tilia americana Linnaeus

THE AMERICAN BASSWOOD, American linden, or lime, forms a compact, symmetrical tree usually seventy to ninety feet high with a trunk two or three feet in diameter. Occasionally trees 140 feet high with maximum trunk diameters of four and one-half feet have been reported.

It is distributed over much of the eastern half of the United States as far south as Tennessee and in the Appalachian Mountains. Its southern range is confused with that of the white basswood, *Tilia heterophylla*, which differs, among other features, in the leaves which are silvery white and covered with fine hairs on the lower surface. The largest and most vigorous trees are found in fertile coves and on low land near streams within the central states. It grows in mixture with other hardwoods and does not form pure stands.

This tree was formerly named *Tilia glabra* by the French botanist Etienne-Pierre Ventenat, the species name referring to the smooth surfaces of the simple, alternate, heart-shaped leaves. The upper surface is dull dark green, and the lower surface paler.

The perfect, five-petaled, fragrant, white or cream-colored flowers appear after the leaves are fully developed in June and early July. They hang in clusters from a stalk attached about midway to a leafy bract. By early October gray, woody, spherical fruits develop.

The buds are dark red or sometimes greenish. While without distinctive flavor, they become mucilaginous

American Basswood forms a handsome, compact, narrow-crowned tree from fifty to one hundred feet high and occasionally higher, with a full, symmetrical trunk two to three feet in diameter

Numerous slender branches, of which those at the base of the trees are strongly drooping, are revealed in symmetrical grace when the leaves have fallen

when chewed. The dark gray bark of old trees is about an inch thick, deeply furrowed into narrow, flat-topped firm ridges with characteristic horizontal cracks. That of young trees is gray, smooth and thin. The bast fibers of the inner bark have long been used in making cords, fish nets, mats and similar articles.

The white to creamy brown wood is valued for its white color, light weight and good working qualities and is used widely for woodenware, slack cooperage, boxes, veneer, excelsior, paper pulp, and many small articles. When air dry it weighs about twenty-six pounds to the cubic foot.

Basswood grows rapidly, and it develops from stump sprouts, as well as from seeds. Trees mature at from ninety to 140 years, and when crowded by other trees they form straight stems with clear lengths up to seventy feet.

While the leaves are frequently disfigured by insects, the tree seldom succumbs to their attacks. Fire often causes trunk scars which permit the entrance of wood-destroying fungi that hollow out the butt logs.

Throughout eastern United States, basswood adapts itself to difficult conditions and is frequently recommended for city streets. It is also satisfactory on the Pacific slope.

U. S. Forest Service

The broad, heart-shaped leaves are smooth on the under, as well as on the upper surface. They are coarsely toothed and taper rapidly to a point. When the leaves have fully formed, clusters of white or creamy, perfect, five-petaled flowers (above) appear, suspended from a leafy bract. Lacking a true terminal bud (right), the smooth, dark red or green lateral buds are about a quarter inch long. The dark gray bark (below) on old trunks is about an inch thick, and is furrowed into flat-topped ridges that are broken by horizontal cracks

U. S. Forest Service

By early autumn, some of the small, fragrant flowers have developed gray, woody fruits (above), which are about the size of a pea. These drop off during the autumn or may remain on the tree well into the winter

U. S. Forest Service

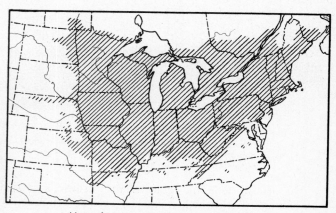

Natural range of American Basswood

BLACK TUPELO

Blackgum, Sour-gum, Pepperidge, Tupelo-gum

Nyssa sylvatica Marshall

BLACK TUPELO grows on a variety of soils, in swamps, bottomlands, and moist uplands through the region east of the Mississippi River, and west through southeastern Missouri to eastern Texas. Best growth occurs in the southern Appalachian Mountains of North Carolina and Tennessee.

branches of the upper crown give reason for the mountain name "wild pear tree." Frequently sixty to eighty feet high and two to three feet in diameter, exceptional trees reach 110 feet and may be five feet in diameter.

In coastal areas, where the tree is subjected to much wind, it often assumes exceptionally picturesque shapes. The top becomes level or horizontal, with the lower branches also being swept into rather horizontal layers that are a distinguishing characteristic.

Of the four American members of the genus *Nyssa*, black tupelo is the most widely distributed, and is commercially the most important. *Nyssa* refers to a Greek water nymph, because all tupelos or gums prefer the swamps, and *sylvatica* designates this tree as "of the woodlands."

Fossil forms indicate that the genus once was distributed over much of North America, Europe, and Asia. A single species is now found in southeastern Asia.

From April to June inconspicuous greenish, five-toothed flowers on slender downy stems appear among the unfolding leaves. Individual trees bear perfect blossoms, while others bear only staminate or pistillate blooms. By September or October blue-black, plum-like

W. R. Mattoon

The well-rounded crown of Black Tupelo contains many small, up-reaching branchlets and, as shown by the winter view, the trunk frequently extends well into the top

The densely foliaged, conical-shaped crown is carried on an erect trunk which frequently extends continuously into the top. The many up-reaching twigs and small

fruits, about half an inch long, are developed, whose thin, oily, slightly acid pulp is attractive to many birds and animals. This may be responsible for the name "blackgum," and also for the name "pepperidge"—an old English corruption of barberry, because, like the barberries, the tupelo berries are acid. Tupelo is an Indian name.

The simple, alternate leaves are oval and pointed, broadest above the middle and with wavy margins. They are of leathery texture, dark green and smooth on the upper surface, slightly downy underneath, and densely clustered on the branchlets.

Resembling somewhat the dogwood, the bark of black tupelo is reddish brown and broken into deep irregular ridges and lozenge-shaped plates. On old trunks the bark may be an inch or more thick. The angular plates are larger than those of dogwood.

The yellow to light brown wood has inconspicuous annual rings and a twisted grain that makes it tough and difficult to split. When air dry a cubic foot weighs about thirty-five pounds. Considerable amounts are cut into veneer to be manufactured into boxes, baskets, and berry crates, and to serve as a core on which veneers of rarer woods are glued. Without natural ability to resist decay, the wood may be successfully treated with creosote or other preservative. Because of its toughness it was formerly used for ox yokes and chopping bowls, and is now used for flooring, rollers in glass factories, hatters' blocks, gunstocks, and pistol grips.

The moist location of most of the trees and the thick bark combine to protect this tree from fire, but the shallow root system frequently causes trees to give way to high winds. Mature trees are often subject to heart rot.

The erect trunk, shapely crown, and gorgeous scarlet or purple autumn foliage combine to make black tupelo an attractive ornamental tree, especially suited to wet or swampy soils.

Warren D. Brush

The yellowish green pistillate or seed-producing flowers occur on trees other than those bearing the staminate

The clusters of small staminate flowers appear in May and June, and are borne on long stalks

Warren D. Brush

The leaves, arranged alternately, are silvery beneath. The fruits, ripe in September, are a half inch long

U.S. Forest Service

Irregular ridges and lozenge-shaped plates build up a reddish brown bark an inch or more thick

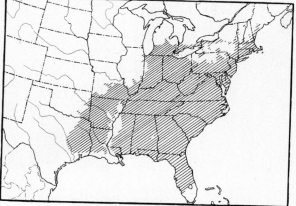

Natual range of Black Tupelo

351

WATER TUPELO

Cotton-gum, Swamp gum, Bay poplar

Nyssa aquatica Linnaeus

WATER TUPELO is an appropriate name for this tree, because it grows in locations that are under water for a large part of the year. A tree of the southern swamps, it may be on dry ground for a short time during the summer but in the fall and winter it stands in water often from three to six feet deep. In the coast region from southeastern Virginia to northern Florida, through the Gulf states to Texas and northward in the Mississippi River region to southern Illinois, the water tupelo reaches its best development in the cypress swamps of western Louisiana and southeastern Texas.

Water tupelo is a large tree sometimes attaining a height of 100 feet and a trunk diameter of three to four feet above its much enlarged base. The swollen base, together with the spreading root system, increases the stability of the trees in loose soil. In the forest it has a long clear bole and a narrow, oblong or pyramidal crown. In the open the trunk is shorter and the crown broader and flatter. The stout twigs are covered with fine, pale, velvety hairs when they first appear, but they soon become smooth and reddish brown. The terminal winter buds are small, one-sixteenth to one-eighth of an inch in diameter, globular in form and are covered with broadly ovate, light chestnut-brown scales. The lateral buds are inconspicuous and nearly embedded in the bark.

The leaves are egg-shaped in outline and sharp or taper-pointed. They measure from five to seven inches in length, two to four inches in width, and the margin may be smooth or irregularly toothed. At maturity thick and firm, they are dark green, smooth and shiny on the upper surface and pale and downy below. The hairy leaf stems are grooved and are from one and a half to two and a half inches in length.

In March or April, as the leaves are developing, the inconspicuous greenish flowers appear on long, slender, hairy stalks. The male or pollen-bearing flowers, are in dense clusters and the female or seed-bearing ones are larger and solitary. The dark purple, plum-like fruit, oblong in shape and about one inch in length ripens in September. It has a tough skin and thin acrid flesh and contains a flattened, ribbed stone.

The dark brown bark, about one-fourth of an inch thick, is longitudinally furrowed and roughened on the surface by small scales. The wood weighs thirty-five pounds to the cubic foot in an air-dry condition, and is hard, moderately strong, stiff and fairly high in ability to resist shock. It has a close, uniform texture and a very interlocked grain which prevents splintering under heavy wear, and makes it difficult to split. This interlocked grain also gives the wood a tendency to warp and twist, and considerable care is necessary in drying to produce straight, flat lumber. The heartwood is light brownish gray and merges gradually into the lighter colored sapwood. The wood is used for furniture and much of it is also utilized for shipping containers.

In the form of veneer, it goes largely into boxes for berries and

Water Tupelo grows in locations which are under water much of the year. It reaches heights up to 100 feet and trunk diameters of three to four feet

other fruits. The ability of the wood to show lettering to good advantage is responsible for its wide use in boxes for export shipments. It has also proved suitable for factory floors and platforms subjected to heavy wear. Some of the wood is used for paper pulp manufacture, and the exceptionally lightweight wood, commonly found in the swollen butts of trees grown in wet locations, is used for fish net floats.

Under favorable conditions water tupelo requires about twenty-five years to reach a diameter of six inches and a height of forty feet, and about fifty years to reach a diameter of ten inches and a height of seventy feet. Trees on moist but well-drained bottomlands grow much more rapidly than those on extremely swampy sites. Mature trees are frequently hollow-butted.

The seeds, which are usually produced in large quantities every year, are distributed principally by water. They become lodged in the mud and many of them germinate when the water has receded. Reproduction is particularly good where baldcypress and other associated trees have been removed.

Other names commonly applied to water tupelo are tupelo gum, swamp tupelo, cotton-gum, sour gum, swamp gum, bay poplar and hazel pine.

Of the four commercially important tupelos in the United States, water tupelo and black tupelo (*Nyssa sylvatica*) provide the bulk of the standing timber and annual cut. Swamp (black) tupelo (*Nyssa sylvatica* variety *biflora*) and ogeechee tupelo (*Nyssa ogeche*) are of much less importance. The stand of black tupelo over most of the southeastern states is much greater than that of water tupelo. The delta region of Louisiana, however, is where the great bulk of water tupelo is located. Much of the lumber produced in Louisiana, Mississippi and Alabama is water tupelo, which is made into furniture, boxes, baskets, crating and dairymen's supplies.

The tree is generally not used for shade or ornamental purposes.

About one-fourth of an inch thick, the dark brown bark is longitudinally furrowed and roughened on the surface by small scales

Photo from Textbook of Dendrology, Harlow and Harrar, courtesy of McGraw-Hill Book Co., Inc.

The purple, plum-like fruit is oblong in shape and ripens in September. It has a tough skin and thin acrid flesh

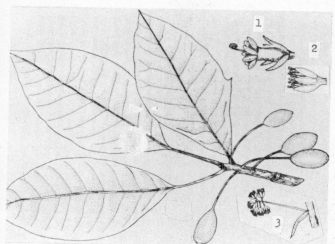

From Guide to Southern Trees, Harrar and Harrar, Dover Publications, Inc., New York

The alternate leaves are five to ten inches long and two to four wide, while the thick skinned, purple fruit is about an inch long, maturing in September and October. (1) The pistillate flower, supported by a short stalk, is solitary. (2) The staminate flower is born on a long, slender stalk and (3) occurs in clusters

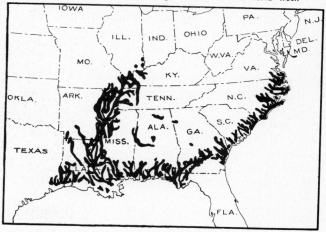

Natural range of Water Tupelo

FLOWERING DOGWOOD

Cornus florida **Linnaeus**

KNOWN best for its showy blossoms, the small irregular crown of slender spreading branches, the brilliant scarlet foliage, and the highly specialized commercial

leaves of flowering dogwood are ovate to elliptical and sharply pointed. They are three to six inches long, two to three inches wide, with prominent midribs and five or six primary veins curving parallel with the contour of the margin. The under surface is light colored and sometimes almost white. In the autumn the upper leaf surface turns bright scarlet.

Large white, pinkish, or rarely rose-red blooms appear in late April, May, or early June shortly before or with the unfolding of the first green leaves. The true flowers are inconspicuous, yellow-green, and perfect, forming a dense cluster in the center of what is usually mistaken for the blossom. What appear to be four large petals with deeply notched tips actually are bracts or forms of leaves.

The flowering dogwood gets its name

Devereux Butcher

A tracery of outreaching small twigs and branches characterizes dogwood in winter

uses of its wood, combine to make flowering dogwood a tree to be remembered. It seldom grows more than forty feet tall, and its short, irregular trunk is usually limited to a diameter of eight inches but occasionally reaches eighteen inches. This slow-growing tree usually occupies the margins of woodlands or the understory beneath open forest growth, and rarely approaches the conditions of a pure stand. It prefers rich, well-drained soils in coves or along the banks of streams from central Florida to eastern Texas and northward throughout the Mississippi Valley and the southern Appalachians to southern Missouri and Michigan, lower Ontario, central New York, and southern Maine. It is also found on the uplands of northern Mexico.

An opposite-branching tree, the bright green simple

Devereux Butcher

The irregularly rounded crown of bright green foliage is seldom taller than forty feet

from its profusion of spring flowers, and for the same reason bears the Latin name *florida. Cornus* is derived from the Latin word for horn, and refers to the hard, tough wood. *Cornus florida* is the most important of some forty or fifty species of shrubs and small trees, of which seventeen are native in North America.

The fruits are often in clusters, each one being small, egg-shaped and scarlet, containing a single hard seed. They ripen in October.

In winter the red terminal buds are like flattened cones and are generally downy near the point. The flower buds are about a quarter of an inch long and broad. They are always terminal and frequently very numerous. The smooth, slender twigs are yellowish green or bright red, often covered with tiny, closely appressed gray hairs.

The dark red-brown to almost black bark is closely ridged and broken into four-sided or rounded scales. It is about an eighth to a quarter inch thick and, with the root bark, has been used as the source of a bitter tonic for treating fevers. The Indians made a scarlet dye from the bark.

The relatively small reddish brown to light chocolate colored heartwood is surrounded by a broad area of pinkish sapwood. Its fine, uniform texture, with narrow annual growth rings, gives a firm, stiff wood that weighs about fifty-one pounds to the cubic foot when air dry. Probably ninety percent of all dogwood cut for commercial purposes is used in the manufacture of shuttles for textile weaving, because the hard, close-textured, smooth wood has little wearing effect upon the thread. It is also used for spool and bobbin heads, small pulleys, skewers, golf club heads, mallet heads, and jewelers' blocks.

Four large, showy, deeply notched bracts surround the cluster of inconspicuous perfect flowers

Deeply ridged and broken, the bark resembles alligator hide

Dogwood reproduces from seed, which is borne nearly every year. It also sprouts from the root collar to form coppice growth, and it may be successfully budded or grafted. Birds feed on the seeds.

The pointed ovate leaves are opposite one another, and the fruit cluster is bright scarlet

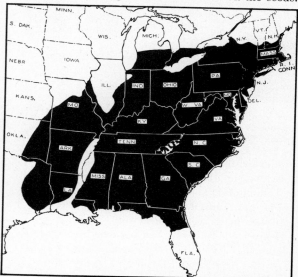

Natural range of Flowering Dogwood

PACIFIC DOGWOOD

Nuttall's dogwood, Western dogwood, Mountain dogwood

Cornus nuttallii Audubon

THE Pacific dogwood resembles its close relative, the flowering dogwood, *Cornus florida*, of eastern United States, the most conspicuous difference being in the petal-like bracts which surround the flower clusters. In the flowering dogwood these bracts are notched at the ends, while in the Pacific dogwood they are entire or more or less pointed. Another outstanding characteristic of the Pacific dogwood is that it often flowers a second time, during the late summer, when the fruit produced by the first flowers is turning red.

The tree occurs from the southern coast of British Columbia (the lower Fraser River Valley and Vancouver

Pacific Dogwood is ordinarily small, approximately 25 feet high, with the unique characteristic of a later-summer second flowering

Island) southward through western Washington, Oregon, and in California on the coast ranges south to the San Bernardino Mountains, and on the western slopes of the Sierra Nevada up to altitudes of 4,000 to 5,000 feet. It is usually found in moist, well-drained soils, on low, gentle mountain slopes, valleys, coves, and bottoms of mountain streams. It reaches its best development in the Douglas-fir forests of the Puget Sound basin and in the redwood region of California.

Pacific dogwood is a small tree, ordinarily from twenty to thirty feet high and six to eight inches in diameter, but rarely thirty to fifty feet high with a fairly straight trunk ten to twenty inches through. When crowded by other trees the long, slightly tapering stem is quite clear of branches and supports a short, narrow crown, but in the open the trunk is short with small spreading branches that form a long, narrow head which in older trees becomes rounded or conical. Occasionally it assumes a bushy habit with several stems.

The slender twigs, minutely hairy when young, are later mostly smooth and dull red purple, often with greenish areas, and the small pointed leaf buds are covered by two light green, narrow, long-pointed, opposite scales.

The egg-shaped leaves, three and a half to five inches long, and one and a half of three inches wide, are borne on stout, grooved, hairy stems, one-half to two-thirds of an inch long with a large, clasping base. The midribs and side veins are conspicuously impressed on their upper surfaces. In the autumn the leaves turn bright orange or pink and scarlet before falling.

The trunk is short and fairly straight with small spreading branches, but when crowded it has a long clear stem and narrow crown

The small, greenish yellow flowers bloom early in spring, and are encircled by from four to six showy white or sometimes pale pinkish scales

The very small greenish yellow flowers, which bloom in early spring, are surrounded by from four to six showy white, or sometimes faintly pinkish bracts, which are popularly thought to be petals. They are, however, flower bud scales which, with the flower cluster, are partly formed during the previous summer. In the spring they grow with the flowers, becoming large and showy when the latter open. It is then that the tree adds a note of exceptional beauty to the wild forests of the mountains that are its natural habitat.

Ripening in September or October, from twenty-five to forty shining red berries are matured in dense clusters. The thin rather dry pulp of the berry encases a hardshelled stone that contains one or two seeds.

The thin reddish brown bark is smooth, except near the base of older trees, where it is broken on the surface into small, thin, appressed scales. The fine-grained wood is heavy, hard and strong, a cubic foot, when air-dry, weighing about forty-five pounds, the heartwood pale reddish brown and the thick sapwood lighter in color. It is used in cabinet work, for mauls and for the handles of tools. The wood has been suggested for the manufacture of shuttles used in weaving in place of the flowering dogwood of eastern United States, although it is somewhat below the latter in hardness and shock resistance.

Pacific dogwood is slow growing. Trees from six to twelve inches in diameter are from fifty to 100 years old, and larger trees from 125 to 150 years. It produces seeds abundantly every year, and seedlings are most numerous in deep shade and on moist stream borders. It is very desirable as an ornamental, not only in early spring when it blooms, but also in late summer and early autumn with the clusters of bright red fruit against a background of bright green or orange and scarlet foliage.

The egg-shaped leaves turn bright orange or scarlet in autumn. Red berries occur in dense clusters of 25 to 40

The thin, reddish brown bark is smooth except near the base of older trees where it is broken on the surface into small scales

Natural range of Pacific Dogwood

PACIFIC MADRONE

Madrona, Madroño
Arbutus menziesii Pursh

PACIFIC MADRONE belongs to the heath family, *Erica-ceae*, which includes also the rhododendron and mountain-laurel or kalmia, azaleas and blueberries. Called Pacific madrone or frequently just plain madrone, or madrona, this colorful tree adds its charm to the greenery of count-less slopes throughout the length of the coastal mountains, from British Columbia south through western Washington and Oregon to southern California. Its orange-colored branches and young trunks and shiny, evergreen foliage distinguish it at once from all other trees or shrubs in its range.

The naturalist John Muir wrote of this tree: "The ma-drona, clad in thin, smooth, red and yellow bark, with big, glossy leaves, seems in the dark coniferous forests of Wash-ington and Vancouver Island like some lost wanderer from the magnolia groves in the South." Its distinctive orange bole is only slightly more eye-arresting than are the foliage and fruit. Sometimes it is described by local people as the tree which sheds its bark instead of its leaves. This descrip-tion has some basis in fact since old leaves persist until the new are fully grown, and the bark on branches and young stems peels into thin, scaly slabs which drop off in the sum-mer and fall in the same way that sycamore bark does. On older trunks, it is brown, covered with loose, thin, gray, plate-like scales that are shed annually.

Because Pacific madrone is found abundantly scattered over sunny hillsides where soils are poor and rocky, people are prone to overlook the fact that it grows much better on fertile, moist sites. Its best growth is attained on well-drained soils, near sea level, where it ranges in height from eighty to 125 feet or even more, and from two to four feet in diameter, breast high. In both the coast ranges and western Sierra Nevada of California, it may be found up to 4,000 feet elevation. This species often forms nearly pure stands, although it occurs in much greater abundance as an understory species in Douglasfir and redwood forests or in association with mixed broadleaf and coni-ferous trees.

In dense stands it is often a stately tree with a straight, clear bole and stout, up-right or spreading branches forming a nar-row, oblong or broad, round-topped head with slender branchlets. The branchlets are light red, pea-green or orange-colored when they first appear, and become, in their first winter, bright reddish brown. In the open, madrone tends to produce a short, crooked or leaning trunk and on dry mountain slopes the tree may be no more than a twisted shrub.

Terminal leaf buds are oval in shape and have numerous scales. The lateral buds are very small. The thick leathery leaves are smooth, dark green and lustrous above and pale or often nearly white below, and meas-ure from three to five inches long and one and a half to three inches wide. They have a thick, pale midrib and conspicuous vein-lets. They are borne on stout, grooved stems one-half to one inch long, are oval to oblong in outline, rounded or contracted into a short point at the apex, and have smooth margins which may, however, be firmly to coarsely toothed on vigorous growth. When they unfold they are light green or often pink, especially on the lower surface. They remain on the tree until the early summer of their second year when they turn orange and scarlet and fall grad-ually and irregularly. A second crop of smaller leaves is often produced late in summer.

Devereux Butcher

When open-grown, Pacific Madrone, one of our most colorful trees, has a short, often leaning trunk and broad crown

The dark green, leathery evergreen leaves contrast sharply with the bright orange-red, berry-like fruit

Philip Palmer

Devereux Butcher

Bark on limbs and young trunks is orange, darkening on old trunks to brown with flaky, gray scales

The small, white, bell-shaped flowers, about one-third of an inch long, appear from March to May in large, showy, nodding, terminal clusters resembling lilies-of-the-valley. Each flower develops into a small, round, bright orange-red, berry-like fruit. Borne in long, loose clusters, each fruit contains several dark brown, angled seeds tightly pressed together.

The heartwood is a light reddish brown and the sapwood white or cream, frequently with a pinkish tinge. The wood is fine-textured, hard, heavy and moderately strong, being similar in these properties to Pacific dogwood, but it has less shock resistance than the latter. A cubic foot of the air-dry wood weighs about forty-six pounds. Together with Pacific dogwood, it has been suggested for the manufacture of shuttles used for weaving cloth in place of the flowering dogwood of eastern United States.

The tree produces large quantities of seed every year. Although difficult to transplant, it is very hardy after it has become established and is often grown in yards and gardens for its bright colors. In the fall, the bunches of brilliant orange-red fruit, with the slender green, red or brown twigs and the reddish older leaves, make pleasing color combinations. It is occasionally cultivated in the gardens of western and southern Europe.

The genus *Arbutus* was first defined by Linnaeus in 1754 and given the old Latin name for the common strawberry tree of southern Europe, *Arbutus unedo*. Of the twelve species, all of them confined to the northern hemisphere, two are found in Mexico and the southwestern United States, and one on the Pacific coast.

The specific name was given by the Siberian-born botanist, Frederick Pursh, in honor of Archibald Menzies, who discovered and collected specimens of the tree at Port Discovery, California, in May 1792. He was the botanist of Captain Vancouver's voyage of discovery in 1790-1795. In his journals he calls it "the oriental strawberry tree" and continues, "this last grows to a small tree and was at this time a peculiar ornament to the forest by its large clusters of whitish flowers and evergreen leaves, but its peculiar smooth bark of a reddish brown color will at all times attract the notice of the most superficial observer."

Pacific Madrone grows naturally from British Columbia to Southern California

SOURWOOD

Sorrel-tree

Oxydendrum arboreum (Linnaeus) de Candolle

J. Horace McFarland Co.

Spreading and drooping branches characterize
the Sourwood tree that is grown in the open

ON WELL-DRAINED wooded slopes and ridges rising above the banks of streams in the southern Appalachians, the sourwood tree reaches a height of sixty to seventy feet and a trunk diameter of eighteen to twenty inches, but its usual height is about twenty-five feet with a trunk diameter not over eight inches. Its range extends from the coast of Virginia to southwestern Pennsylvania, southern Ohio and Indiana, to western Kentucky and Tennessee and south to southeastern Louisiana, the coast region of Mississippi, the shores of Mobile Bay and northern Florida. Most commonly found on hill and mountain sides, sourwood grows to largest size on the western slopes of the Great Smoky Mountains in Tennessee.

It is also called sorrel-tree, both names referring to the sour or acid taste of the leaves and branchlets, resembling that of the herbaceous sorrel. The name *Oxydendrum* is from two Greek words meaning sour and tree, while *arboreum* is from the Latin meaning tree-like. Sourwood has no close relatives; it is the only member of its genus so far as known. It belongs to the heath family, which includes several ornamental trees and shrubs such as the rhododendrons, mountain-laurel and azalea.

In the forest the tree has a tall, straight trunk, the slender branches forming a narrow oblong, round-topped head. When grown in the open, it develops an irregular top with spreading and drooping branches. The smooth twigs are yellow-green at first, marked by numerous, oblong, elevated lenticels, becoming in their first winter orange-colored to reddish brown.

The alternate, oblong, pointed leaves are bronze green when they unfold and dark green at maturity. Five to seven inches long and one and a half to two and a half inches wide, they are very lustrous and smooth with the exception of a slight hairiness on the upper side of the midrib and pale underneath, with a few scattered hairs on the under side of the midrib and on the petioles. They resemble somewhat a peach leaf, are net-veined and finely toothed on the margins and turn scarlet in autumn.

Opening in July or August, the tiny, white, fragrant, bell-shaped flowers, one-third of an inch long, in delicate clusters six to eight inches long, are grouped at the ends of the branches and remind one of the lily-of-the-valley. The fruit matures in September, a month or six weeks after the flowers, as five-angled, grayish capsules, about a half inch long. They hang in drooping clusters, sometimes a foot in length. They hold many pale brown seeds about an eighth of an inch long, and the empty capsules often remain on the branches until late in the autumn.

Terminal buds are lacking and the minute axillary winter buds, about one-sixteenth of an inch long, are

John V. Clancy

Winter reveals the straight trunk and slender
branches which form a narrow oblong head

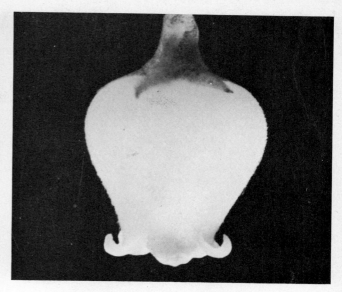

The tiny flowers, one-third of an inch
long, suggest the lily-of-the-valley

The tiny fragrant flowers, in delicate clusters, are grouped at the ends of the branches

covered with opposite, broadly ovate, dark red scales an
inch in length at maturity. The bark on the trunk of
mature trees is gray, tinged with red, from two-thirds to
one inch thick, and is divided by longitudinal fissures
into broad, rounded ridges covered with small, thick,
appressed scales. Young branches are reddish brown.

The heartwood is brown, tinged with red, and the wide
sapwood, with eighty or more layers of annual growth,
is yellowish brown to light pinkish brown. It is fine textured, heavy, hard, stiff, strong in bending and moderately high in shock resistance. A cubic foot of the air-
dry wood weighs about forty-six pounds. It is sometimes

used locally for the handles of tools, machinery bearings
and sled runners.

Sourwood is distinctly an ornamental tree because of
its handsome foliage and large, late blooming clusters of
tiny, bell-shaped flowers, and because of the scarlet coloring of the leaves in the fall. In cultivation it is a small,
slender tree and is often planted in eastern United States,
where it is hardy as far north as eastern Massachusetts.
It is occasionally grown as an ornamental in western and
central Europe.

Arnold Arboretum

The bark on the trunk is divided by vertical fissures into broad rounded ridges

Arnold Arboretum

The grayish capsules of the fruit begin to
develop after the blossoms fall

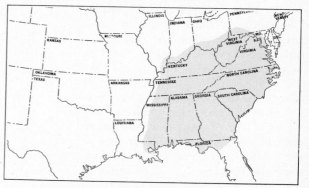

Natural range of Sourwood

PERSIMMON

Diospyros virginiana **Linnaeus**

Ohio Division of Forestry

Persimmon is a tree of moderate height with irregular branches clothed in glossy leaves

A TREE of moderate size, with crooked branches and a round-topped cylindrical crown massed with glossy leaves, the persimmon is the most northern member of the ebony family. It is, however, more generally known for the puckery quality of its immature fruit than for its hard, firm wood. While other true ebonies are largely tropical or subtropical, this tree grows on a wide variety of soils and sites from Connecticut westward through southern Pennsylvania to Illinois, Missouri, eastern Kansas, and south to Florida and eastern Texas. Only one other species of persimmon, *Diospyros texana*, occurs in the United States. This is of no commercial importance, and its range is limited to southwestern Texas.

Frequently a large shrub, forming extensive thickets on abandoned land, it often attains heights of fifty feet and trunk diameters of six to twelve inches. Under favorable forest conditions it reaches 100 to 130 feet in height with trunk diameters of over two feet.

The leathery, alternate leaves are pointedly oval, three to seven inches long, and a deep, glossy green above contrasting with a pale underside. The leaf stems or petioles are a half inch to an inch long. Sheep, goats, and even deer will not browse the foliage. Therefore this tree successfully maintains itself on open land and frequently prospers in spite of pasturing.

U.S. Forest Service

In May or June, when the leaves are partly grown, yellowish green to milky white urn-shaped blossoms appear like small bells on the new shoots. The staminate blossoms are usually on trees separate from those with the pistillate ones, so that there are fruit-bearing trees as distinguished from those that apparently are barren.

The fruit is a true berry, roughly globular and an inch to an inch and a half in diameter, with one to eight oblong, compressed seeds imbedded in the juicy flesh. Early settlers are reported to have roasted the seeds for use as coffee. In summer the big berries become pale orange and often red cheeked, but when ripe turn a blackish purple. Only then does the pulp lose its high content of astringent tannin to become sweet and delicious, with food value second only to the date.

In the same locality there may be trees that are ripening their fruit as early as August or September, while others may ripen in February or even March. Thus persimmons furnish food for birds and wildlife, as well as for such domestic stock as hogs, and to some extent for humans, through the fall and winter. Branches often are weighted down with as much fruit as they can support. The quality varies from tree to tree, some fruits being especially adapted for food.

The name *Diospyros* is from two Greek words—*Dios*, which refers to the god Zeus, and *puros*, for wheat. Freely translated, it means "food for the gods." This applies to the lucious fruits of the 200 or more species of persimmon. *Virginana* refers to that great area of eastern North America, Virginia, named for Elizabeth, "the virgin Queen." DeSoto described the persimmon, in 1557, as a "delicious little plum."

The deep brown to black bark, an inch and a half to two inches thick, is closely divided into small blocks like a rough mosaic.

As with other members of the ebony family, the heartwood of persimmon is dark brown or black, while the larger area of light brown sapwood is often mottled with darker spots. Comparatively little sapwood turns to heartwood until trees are close to 100 years old. The wood is close-grained, hard, strong and tough, weighs about fifty-three pounds to the cubic foot when air dry, and is capable of taking a high polish. The sapwood is used for shuttle blocks, bobbins, plane stocks, and shoe lasts, and is recognized as standard for the heads of golf clubs and other less specialized purposes.

While susceptible to injury from ground fires, persimmon seldom is seriously attacked by insects and is avoided by livestock and rabbits. A fungus disease known as persimmon wilt is causing severe losses among native persimmon trees in the Southeast, notably in Tennessee and North Carolina. Effective control measures have not yet been developed for the dis-

U.S. Forest Service

Chicago Natural History Museum

The leaves are glossy green above and pale beneath, while the fruit is a large berry

ease. Consequently, it is best that plantings of the tree, for wildlife or human food, be scattered. Asiatic species of the persimmon are very resistant to the wilt, but their fruits are not as delicious as those of the native trees.

U.S. Forest Service

The dark brown bark is deeply cut into small blocks

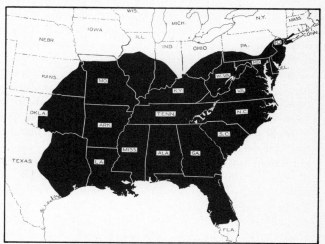

Natural range of Persimmon

WHITE ASH

Biltmore ash, Smallseed white ash
Fraxinus americana Linnaeus

Devereux Butcher

The compact, oval crown of White Ash is clothed with rich green foliage in summer, and in winter it shows a thick growth of upward-reaching branches and twigs

George J. Baetzhold

WHITE ASH, the largest and finest of all the ashes, is one of the leading commercial hardwoods of the United States. It grows from Nova Scotia and Maine, west to Minnesota and south to Texas and Florida. Never in large pure stands, or even a dominant part of the forest, it grows singly or in small groups in association with other hardwoods, or with hemlock, white pine, or spruce. It thrives on a variety of soils, but is most frequently found on comparatively well-drained, fertile sites.

Trees seventy to eighty feet high with broadly rounded or pyramidal crowns, and a straight columnar trunk two to three feet in diameter are common throughout much of its range, but the giants of one hundred and twenty feet in height and six feet in diameter were largely confined to the deep, moist soil of fertile bottomlands in the lower Ohio River Valley. In the forest the straight, symmetrical stem may be clear of branches for more than half the total height of the tree.

Like the other members of the olive family, *Oleaceae*, of which white ash is the chief commercial lumber species, the branching is opposite. The pinnately compound leaves are eight to twelve inches long, with five to nine (usually seven) short-stalked, dark green, oval or broadly lance-shaped, pointed leaflets, each three to five inches long and one and a half inches broad. They are pale

The pistillate or seed-producing flowers, with the unfolding leaves, occur in open clusters, and are borne on trees separate from those that bear the staminate flowers

green underneath, and the edges usually smooth.

The inconspicuous, dark reddish to purple, four-lobed male blossoms are produced on different trees from those bearing the clusters of pistillate flowers. They open before the leaves late in April or May, and the pistillate ones develop by mid-summer into long, drooping clusters of light brown, paddle-shaped fruits, one to two inches long, in which the narrow pointed seed case extends lengthwise to form a wing about a quarter of an inch wide.

Ash may get its name from the dark brown, ashy gray bark which is one to three inches thick, and deeply divided by narrow diamond-shaped fissures into flattened ridges. The thick, opposite branchlets are first dark green or brown and covered with scattered hairs, but later become smooth, ashy gray and marked with pale lenticels.

Fraxinus is the scientific name for ash, while *americana* singles this outstanding American variety from nearly fifty species distributed over the temperate and tropical regions of the northern hemisphere. Eighteen species of ash are recognized in the United States.

The hard, close-grained, light brown wood is strong, tough, elastic. When air dry it weighs about forty-two pounds to the cubic foot. It is used for tool handles, butter tubs, oars, sporting goods, furniture, vehicles, and interior trim.

The wood is relatively free from insect and fungus attack, but the thin-barked young trees are highly susceptible to fire.

Tufts of dark red to purple staminate blossoms appear in early spring before the leaves

White Ash leaves are pinnately compound with five to nine short-stalked leaflets, while light brown paddle-shaped fruits one to two inches long, hang in clusters from the previous year's growth

Deep diamond-shaped fissures cut the ashy gray bark into flattened ridges

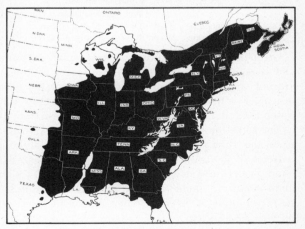

Natural range of White Ash

365

GREEN ASH

Red ash, Swamp ash, River ash, Water ash
Fraxinus pennsylvanica Marshall

GREEN ASH has been recognized as a variety, *lanceo-lata*, of the species *pennsylvanica*, which was called red ash. The only salient feature separating them has been that the leaflets and twigs in the variety are smooth, whereas in the species they are hairy. However, so many trees have varying degrees of hairiness that botanists often do not distinguish between them but include them under the name "green ash," because the variety is more important than the species.

Their areas of distribution are very much alike, and together they extend from Nova Scotia to eastern Alberta, southward through central Montana and northeastern Wyoming to eastern Texas, and east through northern Florida.

Chicago Natural History Museum

Rarely more than sixty feet high and two in diameter, Green Ash is not a large tree

Green ash is principally a tree of moist bottomlands and is commonly found on overflow river bottoms that are not covered with water during most of the growing season. For this reason it is often called swamp ash and water ash. It is most abundant in the Mississippi River basin, sometimes covering banks of streams flowing east from the Rocky Mountains. It also inhabits the river bottoms of the south Atlantic states. In the sparsely forested prairie country of the Middle West it is found almost entirely along streams. In this region it is able to maintain itself in rather dry situations, once it has become established.

Green ash is not a large tree. Rarely more than sixty

feet high and two feet in diameter, it occasionally reaches a height of one hundred feet and a diameter of three feet. Round-topped with slender, spreading branches, it has ashy gray branchlets marked by pale lenticels.

In the pinnately compound leaf, which is from ten to twelve inches long, there are seven or nine oval or lance-shaped leaflets, each two to six inches long and about one inch wide, the edges usually slightly toothed or often smooth below the middle. They differ from those of white ash in that the leaflets are narrower and slender-pointed and the margins are more distinctly toothed.

Male or staminate and female or pistillate flowers are borne in compact clusters on separate trees and the pistillate ones develop into winged fruit a little longer and narrower than that of white ash, generally one and a quarter to two and a quarter inches in length and mostly a little less than a quarter of an inch wide. They are also usually pointed at the apex in contrast to the rounded ones of white ash, although some of both species can be found that are slightly notched at the apex. Ripening in the fall, they often remain attached to the twigs throughout the winter.

The bark, one-half to two-thirds of an inch thick, is ashy gray to brown. As with white ash, it has interlacing ridges, but is more shallowly furrowed.

The wood is heavy, hard, strong, stiff, and has shock-

L. W. Brownell

Green Ash is a round-topped tree with small, slender, spreading branches

Ohio Division of Forestry

The winged fruit is generally about two
inches long and less than a quarter inch wide

L. W. Brownell

The male or staminate flowers are borne
on separate trees from the pistillate ones

resisting ability. In an air-dry condition it weighs about
forty pounds to the cubic foot. Green ash is similar in its
properties to white ash and is used for the same purposes.
As a source of timber, these two species are the most
important ashes and the wood of both is marketed as
"white ash." The most important use is for tool handles.
Other uses are oars, paddles, baseball bats, skis, snow-
shoes and tennis racket frames. Rapid growth wood is
most in demand for these products, having the desirable
characteristics of straightness of grain, stiffness, strength,
hardness, good bending properties and capacity to wear
smooth with use. Slowly growing forest trees, more than
150 years of age have a narrow band of sapwood usually less than two inches wide. Fast growing trees, fairly
open-grown, less than 100 years old and more than twelve
inches in diameter, generally have from three to six
inches of sapwood, and it is the wide-ringed sapwood
that is most in demand.

The commercial supply of green ash is largely in the
South, which is contributing an increasing proportion
of the ash lumber cut.

While the tree is comparatively short-lived and generally grows rather slowly, in favorable locations it makes
rapid growth, especially when young.

Heavy crops of seeds are produced, which germinate
quickly. The seeds also are very light and are carried
far by the wind. Reproduction on bottomlands and on
old fields is especially good where there is sufficient moisture. It is quite free from insect and fungus attack but
is subject to injury from fire, especially when young.
The species has been widely planted as a shade and
ornamental tree in the plains states.

L. W. Brownell

There are seven or nine lance-shaped
leaflets in the pinnately compound leaf

L. W. Brownell

Like white ash, the bark has interlacing
ridges, but it is more shallowly furrowed

Natural range of Green Ash

BLUE ASH

Fraxinus quadrangulata Michaux

THE FOUR-ANGLED twigs, from which blue ash gets its specific Latin name, are the outstanding characteristic of this tree. Its range is quite limited, reaching from extreme southern Ontario, southern Michigan, Illinois and Missouri to southeastern Kansas, locally in southwestern Arkansas, and from Ohio and southwestern West Virginia through Kentucky and Tennessee to northern Alabama and northeastern Mississippi.

It occurs principally on dry uplands through the Ohio and upper Mississippi valleys. It will grow on drier soils than any of the other ashes, but it does well on moist, fertile bottomlands also. Nowhere abundant, blue ash is scattered throughout the hardwood forests, where it is commonly associated with various oaks and hickories. It reaches its best development in southern Indiana, especially in the valley of the lower Wabash River, where it attains a height of 120 feet and a trunk diameter of three to four feet. It is usually a medium-sized tree, however,

Chicago Natural History Museum

Blue Ash usually attains 50 to 80 feet in height, but in the Wabash Valley of Indiana it may reach 120 feet and have a trunk diameter of three or four feet

Chicago Natural History Museum

Small, spreading branches that form a narrow crown, and a short trunk, are characteristics of Blue Ash. They are distinctly noticeable in the winter tree

fifty to eighty feet high and one to two feet in diameter, with a rather short, clear bole and small, spreading branches that form a narrow crown.

The stout four-angled branchlets have a more or less distinct corky wing at each edge. They are dark orange color and are covered with short, reddish, soft hairs when they first appear, becoming gray, tinged with red in their second year, and marked by scattered, pale lenticels. In their third year they are light brown or ashy gray, and gradually become round in cross section. The broadly egg-shaped, pointed, terminal buds are about a quarter of an inch long and have two or three pairs of reddish brown scales. The lateral buds are similar, but much smaller.

There generally are from five to nine (usually seven) narrowly ovate leaflets. Measuring from three to five inches long and one to two inches wide, they are similar in form to those of the black ash, but are borne on short stalks, whereas black ash leaflets have no stalks. When mature they are thick and firm, yellow-green above and paler below, smooth on both surfaces, the margins coarsely and sharply serrate with incurved teeth. They turn pale yellow in the autumn.

In April, as the leaf buds unfold, the flowers appear in loose clusters on shoots of the previous year. They differ from those of other important ash species in that each blossom has both male and female parts. The winged seeds or samaras are one to two inches long and nearly one inch wide, with a wide, thin wing, slightly notched at the tip, extending to the base of the flattened seed. It ripens in September or October and falls soon after.

The scaly bark is a feature which distinguishes blue ash from the other ash species, except black ash, the bark of which is somewhat similar. It is from a half to two thirds of an inch thick, light gray, tinged with red, and is irregularly divided into large plate-like scales which, especially on old trunks, has a shaggy appearance. The inner bark contains a mucilaginous substance that oozes from the stump when the tree is cut, and turns blue on exposure to the air. A blue dye which may be prepared by macerating the inner bark in water was used by the pioneers for dyeing cloth, hence the name blue ash.

The wood is similar to that of white and green ash, a cubic foot weighing about forty pounds when air dry. The heartwood is light yellow, streaked with brown, and the thick sapwood lighter colored. Because of the limited area of distribution and comparatively small size of the tree, it is unimportant as a source of lumber.

Blue ash grows rather rapidly, much faster than black ash and about as fast as white ash on the same sites. It is rather short-lived. Seed is not produced in large quantities, crops occurring every three or four years, and reproduction is poor. As with the other ash species, it is quite free from diseases and insect attack. Because of its unique four-angled twigs, the tree is occasionally grown as an ornamental in parks and gardens in eastern United States. Its ability to thrive in dry locations should recommend it to landscape gardeners and city foresters, particularly in the prairie regions where it has been planted to some extent.

The five to nine leaflets measuring from three to five inches in length are similar to those of Black Ash, except that those of Blue Ash are borne on short stalks

The scaly, light gray bark differs from that of all other ashes except Black Ash to which it is rather similar. It is from a half to two thirds of an inch thick

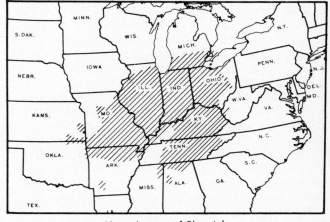

Natural range of Blue Ash

BLACK ASH

Brown ash, Basket ash, Hoop ash
Fraxinus nigra Marshall

Devereux Butcher

Black Ash attains heights up to 80 or 90 feet and trunk diameters that rarely exceed 20 inches. Forest-grown trees have narrow crowns, but open-grown ones have longer, more widely spreading branches

GROWING to a height of from eighty to ninety feet and rarely exceeding twenty inches in diameter, black ash is the slenderest broadleaf tree in the forest. It has a straight columnar trunk with little taper and is often clear of branches for fifty feet. The crown is rounded and is made up of a few short branches; it is narrow under forest conditions, but much wider when grown in the open. The twigs are stout, ashy gray, marked by large pale lenticels and roughened by conspicuous, circular to semi-circular leaf scars.

Black ash is distinctly a northern species, growing from the Gulf of St. Lawrence to Manitoba and south to Minnesota, northeastern Iowa, Pennsylvania and eastern West Virginia. It is primarily a wet-soil tree of northern low-lands and foothills and is usually confined to the borders of swamps, streams and lakes. It makes its best growth on deep, fertile, moist or wet soil, often in company with northern whitecedar, balsam fir, red maple, black spruce and tamarack.

The pinnately compound leaves are from twelve to sixteen inches long with seven to thirteen oblong to oblong-lanceolate, long-pointed leaflets four to five inches long and one to one and a half inches wide. When mature they are thin and firm, dark green and

smooth above, paler and smooth below, with the exception of occasional tufts of rufous hairs along the under side of the broad, pale midrib. The margins of the leaflets have small, incurved teeth pointed toward the tip. With the exception of the terminal leaflet, which has a short stem, the leaflets are attached directly to the leaf stalk. This in contrast to the leaves of white and green ash in which each side leaflet has a short stem of its own. The leaves turn a rusty brown and fall early in the autumn.

The flowers appear before the leaves in slender, branched clusters, on shoots of the preceding season. The black ash is peculiar in that not only are the male and female flowers borne on different trees, but some trees also have perfect flowers—that is, flowers with both the male and female parts.

The flat, winged, one-seeded fruit is narrowly oblong, one to one and a half inches long and about a third of an inch broad; it is surrounded by a wide, thin wing which is rounded or slightly notched at the apex. The seeds are in loose clusters eight to ten inches long. They ripen in August and September.

The ovate, pointed, terminal buds are dark brown to nearly black, about one-fourth of an inch long, covered by four to six scales. The lateral buds are smaller and more rounded, the first pair generally located at some distance from the end of the twig, giving the terminal bud a stalked appearance.

Devereux Butcher

The bark is light gray and smooth at first, later becoming shallowly fissured and divided into large irregular plates with thin, soft, papery scales that rub off easily. Moderately heavy, a cubic foot of air-dry black ash wood weighs about thirty-four pounds. It is moderately hard, moderately strong in bending, moderately stiff, and has high shock-resisting ability. The heartwood is grayish brown to brown and the narrow sapwood is whitish to light brown. Old trees generally have dark colored heartwood, which is well liked for furniture and the interior finish of houses because of its fine grain and pleasing figure. Ash is the standard wood for certain classes of handles, including the shorter handles for shovels and spades, and longer ones for hoes and rakes. Although much black ash is used for handles, other species, principally white ash and green ash, are preferred for long handles because the wood of these species has higher strength values. Black ash has been much used in making splints for baskets because the wood can be easily split between the layers of annual growth. From early times pack baskets have been fabricated by the Indians of the Northeast from such splints, which are obtained by pounding the green wood until it separates along the springwood pores. Black ash is also called brown ash from the color of the heartwood. Other names sometimes applied to it are swamp ash, water ash, basket ash and hoop ash.

The trees are easily injured by fire, from which, however, they are generally protected by the wet locations in which they grow. They are quite free from insect attack and fungus diseases, but the sapwood lumber is subject to attack by powder-post beetles.

Warren D. Brush

A distinguishing feature of Black Ash is the stemless leaflets of the pinnately compound leaves, which are 12 to 16 inches long

The Davey Tree Expert Co.

Bark of the Black Ash is light gray and smooth at first, but later becomes shallowly fissured and has soft, papery scales

Warren D. Brush

Each flat wing contains a single seed that is narrowly oblong, one to one and a half inches in length, ripening in August or September

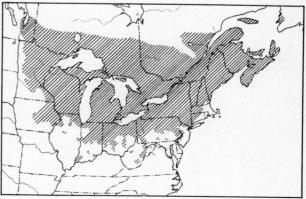

Natural range of Black Ash

371

OREGON ASH

Fraxinus latifolia Bentham

TRAVELERS in western Oregon and Washington often notice pure stands of Oregon ash in its preferred habitat on poorly-drained, moist bottomlands in the innumerable valleys west of the Cascades. Here it follows streams and swamps in ribbon-like fringes. It is also found on sandy, gravelly or even rocky soils in old fields and along roadsides in mixture with bigleaf maple, red alder, lowland white fir and Douglasfir.

Most abundant in Oregon's Willamette Valley, it grows west of Washington's Cascade Range south to Southern California, and from sea level to 3,000 feet elevation.

Oregon ash belongs to the olive family, whose nearly 500 species of trees and shrubs are widely distributed throughout the northern hemisphere and south of the equator in Java. Besides the edible olive, this family includes the lilacs, the forsythias and the privets.

Of over forty ashes in the world, eighteen, of which five or six reach commercial size, are found within the United States. Oregon ash is the only timber ash of the Pacific region.

It is a medium-sized tree from sixty to eighty feet high and from twenty-four to thirty-six inches in diameter at maturity. Under the most favorable conditions, it may become twice as large and reach an age of from 200 to 250 years. Trees grown in the open have short trunks and wide-spreading branches; whereas those found in the forest have long, clean trunks and compact crowns. On dry sites, they are stunted and twisted.

The bark, one to one and a half inches thick, is dark gray-brown, with an interwoven pattern of flat ridges and diamond-shaped fissures. On very old trees the ridges are slightly scaly.

The leaves, as with those of all ashes, appear late in the spring and drop early in the fall after turning a yel-

Oliver V. Matthews

Oregon State Forestry Department

A medium-sized tree, the Oregon Ash has a short trunk and wide-spreading branches when grown in the open. The leaves appear late in the spring and drop early in the autumn

low or russet brown. They are pinately compound with five or seven leaflets, yellowish green above, paler and downy on the under side. The leaflets are three to five inches long, and from one to one and a half inches wide. The leaves almost always have an odd number of leaflets. To find an ash leaf with an even number is considered to be a sign of good luck.

The twigs are stout and densely tomentose, with conical terminal buds and small, ovoid lateral buds.

In April or May, when the leaves begin to unfold, the flowers appear in dense clusters. The male and female flowers are always found on separate trees.

The fruit is an oblong to elliptical samara one to one and a half inches long. It matures in early autumn. Seed is produced at about the thirtieth year; and heavy crops are re-released every three to five years thereafter. New trees are also produced by sprouts from the stump.

A moderately shallow but wide-spreading root system makes the tree unusually wind-firm.

The strong, hard and stiff wood of the Oregon ash resembles that of the other American ashes. The color is a dull yellowish brown, with whitish sapwood. A cubic foot weighs about thirty-eight pounds.

Although not abundant in commercial sizes, the Oregon ash is important by reason of the scarcity of hardwoods in the Pacific Northwest. The wood takes a polish and is used to a limited extent for furniture and interior trim. It is sometimes used for slack cooperage, tool handles, butter tubs, and wagon parts. However, the most notable use is for fuel, as the wood splits easily and has a heat value almost equal to that of oak.

The Oregon ash has been planted as an ornamental in the eastern United States and Europe. For this purpose it is suited because of its handsome shape, rapid growth, and hardiness.

The English botanist, Thomas Nuttall, who first described the species in 1849, records this curious legend: "An opinion prevails in Oregon among the hunters and Indians that poisonous serpents are unknown in the same tract of country where this ash grows."

Philip Palmer

The leaves are pinnately compound with five or seven leaflets, yellowish green above, paler and downy on the underside. The winged fruit is from one to one and a half inches long

Chicago Natural History Museum

Flat ridges and diamond-shaped fissures give the dark gray-brown bark a woven appearance

Natural range of the Oregon Ash. The tree occurs from sea level to 3,000 feet

NORTHERN CATALPA

Hardy catalpa, Cigar tree, Catawba tree
Catalpa speciosa Warder

Devereux Butcher

George J. Baetzhold

Northern Catalpa, picturesque with its large heart-shaped leaves, showy white flowers and long seed pods, may grow 100 feet tall in its natural range

Devereux Butcher

THE word *Catalpa* is a Cherokee Indian name adopted by the early settlers of this continent, and *speciosa,* a Latin word meaning ornamental, has been given this irregular and picturesque tree with large decorative leaves and conspicuous flower-clusters.

In the northeastern states, planted trees reach twenty-five or fifty feet in height with a trunk diameter of six to fifteen inches. The range of northern catalpa extends around the juncture of the Ohio River with the Mississippi. Along the rich bottomlands of the Ohio basin, in southern Illinois and southern Indiana, it attains its maximum size of a hundred and twenty feet with diameters of four or rarely five feet. When growing in the open, the trunk is short and usually crooked, the crown broad and spreading with thick, scraggly branches. In the forest it is taller with a narrow rounded crown and a straight,

374

slightly tapering trunk that is sometimes clear of limbs for sixty feet. In deep, moist, fertile soil northern catalpa grows rapidly, maturing in one hundred years or less. It is tolerant to some shade.

It has been widely planted in the eastern half of the United States as far north as Massachusetts. Never forming pure stands in the forest, it is found singly or in small groups associated with other hardwoods.

Bark on the mature trunk is three-quarters to one inch thick, light grayish brown, broken into longitudinal, scaly, flat ridges. Twigs are stout, smooth or downy, yellowish or reddish brown, with large conspicuous lenticels and large leaf-scars. The small lateral winter buds are embedded in the bark and covered with overlapping scales. Terminal buds are absent, and the tips of twigs in the north are often winter-killed.

The large leaves, which are almost tropical in appearance, are borne on stout cylindrical stems four to six inches long, grow opposite, whorled, or three in a group, and measure seven to twelve inches in length and five to eight inches in width. They are long-pointed at the outer end, round or heart-shaped at the base, and have even edges, or one or two teeth. Mature leaves are light green and smooth above, slightly paler and hairy beneath, and at the axils of the primary veins they have clusters of dark purplish glands which are visited by honey bees.

Appearing in June or early July, the showy flowers, borne on slender terminal stalks, are arranged in pyramidal, many-flowered clusters five to six inches long.

The fruit ripens in autumn. It is a slender two-celled bean-like, cylindrical capsule ten to twenty inches long and one-half to three-quarters inch thick, suspended by a thick stem. Green when young, the pods later turn dark brown and remain on the tree during the winter. Toward spring they split liberating the flat seeds.

Catalpa wood when dry weighs twenty-six pounds to the cubic foot. It is coarse-grained, soft, not strong, but very durable in contact with soil. The heartwood is grayish brown, occasionally tinged with lavender, and the thin sapwood is nearly white. It is ring-porous, and, when cut at right angles to the pith rays, resembles ash. Probably nine-tenths of all catalpa cut is made into fence posts, though occasionally it is used for handles, picture frames, interior finish and furniture.

Often severely injured by frost, its brittle limbs broken by wind, attacked by fungus, and by insects, such as the catalpa sphinx, it is, nevertheless, one of the easiest hardwoods to plant. It is widely grown in parks and along suburban streets and roads in the eastern half of the United States.

Northern catalpa is frequently confused with the smaller common catalpa, *Catalpa bignonioides* of the Gulf of Mexico states from Georgia to Louisiana. Common catalpa has dense clusters of flowers thickly spotted with brownish purple as compared with the more open and less conspicuously spotted flower panicles of northern catalpa. The leaves of common catalpa are smaller, and broader in relation to their length, being only five to six inches long and four to five inches wide. The six-to twenty-inch-long seed pod is more slender and the walls thinner than that of northern catalpa.

George J. Baetzhold

The white flowers bloom in June or July, and are arranged in showy, erect clusters at the ends of twigs

George J. Baetzhold

Bark on the lower trunk of mature trees is three-quarters to one inch thick, light grayish brown, broken into scaly, flat ridges

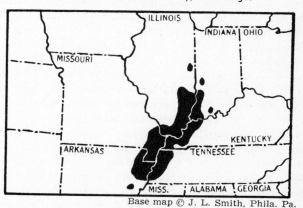

Base map © J. L. Smith, Phila. Pa.

Natural range of Northern Catalpa

ROYAL PAULOWNIA

Princess tree

Paulownia tomentosa (Thunberg) Steudel

THE royal paulownia presents a strikingly handsome appearance in the spring with its large pyramidal clusters of violet-colored flowers which fill the air for a considerable distance with their fragrant perfume. Its broad, ular, elevated leaf-scars and prominent lenticels. The semicircular, compressed, light brown leaf buds are about one-eighth of an inch long, and the much larger velvety flower buds, formed the previous season, are some-

Devereux Butcher

Royal Paulownia is a low, wide-spreading tree with a usual height of 30 to 60 feet. Its trunk is short, thick

Fred Shulley

Some of the thick broad leaves have a single short-pointed lobe on each side

F. W. Besley

long-stalked leaves give the tree some resemblance to catalpa. Introduced into this country from China and Japan, it has escaped from cultivation and occurs chiefly from southern New York and New Jersey southward to Florida and Texas, and occasionally in other localities where the winters are not too severe. It prefers deep, rich, moist soil, and is often seen in yards and vacant lots in towns and villages.

A low, wide-spreading tree with a usual height of thirty to sixty feet, paulownia has a short, thick, trunk, generally from one to two feet in diameter, usually divided within a few feet of the ground into large, stout, spreading branches. In open situations the branches form a wide and often flat-topped open head, but when crowded by other trees the crown is usually rounded and more compact. A maximum height of sixty to seventy feet and a diameter of two to three feet is sometimes attained. The young twigs are covered with soft brown hairs. Later they become smooth and dark brown with large, nearly orbic-

The showy flowers, about two inches long, and borne on thick, densely hairy stalks, appear in large clusters

The olive-brown or bronze two-celled fruit capsules, one to two inches long, are sharply pointed

what egg-shaped and about half an inch in length.

The broadly egg-shaped, short-pointed, oppositely arranged leaves are from five to fifteen inches long, even longer on vigorous shoots, and from four to eight inches wide. They are heart-shaped at the base and are attached to the twig by a petiole which is round in cross-section and from three to eight inches long. At maturity they are thick, dark green above and paler beneath. The margin of the leaf is smooth, but some leaves may have a single short-pointed lobe on each side. Both surfaces of the leaf are finely hairy, but the upper becomes nearly smooth with age.

The showy flowers, about two inches long, are borne on thick, densely hairy stalks. They appear before or with the leaves in dense, erect clusters from eight to twelve inches long. The fruit is a large, leathery, olive-brown or bronze, abruptly pointed, two-celled capsule, one to two inches long and three-fourths to one inch thick, shallowly and longitudinally grooved on each side. At maturity the capsule splits open lengthwise, releasing the numerous small membranous-winged seeds. The open capsules remain on the branches throughout the winter.

On the trunks of mature trees the bark is rather thick, dark grayish brown, and mottled with a shallow, grayish-white network of fissures. The soft, light wood is easily worked, yielding a satiny surface. It is highly valued in oriental countries.

The genus *Paulownia* is named in honor of a Russian princess, Anna Paulowna, daughter of Czar Paul I. *Tomentosa* refers to the hairy or tomentose leaves.

The royal paulownia is commonly grown in the United States as an ornamental, but is not ordinarily grown north of the latitude of New York City because the flower buds are usually killed during the winter. It is often

grown as an ornamental foliage plant farther north, however, by cutting it back to the ground at the end of the growing season. When this is done, a single shoot will sometimes grow to a height of ten to twelve feet during the summer, producing enormous leaves.

On mature trees, the bark is thick, dark grayish brown, and mottled with shallow grayish white fissures

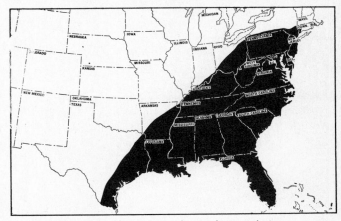

Introduced into this country from China and Japan, Paulownia does best where the winters are not too severe

GINKGO

Maidenhair tree

Ginkgo biloba Linnaeus

THE GINKGO is unique among trees. It is not closely related to any living family or group in the whole vegetable kingdom and is the sole survivor of a family, rich in species, which was distributed over the temperate regions of both the northern and southern hemispheres when the dinosaurs roamed the earth. It has been called a living fossil, for it seems to be identical with fossil species that have been described, and presumably was a common tree in the present temperate and circumpolar regions of the whole northern hemisphere. It seems probable that glaciers caused its extinction in North America, Europe and western

Devereux Butcher

Devereux Butcher

In youth, as in these two trees, Ginkgo has a continuous central column and is sparsely branched with the spire-like habit of conifers. At maturity, the Ginkgo is a stately tree 100 feet or more in height with a cylindric slightly tapering trunk

Siberia, but in the milder climate of the Orient, which the glaciers did not reach, it survived. Even there, however, it no longer exists in a wild state, and in Japan and China it is known only as a planted tree.

The fan-shaped leaf is found in no other flowering plant, but it does suggest the leaflet of the maidenhair fern. Because the tree's method of fertilization of the female flower is similar to what takes place in the ferns, botanists have called the ginkgo a missing link between flowering plants and ferns. The male cell has cilia or minute marginal hairs that propel it with a vibratory movement.

At maturity the ginkgo is a stately tree 100 feet or more in height with a trunk sometimes eight feet in diameter. In youth it has a continuous central column, and is sparsely branched, having the spire-like or pyramidal habit of cone-bearing trees. As it becomes older its form is more or less conical. The main shaft usually divides and the crown is made up of several large ascending and spreading branches.

The slender-stalked leaves are more or less incised or divided at the broad outer end. They have no midrib but numerous branching parallel veins. Usually measuring from two to three inches across, on vigorous young trees and on shoots which develop from the base of the trunks of old trees, they are sometimes from six to eight inches broad. Somewhat leathery in texture, they are bright green when young and dull green at maturity. In autumn they turn a clear yellow. Defoliation occurs late in the season, and is unusually rapid.

Before the leaves are fully developed in the spring, the ginkgo blooms, the male and female flowers borne on separate trees. The pollen-bearing flowers are in arching catkins resembling somewhat those of the oak, but they are stouter and less pendent. The fruit-producing flowers, usually in pairs, are borne under small expanded knobs which terminate long stems.

The orange-yellow, plum-like fruit is about an inch in diameter and consists of a thin, outer fleshy layer which covers a pointed, oval nut from one-half to three-fourths of an inch long, with a smooth, white shell enclosing a soft kernel. On or soon after falling to the ground, the fleshy covering bursts and emits an offensive odor. When the nuts have been cleaned of the pulp they are pure white, and are known in China as white or silver nuts, ginkgo meaning silver fruit in Chinese. These are sold for food in China and Japan and are eaten at banquets, weddings and social gatherings. The ginkgo is the oldest cultivated nut tree.

The bark is fissured into ridges of irregular shape and on old trees it is deeply furrowed. The winter buds are conical and short-pointed with bright brown scales.

Ginkgo wood is white or pale yellow and there is no distinction between sapwood and heartwood. Light in weight, soft, weak, fine textured and easy to work, the wood is of little value. In China and Japan it is used for chess boards and chess men.

The ginkgo was introduced into Europe in 1730 and into England in 1754, from which country, thirty years later, it was brought to the United States. It is desirable for planting and not subject to insect or fungus attack.

Warren D. Brush

The male blooms appear before the leaves are fully developed, and occur in clusters on trees separate from those bearing the seed-producing blooms

Warren D. Brush

The plum-like fruit is yellow, and about an inch in diameter. The fan-like leaves have no midrib, but many branching veins

Devereux Butcher

The bark is fissured into ridges of irregular shape and on old trees it is deeply furrowed. Ginkgo wood is white or yellowish

Because of the disagreeable odor of the fallen fruit, the male trees are preferred. The tree thrives under cultivation in the United States except in northern New England, northern New York, northern Michigan and the northern prairie states, and it will grow in Canada, in southern Ontario and southern British Columbia.

SELECTED BIBLIOGRAPHY

A complete list of the books and periodicals read in the preparation of these tree descriptions would cover several pages. The following, however, comprise the more important sources of technical information used in the text:

Betts, H. S.—*American Woods*. Leaflets on individual tree species. U. S. Forest Service. Govt. Printing Office, Washington, D. C. 20402. 1945-1954.

Bowers, N. A.—*Cone-bearing Trees of the Pacific Coast*. Pacific Books. Palo Alto, California. 1965.

Coker, W. C., and Totten, H. R.—*Trees of the Southern States*. Univ. of North Carolina Press. Chapel Hill, N. C. 27514. 1972.

Critchfield, Wm. B., and Little, Elbert L., Jr.—*Geographic Distribution of the Pines of the World*. U. S. Forest Service. Govt. Printing Office, Washington, D. C. 20402. 1966.

Dominion Forest Service of Canada—*Native Trees of Canada*. King's Printer, Ottawa. 1961.

Eliot, W. A.—*Forest Trees of the Pacific Coast*. G. B. Putnam's Sons. New York, N. Y. 10016. 1938.

Emerson, A. I., and Weed, C. M.—*Our Trees, How to Know Them*. J. B. Lippincott Co. Philadelphia, Pa. 1958.

Fowells, H. A., compiler.—*Silvics of Forest Trees of the United States*. U. S. Forest Service. Govt. Printing Office, Washington, D. C. 20402. 1965.

Graves, Arthur H.—*Illustrated Guide to Trees and Shrubs*. Harper and Brothers (Harper and Row). New York. 1956.

Green, C. H.—*Trees of the South*. Univ. of North Carolina Press. Chapel Hill, N. C. 27514. 1955.

Grimm, Wm. C.—*The Book of Trees*. The Stackpole Co. (Stackpole Books). Harrisburg, Pa. 17105. 1962.

Harlow, W. M.—*Trees of the Eastern and Central United States and Canada*. Dover Publications, Inc. New York, N. Y. 10014. 1942.

Harrar, E. S., and Harrar, J. G.—*Guide to Southern Trees*. Dover Publications, Inc. New York, N. Y. 10014. 1962.

Hough, R. B.—*Handbook of the Trees of the Northern States and Canada*. The Macmillan Co. New York, N. Y. 10011. 1947.

Little, E. L., Jr.—*Atlas of United States Trees*, Vol. I. U. S. Forest Service. Govt. Printing Office. Washington, D. C. 20402. 1971.

　—*Atlas of United States Trees*, Vol. 2. Alaska Trees and Common Shrubs, U. S. Forest Service, Dept. of Agriculture, Miscellaneous Publication No. 1293, Govt. Printing Office, Washington, D. C. 20402. 1975.

　—*Atlas of United States Trees*, Vol. 3. Minor Western Hardwoods, U. S. Forest Service, Dept. of Agriculture, Miscellaneous Publication No. 1314, Govt. Printing Office, Washington, D. C. 20402. 1976.

　—*Check List of Native and Naturalized Trees of the United States (including Alaska)*. U. S. Forest Service. Govt. Printing Office, Washington, D. C. 20402. 1953.

　—*To Know the Trees*. Separate #2156. U. S. Dept. Agriculture Yearbook. Govt. Printing Office, Washington, D. C. 20402. 1949.

　—*Fifty Trees from Foreign Lands*. Separate #2157. U. S. Dept. Agriculture Yearbook. Govt. Printing Office, Washington, D. C. 20402. 1949.

　—*Endemic, Disjunct and Northern Trees in the Southern Appalachians*. The Distributional History of the Biota of the Southern Appalachians. Part II. Flora. Perry C. Holt (ed.) Research Division Monograph 2. Va. Polytechnic Institute and State Univ., Blacksburg, Va. 24061. 1971.

　—*Geographic Distribution of the Pines of the World*, Miscellaneous Publication No. 991, U. S. Forest Service, Govt. Printing Office, Washington, D. C. 20402. 1966.

　—*Southwestern Trees. A guide to the native species of New Mexico and Arizona*, Hand Book, No. 9, U. S. Dept. of Agriculture, Washington, D. C. 20402. 1950.

Mathews, F. S.—*Field Book of American Trees and Shrubs*. G. P. Putnam's Sons. New York, N. Y. 10016. 1915.

McMinn, H. E., and Maino, E.—*Manual of Pacific Coast Trees*. Univ. of California. 1951.

Peattie, D. C.—*A Natural History of Trees of Eastern and Central North America*. Houghton Mifflin Co. Boston, Mass. 02107. 1950.

　—*A Natural History of Western Trees*. Houghton Mifflin Co. Boston, Mass. 02107. 1953.

Preston, R. J., Jr.—*Rocky Mountain Trees*. Iowa State College Press. Ames, Iowa. 50010. 1947.

　—*North American Trees*. Iowa State College Press. Ames, Iowa. 50010. 1961.

Rehder, A.—*Manual of Cultivated Trees and Shrubs Hardy in North America*. The Macmillan Co. New York, N. Y. 10011. 1951.

Sargent, C. S.—*Manual of the Trees of North America*, 2 vols. Dover Publications, Inc. New York, N. Y. 10014. 1965.

Sudworth, G. B.—*Forest Trees of the Pacific Slope*. U. S. Forest Service. Govt. Printing Office. Washington, D. C. 20402. 1908.

Symonds, George W. D.—*The Tree Identification Book*. M. Barrows and Co. 1958.

Wyman, D.—*Trees for American Gardens*. The Macmillan Co. New York, N. Y. 10011. 1965.

INDEX

To serve as a guide in selecting trees which may be grown in any particular locality, sometimes outside their natural range, the various species have been grouped into zones of hardiness. The Roman numerals given under "Hardiness" refer to the zones shown on the map on the inside front cover of this book which is taken by permission from "Trees For American Gardens" by Donald Wyman, published by The Macmillan Company. These zones are based on differences in the average minimum temperatures. There are, of course, many local variations in temperature, such as are caused by altitude, which cannot be shown in these zones. Moisture is also a factor in plant survival as well as type of soil. In general, however, these zones apply correctly to the various species as shown.

As the zone listed for each species is the coldest zone where it will grow normally, it can be expected to grow in many of the warmer zones, but high temperatures and lack of sufficient moisture may prevent it from being grown successfully in some of the warmer zones.

Some species are not as desirable as other more or less similar species, but this is not taken into consideration in this classification. Usually the text indicates whether or not a tree is desirable for planting.

Zone marked with an asterisk (*) indicates tree not listed or zone not given in "Trees for American Gardens." Zone determined or approximated from other source information.

383

386

NOTES

NOTES

NOTES